D0448784

CHRISTIAN DOCTRINE

Also by Shirley C. Guthrie
and published by Westminster/John Knox Press

Diversity in Faith—Unity in Christ

CHRISTIAN DOCTRINE

Revised Edition

SHIRLEY C. GUTHRIE

Westminster John Knox Press
LOUISVILLE
LONDON • LEIDEN

©1994 Shirley C. Guthrie

All rights reserved. No part of this book may be reproduced or transmitted in any form or by any means, electronic or mechanical, including photocopying, recording, or by any information storage or retrieval system, without permission in writing from the publisher. For information, address Westminster/John Knox Press, 100 Witherspoon Street, Louisville, Kentucky 40202-1396.

Scripture quotations from the Revised Standard Version of the Bible are copyright 1946, 1952, © 1971, 1973 by the Division of Christian Education of the National Council of the Churches of Christ in the U.S.A. and are used by permission.

Scripture quotations from the New Revised Standard Version of the Bible are copyright © 1989 by the Division of Christian Education of the National Council of the Churches of Christ in the U.S.A. and are used by permission.

Book design by Publishers' WorkGroup
Cover design by Lisa Buckley

This book is printed on recycled acid-free paper that meets the American National Standards Institute Z39.48 standard.

Published by Westminster John Knox Press
Louisville, Kentucky

PRINTED IN THE UNITED STATES OF AMERICA

09 10 — 18 17 16 15

Library of Congress Cataloging-inPublication Data

Guthrie, Shirley C., date.
Christian doctrine / Shirley C. Guthrie. — Rev. ed.
p. cm.
Includes index.
ISBN-13: 978-0-664-25368-4 (alk. paper)
ISBN-10: 0-664-25368-7 (alk. paper)
1. Presbyterian Church—Doctrines. 2. Theology, Doctrinal. 3. Reformed Church—Doctrines. I. Title.
BX9175.2G88 1994
230' .5—dc20 93-44988

Contents

Preface ix

PART 1
THE METHOD AND TASK OF THEOLOGY
1

1. Who Is a Theologian? 3
   Who Are You? 3
   Who Is the Author? 7
   The Task of Theology 9
   The Reformed Tradition 15

2. Who Says So? The Problem of Authority 20
   Creeds and Confessions 21
   Creeds and Confessions in the Reformed Tradition 25
   The Freedom and Responsibility of Individual Christians 27
   Appendix: Introduction to Reformed Creeds and Confessions 32

PART 2
GOD AND HUMAN BEINGS
37

3. How Can We Find God? The Doctrine of General Revelation 39
   The Problem 40
   The Search for a Solution 44

4. How Does God Find Us? The Doctrine of Special Revelation 53
God's Self-Communication 54
The Word of God 62
The Freedom of God 65

5. Who Is God? The Doctrine of the Trinity 70
Problems and Objections 71
Biblical Roots of the Doctrine of the Trinity 76
The Church's Doctrine of the Trinity 81
One God Who Is Creator, Savior, and Life-Renewer 84
The Social Trinity 88
Trinitarian Thinking about God, Ourselves, and the World 95

6. What Is God Like? The Doctrine of the Attributes of God 97
The Living, Personal God 99
The Loving God of Sovereign Majesty 101
God in Relation to Us 104
God in Heaven 111

7. What Does God Want with Us? The Doctrine of Predestination 118
Three Classical Interpretations 119
Three Basic Rules for Thinking about Predestination 131
The Freedom God Wills for All Human Beings 132
The Meaning of Predestination for Non-Christians 134
The Meaning of Predestination for Christians 136

PART 3
GOD THE CREATOR AND CREATION
143

8. What Are We Doing Here? The Doctrine of Creation 145
God the Creator 147
God's Good Creation 158
Good but Not God 162

9. Why Doesn't God Do Something about It? The Doctrine of Providence and the Problem of Evil 166
The Reality of Evil 167
The Dark Side of Creation 168
The Powers of Darkness 173
The Light That Shines in the Darkness 182

10. Who Are We? The Doctrine of Human Beings 192
Creatures in the Image of God 194

Fellowship with God 199
Human Life in Community 202
Ways Human Beings Relate to Each Other 204
Me, Myself, and I 207

11. Why Don't You Just Be Yourself? The Doctrine of Sin 212
Three Basic Forms of Sin 214
Original Sin 221
The Consequences of Sin 224

PART 4
GOD IN CHRIST AND RECONCILIATION
229

12. Where Is God? The Doctrine of the Incarnation 233
Real God and Real Human Being 234
A Real Human Being 237
God-With-Us 243

13. Is God against Us? The Doctrine of the Atonement 250
The Biblical Images 251
God versus the Gods 256
Were You There? 262

14. Who's in Charge Here? The Doctrine of the Resurrection 270
On the Third Day 271
The Lord and His Kingdom 275

PART 5
GOD THE HOLY SPIRIT AND NEW LIFE
289

15. What's New? The Doctrine of the Holy Spirit 291
Who Is the Holy Spirit? 292
Christian Spirituality 298
The Gifts of the Spirit 302

16. Are You a Christian? The Doctrine of Justification 314
The Problem of Justification 315
Justification by Grace 318
The Justice of Justification 320
Justification by Grace through Faith 322
Postscript: Justification and Social Justice 327

17. Are You a Christian? The Doctrine of Sanctification 330
Christian Faith and Christian Action 332

In but Not of the World 337
The Holiness Jesus Commands 341

18. Living or Dead? The Doctrine of the Church 349
The People of God 351
The Body of Christ 354
A Holy People 356
A United, Catholic People 358
An Apostolic People 363
The Task of the One Holy Catholic and Apostolic Church 366

19. What's Going to Happen to Us? The Doctrine of the Christian Hope for the Future 373
Christian Hope, Hopelessness, and False Hopes 374
Some Guidelines for Asking the Right Questions 381
Christian Hope for the World 386
Christian Hope for Individuals 392

Notes 401

Index 411

Preface to the Revised Edition

The first edition of this book was published in 1968 as part of a church school curriculum for use in adult study groups, primarily in Presbyterian and Reformed churches. I expected that it would be used for a few years until it was replaced by other Christian education resources. But it is still being used as an introduction to theology not only in churches but also in some colleges and seminaries in Presbyterian-Reformed and other denominations—an indication of the hunger of lay church members and beginning theological students for instruction in the Christian faith written in a way that is accessible to them.

Many of those who still find the book helpful have said that if it is to continue to be so, it must be updated to indicate how I would say things differently and how my mind has changed in light of developments in the thought and life of the church and in the world since 1968.

It is not all that important or interesting to talk about changes in "my" theology, but such an update is necessary if the book is to continue to serve the purpose for which it was written—to interpret ecumenical Christian faith as summarized in the Apostles' Creed from the perspective of the Reformed tradition. That tradition itself demands the constant "updating" (reformation) of our always inadequate, time- and situation-bound attempts to understand the Christian gospel. This revised edition of the book, then, is not just an attempt to be up to date, but is an attempt to be faithful to the "always to be reformed" tradition that informs its understanding of the task of theology.

The basic structure and outline of the book have not changed: Christians still confess their faith with the ancient Apostles' Creed. But four kinds of changes make the revised edition different from the first. In this preface I want to identify them and at the same time acknowledge and express appreciation for the help of those who have influenced me to make them.

First, there are changes that are simply attempts to say more clearly what I wanted to say in the first edition, changes not in substance but in expression. Some of them are attempts to clarify by saying the same thing in a more precise and understandable way. Some are attempts to clarify by expanding the discussion of particular questions or issues. Such changes occur throughout the book but especially in chapters dealing with the authority and interpretation of scripture, predestination, providence and evil, and Christian hope for the future (chapters that have provoked the most heated or perplexed reactions). Changes of this kind are mostly the result of many conversations with groups of church people and seminary students who have studied the book. Their questions, objections, requests for "more"—and uncanny ability to spot weaknesses, ambiguities, and sometimes contradictions—have forced and helped me to be more careful in what I say and the way I say it.

Second, there are changes that are the result of my continued study of the Reformed tradition. The first edition was based on a conversation primarily with John Calvin, the confessional documents of Reformed churches, Karl Barth's update of the classical Reformed tradition, and others who stand generally in this theological line. In this revised edition they continue to be fundamental resources for me, but my ongoing conversation with them has resulted both in new learning from them and at some points new critical evaluation of them. I have also learned from confessional statements produced since 1968 (the Declaration of Faith of 1976 and the Brief Statement of Faith of 1991) and from other twentieth-century Reformed theologians. Jürgen Moltmann's work on the doctrine of the Trinity in conversation with the Eastern Orthodox doctrine (along with the work of Eberhard Jüngel and liberation theologians I will mention presently) led to important changes in my own doctrine of the Trinity—and consequently in my understanding of the whole of Christian doctrine based on faith in the triune God. Moltmann's work on the doctrine of creation led me to consider some interesting possibilities for reinterpreting that doctrine for our time. My study of Hendrikus Berkhof's and Moltmann's work on the doctrine of the Holy Spirit resulted in substantial changes in my own discussion of the Spirit's person and work. In this revised edition I continue to write with lay people and beginning theological students in mind and have kept conversation with academic theologians for the most part in the background or in footnotes, but I am happy to acknowledge my indebtedness to them here.

Third, this revised edition is different because it was written in a changed social and historical context. From the time of the Reformation, to be a Reformed theologian has always meant to ask what the living God we come to know in the Bible is saying and doing, and therefore what faithful Christians have to say and do in thankful and obedient response to this living God, in every new time, place, and situation.

In the 1960s that meant for me, as for others, that any faithful and relevant interpretation of Christian doctrine must both speak and respond to: the civil rights movement in the United States; the cold war between the "free" West and the communist East; the real and imagined threat of communist ideology in our own country as well as abroad; the growing gap between the few rich and the many poor in our own country and around the world; the bitter battle between "hawks" and "doves" over the tragic involvement of the United States in Vietnam; the sexual revolution; the chaos that led to the murder of political and spiritual leaders who stood for justice and reconciliation.

In the 1990s we still confront the same fundamental problems but in new, more complex, and more urgent ways. The open racism of the 1960s has been replaced by more subtle, and in some ways more dangerous, forms of racism in church and society, and even those who sincerely oppose it no longer agree on solutions to it. (Now it is often *conservatives* who argue for "integration" and *liberals* who support some form of "separate but equal.") The great cold war has ended only to be replaced by many "little" wars that threaten to become global (and nuclear) wars—surprisingly enough, in our supposedly secularized world—between groups and nations that slaughter each other in the name of Christian, Jewish, Muslim, or Hindu religious commitment. Angry ideological debates in churches, schools, and government about "the communist threat" have been replaced by equally angry debates about the politically correct solution to the conflict between men and women, and between people of different races, classes, and cultural traditions. The gap between the rich and the poor has become even more visible as thousands of homeless people wander the streets of our cities, and even more urgent as we have learned that the economic welfare of every country in the world is inseparable from that of every other country. On the sexual battleground in church and society, the debate is no longer only about sexual freedom and whether "living together" is acceptable for unmarried couples; now it is about AIDS, abortion, the status of women, and homosexuality. We have become aware as never before of the interdependence of all kinds of people that makes an inclusive national and international human community *necessary*, and of the racial, cultural, and religious pluralism that seems to make the achievement of such a community *impossible*. At the same time we are also more aware of the interdependence of human beings and their natural environment, and of the fact that the survival of all life on our planet depends on ecological responsibility we have not yet begun to take with real seriousness. Such is the context in which Christian doctrine must be written today, the context that always lies in the background and often appears in the foreground of this revised edition.

Finally, this edition is different because I have been listening to some new voices in theology: the voices of black theologians such as American James Cone and South African Allan Boesak; feminist and "womanist" theologians such as Rosemary Ruether, Sallie McFague, Letty Russell, and Jacquelyn Grant; and Latin American theologians such as Gustavo Gutiérrez, Jon Sobrino, Leonardo Boff, and Juan Luis Segundo.

These "liberation" theologians, many of them Roman Catholics and representatives of Protestant traditions other than my own, have confirmed and strengthened two convictions I already had and repeatedly emphasized in the first edition of this book (influenced especially by Karl Barth): (1) If scripture is to be for us the normative authority we Reformation Christians confess it to be, we cannot read it only to confirm our own personal, social, and theological biases; we must gladly listen to and be corrected by what fellow Christians who are different from us have learned from it. (2) The God of the Bible is a God whose justice and compassion are exercised especially for the sake of powerless, "marginalized" people who are ignored, excluded, or oppressed by the rich and powerful, and by all who defend any given social, political, and religious status quo.

Liberation theologians have also made me aware of ways I have been unable to hear some of the radical promises and demands of the God of scripture because I have read and interpreted it from the perspective of a white, middle-class, "Euro-American" male who learned my theology from others like me. Of course, those who interpret scripture from other perspectives can and must be criticized for the limited insight, one-sidedness, and biases of their particular race, sex, class, and cultural and religious environment. But this is a different book (and I believe one more faithful to authentic Reformed tradition) because they have helped me learn from the Word of God some things I did not know in 1968 and could not have learned without them. As is the case with other theologians I have mentioned, my conversation with liberation theologians is more often implicit than explicit; but even when I do not mention them, they too have always been with me as I revised this book.

Perhaps the most obvious difference between the first and second editions is the result of what I have learned from the feminist expression of liberation theology. Gone is all talk about "man," "men," and "mankind," and all references to individual human beings in general as "he." Gone too, I hope, are all stereotypes of masculine and feminine characteristics and roles. Gone is all talk about God as "he," and gone is the exclusive and unqualified use of masculine imagery to talk about God. *Of course,* those of us who once used such language to talk about human beings intended to include women. But many women have felt and actually have been excluded by such talk. *Of course,* we did not think of God literally as a big Man up in the sky. But the contemporary debate about appropriate "God-talk" has exposed the fact that some people (including theologians) actually have thought of God as the great heavenly Male made in the image of human males. The task of theology for today is much, much more than learning to use inclusive language to speak of human beings and learning to use feminine as well as masculine images to speak of God. But we cannot get to that much, much more until we get rid of sexist language (and the presuppositions behind it) in speaking about human beings and God.

No Christian theology can claim to speak the last word about God and God's relation to human beings and the world. Every theology is at best a limited, fallible, provisional attempt to speak of the living God of scripture whose truth, justice, and compassion are beyond the very highest and best we can imagine. But I hope the changes I have made in this revised edition will make it for a few more years a theology that is a helpful witness to this living God.

As I have rethought and reworked what I wrote twenty-five years ago, my ongoing conversation and vigorous debates with my colleagues Walter Brueggemann, Will Coleman, Charles B. Cousar, C. Benton Kline, and George Stroup have encouraged and enabled me to keep growing in my theological understanding and commitment. I could not have had a more careful and helpful editor than Harold L. Twiss at Westminster/John Knox Press. Mr. Twiss's work and my own work were made easier because of Ann Titshaw's requests for clarification and suggestions for improvement as she patiently and cheerfully typed the manuscript. My friend, pastor-theologian Richard I. Deibert, generously volunteered to prepare the index.

Shirley C. Guthrie

Columbia Theological Seminary
Summer 1993

PART 1

THE METHOD AND TASK OF THEOLOGY

Sex, politics, and theology—these are the only things worth talking about. This old saying is an exaggeration, perhaps, but it is an attempt to express a deep truth. Sex forces the question, Who am I? Politics asks, How can we learn to live together? Theology, which means literally "a word about God," asks questions like these: What is your only comfort in life and in death? What is the chief end of human life? What are we by nature? In whom do you believe?[1] To risk carrying the exaggeration even further, of the three topics mentioned, theology is the most important and most interesting because it *includes* the questions raised by sex and politics! No theology is interested only in God. *The study of theology is by definition the quest for the ultimate truth about God, about ourselves, and about the world we live in.* What else is there to talk about?

So you should not be awed to hear that you are about to begin a study of theology. Theology is not just an impractical, otherworldly subject for a few dreamy scholars who retire to ivory towers to devote themselves to such irrelevant, hairsplitting questions as, How many angels can dance on the head of a pin? It is the discipline that wrestles with the basic issues and decisions we all face every day, whoever we are, whatever we do. Whether you know it or not, you are already a practicing theologian even before you begin this formal study of theology. The purpose here is to articulate and seek some answers to questions you have been consciously or unconsciously struggling with all your life.

Before we can get to the content of the truth about God, human beings and the world, we have to ask how we should go about discovering this truth. That is the problem we will tackle in the first two chapters.

In the first chapter we will study the method and task of theology and consider the title question, "Who Is a Theologian?" In the second we will ask, "Who Says So?" This will involve a consideration of significant creeds and confessions of the Christian church and their authority over us as church members.

1

Who Is a Theologian?

This first chapter is actually the last. It is written after all the rest of this book has been finished. Its purpose is to tell you what to expect and to give you some guidelines to help you know how to go about your study. We will begin not by talking about the content of the book as such, but by talking about *us*—you and me, the readers and the writer. Theology, of course, does have to do with ideas, truths, and doctrines (doctrine means simply "teaching"). But these ideas, truths, and doctrines themselves point to a living Person who confronts us as persons. So we go straight to the heart of theology when we get personal from the very beginning. As we become clear about who we theologians are, we will also understand our task as theologians and the purpose of this book.

As you read this chapter, make a list of what you need to keep in mind in order to go about your study as a good theologian.

WHO ARE YOU?

Most of you who will study this book are church members, and you probably will be working through it with other members of the church. However, you will never understand Christian theology if you think of yourself and the others only as such.

Your Personal and Social Background

You are not only a Christian; you are either a *male* or a *female* whose life, in fact if not in theory, is as much determined by your sexual as by your religious needs and desires, thoughts, and instincts.

The Christian community is not the only community you belong to. You are a member of a *family* community; you are husband or wife, father or mother, son or daughter, brother or sister. And much more of your life is spent (or should be) concentrating on the success or failure, happiness or misery of your family relationships (or lack of them) than on church activities.

You are a member of one *race* or another, one *economic class* or another; and more than likely even the particular congregation you belong to has been brought together far more obviously on the basis of common racial and class ties than on the basis of common theological convictions.

You are deeply involved not only in the Christian way of life but also in the American way of life, which is something quite different. Not all Christians are Americans, and not all Americans are Christians. But your understanding of the Christian faith is inevitably influenced by your American culture as well as by your reading of the Bible and study of church doctrine.

You are the citizens of a particular nation as well as "citizens of heaven," and your liberal or conservative politics affects your theology as much as your liberal or conservative theology affects your politics.

In short, part of your life is colored by what goes on in the church, but much of it is also colored by what goes on in the home, bank, supermarket, courthouse, and movie and television studios. Even when you leave the "world" to go to church, you take your worldly life with you. Insofar as *you* are in the church, the world is there too. Even when you put aside the newspaper and other secular literature to read the Bible and this book about theology, you bring to your religious studies all your secular problems, desires, and opinions—whether you want to or not.

This means that if Christian theology is to be more than an intellectual game, if it is to deal with you personally, it has to bring the word about God to bear not just on your church life but on your life in the world. At every point in this book, therefore, you will find that I have tried to relate Christian theology not just to purely religious questions and problems but also to family and social and political and economic questions and problems. Christian theology deals with people where they really live because the God we must talk about is a God who is at work to judge and help in every area of our lives.

It follows, then, that as you study the doctrines discussed in this book, your task is to ask at every point what they have to say about your social as well as your individual life, your everyday work and play as well as your private and public worship, your life here and now as well as your life in the "world to come." Only when you do that will you fulfill the task of a good theologian—one who thinks and speaks about both the true God and real human beings in the real world.

I have tried to help you fulfill this task throughout the book, but you will find specific and concrete help especially in the section "For Further Reflection and Study" at the end of each chapter. You might find it helpful to glance first at this section every time you begin a new chapter.

Your Religious Background

You begin your study of theology not only with the whole personal and social background that makes you the particular kind of person you are. You begin also with some sort of religious background. Some of you who read this book are already deeply committed Christians. Some of you have serious doubts about the truth and meaning of the Christian faith. Some of you probably belong to the church because it's the thing to do, without either deep commitment or serious thought one way or the other. Some of you already know a lot about the Bible and the doctrines of your church. Others of you know practically nothing. For some of you, the assertion "The Bible says . . ." or "Our church teaches . . ." carries great weight. Others of you are not impressed with such statements and won't buy anything until you are shown its truth and relevance.

I have been troubled throughout the book about this wide divergence among you. How can I speak relevantly to all of you at once? If you are studying this book in a class with other people, you will soon be confronted with the same problem: How can you discuss theology meaningfully with people whose religious background and faith are different? There is no easy solution to the problem. But as I have written this book, there are two rules I have tried to follow to include all of you in the conversation. I suggest that you keep them in mind as you study the book, and especially as you discuss it with other people. They are general rules for being a good theologian, for "doing theology."

1. *Be honest!* Be honest with yourself and with other people—and above all with God. Don't apologize for, or try to hide, what you believe, whether it is right or wrong in the eyes of others. And don't apologize for, or try to hide, what you cannot believe or have a hard time believing. Growth in understanding and growth in faith are possible only when there is neither self-deception nor an attempt to fool God and other people. An honest doubter is closer to the truth than a superficial or

dishonest believer. To quote the words of the great Christian theologian, P. T. Forsyth, "A live heresy is better than a dead orthodoxy."

2. *Recognize your own limitations.* Theology deals with a God whose thoughts are not our thoughts and whose ways are not our ways (Isa. 55:8). Theologians who are sure that they have all the answers to all questions and that their task is simply to convince others that this is so are bad theologians. They only prove that they know nothing at all of the majesty and mystery of the God who cannot be captured and mastered by any human system of thought. Sometimes it is more believing to say "I just don't know" than to be too smugly sure. Sometimes it is better to leave some questions open until we have more light. It is often the case that sincere, serious Christians disagree even on very important questions, so that it simply cannot be said that this or that is *the* Christian position. In other words, we will be good theologians when we are modest theologians, acknowledging our own limitations, recognizing that we may be wrong at this or that point, knowing that we need to be open to let ourselves be helped by as well as to help, to be changed by as well as to change, those who think differently from us.

I have tried to follow these rules myself. I have tried to be honest about what I think myself, yet to invite you to examine and criticize the positions I have taken. Instead of trying to give one right solution to every problem, I have often described several possible solutions, suggesting the arguments for and against each and leaving it up to you to decide. Sometimes I have only raised questions, suggesting some factors that have to be taken into consideration in searching for answers, without giving any answers as such.

You will be fortunate if different members of your study group choose different alternatives and different answers, and if you are willing to give them the same freedom to be honest about their faith and doubts that you want for yourself. You will learn far more from genuine open debate than from total agreement.

All this means that when you have finished your study, you will not have a nicely wrapped-up system of theology with every question answered and every problem solved. You will not have "arrived" in your understanding of the Christian faith; you will only be a little further along the way. Moreover, you will be better theologians just because you have learned that our faith must be in the God who is beyond all that any of us can ask or think, and not in our simple or complicated, liberal or conservative, orthodox or heretical theology.

WHO IS THE AUTHOR?

Your task as theologians is clarified not only by reflection about who you are, but also by some things you ought to remember about the theologian who wrote the book you are studying. One of the things you ought to keep in mind about me is that I am an ordained minister and professional theologian. This carries with it some advantages and disadvantages.

Professional Limitations

On the one hand, it means that I am at least supposed to have more competence than most of you in understanding and explaining the teachings of the Bible and the church. But on the other hand, it means that most of my time and work are spent in an ecclesiastical and academic environment. If, as we have said, theology has to do with the truth of God in relation to every aspect of life *in the world,* then many of you know more about that side of the theological task than I do. I have done my best not to write from an ivory tower, but I have been very much aware of the limitations of my profession. You should keep this in mind also. And you can help counterbalance my limitations by carefully examining what I have written in the light of your own experience and by listening seriously to those who have competence in other fields. What are the reactions of a homemaker, a medical doctor, a public official, a business leader, a sales clerk, a scientist, to what you read in this book? You will study the book as good theologians, not when you study it as if it had nothing to do with what people in such "worldly" vocations know, but when you constantly invite criticism and additional information from them. Good theology is a two-way conversation between preachers and lay people, church and world, professional theologians and experts in other areas. So take advantage of whatever help is available to you from both sides.

The Problem of Language

Part of my job is to interpret the language of the Bible and the technical terminology of the church. I have tried to do that in this book. You will find such words as *justification, sanctification, sin, grace, salvation,* and *eschatology* throughout the book. I have used such religious language deliberately. Just as you have to learn the vocabulary of psychology or physics or sociology if you are going to study those sciences, so you have to understand the vocabulary of the Bible and the church if you are to understand the science of theology.

On the other hand, you must watch us professional theologians very carefully! Sometimes *we* know what we are talking about when we use the language of our profession, but do not explain it so that other people can understand it. And sometimes we unconsciously use technical jargon to avoid difficult problems, or to hide from ourselves and others the fact that we ourselves do not know what we are talking about. I have done my best to avoid both faults, but may not always have been successful. So read this book very critically. Keep asking all the way through: Does it make sense? What is the meaning of this biblical or technical word? Has the author explained it adequately? Is it my fault or his that I do not understand? And be just as hard on other members of your study group. Don't let anyone get by with meaningless or ambiguous jargon. Keep asking for definitions and explanations—even of the most basic words, such as *God* or *Christ* or *Spirit* or *sin*. Theology that is only intellectual or pious or undefined biblical jargon is always *bad* theology. It is not enough to say "The Bible says . . ." or "The church teaches . . ." or "Theologians say . . ." The job is not done until the meaning of such statements is clear.

The Problem of Personal Bias

No matter how seriously theologians try to put aside their personal wishes, feelings, and opinions in order to understand the truth about God and God's ways with the world, their understanding of the truth is always distorted because they see or hear from the perspective of their particular race, sex, economic class, religious and national heritage. That is also true of the white, male, middle-class, North American Presbyterian who wrote this book. Even when I have left questions open and have presented several alternative solutions, you will probably see what my own personal preferences are. Even when I have quoted scripture or the teachings of the church or the writings of other theologians, what comes out is inevitably *my* interpretation of them. I have tried to be fair in describing the position of those with whom I differ and to recognize the limitations and difficulties of my own position. I have tried not to twist what others have written to suit my own taste and fancy. Many of the changes in this revised edition are the result of my trying to listen especially to the voices of people who are different from me: women, members of racial and ethnic minorities, the poor and oppressed, and theologians of the third world. But still my biases and limitations will show through—more clearly to those of you who are different from me than to me.

This means that you must study this book with a critical eye. Your task is not to learn just what I think, but what the truth is. But how can you distinguish between the truth itself and my biased interpretation of it? You must be careful here, because the temptation is to judge what the book says by *your* personal biases. If you do that, you still will not discover the truth, but only the confirmation of your own likes and dislikes. You will finish exactly where you began, having learned nothing. What are the criteria, then, by which you can at least honestly try to get past both my *and* your own prejudices? There are some. They are the criteria by which both what I have written and your study of it should be guided—criteria that define the task of Christian theology as such.

THE TASK OF THEOLOGY

What we have to do and the way we should go about it comes into focus as soon as we say that what we are concerned with is not just theology in general but *Christian* theology. Our task is to try to understand a particular view of God, human beings, and the world, the content and nature of which is no more a matter of personal opinion than is the content and nature of Marxist communism or Freudian psychology. As with the teachings of Marx or Freud, so with the religion identified with the name of Christ—we may like or dislike what we are told. We may believe it or not, accept it or not. We may and should criticize any particular interpretation of it. But when we are asked to say what Marxism or Freudianism or Christianity is, we are neither asked nor allowed simply to express our own likes, dislikes, wishes, opinions, or prejudices about politics, psychology, or religion. We have to try to understand a way of thinking and living that is identifiable quite apart from our own personal preferences and ideas.

In the case of Christian theology, there are three objective factors that have to be taken into consideration. They are the criteria that have guided me as I have tried to say what the Christian faith is. And they are the criteria that can help you evaluate both what I have written and your own reactions. My purpose in writing and your task in studying this book is to understand the truth about God, human beings, and the world as it is made known, believed, and experienced in Jesus Christ, the Bible, and the church.

Jesus Christ

The name *Christ* is by definition the clue to what Christian faith is. If you want to know what God is like, Christian theology says—look at Christ. If you want to know what real humanity is and how you can live a genuinely human life—look at Christ. If you want to know what God is doing in the world and in your individual lives—look at Christ. For Christian theology, the person and work of Christ is the key to *all* truth about God, ourselves, and the world we live in.

To say this does not mean that all questions are automatically answered, all problems automatically solved by repeating the magic words *Jesus Christ*. Christ is himself the question and problem of Christian theology, the mystery we must try to understand. But to say that he stands at the center of all Christian theology does mean that at every point we must let all our own ideas, feelings, and experiences be examined, measured, judged, and interpreted by the problem, question, and mystery of who he is and what he does.

Again, the claim that for Christian theologians everything turns around the truth to be discovered in Christ does not imply the arrogant claim that only we Christians know anything about God, human beings, and the world, and that we have nothing to learn from anyone else. We learn from scripture itself that the whole world is God's world and that there is no place where God is not at work creating, reconciling, and renewing—even among people who do not know or believe in God. Therefore, in this book we will also listen to and be open to learn from the natural sciences, psychology, political science, secular novels and plays, and even other religions. Consistent with our Christian standpoint, we will do so in the light of the truth about God, human beings, and the world given in Christ. But as we listen to these "outsiders," it will be vital not to confuse Christian truth with our own biased interpretation of it.

This, then, is the first objective reference point for our theological work. Recognizing that it is the problem as well as the answer of Christian theology, being wide open for the insights of other points of view, everything we do must be done with reference to the truth that is *in Christ Jesus* about God, about ourselves, and about the world.

The Bible

In the Bible we come to know the Person who stands at the center of the Christian faith. The whole of the Old Testament looks forward to him and is fulfilled in him. The whole of the New Testament is an expression of the faith that in him is hid the secret of the past, present, and future not only of Christian individuals but of the whole world. Christian theology is different from theology in general in that of all books this particular book is the source and norm of its attempt to understand the truth about God, human beings, and the world. The fact of the Bible means that we are not left alone to talk about a God who is only the projection of our own desires and fears, a humanity that is only the result of our wishful thinking about ourselves, or a world that is only the reflection of our own pessimistic or optimistic view of life. If we want to know what Christians believe, we cannot look only to our own minds and hearts and personal experiences; we have to go to the Bible.

You will find, therefore, that Bible study is an essential part of the theological work ahead of you. Take the trouble to look up the passages mentioned and to do the Bible study suggested. Use the various Bible dictionaries and word study books at your disposal. That will give you a constant way of checking my biases and presuppositions as well as your own and of exposing both of our subjective interpretations of Christian truth to the source and norm of that truth.

But Bible study in itself is no automatic guarantee of good theology—for two reasons that have to do not so much with the *authority* of scripture as with the more difficult problem of the right *interpretation* of scripture.

First, there is always the danger that we will find *in* the Bible only what we take with us *to* it—that we will use it to confirm what we already think and will hear only what we want to hear. Because they already hated Jews before they read the Bible, some German Christians once found in the Bible justification for slaughtering millions of Jews. Because they wanted to keep their human property, some American Christians once argued from the Bible that it is right to buy and sell human beings as if they were animals. Mean people usually find a mean God in the Bible, and superficial people usually find a superficial God. Comfortable, powerful people usually find that the Bible supports social and political conservatism; poor, exploited people usually find that it supports social and political reform or revolution. What is to keep us from simply using the Bible to give authority to our own religious, social, political, and economic prejudices? What is to prevent us from using the study of this ancient book as a pious excuse for refusing to face the radical claims of the living God on every area of our lives, here and now?

But the difficulty of faithful biblical interpretation lies not just with us; it lies in the Bible itself. It is not one book but a collection of writings composed by and for ancient Near Eastern people over a long period of time. It bears witness not to general, timeless truths about God, but to the way different people and groups, using different ways of speaking and thought forms, discerned the word and work of God in their particular time, place, and situation. All of them lived with a prescientific, preindustrial worldview, in a patriarchal-hierarchical society that generally treated women as inferior, accepted slavery as normal, and did not even dream of all the complex problems and needs of the kind of modern technological society we live in. How are we to discern in this ancient book what the living God is saying and doing in our quite different time and place? How are we to distinguish within scripture what is the will of God in all times and places from what was God's specific will for particular people in one or another of the particular historical situations we read about in the Bible?

Both these problems raise very difficult questions about how scripture is rightly interpreted. But the confessions of the Reformed tradition (which we will discuss presently) give us some widely accepted rules of interpretation that can help as you evaluate the way I have used the Bible and the way you use it.[1]

1. *Scripture is to be interpreted in light of its own purpose.* All Reformed confessions agree with the Westminster Confession (1.2) that scripture is "given by the inspiration of God to be *the rule of faith and life*." We read the Bible rightly when we read it to learn who God is and how we may live faithfully in the presence of God. We do not read it properly when we read it as if it were a textbook of scientific information about the structure of the world and human life in it, or a book about world history in general. Therefore we should be neither surprised nor offended when we encounter in this ancient book a prescientific or unscientific worldview and understanding of history. It tells us about the ultimate origin, meaning, and goal of human life that lie beyond the scope of modern scientific and historical disciplines.

2. *Scripture interprets itself.* "When there is a question about the true and full sense of any scripture, it may be searched and known by other places that speak more clearly" (Westminster Confession, 1.9). When we encounter passages that are hard to understand, we can look at other passages that throw a different light or more light on the question at hand. This rule also means that we must listen to the *total* witness of

scripture, not just to selected passages that support what we already think and want to hear. When anyone argues that "the Bible says" this or that, it is always important to ask, "Is that *all* the Bible says, or have you picked only passages that support your own ideas and preferences? What other passages might give us a better and fuller understanding of the biblical message?"

3. *The christological principle.* Jesus Christ is the clearest revelation of who God is and what God promises and wills for faithful Christian life. Therefore all scripture is to be interpreted in light of "what Christ Jesus himself did and commanded" (Scots Confession, 18), "in the light of its witness to God's work of reconciliation in Christ" (Confession of 1967, I.C.2). "When we encounter apparent tensions and conflicts in what Scripture teaches us to believe and do, the final appeal must be to the authority of Christ" (Declaration of Faith, 6.3). This christological principle of interpretation can help us with many questions. For instance, would it help to read some Old Testament texts that seem to point to the brutality of God in dealing with God's enemies in light of the New Testament witness to God's love in Christ for sinners and Christ's command that we are to love our enemies? Does the way Jesus dealt with women help us interpret texts in both the Old and New Testaments that suggest the inferior status of women?

4. *The rule of faith.* Referring to such central Protestant convictions as confession of the unique authority of scripture and salvation by God's grace alone, the Scots Confession (chap. 18) says, "We dare not receive or admit any interpretation which is contrary to any point of our faith." The Declaration of Faith says more generally, "listening with respect to fellow believers past and present, we anticipate that the Holy Spirit will enable us to interpret faithfully God's Word for our time and place" (chap. 6.3). We interpret scripture rightly when we do not try to interpret it by ourselves, as if we were the first ever to ask what it means. Seeking the guidance of God's Spirit, faithful Christians before us and other faithful Christians in the church around us have also struggled to understand and be led by it, and we are to listen to them "with respect." In our time we have learned the importance of listening also to fellow Christians, past and present, who are different from us in gender, race, class, cultural background, and national origin. They help us avoid confusing biblical truth with our own limited perspective on it.

5. *The rule of love.* "We hold that interpretation of scripture to be orthodox and genuine which agrees with . . . the rule of faith and *love*"

(Second Helvetic Confession, chap. 2). An often forgotten rule, this one is based on the fact that the fundamental expression of God's will is the twofold commandment to love God and neighbor. Any interpretation of scripture is wrong that shows indifference toward or contempt for any individual or group inside or outside the church. All right interpretations reflect the love of God and the love of God's people for all kinds of people everywhere, everyone included and no one excluded.

6. *The study of scripture in its literary and historical context.* Already the classical confessions of the sixteenth century knew that it was important to interpret the scripture "from the nature of the language in which they were written, likewise according to the circumstances in which they were set down" (Second Helvetic Confession, chap. 2). But it is especially contemporary confessions that recognize the importance of the literary and historical investigation of scripture:

> The Scriptures, given under the guidance of the Holy Spirit, are nevertheless the words of men, conditioned by the language, thought forms and literary fashions of the places and times at which they were written. They reflect views of life, history, and the cosmos which were then current. The church, therefore, has an obligation to approach the Scriptures with literary and historical understanding. As God has spoken his word in these diverse cultural situations, the church is confident that he will continue to speak through the Scriptures in a changing world and in every form of human culture. (Confession of 1967, I.C.2)

> God has chosen to address his inspired Word to us through diverse and varied human writings. Therefore we use the best available methods to understand them in their historical and cultural setting and in the literary forms in which they were cast. (Declaration of Faith, 6.3)

We need not be afraid to learn from scholars who are skilled in investigating scripture in its original literary and historical context. They help us to understand that God spoke to our ancestors (Heb. 1:1), and they help us to discern what the God who spoke and acted "back then" is saying and doing here and now.

I have tried in this book to follow these rules of interpretation, and you will be on your way toward becoming honest and faithful biblical theologians as you use them to evaluate and correct my, your own, and others' interpretation of scripture.

Our discussion of scripture as a second criterion of faithful Christian theology has underlined what we said about God's self-revelation in Christ as the first criterion, and it has already anticipated what we now have to say about a third criterion.

The Church

As soon as we say *Christian* theology we also say *church* theology. To be a follower of Christ has meant from the very beginning to join the community of disciples he draws together around himself. Christ himself promised to make himself known especially where people were gathered together in his name. The Bible was not written for and about isolated individuals; it was written for and about a *community* of people—Israel in the Old Testament, the church in the New Testament. You cannot be a Christian by yourself; you can only be a Christian together with other Christians who serve God in the world. It follows, then, that you cannot be a Christian theologian by reflecting on the meaning of Christ and studying the Bible only by yourself, to suit yourself. You can be a Christian theologian only as you do your work in conversation with other Christians in the Christian community, as together with them you seek to learn what God is doing and what God also has for you to do in the world outside the church.

There are several ways in which this book seeks to be church theology—and invites you to be theologians of the church. First, I have tried—and invite you to try—to listen to and learn from fellow Christians in the church, including especially those who are different from us in all the ways that set people against each other in contemporary secular society. Second, I have constantly depended on the work of the great theologians of the church, both past and present. Whether I have interpreted them correctly is always open to question. But the fact that they are there is at least a check on my and your ignorance, narrowness, and personal prejudices. Finally, this is church theology in that it constantly depends on the creeds and confessions that are the official statements of what the church believes. This is still another way in which my own and your private opinions will be subject to examination and correction.

THE REFORMED TRADITION

I acknowledge that it is especially the creeds and confessions of the Reformed-Presbyterian churches that will guide us. Does this mean that we have been trying to overcome personal theological biases only in order to substitute a narrow denominational bias? Several things need to be said from the very beginning about the particular place we will stand to do our church theology.

Christians Among Fellow Christians

All Christian theologians work from some one concrete part of the one "holy catholic church." They may be Roman Catholic, Lutheran, Methodist, Anglican-Episcopalian, Baptist, or some other "brand" of Christian, but none of us can belong to *the* church without belonging to *a* church. If we do our work from a particular perspective, this does not mean to claim that we are the real Christians whereas those others are false Christians, or that we have a monopoly on the truth. We can and we will learn also from the thinkers and creeds and confessions of other parts of the church. Even when our tradition differs from theirs, we will not question the fact that they are truly and sincerely Christian, too. But genuine and helpful conversation within the whole church is possible only where the individual partners in the conversation do not try to hide who they are and where they come from. In this book, we will enter the conversation honestly and openly identifying our perspective as Presbyterian-Reformed—the tradition springing especially from John Calvin and guided by the creeds and confessions of the Calvinistic branch of the church.

An Ecumenical Tradition

At the heart of the Reformed tradition stands the one confession of faith that nearly all Christian churches everywhere have in common—the Apostles' Creed. The articles of this creed form the main outline of this book. This means that although you may expect some typically Reformed emphases in this book (for instance, the free sovereign grace of God, our total dependence on God, the claim of God on every area of our life in the world), nevertheless you are not beginning a narrow denominational study. In following the Apostles' Creed, I have tried to write not just Reformed theology, but ecumenical (worldwide) *Christian* theology—from a Reformed point of view.

The Reformed Family

The word *Reformed* itself excludes narrowness and one-sidedness. There is no such thing as *the* Reformed position; there is only a generally recognizable Reformed "perspective" or "orientation" or, perhaps best of all, "family."

All Reformed Christians recognize especially John Calvin as their father. But Calvin can be understood in different ways, and, as is the case in any family, his children feel different degrees of dependence upon him. So, for instance, the American Reformed theologians Charles Hodge (died 1878) and Benjamin Warfield (died 1921) stuck closer to home than have Karl Barth and Jürgen Moltmann, two twentieth-century Reformed theologians. But there is no doubt that Barth and Moltmann are legitimate children and still belong to the family.

Moreover, there is no one authoritative statement of faith to which all Reformed churches subscribe. There are many different statements. They all bear a common family resemblance, but they differ from each other in emphasis, in the spirit in which they are written, and sometimes in theological content. We will consider all of them, recognizing all as genuinely Reformed, honestly acknowledging their differences, refusing to let any one statement become the standard by which the others are judged. There is plenty of room in the Reformed family, in other words, for individual differences and freedom of movement.

Finally, strictly speaking, "Reformed" is a theological, not a denominational, title. It is a mistake to limit it to any one denomination. More than a hundred churches around the world belong to the World Alliance of Reformed Churches, representing millions of Christians who identify themselves as Reformed Christians. "Reformed" is a doctrinal-theological description that cuts across all linguistic, national, racial, class, political, and cultural distinctions.

In other words, when we say that we will be doing Christian theology from a Reformed perspective, we do not mean that we will be talking about just "me and my denomination, and those within it who think and live exactly like me." The Reformed perspective aims not at setting up but at breaking down barriers between Christians.

This brings us to a last point, which summarizes everything I have been trying to say about the task of theology in this whole chapter.

Reformed and Always Being Reformed

The heading echoes an old slogan of the Reformed tradition. To say that this book is Christian theology from a Reformed point of view does not mean that our task is to try to master an already fixed system of theology that Reformed Christians believe has once and for all captured the truth about God, human beings, and the world. According to the Reformed faith, no system of theology can ever do that. *The* truth is the truth about God, human life, and the world in Jesus Christ as we know him in the Bible. All theology, whether that of an individual or of the whole church, is at best an inadequate, fallible, human attempt to understand that truth. According to the Reformed churches, therefore, there always has been and always will be the right and responsibility to question any individual's, any denomination's, any creedal document's grasp of the truth—not for the sake of our freedom to think anything we please, but for the sake of the freedom of biblical truth from every human attempt to capture and tame it.

To work at Christian theology from the Reformed perspective, then, does not mean that we are asked to hold the fort and defend what Calvin and his followers thought three or four hundred years ago. Being loyal to them means that we do not simply repeat what they said, but that we take seriously what they themselves taught us about the superiority of the Word of God over every human word—including theirs! It means to ask the question they themselves taught us to ask: "What is the living God we know in Christ and in the Bible doing and saying in *our* time, *here* and *now,* where *we* have to think and live as Christians?" And that means that we will be faithful to the Reformed tradition when we continue the reformation begun in the sixteenth and seventeenth centuries and are willing when necessary to say things differently in the twentieth century.

Reformed means *always being reformed.* That is the task—and the freedom—to which you are invited as you study in this book *Christian* theology from a *Reformed* point of view.

But what is the relation between the authority of Christ, the authority of the Bible, the authority of the church, and the authority of our individual attempts to measure the teachings of the church by the truth given in Christ and in the Bible? That is the problem we have to wrestle with in the next chapter.

FOR FURTHER REFLECTION AND STUDY

1. In light of what you have read in this chapter, evaluate the following statements:
   a. Religion is just a matter of personal opinion. It doesn't really matter what you believe so long as you are sincere.
   b. All religions are basically the same.
   c. Christ is the answer.
   d. The church ought to stick to spiritual concerns and not meddle in social, political, and economic problems.
   e. "My reading is very limited and yet very extended; it begins with Moses and ends with John. The Bible and the Bible alone I read

and study. . . . For it does not matter to me to learn how Ursin or Luther or Anselm or Augustine or Irenaeus [that is, great theologians in the history of the church] thought about the matter and formulated and determined it—they and their decisions are too new. I want that which is old, original and solely authentic: Holy Scripture itself" (G. Menken, nineteenth-century theologian).[2]

2. What should your attitude be toward someone whose theological beliefs are different from yours?
3. What should be the attitude of Christian theology toward such secular disciplines as science and psychology? Toward other religions?
4. What is the difference between "Reformed" and "Presbyterian"?
5. Is "Always reforming and being reformed" a dangerous slogan?
6. Would "I believe; help my unbelief" be a good motto as you study Christian theology?

2

Who Says So?

The Problem of Authority

Who has the right and the ability to decide what is genuinely Christian? The biblical writers? But whose *interpretation* of the Bible? The church? *Which* church? Every individual Christian for himself or herself? But how can we tell the difference between what is *Christian* and what is only *personal opinion?*

These questions point to the problem we are going to tackle in this chapter—the problem of authority. It confronts us most directly and concretely with the question of our attitude toward the various creeds and confessions of the church, so we will deal with the problem of authority in terms of the question of their authority. (A creed or confession is an officially adopted statement that spells out a church's interpretation of what it means to be faithful and obedient Christians. A creed is a brief statement; a confession of faith, a more developed one. Both are "confessional statements.")

Our perspective will be that of the Presbyterian-Reformed tradition. But Presbyterian and Reformed churches are not the only churches with confessional standards. The Roman Catholic, Eastern Orthodox, Lutheran, and to a lesser extent the Anglican, Episcopal, and Methodist churches are also confessional bodies. Even so-called free churches like the Baptist churches that acknowledge only the Bible as their creed have often made semiauthoritative confessional statements. Most Christian churches officially or informally share the faith of the ancient Nicene and Apostles' Creeds. Therefore, before we speak of the uniquely Presbyterian-Reformed understanding of creeds and confessions, we must speak of the origin, nature, and purpose of creeds and confessions in the history of the Christian church generally.[1]

CREEDS AND CONFESSIONS

> We want a living People's Church which is the expression of all the religious powers of our nation. . . . We demand a change in the legal constitution and open battles against Marxism, hostile to religion and to the nation, and against its socialist-Christian fellow travelers of all degrees. . . . We see in race, national character and nation orders of life given and entrusted to us by God, to maintain which is a law of God for us. Therefore racial mixing is to be opposed. . . . We know something of Christian duty and love toward the helpless, but we demand also the protection of the nation from the incapable and inferior. . . . We want an Evangelical Church which roots in the national character, and we repudiate the spirit of a Christian cosmopolitanism.[2]

These sentences, written in 1932, were a part of the platform of a group called "German Christians," who wanted to make the church into the religious arm of Hitler's Nazi regime. In 1934, another group of Christians in Germany from the Reformed, Lutheran, and United Churches made a "confession of faith" in what was called the Barmen Declaration. It said in part:

> Jesus Christ, as he is attested for us in Holy Scripture, is the one Word of God which we have to hear and which we have to trust and obey in life and in death.
>
> We reject the false doctrine, as though the Church could and would have to acknowledge as a source of its proclamation, apart from and besides this one Word of God, still other events and powers, figures and truths, as God's revelation. . . .
>
> As Jesus Christ is God's assurance of the forgiveness of all our sins, so in the same way and with the same seriousness he is also God's mighty claim upon our whole life. Through him befalls us a joyful deliverance from the godless fetters of this world for a free, grateful service to his creatures.
>
> We reject the false doctrine, as though there were areas of our life in which we would not belong to Jesus Christ, but to other lords. . . .
>
> The Christian Church is the congregation of the brethren in which Jesus Christ acts presently as the Lord in Word and sacrament, through the Holy Spirit. As the Church of pardoned sinners, it has to testify in the midst of a sinful world . . . that it is solely his property, and that it lives and wants to live solely from his comfort and from his direction in the expectation of his appearance.
>
> We reject the false doctrine, as though the Church were permitted to abandon the form of its message and order to its own pleasure or to changes in prevailing ideological and political convictions.

The Nazis got the point! Those who stood by this creed were considered traitors, and many of them gave their lives because they refused to compromise their faith in Jesus Christ to make it compatible with the Nazi ideology.

This Barmen Declaration is a modern example of what "creed" or "confession of faith" has always meant in the history of the Christian faith. It suggests several things about the origin, nature, and purpose of creeds and confessions in general.

1. *The great creeds and confessions are rooted in concrete historical situations.* They are not the work of otherworldly theologians who sit down to think up a creed, but the work of theologians faced with crucial issues of the church's life and witness in the world. To know and confess the God of the Bible is to know and confess the living, acting God who confronts us in the events of history—"secular" as well as "religious" history. The earliest Christian confession and the basic Christian affirmation repeated in different ways, in different times and places, in *all* the creeds of the church is the simple New Testament confession "Jesus is Lord" (Rom. 10:9; Phil. 2:11).

That sounds admirably pious and comfortably harmless until its meaning is spelled out in the concrete situation of the church at various periods in its history. Then it has always become "subversive," "fanatical," "ridiculous," "explosive"—*alive! Jesus Christ* is Lord: not Caesar, not the pope, not Hitler, not Jim Crow! *Jesus Christ* rules our thinking and living: not the ancient Jewish, or the classical Greek, or the medieval European, or the modern American way of life. *Jesus Christ* is to be served and obeyed: above nation, above generally accepted ethical and religious values, above family, above economic prosperity—above everything else. We understand the creeds and confessions of the church only when we see that they have to do with life-and-death decisions of individual Christians and the Christian community, not just with some abstract intellectual theories.

2. *The great creeds and confessions are also a form of worship.* "I believe in God, the Father Almighty, Creator of heaven and earth" does not mean only "I believe that God exists." It means "I put my ultimate trust and confidence in this God—and no other." If I confess that Jesus Christ is Lord, I thankfully and prayerfully commit myself to his care and to his authority. "In confession the believer takes his stand, commits his life, declares what he believes to be true, affirms his ultimate loyalty, and defies every false claim upon his life."[3]

3. *The great creeds and confessions are intended to be a guide to the proper interpretation of scripture for Christian preaching and witness.* They assume that the Bible is the norm for living and proclaiming Christian truth, and they seek to preserve its authority by ruling out false interpretations that in fact "put the word and work of the Lord in the service of some self-determined wishes, purposes or plans" (Barmen Declaration, par. 6).

4. *The great creeds and confessions of the church are usually polemical.* They defend and clarify Christian truth against attacks and perversions both from without and from within the church. Heresy from within has often been more difficult to recognize and fight than heresy from without, and therefore it is more dangerous. The most dangerous heretics the creeds have had to fight are not the openly godless, immoral people who attack the church and the Christian faith from the outside. They are the people within the church (like the "German Christians") who are enthusiastically in favor of the Bible, religion, morality, and the church—but use them to lend authority and respectability to ideologies and methods they consciously or unconsciously want to enthrone *in place of* God in Christ.

On the other hand, heretics, both within and without, have performed a real service to the church. They have forced the church to formulate and clarify its beliefs. Sometimes, by overemphasizing some aspect of Christian truth neglected by the church, they have forced the church to correct its own one-sidedness.

5. *The great creeds and confessions are creeds and confessions of the church.* Even when they have been composed by an individual or several individuals, and even when they say "I believe," they are intended to articulate the faith of the *whole community* of Christians. They do not aim to confess the faith of a few extraordinarily orthodox or pious individuals, or the faith of a group within or among the churches who consider themselves spiritually and intellectually superior. They aim to be the voice of the *"one holy catholic"* church. And even when they have to exclude, the great creeds and confessions do so for the sake of the "one *holy* catholic" church. We misunderstand and misuse the creeds when we use them intentionally to divide and set Christian against Christian, rather than as an attempt to express the unity of the Christian community.

6. *The great creeds and confessions have been intended for the instruction of Christians as manuals of education.* The earliest creeds

grew out of the need to teach new converts the meaning of the Christian faith before they were baptized. Creedal and confessional statements throughout the history of the church have therefore often been in the form of catechisms used in the instruction of children, new Christians, and mature Christians who need to learn to articulate their faith.

7. *The limitations of creeds and confessions.* The church's creeds and confessions have united and equipped the church to deal with the issues, problems, dangers, and opportunities of the specific historical situation in which they were written. But historical *concreteness* also means historical *limitation.* The language and thought forms that made sense in an earlier time may be very difficult for Christians in a later time to understand (as anyone knows who tries to understand the seventeenth-century Westminster Confession today). The great classical confessions, written before the discoveries of modern science, reflect an understanding of the world and natural processes that seem outdated and "primitive" to us "modern" Christians (just as our confessions will seem outdated and primitive to Christians in centuries to come!). The theology and ethics of confessions of every age are shaped by the sexual, familial, social, economic, cultural, and political patterns and norms of a particular society (or particular segment of that society) in a particular period of history. Even those confessions that claim to be based exclusively on biblical revelation have often confused the revelation itself with various historically and socially conditioned thought forms and cultural patterns of the time in which the biblical revelation was first received.

The confessions of the church, in other words, have indeed interpreted, defended, and preserved biblical-Christian truth. They have united the Christian community in its one task of bearing witness to the one Christian confession that Jesus is Lord. But at the same time, because of their limited historical and social perspective, they have also inevitably distorted the truth revealed in Jesus Christ, been unable to grasp or even see some parts of the biblical witness to God's presence and work in Christ, and divided the church into churches with conflicting views of what Christian faith and life are all about.

Is there any way to distinguish between the biblical-Christian truth to which confessions of faith seek to bear witness and their always partial and inadequate witness to the truth? Christians in the Reformed-Presbyterian tradition believe that they know at least how to go about this task.

CREEDS AND CONFESSIONS IN THE REFORMED TRADITION

Everything we have said about the nature and purpose of creeds and confessions in general applies also to those of Presbyterian and Reformed churches. But the Reformed confessional tradition is unique among other Christian traditions in two ways: in the *doctrinal content* of its confessional statements and in its understanding of their *authority.*

The unique doctrinal emphases will appear in the following chapters, so we will not discuss them now. It is important, however, to say once again that we ought not overemphasize the uniqueness of the doctrinal content of Reformed confessions. From the very beginning and throughout their history, Reformed churches have sought to represent the worldwide "catholic" church. Their confessions do not speak of what "the Reformed Church" or "Presbyterians" believe, but of what *Christians* believe. When Reformed Christians have been true to their own confessional tradition (unfortunately not always the case!), they have always been open to learn from other churches and traditions, and eager to participate in conversations with them that could lead to mutual correction and reconciliation.

This doctrinal openness follows precisely from the Reformed tradition's unique understanding of the authority of its confessional statements. The most revealing clue to this uniqueness is the fact that (in contrast to all other Christian traditions) the Reformed tradition has produced a great number of creedal and confessional statements, written by many different people, in many different places, over a long period of time (see the partial list of them in the Appendix to this chapter). This means that the Reformed tradition has never been content to recognize any one confessional statement as an absolute, infallible statement of faith for all Reformed Christians for all time. Confessional statements do have authority for Reformed Christians, and there is a remarkable consistency in the fundamental content of their many confessions. But for them all creeds and confessions have only a *provisional, temporary, relative* authority and are therefore subject to revision and correction. There are three reasons for this attitude toward their confessions.

1. *Reformed Christians believe that their confessional statements are subject to revision and correction because they know that all confessions are the work of limited, fallible, sinful human beings and churches.* In our time we have become more aware than most of those who wrote and

adopted Reformed confessions in the past that even when confessions intend to serve only the revealed truth and will of God, they are also influenced by the sexual, racial, and economic biases and cultural limitations of a particular historical situation. But from the very beginning and throughout their history, Reformed Christians and their confessions have acknowledged with the Westminster Confession of 1646: "All synods or councils since the apostles' times, whether general or particular, may err, and many have erred; therefore they are not to be made the rule of faith and practice, but to be used as a help in both" (33.3).

2. *Reformed Christians believe that their confessional statements are subject to revision and correction because they believe that faith in the living God who is present and at work in the risen Christ, through the Holy Spirit, means always to be open to hear a new and fresh word from the Lord.* Reformed Christians have never been content to learn only how Christians before them discerned and responded to the word and work of God. They have continually asked in every new time, place, and situation, "What is the living Lord of scripture saying and doing *here* and *now,* and what do *we* have to say and do to be faithful and obedient in *our* time and place?" So, for instance:

> But where something is brought before us by our pastors or by others, which brings us closer to Christ, and in accordance with God's word is more conducive to mutual friendship and Christian love than the interpretation now presented, we will gladly accept it and will not limit the course of the Holy Spirit, which does not go backwards toward the flesh but always forward towards the image of Jesus Christ our Lord. (Confession of the Synod of Berne in 1532)[4]

3. *Reformed Christians believe that their confessional statements are subject to revision and correction because they are subordinate to the higher authority of scripture.* A frequently repeated theme in Reformed confessions is the subjection of Reformed Christians' own theological and ethical thought (including their interpretation of scripture itself) to the higher authority of scripture or, more accurately, to the higher authority of the Holy Spirit who speaks through scripture.

> We protest that if any man will note in this confession of ours any article or sentence repugnant to God's holy word, that it would please him of his gentleness and for Christian charity's sake to admonish us of the same in writing; and we upon our honor and fidelity, by God's grace, do promise unto him satisfaction from the mouth of God, that is, from his holy scriptures, or else reformation of that which he shall prove to be amiss. (Preface to the Scots Confession, 1560)

> The Supreme Judge, by which all controversies of religion are to be determined, and all decrees of councils, opinions of ancient writers, doctrines of men, and private spirits are to be examined, and in whose sentence we are to rest, can be no other but the Holy Spirit speaking in the Scripture. (Westminster Confession, 1.10. Note that this applies also to the Westminster Confession itself!)

> Confessions and declarations are subordinate standards in the church, subject to the authority of Jesus Christ, the Word of God, as the Scriptures bear witness to him. No one type of confession is exclusively valid, no one statement is irreformable. Obedience to Jesus Christ alone identifies the one universal church and supplies the continuity of its tradition. This obedience is the ground of the church's duty and freedom to reform itself in life and doctrine as new occasions, in God's providence, may demand. (Preface to the Confession of 1967)

Now we see the reason for the slogan "reformed and always being reformed" that was mentioned at the end of the last chapter!

But this uniquely Reformed understanding of the provisional, temporary, and relative authority of creeds and confessions puts individual members of Presbyterian and Reformed churches in a difficult position. We turn now from talk about "the church" and "the Reformed tradition" to speak about *you* and *me*, and the attitude *we* should have toward the church's confessional statements.

THE FREEDOM AND RESPONSIBILITY OF INDIVIDUAL CHRISTIANS

How should individual members of Presbyterian and Reformed churches deal with the official teachings of their church? If I want to be a faithful Christian and member of the church, to what extent am I free either to agree or disagree with them, and to what extent am I required to accept them? There are three possible answers to this question—the first two easy and wrong, the last difficult and correct!

One could argue in the first place that the task of theology is simply to restate and interpret the given teachings of the church. They are not to be criticized or questioned. The possibility of error and inadequacy is not to be considered. Perhaps they can be understood in a deeper and more complete way than they have been understood in the past. Perhaps they could be expressed in different language. Perhaps new additions could even be made. But the task of individual Christian thinkers is essentially one of holding onto and defending what the church has said in the past. They are totally bound to it, not free to challenge or contradict it.

This is the conservative Roman Catholic understanding of the theologian's task (an understanding rejected by many contemporary Catholic theologians). Some Reformed thinkers have also considered it to be their task, but only in contradiction to the very Reformed creeds and confessions they want to defend. This position may admit that Christ as he is given to us in scripture is Lord *in* and *through* the church, but it does not see that he is also Lord *over* the church. Ultimately it defies the church, because it attributes to its teachings an infallible authority that belongs to God alone.

A second simplistic solution to the problem goes to the opposite extreme and says that the theologian's task is not to deify but to ignore the church's creeds and confessions, to insist on total freedom from them. What the church has said in the past is of no great importance; what *I* think *now* is what is important. Protestantism in general has tended toward such individualism. It can be expressed in either a conservative or a liberal way.

Conservative Protestant individualism appeals to the Reformation principle that every individual has immediate access to scripture through the Holy Spirit and argues that we do not need and should not allow the interference of the church. The good theologian is the theologian alone with his or her Bible. Good theology is *my* interpretation of the Bible, not the church's interpretation.

Liberal Protestant individualism argues that good theology is not the work of Christian individuals alone with the *external* authority of the Bible but the work of Christian individuals alone with the *internal* authority of their own reason, personal religious experience, conscience, or innermost understanding of themselves. Neither the church nor the Bible can have a higher authority than what I know to be true in one way or another deep within myself.

But neither the conservative nor the liberal individualist can be a Reformed theologian. If Roman Catholic theology of the past tended to deify the *church,* both conservative and liberal Protestant individualism tends to deify the *Christian individual.* Both Roman Catholic "collectivism" and various expressions of Protestant individualism give final authority to a human word that according to the Reformed churches belongs to the Word of God alone.

The third, more difficult, answer is that Reformed theologians are therefore neither totally bound to the church and its confessions and creeds, nor totally free from the church and its teachings. They are *relatively* bound and *relatively* free. In saying what this means, we at the same time summarize everything we have been saying about how we are to understand and use the creeds and confessions of our churches.

Relatively Bound

The individual Reformed Christian is relatively bound to the confessional teachings of the church in four ways.

1. The creeds and confessions are attempts to understand and interpret scripture. They help to preserve respect for the authority of scripture by being a constant check on theologians' tendency to let their own opinions and feelings instead of scripture determine their thinking.

2. God in Christ promised to be present and known in the church. To ignore the creeds of the church is to cut oneself off from the community to which is promised the truth the theologian seeks to understand and interpret.

3. The Holy Spirit who enlightens my mind, here, today, is the same Spirit who has been at work among other Christians in other places and times. To ignore the creeds and confessions of the church would mean that I am not really interested in what the Holy Spirit is saying and doing, that I run the risk of confusing the Spirit of God with some other spirit.

4. To be a Reformed Christian means to belong by free decision to the community of Reformed Christians who confess their faith through their creeds. To ignore the creeds is to contradict my own decision to participate in *this* Christian community.

Relatively Free

The individual Reformed Christian is relatively free in relation to the confessional teaching of the church in the following ways.

1. The creeds and confessions of the church are the words of fallible, human beings—people who are "of themselves liars," as the Belgic Confession strongly puts it. The church's understanding of Christian truth is therefore always subject to possible improvement and correction.

2. The final truth of the Christian faith is the truth mediated to us by scripture, not the truth of the church. Our first loyalty must be to God's Word, not to the words of Christians.

3. We can serve the church only when we are free to remind it of the One who stands above it. Christians who want only and always to defend the church's past and present decisions contribute to the idolatrous substitute of the church's word for the Word of God, and thus help corrupt instead of serve the church.

4. The Holy Spirit who was at work guiding the church's thought and life in other times and places is still at work. The Spirit did not retire when Calvin died or when the great confessions of the past were completed. We must be open to the Spirit's guidance here and now.

5. The Reformed confessions and creeds acknowledge their own authority to be relative and invite continually renewed examination and, if necessary, correction in the light of scripture. To deny freedom to perform this task is to contradict what the creeds themselves teach.

Another way of describing what it means to be relatively free and relatively bound in relation to the creeds and confessions of the church is to say that Reformed theologians (that means *all* members of a Reformed church) stand at the same time under the First and Fifth Commandments: "You shall have no other gods before me," but at the same time "Honor your father and your mother." We should honor our theological "fathers and mothers" who were responsible for the creeds and confessions of our church. That means to respect them and to consider very carefully and seriously what we are doing when we disobey or contradict them. But we cannot make gods of them. There is still a higher authority to whom we are responsible, and we do our parents no honor when we treat them as gods. We honor them precisely when we learn from them to be free *from* them—not free to think and live however we please, but free for the God whom they themselves have taught us to love and obey above all. We serve and obey our heavenly Parent when we give our human parents no less but also no more honor than is due them.

It is not an easy task to which we are called. When we criticize and disagree with the church's teaching at this or that point, how can we be sure that we really are doing it in obedience to Christ or scripture and not just as an expression of our own personal biases? When we hold tenaciously to what the church teaches, how can we be sure that we really are doing it because we respect the truth of God and not just because we are afraid or unwilling to subject our understanding of the truth to revision and correction? It is never easy to keep freedom and responsibility in proper balance. And it is especially difficult when we are trying to learn what it means to be properly free and properly bound in relation to the authority of the church.

But it is an exciting task to which we are called. How dull it would be if Christian truth were a neat package of information handed to us by the church to be memorized, mastered, and dutifully recited when called upon. How exciting it is to know that we never "arrive" in our understanding of the depths of the truth of God, that we are a part of a church whose motto is "always being reformed." Growing up is painful sometimes. It is easier not to grow. But not to grow is to stagnate and die. The confessional teachings of the Reformed churches are not an invitation for us to stop growing, asking, seeking, moving, changing. They are not our final destination but signposts that lead to maturity to "the measure of the stature of the fulness of Christ" (Eph. 4:13, RSV). Difficult as it is, we will use them correctly when we struggle to learn what it means to respect them as trustworthy signposts (being bound to them), but *only* as signposts that point beyond themselves (being free in relation to them). This will be our attitude toward the creeds and confessions of the church throughout our study of Christian doctrine according to the Reformed churches.

FOR FURTHER REFLECTION AND STUDY

1. Scholars believe that the very earliest confessions of faith (used even before the New Testament was written down) are preserved in the following passages: Phil. 2:5–11; 1 Cor. 15:3–8; Rom. 10:9; Eph. 4:4–6. Make a list of the affirmations these brief confessions make about God and about Jesus. Which of these affirmations are included in the Apostles' Creed? Which affirmations in the Apostles' Creed are *not* mentioned in these passages? Do you think the added elements in the Apostles' Creed are essential additions for a full summary of the Christian faith?
2. In view of the fact that the great creeds and confessions of the past were formulated to bring the truth of the Christian faith to bear on the needs and problems of a concrete historical situation, do you think that it is legitimate for your denomination to try to formulate a new confession for our time?
3. What heresies (perversions of the Christian faith and life) in the modern world and in the modern church would need to be dealt with in a contemporary confession of faith? List them.
4. Should a good Reformed Christian ever question the authoritative confessional statements of the church?
5. How can we reconcile the basic Christian affirmation "Jesus is Lord" (or King) with the democratic structure of the church?
6. To what extent is your personal faith (your "creed") determined by

an official creedal statement of the church? By the liturgy and especially the hymns of your church? By your pastor's views? By the prevailing local sentiment in your community? What are the advantages and disadvantages of being guided by a written creed or confession?

7. Members of the Presbyterian Church (U.S.A.), as you look at the following list of Reformed creeds and confessions, which of them are a part of your church's Book of Confessions?

APPENDIX
INTRODUCTION TO REFORMED CREEDS AND CONFESSIONS

Ancient Ecumenical Creeds

The three creeds listed below come from the ancient church and became the common root from which later creeds and confessions have grown. In our time they are still formally or tacitly acknowledged by most Christian churches—Roman Catholic, Eastern Orthodox, and the various Protestant denominations. Because they contain the most basic articles of faith, they are an expression of a fundamental unity despite all the differences among the churches. Here Reformed Christians stand together with other Christians everywhere, in all times. The first two are included in the Book of Confessions of the Presbyterian Church (U.S.A.).

The Apostles' Creed. By legend attributed to the original apostles. Present form not found before the sixth or seventh century, but probably goes back to an ancient Roman baptismal creed of the second century.

Nicene Creed. As we recite it now, formulated at the Council of Nicaea in 325 and completed at the Council of Constantinople in 381. Defined the relation between Father, Son, and Holy Spirit.

Creed of Chalcedon. Formulation in 451 of the "two natures" of Christ, the relation between his humanity and deity.

Reformed Confessions of the Sixteenth Century

Whereas the ecumenical creeds, with the exception of the Apostles' Creed, concentrated on particular theological problems, most of the Reformation and post-Reformation confessions were attempts to summarize the whole of the Christian faith in extended form. We list only some of the most widely influential.

SWITZERLAND:

Catechism of Geneva, 1541. Calvin's summary of the Christian faith written for children.

Second Helvetic Confession, 1566, by Heinrich Bullinger, reformer from Zurich. One of the most widely adopted of all continental Reformed confessions. Summary of central affirmations with a pastoral emphasis. Included in the Book of Confessions of the Presbyterian Church (U.S.A.).

GERMANY:

The Heidelberg Catechism, 1563, by Zacharia Ursinus and Casper Olevianus (who were twenty-eight and twenty-six years old when the catechism was composed). A guide intended for instruction of youth, preachers, and teachers, and for use in public worship. Most widely accepted of all Reformed confessions. Included in the Book of Confessions of the Presbyterian Church (U.S.A.).

FRANCE:

The Gallican (or French) Confession, 1559, prepared from a rough draft by Calvin.

NETHERLANDS:

The Belgic Confession, 1561, by Guido de Bres. Similar in form to the French Confession. An official standard of the Reformed Church of America.

SCOTLAND:

The Scots Confession, 1560, by John Knox with a committee. First English-speaking Reformed confession. Included in Book of Confessions of the Presbyterian Church (U.S.A.).

Reformed Confessions of the Seventeenth Century

One has only to read the major confessions of the sixteenth and seventeenth centuries to notice the difference. The sixteenth-century confessions and catechisms were usually written in the form of warm personal affirmation, with an obvious feeling of personal involvement. The seventeenth-century confessions and catechisms were written in a more impersonal, rationalistic style. They were more concerned with right thinking about the truth than with personal involvement in it. In the seventeenth century the sense of joyous excitement of a new discovery of the gospel gave way to bitter arguments not only between Protestants and Catholics but also between Reformed and Lutheran and even between Reformed and Reformed Christians. It now seemed necessary not simply to confess the new insights of the Reformation but to define them very precisely and defend them against other views. The seventeenth century is identified by the term "Protestant Orthodoxy" or "Protestant Scholasticism." A proper understanding of Reformed confessions includes the joyful, modest, thankful, free, personal character of the sixteenth century and the careful, hard-thinking character of the seventeenth century. Two documents from the latter period have been most influential:

The Canons of the Synod of Dort, 1619. Result of an international conference of Reformed theologians in the Netherlands. Dealt with problems related to predestination.

Westminster Standards, 1646. Came from the Westminster Assembly, meeting in London from 1643 to 1649, called to deal with issues of the Puritan conflict. The Westminster Confession of Faith, with the Larger and Shorter Catechisms, became the most influential confessional standard in the English-speaking Reformed world and in Reformed churches in Africa, Asia, and Latin America begun by missionaries from American Presbyterian churches. Included, with various modifications, in the Book of Confessions of the Presbyterian Church (U.S.A.).

Reformed Confessions of the Twentieth Century

The writing of Reformed confessions came to an end for two centuries after the seventeenth century. Under the influence of Protestant Orthodoxy, the Reformed churches lost sight of the reason for multiple confessions, and the liberal theology that dominates the eighteenth and nineteenth centuries was suspicious of any confessional restraint. But the cataclysmic events of history in this century and all the complex social, political, economic, scientific, and technological problems of life in our time have led Reformed churches around the world to discover again the original Reformed conviction that the church must confess its faith afresh in every new time and situation. We list only a representative sample from the explosion of new Reformed confessions written in this century.

GERMANY:

The Barmen Declaration, 1934. Written primarily by Karl Barth, representatives of both Reformed and Lutheran churches confess here the lordship of Christ in the political and economic sphere, protesting against the modern heresies of nationalism and racism. Included in the Book of Confessions of the Presbyterian Church (U.S.A.).

UNITED STATES:

The Confession of 1967. First American confession of faith for the Reformed tradition. Summarizes the central affirmations of the Reformed tradition in terms of the doctrine of reconciliation, relating it to concrete areas of alienation in modern American life. Included in the Book of Confessions of the Presbyterian Church (U.S.A.).

The Declaration of Faith. Contemporary confession written for the old Presbyterian Church in the United States (the "Southern" Presbyterian Church). Approved for study and use in the reunited Presbyterian Church (U.S.A.).

A Brief Statement of Faith, adopted in 1991 as an expression of the faith of the reunited Presbyterian Church (U.S.A.).

SOUTH AFRICA:

Theological Declaration, 1979. Statement of the Dutch Reformed Church.

A Declaration of Faith for the Church in South Africa. Presbyterian Church of Southern Africa.

JAPAN:

Confession of Faith, 1954. United Church of Christ in Japan.

KOREA:

Our Confession of Faith, 1976. Presbyterian Church in the Republic of Korea.

TAIWAN:

Confession of Faith, 1979. Presbyterian Church in Taiwan.

CUBA:

Confession of Faith, 1979. Presbyterian-Reformed Church in Cuba.

PART 2

GOD AND HUMAN BEINGS

"There are many gods" (1 Cor. 8:5). "God" is whatever is more important than anything else, something for which we will sacrifice everything else, something from which we expect everything worth having.[1] My god may be my own individual success or pleasure or happiness. It may be my family, my nation, or even my church. It may be an ethical idea or a political cause. In our time it may even be "nothingness" or "meaninglessness." But whatever it is, our understanding of our god shapes our understanding of ourselves, and our understanding of ourselves shapes our understanding of our god. When I talk about what is most important to me, I give away what I think about myself. And when I talk about myself, I give away what my god really is (it may turn out to be a different god from the god I claim I believe in!).

If, for instance, I understand myself basically as a kind of animal, my god will be something that fulfills what I consider my most essential animal needs: sex, hunger, or self-preservation. And my god will in turn shape my life. I will use and sacrifice family, friends, the welfare of the society in which I live—everything—for sexual pleasure or economic security or sheer power. If some political cause is my god, I will understand myself as an exclusively political being and other persons not so much as fellow human beings but rather usable or not usable means in achieving my cause's victory. My self-understanding will lead me to make of my cause a god that demands and receives the sacrifice of anything or anyone who gets in the way. Understanding of my god and understanding of myself shape each other.

"There are many gods . . . yet for us there is one God" (1 Cor. 8:5–6).

What we have said in general about human beings and their gods is true also of Christians and their God. John Calvin begins his *Institutes of the Christian Religion* with the statement that "true and sound wisdom, consists of two parts: the knowledge of God and of ourselves."[2] Without the knowledge of self, Calvin says, there can be no knowledge of God, and without the knowledge of God, there can be no knowledge of self.

This suggests that we could go about trying to understand the Christian faith in one of two ways. We could begin with the Christian understanding of human life and try to grasp the Christian understanding of God from that point of view. Or we could speak first of the knowledge of God and in light of that try to reach the knowledge of ourselves. Calvin himself, and following him, the Reformed confessional writings, chose the second alternative. That will be our approach also. A glance at the table of contents will show that throughout we will speak first of God and then of ourselves. But we must be careful that we do not make a separation here, as if we could ever talk only about God without at the same time talking about ourselves, or vice versa. We must always keep asking both questions at the same time: What do our statements about God have to do with the way we understand ourselves, and what do our statements about ourselves imply about our understanding of God?

"There are many gods, but for us there is one God." If Christians make such a claim, there is a series of questions we must answer before we do anything else: How do we know this one God? Who is God? What is God like? What does God want with us? These are the questions we will try to answer in this part of our study. As we answer them, some other questions will arise that will determine where we have to go from here.

3

How Can We Find God?

The Doctrine of General Revelation

"Brother, have you found God?" a street-corner preacher once asked a man passing by. The man, who happened to be a Christian, answered, "I didn't know God was lost." For Christians the problem is not that *God* is lost, but that *human beings* are lost. Although the man gave a good Christian answer, still we can understand the question. We too can share the anguish of Job when he cried, "Oh, that I knew where I might find God!" Moreover, even when we do believe we know God, we have the responsibility to explain *how* we know. This is usually the first question taken up in Christian theology, and it is the first question we must wrestle with: How do we Christians—or anyone else—come to know God?

The broad stream of Christian thought, like the confessional writings of the Reformed churches, gives two answers to this question.

First, God is known by the "light of nature and the works of creation" (Westminster Confession, 1.1). Or God is known "by the creation, preservation and government of the universe" (Belgic Confession, Art. 2).

Second, God is known because "it pleased the Lord, at sundry times, and in diverse manners, to reveal himself and to declare his will unto his church; and afterwards . . . to commit the same wholly unto writing" (Westminster Confession, 1.1). Or more briefly: "Secondly, he makes himself known by his holy and divine Word" (Belgic Confession, Art. 2).

Another way of identifying these two ways of knowing God is to speak of a general revelation and of a special revelation. Because we will be using these technical terms and some concepts connected with them throughout this chapter, it is important that we get their meaning clearly in mind now.

General revelation refers to the self-disclosure of God that all people can perceive by contemplating evidences of God's presence in the world of nature, history, and human life in general. The knowledge of God derived from this revelation is sometimes called the *natural knowledge* of God. The movement of theological reflection here is from us to God; we seek God.

Special revelation, on the other hand, refers to the unique self-revelation of God through God's word and action (1) in the history of Israel and above all in Jesus Christ, (2) through the Bible, which tells us of the God who came to us in this way, and (3) through the Christian church, which preserves and interprets the biblical witness. The knowledge of God derived from this source is called the *revealed knowledge* of God. The movement of theological reflection here is from God to us; God seeks and finds us.

In this chapter we will discuss the knowledge of God that comes from general revelation. We will save consideration of special revelation until chapter 4. Now we ask, How can we find God? In chapter 4 we will ask, How does God find us?

THE PROBLEM

"Why am I here? Where did I come from? Where am I going? What is the meaning of my life?" We do not ask such ultimate questions every day, but they plague us especially at times of crisis—when we face death, or war, or an important decision that will alter the course of our lives and affect the lives of others. And sometimes such questions crop up in an unexpected way in the normal routine of our lives.

We read the newspaper at breakfast: violence, corruption, injustice, tragedy, ruined lives everywhere. What is it all about?

We drive to work, do the same thing today that we did yesterday, drive home—and do it all over again the next day. We make beds, wash dishes, vacuum rugs—over and over again. And suddenly the question is there: What am I doing here?

We make money, spend money, fulfill our responsibilities, enjoy simple and great pleasures, do what has to be done, look forward to the next weekend or the next vacation. We are alternately happy and depressed, frustrated and successful, resigned to our place in life and hopeful that things will get better. But sometimes at night we cannot sleep because the questions come: Why? Where? What? Who? How?

These questions are religious questions. They very easily become: Is there a God? Is there Someone at the beginning and end of my own life and of the world in general who can make sense out of it all? Is there Someone in charge here who can help me to understand who I am, why I am here, and how I can go about living as I should?

Not only Christians but probably all people, in all times, everywhere, have asked these questions. Some have come to the conclusion that there is no God, or that if there is, God's character and will are unknown to us. But others (non-Christians as well as Christians) have come to the conclusion that there is good evidence of God's existence, some indications of what God is like, and therefore some helpful answers to our questions about the meaning and purpose of our lives. In other words, they say that a "natural knowledge" of God is possible, if only people are open and sensitive enough to perceive God's presence in and around them. What, then, are the evidences for the existence of God?

The Evidence

The following arguments have been given by philosophers and theologians through the centuries.

1. *The world is not self-explanatory.* When we look around us, we ask, Where did it come from? What holds it together? There must be a God who is the source and ground of all things. Behind all the change and decay we see around us, there must be an Ultimate Reality that is eternal and unchanging. We are born; we work, love, hate, suffer, and die. But we may find comfort, strength, and hope from the fact that we do not come from nothing and return to nothing. We come from God, live in a world created and governed by God, and return to God.

2. *The universe displays a purpose.* When we look at the world around us, we feel that it must have an origin and ground. There are many signs of order and design in the world of nature. Think, for instance, of the regularity with which the earth turns on its axis and how it orbits around the sun at precisely such a distance that life is possible on earth. Or think of the wonderful structure of the human body, with all of its parts so exactly coordinated to function together. It cannot be sheer accident that there is order and harmony and not chaos in the world. There must be a God with a purpose at work here.

3. *World history and personal experience point to God's existence.* Over

and over again throughout the course of history, forces of injustice and evil have been defeated and forces of justice and righteousness have finally prevailed. In my own life and that of my family, sickness has been surprisingly healed, needs unexpectedly met, apparently insoluble problems solved, a way out provided when there seemed to be a dead end. If we study history and analyze our own experience, we must conclude that there is a good God at work in the world providing for human welfare.

4. *Conscience bears witness to the existence of God.* In contrast to animals, all human beings feel within themselves a sense of moral responsibility, a sense of right and wrong, a feeling of duty to do what is good and true. Is that not an indication that some great Moral Power is at work in us? We can discover what it means to live as true human beings if we listen to the voice of God directing our lives through our consciences.

5. *We have a spiritual awareness of a divine presence deep within ourselves.* We are not only rational, moral, and physical beings, but spiritual beings as well. An important dimension of life is left out if we ignore the creative presence of a Spirit that we cannot explain, but one we are all intuitively aware of. This awareness of God is more like the knowledge of a poet or artist or religious mystic than the knowledge of a philosopher or mathematician or scientist. But why should it be any less trustworthy? Why should it not be *more* trustworthy?

6. *The world seems to function in a rational way.* There is a strange agreement between the way our minds work and the structure of the world. We are rational beings. We can formulate in our minds certain logical rules, and we discover that the world of nature operates according to these rules. Must there not be a great Mind behind both rational human beings and a rational world? If we carefully analyze the laws of nature and of reason, we can learn how the mind of the Maker works, and therefore what the world is all about and how we can live in it meaningfully. If we learn what it means to live as rational human beings in a rational world governed by a rational God, we will live according to the will of God.

By way of summary: An analysis of the world around us and of our own lives points to the fact that there is a God. Such an analysis gives us evidence of God's eternity, wisdom, power, and goodness. It furnishes us with at least a foundation upon which we can discover the answer to those disturbing questions we cannot escape: Why am I here? Where did I come from? Where am I going? How should I live?

Three Christian Positions

What can we make of the knowledge of God to be gained from "the light of nature and the works of creation"? How is it related to the knowledge given to us by God's self-revelation in the "holy and divine Word"? Christian thinkers have taken three basic attitudes toward the knowledge God gives by general revelation and the relation of this knowledge to that given by special revelation.

The first position is a radical one taken by only a few. It was especially typical of the Deists in the eighteenth century, but it is not unknown today. According to this view, what we know about God from our observation of the world and from a study of ourselves is the most certain knowledge we have. Anything else we are told about God must be measured, judged, and corrected by this knowledge. There may be a special revelation such as that recorded in the Bible. But anything the Bible says about God can be true only if it does not contradict what we already know by rational or natural religion. If there is a contradiction, it is the Bible that must be rejected, changed, or reinterpreted—not our analysis of the world and our experiences in it.

In the same way, the surest guide we have to right living is given to us in our consciences and the natural laws of the world. There may be a specially revealed will of God, but it can be valid only insofar as it agrees with the moral law of the universe that any rational person of integrity can figure out for himself or herself. Insofar as the biblical ethic does not conform to that, it must be either rejected or corrected.

So, for instance, if I think I have learned what is possible and impossible according to the God-given physical laws of the natural world and I read in the Bible about a God who breaks those laws and does the impossible, I must automatically conclude that the Bible is wrong in what it says, or explain it in such a way that it only *seems* to speak of a God who acts in an unnatural way. Could God break God's own law—the law we find operating in the world God made?

If I decide that according to the laws of nature it is unnatural for us to love our enemies, then I must refuse to accept the biblical claim that God loves God's enemies and commands us to do the same. Or perhaps I can interpret the biblical claim so that it becomes only a great spiritual ideal that is not meant to apply to the practical issues of everyday life.

The main stream of Christian thought has, of course, rejected the extreme position that special revelation is to be judged by and made to conform to "natural religion." It obviously is a subtle way of our deciding what God can and must be and do. We ask ourselves the questions and give ourselves the answers. There is no place for a real revelation at all. Revelation means that something *new* is made known. But this extreme position will hear and accept only what we already know or think we know or can learn by ourselves.

A second position is a less extreme affirmation of the validity of the knowledge of God given through general revelation. General revelation cannot dictate what special revelation can and must be, but it can give us an *incomplete, preliminary, preparatory* knowledge of God. It can at least show us that there *is* a God, and it can tell us *something* of God's power, wisdom, and goodness. This knowledge is not enough in itself. Contrary to the position of natural or rational religion, the knowledge derived from general revelation must be interpreted, supplemented, and perhaps even corrected by that derived from special revelation. Nevertheless, we really can know something of God through natural evidences, and this knowledge can at least prepare us to recognize and receive the full knowledge given in Christ, the Bible, and the Christian church. This "moderate" position is taken by Roman Catholic and most Reformed theologians, including Calvin himself.

The third position is the denial of any validity at all to the natural knowledge of God. Perhaps it is true that all people have some sense of the existence of God from their observation of nature and history, and from an analysis of their own minds, hearts, consciences, and personal experience. But as soon as we try to say anything about this God, we talk only about our own ideas and feelings, not about God. There is *no* way from us to God, not even a beginning. The only way to any true knowledge of God is from God to us through God's self-revelation in the events recorded in the Bible. True Christian theology must depend completely and exclusively on the grace of God in Christ. This is a position relatively new in the history of theology. It has been taken especially by the Swiss Reformed theologian Karl Barth and those influenced by him.

THE SEARCH FOR A SOLUTION

The debate about the validity of general revelation is more important than may appear at first glance. It was because he rejected all natural theology that Barth was able to speak so effectively as he called the churches in Germany to acknowledge the sole authority of Jesus Christ over their thought and life. The "German Christians" claimed to find the "will of God" in an ideology of "blood and soil" and in the destiny of a "super race." Barth wrote:

> The fellowship of those belonging to the Church is not determined by blood, therefore, not by race, but by the Holy Spirit and Baptism. If the German Evangelical Church excludes Jewish-Christians, or treats them as of a lower grade, she ceases to be a Christian Church.[1]

But we only have to change two words to make the last sentence read:

> If the American Church excludes members of any racial-ethnic minority, or treats them as of a lower grade, she ceases to be a Christian Church.

We see then that the discussion of the place of natural theology is not a hairsplitting debate of interest only to technical theologians. Important issues are involved here for all Christians. How we understand God and the meaning of our lives, how we relate Christianity to other religions, how we go about evangelism and missions, and even how we stand on political, social, and economic issues—every area of Christian thought and life will be influenced by the decisions we make at this critical point.

Let us examine the alternatives more carefully. In what follows, we will look at the arguments both for and against general revelation, and then suggest some guidelines for making a decision on this issue.

Arguments for the Natural Knowledge of God

The light of nature and the works of creation are admittedly "not sufficient to give that knowledge of God, and of his will, which is necessary unto salvation" (Westminster Confession, 1.1). They do not tell us about the love, grace, and forgiveness of God that we know only by God's special self-revelation in the history of Israel and in Christ. Nevertheless, it is important to take seriously what can be known of God in this way for the following reasons.

1. It would be arrogant and blind to argue that there is no knowledge of God at all except in Jesus Christ and biblical revelation. Awe, wonder, and joy in the presence of a creative Power that people know is not drawn from their own resources but is a gift from outside themselves; worshipful awareness of a dimension of life that transcends everything we can know by our five senses; obedient response to a Spirit of love and justice that frees people to become courageous and compassionate human beings—all this is no monopoly of Christians. Without any reference to Jesus, the Bible, or the Christian church, many philoso-

phers, scientists, psychologists, artists, and followers of other religions have convictions about God and the purpose of human life in the world that are remarkably similar to Christian convictions. How can we deny that, however imperfectly, they have some awareness of the same God we worship—even when they call God by a different name? Does not the Bible itself teach us that God the Father, Son, and Holy Spirit is not trapped in the church or able to be present only in the lives of Christians but is at work "out there" in the world creating, preserving, loving, forgiving, reconciling, helping, making things new? Should not Bible-believing Christians above all expect evidences of God's presence and work outside the Christian circle? Should we not be glad when others, however dimly and without awareness of the true source of what they know and do, recognize and participate in what the God of Christians is doing in the world?

2. Some Christians are eager to recognize that a limited knowledge of God is available to all people, because they want to show that nonbelievers are "without excuse" in *not* knowing and serving God. Look at Rom. 1:18–23 to see how Paul makes this point.

3. The knowledge of God's existence that is available to all furnishes us with a good beginning point in evangelism. We can best help nonbelievers to become Christians when we begin "where they are," pointing to the evidences for the existence of God in their own experience of the world, in their reason, conscience, and spiritual intuition. Having thus helped them to see that belief in God is at least possible, we can then go on from there to tell them who this God is. God is not just some kind of powerful, wise, good Creator and Ruler of the world out there somewhere, but the gracious and loving God we Christians know in Christ. The natural knowledge of God, in other words, enables us to lead non-Christians gradually to understand and accept the full truth of the Christian faith. This is a far more sympathetic approach, and far more likely to be a successful form of evangelism, than an arrogant presentation of the Christian gospel with a "take it or leave it" attitude. Look at Acts 17:22–31 to see how Paul used this approach in talking about God with nonbelievers.

4. Finally, we must take seriously what can be known about God from the light of nature and the works of creation, because the Bible itself invites us to do so. Look up the following passages that are cited by those who defend this point of view: Psalm 19; Acts 14:16–18; 17:22–31; Rom. 1:18–23; 2:12–16.

Arguments Against the Natural Knowledge of God

The case against any dependence at all upon general revelation, and for exclusive dependence on biblical revelation, rests on the following arguments.

1. The arguments for the existence of God are not convincing, and therefore it is very questionable whether an analysis of the world and of ourselves leads us even to preliminary knowledge of God. It has been argued, for instance, that what we once thought was the plan and purpose of a divine mind in nature was in fact only a pattern we falsely read into nature with our human minds. Again, modern anthropologists have shown that people's sense of right and wrong varies in different cultures and in different times and places. Conscience is not the "voice of God"; it simply reflects the particular environment in which we live and our practical experience in learning how to live together. All the other arguments for the existence of God can be criticized in a similar way. The point of such criticisms is not to deny that God exists. The point is that if we are to have any certainty of God's existence, we cannot depend on any of the highly debatable arguments for it. They all tell us more about the people who are searching for God than about God.

2. The result of looking outward at the world or inward at ourselves is not only uncertainty about the existence of God but also uncertainty about God's nature. If lovely sunsets and flowers are evidences of a good God, what kind of God do earthquakes and hurricanes point to? If events in history such as the defeat of Hitler's Nazi regime are evidences of the rule of a just God, what kind of God is it who allows the slaughter of six million Jews before the Nazis were defeated? If the miracle of a baby's birth and the laughter of a little child suggest one kind of God, what kind of God is suggested by the suffering of a child born tragically deformed? Evidence for the natural knowledge of God is contradictory and ambiguous. And for that reason, the very arguments that lead people to think about God also lead them to doubt whether God exists at all.

3. The knowledge of God we think we derive from an analysis of the world around us or from our own experience is untrustworthy not only because it is uncertain and ambiguous, but also because it is inevitably distorted by our sinfulness. Real evidences of God may be manifested in God's works of creation and in history, but we look at those evidences with hearts and minds clouded by our own corrupt ambitions and prejudices. The result is that instead of discovering the true God, we

make for ourselves false gods to lend respectability to our sinful desires and opinions.

For example, we may find evidence of a God guiding the destiny of our nation. But the "God of our forebears" very easily becomes an idol. We have a tendency to think that instead of our being here to serve God, God is there to serve us. God's function is to give success to all our self-chosen economic, political, and military enterprises. And if someone suggests that God is not automatically on our side, and may even be against us in this or that enterprise, we suspect that such a person is probably an atheist or communist. Our national idol prevents us from knowing the true God.

Another example: We may find evidence of the providence of God at work in the world. But some people make use of providence to justify any given social situation, especially when it is to their own advantage. If some people are poor and exploited and if others are comfortable and secure, that is the way God wills it. Those "on top" should be thankful, and those "at the bottom" ought not complain or rebel against their divinely appointed position in life. The idol Providence sanctifies the status quo as the "will of God" and prevents people from knowing the true God who just might be against the status quo.

In short, sinful people use the natural knowledge of God they think they discover in creation to avoid being open to hear and accept the God we come to know in Christ through scripture.

4. A natural knowledge of God based on our own reason and experience is impossible not only because of our sinful nature but because of God's transcendent nature. According to the Bible, God is far beyond and above anything we can think or imagine. We cannot hope to bridge the gap between our finite humanity and God's incomparable deity. The God whom we think we can discover for ourselves always turns out to be a God made in our own image, a magnified copy of ourselves. True knowledge of the true God, therefore, can come only from God's side, when the God who is unknown and unknowable comes to us in self-revelation. How is this transcendent hiddenness of God expressed in Isa. 55:8; Matt. 11:27; John 14:6; 1 Cor. 1:20–25; 2:9–16?

5. Those who want to depend only on special revelation argue that their position is supported and not undermined by the texts that at first glance seem to indicate a general knowledge of God. Psalm 19:1 says that "the heavens are telling the glory of God; and the firmament proclaims his handiwork." But the psalmist was a member of the community of Israel that drew its very life from the special revelation of

God to God's chosen people. He could recognize God everywhere because he already knew who God was. In Romans, Paul speaks of the knowledge of God in creation "not as a knowledge which men actually have and from which they can advance to further knowledge, but as a knowledge they have lost; for by their failure to act on it they have forfeited it, and . . . unable to recover it, they are driven in their blindness to fashion idols (and ideas) as substitutes for the reality (Rom. 1:21–25). . . . Paul appeals to the religiosity of the Athenians as evidence, not of a knowledge of God, but of ignorance of God, for which he calls them to repentance (Acts 17:22–31)."[2]

To summarize the whole argument against a natural knowledge of God: All people everywhere may have some idea of God, but what we can know by ourselves is at best uncertain and ambiguous, and at worst a dangerous hindrance to real knowledge of the true God. The only trustworthy and sure knowledge we can have of God comes by God's breaking into our lives in a special way that is not at all dependent upon what we can tell ourselves about God.

Some Guidelines for Making a Decision

We have seen that convincing arguments can be made both for and against general revelation and the natural knowledge of God. How can we decide between them? We conclude this chapter with some guidelines for making a decision. Do you agree with them? How would you change or correct or add to them?

1. *We must take seriously all the passages of scripture that are relevant to this problem.* We can never hope to find a true solution if we listen only to those passages that support our personal bias and ignore those passages that do not, or if we twist the passages that cause us difficulty to make them say what we would like for them to mean. Good Christian theology is possible only when we listen with open minds to the *whole* witness of scripture—in this case to passages that speak both for and against general revelation and the general knowledge of God.

2. *In agreement with those who deny general revelation and the natural knowledge of God, we must take seriously their emphasis on the transcendence of God on the one hand, and on the limitations of human beings on the other.* God's thoughts are not our thoughts, and God's ways are not our ways. God's love, power, goodness, and truth are far beyond even the very best and highest finite human thinking and feeling can imagine. We will never know God and God's will so long as our knowledge is based only on our analysis of our personal experience and the world around us.

Moreover, we must never forget the tendency of all of us—Christians as well as non-Christians—to use "God" and the "will of God" to serve our personal sinful prejudices, plans, and desires and those of others who are like us. We must always be very modest about what we think we know of God and God's will, and constantly subject everything we think we know to the correction of God's "special" self-revelation. Or to put it positively: We do not have to depend upon the uncertain, ambiguous, and contradictory knowledge of God we can discover for ourselves. We can live by the promise that God comes to the community of those gathered in the name of the Christ, whom we meet in scripture, to show us who God is and what God is doing in the world and has for us to do.

3. *In agreement with those who defend general revelation and the natural knowledge of God, we must take seriously those who insist that the truth of God makes sense.* It is not irrational or antirational truth we are asked to swallow at the cost of intellectual honesty and understanding. It does not simply contradict but illumines and interprets our personal experience, the restless longing of our hearts, and the inexpressible Presence we sometimes feel in the depths of our being. However unexpected and surprising it may be, Christian truth does not ignore but really answers the questions all people ask about the meaning and purpose of life. Talk about "God" or "Jesus Christ" or "what the Bible says" or "what Christians believe" should not be just meaningless jargon or pious clichés. If the Christian faith claims to speak of the truth, it must have some correspondence with the truth we can learn from the natural sciences, philosophy, modern psychology, and the attempts of artists to grasp the mystery of life. It must be able to acknowledge the insights of other religions into the truth. After all, we Christians must remember that we too are only finite, sinful human beings, and that our understanding of God and God's will is also limited. It would be sheer arrogance to assume that our wisdom and virtue is so superior to that of non-Christians or "secular thinkers" that we can instruct them but have nothing to learn from them. God is not the prisoner of the Christian church. We must expect God to be present and at work also outside the sphere of those who know about and depend on Christ and the Bible.

Is it possible to follow all three of these guidelines? At the end of the next chapter, after we have considered special revelation, we will attempt to take all three with proper seriousness. See the section titled "The Freedom of God" in chapter 4.

Meanwhile, the questions and suggestions that follow are intended to help you get clear in your mind the issues involved as you struggle to formulate your own position regarding general revelation and the natural knowledge of God.

FOR FURTHER REFLECTION AND STUDY

1. How would you as a Christian try to speak meaningfully and helpfully to someone who said to you, "There is no God"? Would you try to prove the existence of God to this person?
2. If you tend to agree with the arguments *for* a natural knowledge of God, how would you answer the arguments *against* it?
3. If you tend to agree with the arguments *against* a natural knowledge of God, how would you answer the arguments *for* it?
4. Read Rom. 1:16–32 and Acts 17:23 with this question in mind: Does Paul defend, reject, or accept with certain reservations (what are they?) a natural knowledge of God?
5. What difference would the affirmation or denial of a natural knowledge of God and God's will make in evaluating as Christians the following statements:
   a. "Whatever your sickness is, know certainly that it is God's visitation" (Anglican *Book of Common Prayer,* seventeenth century).
   b. The lower classes should accept social inequality with humility and patience, knowing that "their more lowly path has been allotted to them by the hand of God" (William Wilberforce).[3]
   c. "When in the Course of human Events, it becomes necessary for one People to dissolve the Political Bands which have connected them with another, and to assume among the Powers of the Earth, the separate and equal Station to which the Laws of Nature and of Nature's God entitle them, a decent Respect to the Opinions of Mankind requires that they should declare the causes which impel them to the Separation.

      "We hold these Truths to be self-evident, that all Men are created equal, that they are endowed by their Creator with certain unalienable Rights, that among these are Life, Liberty, and the Pursuit of Happiness" (The Declaration of Independence of the United States of America).
   d. "In the long run it is only to the man of morality that wealth comes. We believe in the harmony of God's universe. We know that it is only by working along His laws natural and spiritual that we can work with efficiency. Only by working along the

lines of right thinking and right living can the secrets and wealth of nature be revealed. . . . Godliness is in league with riches. . . . Material prosperity is helping to make the national character sweeter, more joyous, more unselfish, more Christlike" (Bishop Lawrence of Massachusetts, 1900).[4]

e. See the statement of the German Christians in chapter 2 at the beginning of the section titled "Creeds and Confessions."

4

How Does God Find Us?

The Doctrine of Special Revelation

"I didn't see God up there," says a cosmonaut who returned to earth from the heavens.

"God is dead," says a theologian, speaking for a secular world that thinks it no longer needs God because it has learned to answer all questions and solve all problems without "God."

"Religion is the opiate of the people," said Karl Marx, speaking also for many people since his time, communist and noncommunist alike, who have seen that "God" is often only an excuse for the rich, comfortable, and powerful to maintain the status quo, and to persuade or force the poor and exploited to stay "in their place."

Consider the following pairs of contradictory statements:

There is one true and living God. There is no God.

Human beings cannot be truly human without God. We can achieve a more just and more human world without dragging God in as a sop or as a weapon.

Look around you: There are evidences everywhere of a wise, good, and powerful heavenly Father. Take another look: A world so filled with suffering, injustice, and evil screams that God does not exist—or must be either unable or unwilling to do anything in response.

All these statements raise the issues and problems involved in our search for God. They are the issues and problems debated by those who affirm or deny a natural revelation of God in the world and a natural knowledge of God made possible by such a revelation. We have seen in the last chapter that Christians differ among themselves about the result of such a conversation.

However Christians may differ in their answer to the question how and whether we can find God, they agree that in the last analysis we know that God exists because God has found us, not because we have found God. And we know what God is like, not because we have figured out for ourselves what qualifications a "divine being" must fulfill in order to be truly divine, but because God has revealed God's innermost self by speaking and acting in the world in a special way.

How does this special divine self-communication take place? Christians give three answers: It happened and still happens (1) in *history*—the history that leads up to, centers in, and follows from a man named Jesus; (2) in the *book* that bears witness to what God said and did, and promises to say and do, in that history and in that man; (3) in the *community of people* who through the centuries have listened to, proclaimed, and lived by faith in Jesus and the biblical message. In this chapter we will discuss the meaning of this special revelation and the three ways it comes to us.

GOD'S SELF-COMMUNICATION

We said at the beginning of our study of revelation and the knowledge of God that two things are always involved at the same time: knowledge of God and knowledge of ourselves. What we think about God influences what we think about ourselves, and what we think about ourselves influences what we think about God. It is especially important in this section to keep asking what new understanding both of *God* and of *ourselves* is given in God's self-revelation to us.

The content of revelation is a Person. God reveals God's *self.* Revelation is not the giving of some supernatural information about God and human life in the world. It means that God confronts us person-to-person. To receive God's self-revelation is to know not *something* but *someone* we did not know before. The revealed truth Christians believe in is not an "it" but a "Thou." This is most clearly seen in Jesus' strange saying, "I am the truth." The truth is a person, not an idea or concept. In God's self-revelation we are of course given some new thoughts and ideas about God and God's will, but a theology based on special revelation differs from a theology based on general revelation in that it does not have to do with an explanation of the world, a list of ethical laws and principles, or a liberal or conservative social-political-economic ideology. It has to do with the work and word of a living, personal God. (In chapter 6 we will discuss more fully just what it means to believe in a "personal" God.)

The knowledge that results from revelation is not theoretical but personal. If the content of revelation is the living personal God, then we must have a particular understanding of the "knowledge" of God given in revelation. In the Bible, where we learn about the self-revealing God, "to know" God does not mean to know *about* God, to believe intellectually and grasp rationally that "there is" a God, to have information about God's "attributes" and will. To know God means to *experience* God, to have a personal relationship with God. To know God's judgment, for instance, is not simply to believe that there is a divine Judge; it is to have God's judgment happen to you (Jer. 16:21; Ezek. 25:14). To know God's love is not just to believe in a theory of the love of God; it is to experience God's loving action (Deut. 4:32–40). To know God is to acknowledge, confess, honor, thank, and serve God.

On the other hand, those who know only theoretically do not know at all. The sons of the priest Eli (preacher's sons!) "grew up in the church" and knew all about God, yet because they were faithless and disobedient, it is said: "they knew not the Lord" (1 Sam. 2:12, KJV). The people of Israel (like some Christians today?) had all the information they needed about God, believed all the right things about God, and were very careful in their religious practices. But Isaiah said that they did not "know" God (Isa. 1:3). Despite their orthodox beliefs and proper religious rituals, they rebelled against God and were guilty in their social and political lives of oppression, injustice, and indifference to the needs of the poor and defenseless. Jeremiah even dared to say that the prophets and priests (preachers!) who handled the Law did not know God, because their knowledge was only a matter of correct doctrine, not an obedient, thankful, personal relationship with God (see Jer. 2:8).

The situation is the same in the New Testament. What is the meaning of "knowledge" in 1 John 2:4; Phil. 3:8–11; Eph. 3:14–19? Look again at Rom. 1:18–23, the passage referred to earlier when we were considering the natural knowledge of God. Do those who "knew" God but "did not honor him as God or give thanks to him" really know God at all?

The knowledge given with revelation is the knowledge of something (or better: someone) new and unexpected. The word *revelation* itself suggests that something hitherto hidden or unknown has come to light. Our thoughts are not God's thoughts and our ways are not God's way (Isa. 55:8–9). Therefore, when revelation happens we are confronted with "what no eye has seen, nor ear heard, nor the human heart conceived" (1 Cor. 2:9). The self-revelation of God is in fact so new and unexpected that it is often offensive to those who think they already know who God is and what God must say and do if God is really God. Thus, in the first century (and in the twentieth?) the truth about God in a crucified Jesus who suffered and died for ungodly sinners seemed "foolishness" to intellectuals and an ethical scandal to those who stood for law and order and moral seriousness (1 Cor. 1:23).

If we are to know God in God's self-revelation, we must be willing to hear and accept something brand new, even if it contradicts our previous ideas about what the truth, love, and justice of God must be. Only then can we learn that the "news" given us in revelation is astonishing *good* news. We may hear *gladly* that God is not imprisoned in an otherworldly "spiritual" realm shut out from the physical, flesh-and-blood world we live in, but rather God-with-us and God-for-us *in* the world. We may hear *gladly* that God is not a great heavenly bookkeeper who pays off for credit earned and exacts the penalty for payment due, but a God who loves the unworthy and undeserving and forgives debts. We may hear *gladly* that God is present and at work not just where there is power, success, and happiness but also in the midst of failure, weakness, and suffering.

God's self-revelation comes to us as God's word-with-action and action-with-word. We open up or reveal ourselves to one another in speaking and in acting. But with us, what we say and what we do are often not the same thing and may even contradict each other. When our words are not followed by corresponding actions, we lie. Our words do not reveal but cover up who we really are. On the other hand, if we act without corresponding words, our actions are often ambiguous. If a parent disciplines children, for instance, the action without explanatory words might convince the children that the parent does not love them when in fact the discipline may have been an expression of love.

God reveals God's self to us both in words and in actions. It is a true self-revelation because God's words and actions agree with and confirm each other. God *does* what God says, and God's word is accompanied by an interpretative action. Thus the central revelation for the ancient people of Israel was their deliverance from Egypt. God *said,* "I will be your God and you shall be my people." And God *acted out* what God said: "I am the Lord your God, who brought you out of Egypt, out of the house of bondage."

This unity of word and act is even more clearly seen in God's self-revelation in Jesus, who is himself the "Word" of God (John 1:1). What God has to *say* to us in him is what God *did* in his life, death, and resurrection. Jesus not only *talked* about the coming of the kingdom of God's love, justice, and peace; he *demonstrated* the coming of the kingdom as he healed the sick, forgave sinners, befriended the poor and the excluded. Jesus not only spoke about God's love; he himself loved with the love of God.

We may always expect God's self-revelation to come to us both in mighty acts and in spoken words that interpret these acts. To know God, therefore, is both to hear what God has to say and to experience and participate in what God is doing. Revelation and the reception of revelation involve a personal encounter in which God speaks and we hear; God acts and we actively respond.

God's self-revelation is given and received in an earthly, worldly, human way. As you have read what we have said so far about the meaning of revelation, perhaps you have thought to yourself: "That sounds right theoretically, but it just does not agree with my experience. I can't really think of God as a person except when I slip back into a childish view of an old man with a white beard up in the sky. There may be such a thing as a "personal relationship" with God in which God speaks and people hear, God acts and people recognize God's activity in their lives. But God never spoke personally to me, and I can never be sure whether God is doing anything in the events of my life. Maybe I'm just not a real Christian. Or maybe God's self-revelation happened only long ago in biblical times. Or maybe God still speaks and acts in the lives of some people, but I have been left out."

There is another aspect of God's self-revelation that helps us with this problem—a problem all honest people must admit they have at least sometimes. (Even Jesus himself could cry out, "My God, my God, why have you forsaken me?")

Let us put it bluntly: God is never *directly* present to us in self-revelation, and no one (with one exception) ever had a *direct* personal relationship with God. God comes to us and we can know God only *indirectly.* It is in this indirect way that we come to know and enter into a personal relationship with God. Why is this so?

God is not a human being (not even a very big or very good one), and we human beings are not divine (not even as little "chips off the old block"). God's deity is so different from our humanity, and we are so different from God, that God is unknown, unknowable, unimaginable to us. But God wants to be known and knowable to us, wants to enter into a "personal relationship" with us. How can that happen? Revelation means that God "comes down to our level" (Calvin: "condescends") to be with us in the human, earthly, worldly sphere where we live. The human-earthly-worldly "form" in which God is present with us is not God, but God is truly present and revealed in this human-earthly-worldly form. God "hides" God's self in this way in order to "reveal" God's self, and just in this "hiddenness" God is truly "revealed." How else except in this indirect ("mediated") way could the God who is not human be present and known to us human beings who are not divine? Perhaps this difficult paradox will become easier to understand if we look at some of the specific ways in which God's self-revelation happens.

1. *God comes to us and is revealed to us above all in the man Jesus.* How do we come to know the Creator of heaven and earth? Where do we meet this God personally? In a weak, helpless baby lying in a cradle in a barn! In a Jew who was the friend of dishonest business people, prostitutes, and social outcasts! In a man condemned to die by capital punishment between two thieves! What an inappropriate place to meet "Almighty God"! How unspiritual! But hidden in this peasant baby, this ancient Jewish preacher, this "criminal"—there is *God* speaking, acting, personally present. God is not a man, but *this* man is God-with-us. "No one has ever seen God; the only Son . . . has made him known" (John 1:18, RSV). Whoever has seen me has seen the Father" (John 14:9).

2. *God is revealed by God's mighty acts in the history of Israel and in the words of the prophets.* But God's "mighty acts" coincided with the mighty acts of heathen kings and armies that can just as well be explained by the political and economic conditions of the ancient world. And when the prophets said, "Thus saith the Lord . . .," people in their time as well as in ours could say, "I didn't hear the Lord. All I heard was Jeremiah or Isaiah." In the history of Israel God truly spoke and acted—but only *indirectly,* in ordinary historical happenings and through ordinary human beings.

3. *God is revealed in the Bible.* Christians believe that God speaks to us in this book. But God speaks through human writers who used the

languages of an ancient Near Eastern people and of an ancient Western civilization. Moreover, the biblical writings reflect their writers' education or lack of it, their local environment and culture, their ancient views of geography, physics, and astronomy. As God in the infant Jesus came to us wrapped in swaddling clothes lying in a manger, so the word of God comes to us in the words of these human beings (Luther's analogy).[1] It would be just as foolish to confuse these human words with the word of God as to confuse the swaddling clothes and manger with the child. Yet, just as God-with-us was in them, so God's word comes to us in these human words.

4. *God is revealed in and through the Christian community, the church.* But God's word comes to us in the all-too-human words of preachers. In baptism and the Lord's Supper, God is at work calling, renewing, forgiving, nourishing, and helping us through the use of plain old tap water, grocery store wine (or grape juice), and store-bought or homemade bread. The preacher is not God, and the preacher's word is not God's word. The few drops or a tubful of water do not in themselves do what only God can do—wash away sins or drown the old self in us to create a new self. The bread and wine are not literally the body and blood of Christ. But through the church's word and sacrament, in these indirect ways, God really speaks and acts.

In the same way, the church is not in itself the "Body of Christ," the community in which God in Christ is visibly present and at work in the world. It is an all-too-human—sometimes all-too-*inhuman*—organization. All the sinful self-interest and power politics; all the personal rivalries, envy, jealousy, and animosities; and often the same patterns of sexual, racial, class, and cultural arrogance and discrimination that can be found in other clubs and organizations—all that can be found in the church too. Yet Christians believe that in *this* organization, despite everything that it is and is not in itself, God still speaks and acts—not just for the good of the church and its members but for the good of the world God loves and for whom Christ died. Here too—very indirectly!—the self-revelation of God happens.

Now, what does all this have to say about the question with which we began? Can this human-earthly-worldly character of God's revelation help us with our difficulty in knowing what a personal relationship with God means? Three things follow from what we have said.

First, we ought not be surprised that we do not have the kind of personal relationship with God that means God speaks to us directly "out of the blue." We ought not be surprised that we cannot always positively identify what God is doing in our lives or the world around us. We are human beings and not God. We cannot and should not expect to meet God in a direct, unambiguous way.

Second, if we want to have a personal relationship with God, experience God's presence and work in our lives, we should *expect* it to happen in a disguised, indirect way. God comes to us in the world; and if we want to meet God, it must be in the world—not in a vain attempt to escape our earthly human existence to ascend to the heavenly heights. As we listen to the words of a book written in human language, growing out of the experiences of an ancient human people; as we focus our attention on the story of the words and deeds of an ancient Jewish preacher; as we participate in the life of an all-too-human and sinful community gathered in his name to listen to that book; as we interpret all the events of our lives and the world around us in the light of this book, this man, and participation in this community—*there* God promises to be revealed to us. Indirectly, to be sure. "Only" in a book written by human beings. "Only" in a human being named Jesus. "Only" in a very questionable community of people. But "only" in these worldly ways, God really reveals God's self and acts in our lives.

How can we have a personal relationship with God? Could it be that God becomes real to us only in and with and through our personal relationships with *other people*—the people who wrote and collected the books of the Bible, the one person who is God-with-us, the people around us in the Christian community, the people we encounter in our daily lives? Could it be that the kind of relationship we have with God is indicated by the kind of relationship we have with these past and present human beings? Could it be that our openness or closedness to them, our love or indifference or contempt in relation to them, is the indication of what our relation to God is? "No one has ever seen God; if we love one another, God lives in us, and his love is perfected in us" (1 John 4:12).

On the other hand, if we want to have a personal relationship with God, we must be very careful not to confuse God with the worldly "clothing" in which God comes to us. God comes to us in the man Jesus, but the man himself (his "human nature") is not God. God speaks to us in the Bible, but these human writings are not in themselves the word of God. God speaks and works through the worship, witness, and work of the church, but none of these is the word and work of God as such. God works through the social and political movements of our time and meets us in our encounters with other people, but no nation, party, movement, program, or individual can claim our ultimate loyalty. If we confuse God with any of these ways in which God comes to us, we make false gods and cut ourselves off from the true God.

There is no such thing as a personal relationship with God without a personal relationship with our fellow human beings. But our fellow human beings are not themselves God. *In, with,* and *through* these relationships God comes to us—judging, forgiving, renewing, doing among us and for us what we can never do for ourselves or for one another.

Revelation is the revelation of a mystery. Even as the self-revealing God, God remains one who is beyond all our thinking and imagining. Even as one who draws near to us, God remains a Stranger in our midst. So do not be surprised if the paradox of the worldliness of God's self-revelation is difficult to grasp. What is important is this: To have *faith* in God means to expect, find, accept, and know God as God has chosen to be known by us, on our level, in an earthly-worldly-human way. And to have faith in *God* is to do this without idolatrously confusing the indirect, mediated way God comes to us with the mysterious One who comes in this disguised way.

One last word about this mystery. The question has been asked whether the experience of the Holy Spirit in the hearts and minds of individual Christians is not a direct, "unmediated" revelation of God to them. Answer: In a sense the "internal" experience of the guidance and help of the Spirit is indeed a more immediate experience of revelation than the experiences of revelation in the various "external" means we have been discussing. But the Holy Spirit is not just any spirit, saying and doing just anything. The Spirit is the Spirit of the crucified and risen *Jesus of Nazareth,* the Spirit who enlightens our minds and fills our hearts as we listen to the words of the *Bible,* the Spirit promised to the *Christian community* as Christians *come together* in Jesus' name to be led by scripture—the Spirit who is recognized and experienced just as we pay attention to the external ways God comes to us.

A very important issue is involved here. How do we know whether talk about the Holy Spirit within us is not really just a self-deceptive way of talking about our own feelings, wishes, desires, personal opinions, and preferences? We must ask whether what we think the Holy Spirit is saying and doing in our lives is consistent with what we know about God and God's will in the man Jesus, the Bible, and the church's attempt to discern the revelation of God in Jesus and the Bible. It is just these indirect, human-earthly-worldly means of God's self-revelation that enable us to recognize and experience the word and work of the Holy

Spirit in our hearts and minds, and to distinguish between the guidance and help offered by God's Spirit and the self-instruction and self-help that come from our own spirits. We will discuss the person and work of the Holy Spirit in more detail in chapter 15.

THE WORD OF GOD

We have seen that God's self-revelation happens in three ways: (1) in the history of God's words and actions centered in Jesus Christ, (2) in the Bible, and (3) in the Christian community. So far we have put all these ways of revelation more or less on the same level. Now we must talk about how they are alike and how they differ.

One way of pointing to the *unity* of the different forms of revelation is suggested by a phrase we have frequently used in speaking about it, "word of God." What comes to mind when we hear this phrase? Word of God—that is Jesus himself, the Word made flesh. Word of God—that is the Bible. Word of God—that is what is proclaimed on Sunday morning in preached word and sacrament. It is no accident that the phrase suggests all three to us, because scripture itself suggests this threefold interpretation. Compare John 1:1–14; 2 Tim. 3:16; 2 Peter 1:19–21; and Acts 13:44. The same threefold understanding of the word of God is recognized also by the confessional statements of the Reformed tradition.[2] Christ, Bible, and preaching and sacrament—all three are ways in which the one word of God comes to us.

But we must obviously make a *distinction* between these three forms of the word of God. A word identified with a person is not the same as a word that refers to the words in a book, and neither of them is the same as the word Christians speak and act out when they communicate the truth of God in word and sacrament. Moreover, there is a certain historical order and priority among these three forms of the word of God. *First,* God was revealed in God's words and actions in the history of Israel and its fulfillment in Jesus Christ. *Then,* under the guidance of the Holy Spirit, a written record and interpretation was made of this original revelation. *Finally* comes the church's word and action. Within the unity of the three ways in which the word of God comes to us we have to make distinctions in *form* and distinctions in *priority.*

Instead of talking theoretically about the unity and distinctions between the three forms of the word of God, we will try to understand them by dealing with two familiar questions.

Do you believe in the Bible? Strictly speaking, Christians whose faith is in God's self-revelation have to say *No*—precisely when we take the Bible seriously. Our faith is not in the book but in the God we learn to know in it. It is *God,* not the Bible, who rules and judges, helps and saves, in whom we trust. We do not "believe in" Isaiah or Paul or John; we believe in Jesus Christ. He and he alone is God-with-us in person. The biblical writers are not themselves God's self-revelation; they are witnesses to it. We would completely miss the point of what they want to tell us, and do them no honor, if we believe in *them.* They ask us to place our hope and confidence not in them but in the God to whose speaking and acting they point, the God made known above all in the life, death, and resurrection of Jesus Christ. We believe the Bible just when we do not believe *in* the Bible but in the living, acting, speaking God to whom the biblical writers introduce us.

On the other hand, we who are not prophets and apostles and were not the direct recipients of the self-revelation of God that happened in the history of Israel and Jesus—we have access to this original revelation only through the biblical witness to it. We know the living God and the Christ who is God-with-us only through this witness. The Bible makes present to us here and now the self-revelation of God that happened back there and then. In this sense—a secondary sense—the Bible is not only a witness to revelation; it is itself revelation.

There is thus a *distinction* between the Bible as the word of God and Jesus Christ as the Word of God. It is the distinction between the one who is himself God's self-revelation and the book that bears witness to him. But there is also a *unity* here: We know the Word of God in person only in and through the written word of God.

Did revelation cease when the Bible was completed, or does it still go on in our time? We have already answered this question. The God we come to know in the history of Israel and Jesus Christ still speaks and acts—above all in and through the church. We learn in the Bible itself that God is a living God, that Christ is a risen and living Lord, that God's promised Holy Spirit will continue to guide the people of God. God did not retire from history when the biblical story was completed. Christ did not disappear with his ascension to sit and wait with nothing to do until the "last day." The Holy Spirit was promised not only to Christians "back then" but to all Christians ever since. God the Father, Son, and Holy Spirit is always a God of the present, a God who goes with the people of

God in every time and place, promising to reveal to them what they need to know, say, and do in their particular situation. So God's self-revelation does continue.

On the other hand, it is only by listening to the story of the past revelation of God recorded in the Bible that we are able to *recognize* what God is saying and doing in and through the church in our time. The past revelation is the "normative" revelation that enables us to distinguish between what God is saying and doing in our time and what is only the questionable human word and work of the church, its ministers, and/or its members.

Let us illustrate. Does the church speak and act as if physical human life is cheap and unimportant? To that extent it is not speaking and doing the word of God. For we learn in the Bible that God is the *Creator* who willed and created physical life and saw that it was "very good." The church proclaims the word of *God* only when it speaks and acts to value, defend, and preserve the physical welfare of human beings—all human beings.

Does the church speak and act as if the alienation of individuals, races, classes, and nations from one another is unimportant or even desirable? To that extent it is not speaking and doing the word of God. For the God of the Bible is God the *Reconciler* who is at work in the world to overcome the hostility and alienation of human beings in relation to each other as well as in relation to God. The church proclaims the word of *God* only when its speaking and acting is reconciling and healing.

Does the church speak and act as if its only task is to serve itself—to make itself a big, successful, influential institution; or to tend to the spiritual and psychological needs of its own members? To that extent it is not speaking and doing the word of God. For God was and is a *liberating Spirit* who sets people free from enslaving preoccupation with their own power and security, free for service of God and fellow human beings. A truly "spiritual" church proclaims the word of *God* only when it speaks and acts to serve not itself but the kingdom of God's liberating justice, compassion, and peace in and for the world, outside as well as inside the church.

What specifically will the church and individual Christians do and say when they proclaim in word and in action the word of God the Creator, Reconciler, and Liberator? No program can be outlined, no specific answer given. That would be to claim that we have the word of God at our disposal. The church will be able to speak and do the word of

God only when in every new situation it confesses that it does not have all the answers to every question or know the solution to every problem. Then and only then will it be ready and open to *learn* what the living God is saying and doing, and to participate in God's word and work.

In other words, there will be a *unity* between the word of the church and the living Word of God just when, and only when, we acknowledge the *distinction* between the speaking and acting of Christians and the speaking and acting of God. But when we do recognize this distinction, then we may be confident that the same living God who once spoke and acted long ago in the history of the people of God continues to speak and act in our time, among us, in and through the Christian church.

THE FREEDOM OF GOD

In this chapter we have been speaking about special revelation. Special revelation means that God's self-revelation does not happen just anywhere and everywhere, and that God is not known by just anyone and everyone. Christians believe that for God's own good reasons, God chose to be known in the history of one particular people among all the peoples of the earth, in one particular man, in one particular period of history. We believe that this revelation is recorded and preserved in one particular book. And we believe that since the time of the original decisive revelation God has chosen one particular community of people to discern and participate in what God is saying and doing in every new time and place.

We must not forget that the one people and the one man God chose as vehicles of God's self-revelation were Jews. We must not forget that the one book contains the scriptures of the synagogue as well as those of the Christian church. Nor must we forget that according to the apostle Paul in Romans 9—11 the chosen people of God are still first of all the people of Israel. Both Israel and the church are called in their different ways to be a "light to the nations," to discern and participate in God's ongoing self-revelation. We concentrate on Christians and the church in this book, but we must not forget that God has an ongoing story with Israel too and that to the extent we forget or reject the Jews, to that extent we close our eyes and ears to the self-revelation of our own God, the God of Jesus Christ who is also the God of Abraham, Isaac, and Jacob.[3]

The particularity and exclusiveness of biblical faith is offensive to many people, including many Christians. Why Israel and not also other nations? Why Jesus Christ and not also other holy men or women throughout history? Why the Bible and not also other inspired and inspiring writings? Why the Christian church (with the synagogue) and not also other religious communities? We stumble here on the mystery of election and predestination, which we will discuss later. But already now at the end of our discussion of revelation we need to make some remarks that will help guard against misunderstanding of the particularity and exclusiveness of God's special self-revelation. Some of them underline points we have already made.

God is at work even where God is not known. The particularity and exclusiveness of God's self-revelation in the history of Israel, Jesus Christ, the Bible, and the church does not mean that God was and is at work only in these particular times, places, and people. It means that God is fully known, recognized, and honored especially here. The Bible tells us that God is the Creator and ruler of all people, everywhere. God is at work in the history of all nations, in all times, to judge and help. The difference between "us insiders" and "those outsiders" is not that God loves and works among "us" and does not love and work among "them." The difference is that we know about God's love and what God is doing and promises to do for the welfare of all humanity. Just because we have learned who the God of the Bible and Jesus Christ is, we can recognize signs of God's work not only in the religious affairs of the church but also in the secular affairs of the world, not only in the community of believers but also in the political and social community, not only in countries where the Judeo-Christian tradition is predominant but also in countries where it is not.

Here is no ground for Christian arrogance. The particularity and exclusiveness of God's special revelation is no ground for Christians to feel superior to other people. On the contrary, it means that we stand under a special judgment of God and have a special task to perform. Even more than others we stand under the judgment of God. If we know as they do not about the justice, compassion, healing, reconciliation, and peace that God in Jesus Christ wills for the welfare of all humanity, we are more severely judged by God when we do not work for these goals—especially when people who do not know our God sometimes seem more committed to these goals than we Christians and are more willing to pay the cost of working for them. Our special knowledge also means not just special privilege but a special task. If we know about a God who offers help and hope not only to us Christians but to all humanity, how can we not live by that knowledge ourselves and share it with others? If we withhold it from them or live as if the good news is only for us, do we not deny the very God we claim to know?

We are limited but God is not. The particularity and exclusiveness of special revelation is a limitation placed on us, but not on God. God chose to be known especially in the history of Israel, in Jesus Christ, in the Bible, and in the church. Therefore, if we want to know God we are bound first to look here and no place else. It is true that we learn from these particular sources to recognize God's work everywhere around us. But we are not free to look first just anywhere and everywhere to discover God, God's will, and what God is up to in the world. To use an old analogy, we must look at ourselves and at the world through the "spectacles" of God's word if we want to see clearly what is going on around us. Without these spectacles, we will receive a distorted image of God and the work of God in our individual lives and in the world. In this sense, we are limited to the particularity of special revelation. These spectacles and no others enable us clearly to see God, ourselves, and the world.

But having spoken so exclusively of God's special self-revelation in and to a particular nation, a particular man, a particular book, and a particular community; and having so exclusively limited the knowledge of God to these particular sources, we cannot end our discussion without an important qualification. God is free! We are bound to seek God first of all here and no place else. But God is not bound. The Spirit "blows where it chooses" (John 3:8). In absolute freedom, God can and does speak and act to reveal God's self even where we might never expect it (not because people have sought and found God, but because God seeks and finds them). This is true also of non-Christians who do not know Christ or read the Bible or belong to the church.

John Calvin wrote of the "admirable light of truth" shining in secular thinkers, even "ungodly" ones, from whom we can learn that

> the mind of man, though fallen and perverted from its wholeness, is nevertheless clothed and ornamented with God's excellent gifts. If we regard the Spirit of God as the sole fountain of truth, we shall neither reject the truth itself, nor despise it wherever it shall appear, unless we wish to dishonor the Spirit of God. For by holding the gifts of the Spirit in slight esteem, we contemn and reproach the Spirit himself. (*Institutes* 2.2.15)

Or again: "We ought not to forget those most excellent benefits of the divine Spirit which he distributes to whomever he will, for the common good of mankind" (*Institutes* 2.2.16).

This reminder of the freedom of God to be known wherever and however God pleases does not mean that we are free to seek God wherever and however we please. But why should we not rejoice when we see, also among unbelievers or the followers of other religions, something of the beauty, truth, goodness, justice, and compassion of God at work? Why should we not see in them the confirmation of our faith that the world really does belong to the creative, helping, and liberating God of the Bible and Jesus Christ? And why should we not be willing to listen as well as speak to such "outsiders," learn from them as well as instruct them?[4]

We have been talking about how we know God. But who is God? What is God like? What specifically is God up to in our individual lives and in the world? That is what we have to talk about in the following chapters.

FOR FURTHER REFLECTION AND STUDY

On "God's Self-Communication"

1. Why is it wrong to ask "*What* is God"?
2. In light of our discussion of what it means to "know" God, would you say that everyone knows God who believes everything the Bible and the doctrinal standards of the church say?
3. What new and unexpected things does God's self-revelation tell us about God?
4. How is the meaning of revelation made clear by saying that Jesus is the "Word of God"?
5. How would you teach a child to know God and have a personal relationship with God?
6. How would you answer someone who said, "The Bible cannot be a trustworthy source of the revelation and knowledge of God because it presupposes an outmoded scientific view of the universe"?
7. How could the Bible or the church become "idols" that prevent us from knowing God and having a personal relationship with God?

On "The Word of God"

1. In what sense are true Christians "Bible believing"?
2. What would you say to someone who says, "I don't need to go to

church to hear the word of God. I would rather stay home and read the Bible than hear some preacher talk"?

3. Is revelation still going on in our time? If so, is what it tells us different from past revelation?

On "The Freedom of God"

1. What is the difference between saying that people can discover God for themselves by natural revelation and saying that God is free to make something of God's self and God's will known, even to non-Christians, whenever and wherever and however God chooses?
2. Do you think Jesus was too exclusive when he said, "I am the way, and the truth, and the life; no one comes to the Father, except through me" (John 14:6)?
3. Is Christ at work only in the church, among those who know him? For help in answering this question, look up Eph. 1:16–23 and Col. 1:15–20.
4. Do you think Christians can learn anything about God from Jews? Muslims?

5

Who Is God?

The Doctrine of the Trinity

"Holy, Holy, Holy! Lord God Almighty. . . . God in three Persons, blessed Trinity."

"I believe in God, the Father Almighty . . . and in Jesus Christ, his only Son, our Lord. . . . I believe in the Holy Spirit."

"I baptize you in the name of the Father, and of the Son, and of the Holy Spirit."

"O God, our Father in heaven . . . by the inspiration of your Holy Spirit . . . through Jesus Christ our Lord. Amen."

"Glory be to the Father and to the Son and to the Holy Ghost."

"The grace of our Lord Jesus Christ, and the love of God, and the communion of the Holy Spirit be with you all."

For centuries Christians have sung, confessed their faith, prayed, received new members into their community, and gone out into the world to live—with worship of a Trinitarian God who is Father, Son, and Holy Spirit. If we move now from the question, How do we know God? to the question, Who is God?, it is with the doctrine of the Trinity that we must begin.

But for many Christians in our time, the doctrine of the Trinity has become more an embarrassing or even offensive problem than a joyful affirmation of Christian faith and a firm foundation for Christian life. So if we are to defend and make sense of this ancient doctrine today, we must first deal with some problems and objections that make it an obstacle rather than the entrance to faith in the God whom Christians worship and serve.

PROBLEMS AND OBJECTIONS

Is This Doctrine Necessary?

Many of us have heard a conversation in a church school class or study group that goes something like this:

"Do we *have* to believe all this business about three-in-one and one-in-three to be Christians?"

"Yes, the church has always held that the doctrine of the Trinity is essential."

"Well, what does it mean? How can you put three persons together and get one, or divide one into three and still have one?"

The defender of the faith then blunders through a fuzzy explanation and concludes hopelessly: "It's a mystery no one can understand. You have to accept it by faith."

Then some people say, "Well, if you're supposed to believe it, I guess I do—whatever it is." And more honest people think to themselves, "If no one knows what it means and no one can explain it, it can't really be all that important."

It is true that "three persons in one Godhead" is a mystery no one can understand. But this mystery is far too central to the Christian faith to be either unthinkingly accepted because we are supposed to accept it or casually shrugged off because no one can explain it. If it were only a mathematical puzzle or a numbers game, we might take someone's word for the solution or simply say that we are not interested. But the doctrine of the Trinity is far more than that. It is the church's admittedly inadequate way of trying to understand and guard against false interpretation of the uniquely biblical-Christian understanding of who God is, what God is like, how and where God is at work in the world, what God thinks about us human beings, does for us, requires of us, promises us.

Christians do not "believe in" the doctrine of the Trinity (or any other doctrine). We believe in a living God. But the God we believe in is the God this doctrine confesses, the one living and true God who is Father, Son, and Holy Spirit. Faith in *this* God—and lives shaped by faith in this God—is what distinguishes Christians from people who do not believe in God at all and from other religious people whose faith and life is shaped by other views of God. Moreover, within the Christian circle itself it is faithfulness to the will and word and work of the one "triune" God that distinguishes authentic Christian faith and life from misunderstandings and distortions of it.

We will see that the ancient doctrine of the Trinity was formulated in language that is meaningless and misleading for most Christians in our time, and that this ancient language must be translated and reinterpreted if the doctrine is to be the powerful expression of faith for us that it has been for Christians in the past. But it is worth the effort it takes to do this—not because we have to or because we are supposed to, but because here we are confronted with the very heart of what the Bible tells us about God and the meaning and purpose of our lives in the world.

The Problem of Interreligious Dialogue

More than ever before we are aware that we live in a religiously pluralistic world in which we Christians must learn to live in peace and cooperate with people who have religious beliefs different from ours. But does not our Christian faith in a *triune* God make it very difficult if not impossible for us to talk about the things that matter most to other religious people, especially Jews, Muslims, and other "monotheists" who believe in *one* God? Does not our doctrine of the Trinity almost inevitably lead us to the arrogant and intolerant claim that ours is the only true God, whereas theirs are false gods or idols? Would it not be better to try to discover what we have in *common* with people of other faiths instead of concentrating on what *separates* us from them, and thus to set aside our unique doctrine of the Trinity?

Without going into a detailed discussion of the complex issue of interreligious dialogue, we can say three things about genuinely Christian participation in it:

1. Interreligious dialogue becomes really interesting and helpful when representatives of different religions know who they are and what they believe, and are able to articulate their own particular religious perspective in conversation with those who are different from them. Dialogue does not have to be a battle about who is right and who is wrong, who is superior and who inferior. It can be a way for people of various faiths to explain themselves to each other, learn to understand and appreciate each other, express genuine care for each other. If we Christians are truly interested in people of other faiths, we will be open to listen to them, learn from them, be changed by them as they explain themselves and their faith to us. If we are truly interested in them, we must also be able to hold up our side of the conversation. We must be able to say who *we* are and what *we* believe. That is what the doctrine of the Trinity prepares us to do. It is not an excuse for having nothing to do

with people of other faiths, much less a club for rejecting and defeating them. It is what prepares us to tell them who we are and helps us enable them to get rid of false perceptions of what we mean when we say that we too believe in one God—the God who is Father, Son, and Holy Spirit.

2. Christians believe that the Trinitarian God in whom we believe is not just "our God," but the God who is over and for and with all people, of all religions (or no religion), everywhere—even before and whether or not they know this God. The doctrine of the Trinity tells us about this God's compassion, justice, and promise of renewing power for them as well as for us. Precisely this doctrine leads us not to exclude those who are different from us but to include them as fellow human beings who, just like us, are created, judged, loved, forgiven, and promised new life by the God who is Father, Son, and Holy Spirit. We can gladly bear witness to the God we believe in because we know that what we have to say is good news not just for us Christians but for all people.

3. Talk about a God who is three-in-one and one-in-three will indeed sound strange and even offensive to followers of other religious traditions, and will indeed distinguish us Christians from them. However, if, as we said in the last chapter, the triune God we believe in is present and at work everywhere in the world, even outside the Christian circle, we may expect others to have discerned something of this God's presence and work in their own religious experience. We may therefore hope that when we talk about this God, other religious people will discover that they have more in common with us, and we with them, than either of us realized before we began talking with each other.

In other words, we try to understand the uniquely Christian doctrine of the Trinity not to cut off but to prepare for a genuinely honest, open, friendly, mutually helpful dialogue with believers of other religious traditions.

The Gender Problem

A relatively recent objection to the traditional doctrine of the Trinity is that it is both sexist and idolatrous because it makes God in the image of a male human being. This is an objection that all Christians (not just "radical feminists") must take seriously because it helps us correct a very distorted understanding of what we mean when we speak of God as "Father," "Son," and even "Holy Spirit." In responding to this objection we will first defend the language of the classical doctrine of the Trinity. Then we will acknowledge how it has in practice been widely misunderstood and misused, and look at some suggestions for alternative ways of talking about the triune God. Finally, we will indicate how we deal with the issue here (with the understanding that not everyone will agree with us!).

When the theologians who formulated the doctrine of the Trinity spoke of the "Father," they did not think of a great big Male up in the sky (with great big male "parts"). When they spoke of the "Son," they did not think only of the man Jesus but of the eternal "Word" that was with God and was God from the foundation of the world—the Word that came to us in the man Jesus but was the "second person" of the Trinity, part of God's self, long before this male human being was born. When they spoke of the "Spirit," they used a word that is masculine in the Latin of ancient church theology but feminine in the Hebrew of the Old Testament and neuter in the Greek of the New Testament. Maleness is not an essential characteristic of any of the members of the Trinity.

At its deepest and best, traditional Christian theology has always remembered that according to the Genesis story of creation, both male *and* female human beings are created in the image of God. But it has also known that according to the Second Commandment, we are forbidden to make God in the image of *any* earthly creature: women *and* men are made in the image of God, but God is not made in the image of men *or* women. The reality of God is beyond everything we can conceive or even imagine (Isa. 55:8–9; 1 Cor. 2:9–13).

So how can we speak truly about God at all? The best theologians of the church have said that we can do so only when we remember that all our language about God is analogical or metaphorical language, language that expresses both the similarity and the dissimilarity between God and human beings. Like male and female human beings, God is a living, acting, speaking, personal God who lives in relationship with other persons. But God's personalness is different from that of the two kinds of persons we know; it is personalness that transcends the distinction between male and female human beings.

With respect to the doctrine of the Trinity, this means that when we speak about God as "Father," when we speak about the eternal "Son" who comes to us in the man Jesus (who taught us to call his Father "our Father"), and when we speak about the "Spirit" who is the Spirit of the Father and of the Son, we are not talking about the *gender* of God (for God is neither male nor female). We are using analogical language from human experience to talk about the *kind of relationship* that exists between the members of the Trinity and between the triune God and us human beings—a relationship that is like the intimate relationship between parents and their children. Speaking of God's relationship to us, the Brief Statement of Faith of the Presbyterian Church (U.S.A.) expresses this analogical understanding of God when it says that God is "like a mother who will not forsake her nursing child, like a father who welcomes the prodigal home."

This last statement exposes the reason many people today, women and men alike, object to the traditional Christian doctrine of God. If with scripture itself the "best theologians" have "always known" that God is not made in the image of either male or female, and if they have "always known" that our language about God's personalness can only be analogical language that acknowledges the difference as well as the similarity between God's personalness and that of human males and females, then why have they spoken about God almost exclusively with masculine imagery? Why have they thought of God not only as father but as king, shepherd, mighty warrior, and so on? Has this not misled many ordinary Christians (not to mention the theologians themselves!) to assume that God is literally the great heavenly Male? Especially in a church and world that for centuries have ignored, excluded, devalued, or subjugated women (often in the name of a male God), would it not be better theology to give up "patriarchal" masculine imagery in thinking and speaking about God and substitute *feminine* imagery for it, or at least use both masculine and feminine images?

Should we not learn to think of God also as "Mother," especially because the Bible itself can compare God with a mother (see, e.g., Isa. 42:14 and 66:13)?[1] Should we not at least try to combine masculine and feminine imagery to think of God as a "paternal Mother" and "maternal Father"?[2] (An instructive example of this "confusion" is found in the statement of the Council of Toledo in 675 that the Son was created "out of the womb—uterus—of the Father"!)

Similarly, in thinking of the second person of the Trinity, instead of thinking only of the eternal "Son," should we not think also of the external "Wisdom" of God (a feminine word in the Bible) that according to scripture goes out from God to reveal and accomplish God's will, and comes to dwell within us?[3]

Should we not remember that the Hebrew word for "spirit" is feminine, think of the Spirit as the "feminine side of God," and think of Jesus as being conceived and born from the "motherhood of the Spirit"?[4]

All such uses of feminine imagery may sound strange to us who are used to hearing only masculine references to God. But so long as we remember that feminine language for God is also analogical and not literal language used to speak of the God of scripture who is personal but neither male nor female, it is a much-needed corrective of a centuries-long tendency of Christians idolatrously to make God in the image of a human male.

In this chapter and throughout this book we will continue to use traditional Trinitarian language to speak of God as Father, Son, and Holy Spirit. We will do this for two reasons: (1) It is the language of the Bible itself, and if we take scripture seriously as the norm of Christian faith and life, we must try to understand and interpret this biblical way of speaking of God. (2) It is language that has been deeply embedded in the worship, thought, and life of the church for centuries, and we ignore or reject this language at the cost of cutting ourselves off from our fathers *and* mothers in the faith who have gone before us.

On the other hand, faithfulness to scripture and the deepest intent of traditional Christian theology require us to try to correct distortions of the doctrine of God and reinterpret it for our time and place. In this chapter and throughout this book we try to do this in several ways: (1) We try to avoid confusing the personalness of the triune God with the personalness of either male or female human beings. You may have noticed that from the beginning we have avoided referring to God either as "he" or "she." (2) When we speak of God the Father, Son, and Holy Spirit, we refer not to the gender of God but to the kind of relationship that exists between them in the inner life of God, and between the triune God and us. (3) In a later section of this chapter, entitled "The Social Trinity," we will consider some insights from Eastern Orthodox and from contemporary feminist and liberation theologies that help us overcome some of the consequences of the one-sided use of masculine imagery to talk about God in traditional Roman Catholic and Protestant theology. (4) In the following chapters we will (in agreement with the Brief Statement of Faith) remember that God is "like" both a father *and* a mother to us.

Having dealt with some of the objections to the doctrine of the Trinity, we will now look at the doctrine itself.

BIBLICAL ROOTS OF THE DOCTRINE OF THE TRINITY

The Bible does not teach the doctrine of the Trinity. Neither the word "trinity" itself nor such language as "one-in-three," "three-in-one," one "essence" (or "substance"), and three "persons" is biblical language. The language of the doctrine is the language of the ancient church taken from classical Greek philosophy. But the church did not simply invent this doctrine. It used the language and concepts available to it to interpret what the Bible itself says about who God is and how God is present and at work in the world. Although scripture does not teach the doctrine itself, it says some things about God that made the doctrine necessary.

One God

"Hear, O Israel: The Lord our God is one Lord" (Deut. 6:4, RSV). That was the "Apostles' Creed" of ancient Israel, its central confession of faith in a time when most people believed in many gods. "I am the Lord your God, . . . you shall have no other gods before me" (Ex. 20:2–3). That was the First Commandment Israel lived by. "I am the Lord, that is my name; my glory I give to no other" (Isa. 42:8). That was the warning the prophets repeated again and again as the people of Israel were constantly tempted to fall back into the superstitious worship of other gods.

When Jesus was asked what is the first and greatest commandment, he simply summarized the creed of Israel: "Hear, O Israel: the Lord our God, the Lord is one; you shall love the Lord your God with all your heart, and with all your soul, and with all your mind, and with all your strength" (Mark 12:29–30). The writers of the New Testament said the same thing: "There is no God but one" (1 Cor. 8:4). There is "one God and Father of all" (Eph. 4:6).

"We confess and acknowledge *one God alone,* to whom *alone* we must cleave, whom *alone* we must serve, whom *only* we must worship, and in whom *alone* we put our trust." The opening statement of the Scots Confession of 1560 summarizes the faith of both Christians and Jews in all times and places.

Biblical faith stands or falls with this confession of one God. Christians are by definition people who are freed *from* the superstition, fear, and slavery of believing in all kinds of visible and invisible powers and authorities. And they are people who are freed *for* loving, trusting, and obeying the one true God. Under no circumstances can we allow other gods to stand over or alongside of this one true God. "Other gods" include not only the wood and gold idols of primitive people but also the more sophisticated idols of modern people, often represented by *both* sides of the "ism" debates of our time: socialism *and* individualism, communism *and* capitalism, secularism *and* otherworldly spiritualism, militarism *and* unqualified pacifism, liberalism *and* conservatism, racism of *any* racial-ethnic group. To know the one God who alone is God means that we neither *have to* nor are we *allowed to* be dominated and controlled by *any* of the political, social, economic, or religious ideologies of our time, all of which separate people from God and set them against fellow human beings. The first Christians were denounced as atheists because they rejected all the tyrannical, dehumanizing gods that people around them anxiously or fanatically worshiped and served; because as Christians they worshiped and served the one God in whose exclusive, total claim on their lives they found true freedom, self-fulfillment, and genuine human community. How many such "atheist Christians" can be found in our time?

God the Son

Who is this one true God? The first Christians could not talk about the God of Israel who was their God too without talking about a man named Jesus. They did not speak of Jesus' "deity" or "divinity," nor did they speculate theoretically about his divine "nature" or "essence." They thought about what Jesus *did.* Here is a man who *acts* like God, does what only God can do. He speaks with the absolute authority that belongs only to God—even to the extent of calling into question the ethical teachings the people believed to be the will of God made known to Moses. He heals and raises the dead with the life-giving power that belongs only to God. He dares to forgive sin as only God has the right to do. He speaks and acts as if his coming means that the kingdom of God is breaking into the world. He speaks and acts as Judge, Reconciler, Redeemer, Liberator, and Lord over life and death. It is not surprising that religious people of his day accused him of blasphemy: he claimed that in what he said and did God was speaking and acting.

During Jesus' life, his disciples were confused and uncertain about what all this meant. After his death and resurrection it became clearer to them. They still did not try to explain it, but they now confess that the risen Jesus is "Lord" and "Savior" who is "far above all rule and authority and power and dominion, and above every name that is named" (Eph. 1:21). That is, they now give Jesus the same names, the same authority, the same saving power that they had reserved for God.

But there is an obvious problem here. There is only one God, the Creator of heaven and earth, the Lord and Savior of Israel. Now we hear that *Jesus* is Lord and Savior. If we say that there is one God, how can we say that God is really present and at work in Jesus; and if we say that God is really present and at work in Jesus, how can we avoid saying that there are in fact two Gods—one "up in heaven" and one who appeared down here on earth?

The New Testament does not solve this problem. But it does give a clue that helped the ancient church in its later struggle to find a solution as it moved toward what became the doctrine of the Trinity. According to the New Testament, we must speak of both a *unity* and a *distinction* between God and Jesus.

Unity with God

On the one hand, Jesus is Immanuel, "God with us" (Matt. 1:23). According to John 1, in Jesus the "Word" that from all eternity *was* God has come to dwell among us in a flesh and blood man. Jesus himself can say "The Father and I are one" (John 10:30) and "Whoever has seen me has seen the Father" (John 14:9). According to Colossians 2:9, "in him the whole fullness of deity dwells bodily." In Jesus we have to do with *God,* not just a great and good man sent from God, or a prophet, or an angel. When we meet this human being we meet God. If we want to know who God is and what God does, we have to look at this man Jesus and what he does.

Distinction within God

On the other hand, neither the eternal Word nor the man Jesus is simply identical with God. John 1:1 says that the Word was *with* God, suggesting that the two can be distinguished from one another. According to Jesus himself, the Son is not the same as the Father; he is *sent by* the Father, and his sonship is in obedience "to do the will of him who sent me and to complete his work" (John 4:34). "The Son can do nothing on his own, but only what he sees the Father doing" (John 5:19). These and other similar passages suggest that if we want to know who God is and what God is like, we have to look at Jesus. But we also have to distinguish between the Father who "sends" and the Son who is "sent," between the will of the Father and the Son who does the Father's will.

Could it be that the solution to the problem of confessing one God yet confessing that Jesus is God-with-us lies in trying to understand both the unity and the distinction between Father and Son? That is the way the ancient church tackled the problem. But before we look at how it did so, we must look at a similar problem—and similar clue to its solution—in what the New Testament says about the Holy Spirit.

God the Holy Spirit

Just as the first Christians could not talk about the one God who is the God of Israel and their God too without talking about the "Word" or the "Son" of God, so they could not talk about their God without talking about the Holy Spirit. The same God who is God *over* us as God the Father and Creator, and God *with* and *for* us as the incarnate Word and Son, is also God *in* and *among* us as God the Holy Spirit. But how are we to understand this Spirit? On the one hand, the Spirit is the Spirit of God (1 Cor. 2:11; 6:11; 7:40). On the other hand, the Spirit is the Spirit of the Son (John 14:16; Rom. 8:9; 2 Cor. 3:17). In John 14:15–18 Jesus promises his disciples that he will pray to the Father to send "another Advocate . . . the Spirit of truth" to be with them, but then says, "*I* am coming to you." Is the Spirit the Spirit of the Father or the Spirit of the Son—or a third party (the "Advocate") besides the Father and the Son? Is what the Holy Spirit wills and says and does the same thing, something additional to, or even perhaps something different from what the Father and the Son will and say and do? That is not only a very important question for all Christians who seek the guidance of the Spirit, but also a very important question for Christians who believe in one God, yet want to talk about God as Father *and* Son *and* Holy Spirit. Could it be that the answer lies in thinking about both the unity and the distinction between the three? That is the way the ancient church thought about it as it worked out the doctrine of the Trinity.

Father, Son, and Holy Spirit

All the questions raised by the "three names" of God become all the more pressing when we look at the numerous passages in the New Testament in which the Father (or God), Christ (or the Lord), and the Spirit are mentioned together. Look for instance at the following passages: Matt. 28:19; 2 Cor. 13:13; Eph. 4:4–6; 1 Cor. 12:4.

The doctrine of the Trinity is not found in the Bible. But the Bible does speak of the one God who is present and at work in three ways. What is the meaning of this "one" and this "three"? How are the three united yet distinct in who they are and what they say and do? These are the questions that led to the church's doctrine of the Trinity. It is as important for us modern Christians as it was for ancient Christians to struggle with this doctrine not only because scripture itself lies behind it but also because we too have to contend with the charge of Jews and other "monotheists" who believe that we Christians are "polytheists" who believe in three Gods.

THE CHURCH'S DOCTRINE OF THE TRINITY

We will not try here to follow the centuries-long debate in the ancient church that finally resulted in the doctrine of the Trinity.[5] It involved trying out and then rejecting various answers that proved unsatisfactory for one of two reasons: (1) They so strongly emphasized that Father, Son, and Holy Spirit are *all three* God that they compromised faith in *one* God. Or, (2) they so emphasized faith in *one* God that they compromised faith in the real presence and work of God in *each* of the three. The Greek-speaking church at the eastern end of the Mediterranean (which later became the Eastern Orthodox church) emphasized the threeness of God, whereas the Latin-speaking church in western Europe (which became the Roman Catholic and Protestant churches) emphasized the oneness of God. This difference between the churches of the East and the churches of the West still exists, and we will presently see that we need the emphasis of each. First we will discuss the "wrong answers" both sides rejected. (In seeking to understand what the church *does* believe, it is helpful if we can be clear about what it *does not* believe.) Then we will discuss the "right answer" they (more or less!) agreed on.

Unsatisfactory Answers

Instead of trying to define and analyze the technical language the church used to identify the positions it rejected, we will discuss them as we are most likely to hear them expressed today. Because everyone tends to emphasize either the unity-oneness or the distinction-threeness of God, we all tend toward one or another of these heresies. Which tends to be *your* heresy?

1. God is like a heavenly board of directors of a corporation made up of three equal partners, each of whom has a particular responsibility. The Father handles creation (production and maintenance?), the Son handles salvation (sales and distribution?), and the Spirit handles the reception and enjoyment of salvation (customer satisfaction?). To propose one committee or board, with three members and three tasks, is obviously to think of three different gods who perform three different tasks. This approach does not understand that there is one God whose "works" may be distinguished but not separated from each other.

2. God is like a committee or board in which there is one big boss and two subordinates who go out to do what the boss orders: one God (the Father) and two "agents" of God (the Son and the Spirit) who are invested with divine authority and power but are still less than God. This protects the oneness of God, but at the expense of suggesting that neither the Son nor the Spirit is really *God*-with-us, and that there might be a conflict between what the "top God" and God's inferior "representatives" will and do (between the Father's sovereign power over and above us, the Son's self-giving love for us, and the Spirit's intimate presence within and among us, for instance).

3. God is like three players on a football team sitting on the sidelines and waiting their turn to get into the game, one after the other going out onto the field to substitute for each other. First comes the Father, who does the work of creation (the God of the Old Testament). Then the Son takes over to do the work of salvation (Jesus and the Gospels). Finally, the Spirit comes along to take up where the Son left off (Pentecost and the Epistles). But this too suggests three different Gods, doing three different and perhaps even contradictory things. It forgets that from the very beginning there has been only one God "in the game," a God who at every moment is simultaneously Creator and Sustainer of all life, Helper and Redeemer of needy and sinful human beings, and life-renewing Presence.

4. God is like a man or woman who "wears three hats" or fulfills several functions at the same time—spouse, wage earner or member of a profession, church officer or civic leader. Or God is like an actor who changes costumes to play three different roles in a drama. One God carries three different functions or roles. This analogy recognizes distinct activities of God, but it could suggest that the really true God is hidden *behind* these functions—like a person who says that the "real me" is not the same as what I do in my various roles. It suggests that God may play the part of a caring heavenly Father, a self-giving Son who loved and died for us, and a comforting and empowering Spirit. But what if God were to get tired of playing these roles of a "good" God and decided at least sometimes, with some people, to be an uncaring, hostile, vengeful God? How can we be sure that the roles God plays as Father, Son, and Holy Spirit express who God really is behind these roles? Moreover, this role-playing analogy forgets that although we can perform only one or another of our roles in life at a time, often being forced to choose between them to neglect one for the sake of another, God is always at the same time, with all people, powerful Creator and Ruler

over us, loving Friend and Companion with and for us, and Giver of a new life within and among us.

None of these answers will do, though each sees something of the truth. All of them suggest three different gods willing and doing different things, or one God who is not really revealed, present, and at work in all three of the ways God comes to us and works among us. So what is the alternative?

The Church's Answer

Having rejected false solutions to the problem, the ancient church used the language and concepts available to it to insist both on the oneness-unity and on the threeness-distinction of God the Father, Son, and Holy Spirit. The Westminster Confession preserved this answer when it says, "In the unity of the Godhead there are three persons of one substance, power and eternity" (2.3). One divine "essence" (or "substance") and three "persons"—that is the orthodox doctrine of the Trinity for Christians in the West. (The Eastern Orthodox church means the same thing but says one substance, or essence, and three divine "hypostases," or individual ways of being God.)

From the beginning there have been arguments about the implications of this language, but it is especially difficult for us because the words mean something quite different now from what the ancient church intended to say.

Talk about one substance, or essence, suggests to us modern people that God is composed of some kind of divine "stuff." But that suggests a lifeless divine "something" rather than a living, acting person. Or we might think (as did some in the ancient church) of Father, Son, and Holy Spirit as three different persons who share a common "nature," just as three human individuals share a common human nature. But that would imply a crude tritheism that contradicts the very oneness of God that the statement wants to defend. However meaningful it may have once been, language about one divine essence, substance, or nature no longer helps us understand faith in one living, acting, speaking God.

Language about "three persons" is even more confusing. We inevitably think of three individual, self-conscious personalities—three gods. The ancient church did not mean to say that God is three persons in our sense of the word. It borrowed the word *persona* from the theater, where it was used to refer to the masks actors wore to identify the various roles they were playing. (We still see the *dramatis personae,* cast of characters, listed in theater programs.) So in the language of the church "three persons" did not mean three different personalities; it meant three different "roles" God plays or three different functions God fulfills. This may sound suspiciously like the third or fourth of the rejected heresies we mentioned, but the church's doctrine differs from them in two ways: (1) These roles, or persons, are true self-expressions of God, not just God's "acting like" or "pretending to be" one or the other, with the possibility that God might just as well decide to play other roles and be a different kind of God. (2) God's actions as Father, Son, and Holy Spirit are *simultaneous,* always going on at the same time, not actions in a temporal sequence. But even with these qualifications and explanations, talk about "three persons" in the Godhead still sounds like tritheism to us.

If we want to translate the ancient doctrine of the Trinity into language that is meaningful to us, we could say something like this: "One God in three persons" means *one personal God who lives and works in three different ways at the same time.* Now perhaps this still sounds like a numbers game that tries to put three together and get one, or divide one into three and still have one. But the doctrine of the Trinity does not try to *explain* the mystery of the triune God; it tries to *preserve* a mystery that cannot be explained without "explaining it away" in one false direction or another. What is finally important is not that we comprehend the mystery itself but that we see how the doctrine of the Trinity functions in Christian thinking about who God is and what God is doing in our lives and in the world around us. This is what we will try to do in the last two sections of this chapter.

In the next section we will discuss the "works" of the Trinity, emphasizing (with the Western church) the oneness, or unity, of Father, Son, and Holy Spirit. In the last section we will emphasize (with Eastern Orthodox churches) the threeness, or distinctions, that exist both in the inner life and in the work of God in the world.

We come now to the "payoff" of the church's doctrine of the Trinity—the practical consequences that make all this talk about oneness and threeness worth the trouble, the goal of our struggle with this difficult doctrine.

ONE GOD WHO IS CREATOR, SAVIOR, AND LIFE-RENEWER

We think first of what the one God who is Father, Son, and Holy Spirit *does.*

Three Works of God

Following scripture, Trinitarian theology "assigns" or "attributes" different works to the Father, Son, and Holy Spirit. We have not been able to talk about the triune God without mentioning them; and even if you think you do not know much about the doctrine of the Trinity, you have probably been deeply influenced by it to the extent that you automatically follow this "division of labor" in your own thinking about God.

When we think about God the Father, we think about "God, the Father Almighty, Creator of heaven and earth." We think about God's work as powerful Creator, just Ruler, Protector, and Preserver of the world and all living things in it. We think about God's presence and work *over* us.

When we think about God the Son, we think of God's loving, self-giving work in Jesus Christ to reconcile, save, and liberate needy, sinful creatures and the created world. We think about God's presence and work *with* and *for* us.

When we think about God the Holy Spirit, we think of God's work to renew and transform human beings, human communities, and our whole natural environment in order to achieve a new humanity in a new creation. We think of God's presence and work *in* and *among* us.

Three "persons"—Father, Son, and Holy Spirit. Three works—creation, reconciliation-salvation, and renewal-transformation. If that were all we could say about who God is and what God does, we would turn the triune God into a committee of three gods, each of whom has a special committee assignment or responsibility that is different from and unrelated to what the other two are doing. But the doctrine of the Trinity emphasizes the unity of the three things God is and does.

Three Works of ONE God

According to scripture, *all* of God is involved in *everything* God does.

The work of creation is not only the work of the Father; it is also the work of the Son: "All things came into being through him" (John 1:3). "All things have been created through him and for him" (Col. 1:16). And according to Gen. 1:2, creation is also the work of the Spirit ("wind") of God moving across the waters of chaos.

The work of reconciliation and redemption is not only the work of the Son but the work of the Father and the Spirit too. "In Christ *God* was reconciling the world to himself" (2 Cor. 5:19). It is through the Spirit that we "have access in one Spirit to the Father" (Eph. 2:18).

The Spirit's work of "sanctification" that renews us for fellowship with God and thankful service of God and neighbor is also attributed to the Father (1 Thess. 5:23) and to the Son (Eph. 5:26).

In other words, we may associate different works especially with the Father, the Son, or the Spirit, but we cannot separate them. They are different aspects of the total work of *one* God. What one wills and does, the other two will and do also. We never have to do with one without the other two. Where one is at work, there the other two are at work also, and the purpose and goal of any one is the same as the purpose and goal of the other two.

This understanding of the unity of the works of God led the ancient church to formulate a fundamental rule for Trinitarian thinking that is still absolutely essential if we are to understand who God is and what God is doing in our lives and the world around us: *The works of the Trinity are indivisible.* The importance of this rule becomes clear when we see how it exposes and corrects widespread false interpretations or heresies that result from separating what the Father, Son, and Holy Spirit do. Here are three examples.

Heresy: For us Christians in the church, God is the loving Father of Jesus Christ who loves us, forgives our sins, saves us, and promises the Holy Spirit to help and guide us. But for non-Christians outside the church, God is a powerful, righteous Creator and Judge who does not love, forgive, and help but who condemns and punishes them for their sins. That is why we must have missions and evangelism—to tell them about Christ so that they may be included among those whom God loves and promises to help.

But the doctrine of the Trinity teaches us that what God the Savior and Helper of Christians wills and does is not different from what God the Ruler and Judge of the whole world wills and does. What we Christians know about God's love in Christ, and about God's helping and renewing power in the Holy Spirit, tells us what the Creator of heaven and earth wills and is doing in the lives of all people everywhere (even before they know about it). And on the other hand, the warning of God's just judgment against the sinfulness of all those non-Christian outsiders is also directed against the sinfulness of us Christian insiders. There are not three Gods, one who wills and does one thing in relation to non-Christians, and a second and third who will and do something else in relation to Christians. There is only one God who rules with just judgment against us sinful Christians as well as against those sinful non-Christians; and who at the same time loves, forgives, and helps them as well as us. We cannot separate what God the Father-Creator wills and does out there in the world and what God the Son-Redeemer and Spirit-Renewer will and do in the church, for they are one and the same God. Would our understanding of ourselves and of unbelievers in the world outside the church and our understanding of the task of missions and evangelism be different if we learned not to separate but to connect the work of God the Father, Son, and Holy Spirit?

Heresy: God is an angry God who wanted to punish us because we have been bad and disobeyed God's laws. But Jesus loved us and took God's punishment on himself, so God had to let us go free. Jesus our Savior who loves us saves us from God the righteous Judge who hates us.

But the doctrine of the Trinity means that the will and action of God the Son in our behalf are not opposed to the will and action of God the Father; they *are* the Father's will and action. Christ does not *change* the attitude of God toward us sinful human beings and force God reluctantly to be for us instead of against us; Christ is the *deepest expression* of God's desire to be with and for us. If Jesus is the friend of sinners, then so is God. If God the Son takes the consequences of our sins on himself in self-giving, suffering love, then that is what God the Father does too. We cannot separate the power and righteousness of the Father from the self-giving suffering love of the Son, for Father and Son are one and the same God. Would this understanding of the unity of Father and Son help us in discerning what the "will of God" is when bad as well as good things happen in our own lives, in the lives of those whom we love, and in the world around us?

Heresy: The Holy Spirit makes us be "spiritual" people by helping us be concerned about such things as prayer, worship, and church activities. The Spirit has nothing to do with such "worldly" things as sexual needs and pleasures, the way we make and spend money, and issues of political and economic justice. On the contrary, the Spirit helps us to rise above all that to find comfort and peace in lives devoted to a deeper spirituality in our personal walk with God.

But the doctrine of the Trinity teaches us that the Holy Spirit is the Spirit of the God who is Creator and Ruler of heaven *and* earth, human souls *and* bodies, individual persons *and* social-political communities. The Spirit is the Spirit of the Son who became a flesh-and-blood human being who went to parties, healed the sick, fed the hungry, liberated the oppressed, forgave sinners, came to bring the kingdom of God's justice, compassion, and peace into and for the sake of the world. The Holy Spirit is the Spirit of the God who is the Creator and Redeemer of *this* world, and therefore the Spirit who enables us not to escape from but to work for the renewal of human life that is lived out in the realm of the bodily, physical, and material; in the arena of the social, political, and economic affairs that shape our lives for good or ill. Would our understanding of "spiritual growth" in our personal devotional lives and in the church be different if we understood that the work of God the Holy Spirit cannot be separated from the work of God the Father and God the Son?

It has been said that all Christian heresies are at bottom Trinitarian heresies. Many of them come from separating the will and work of God the powerful and just Creator and Ruler of the world, God the loving Reconciler and Savior of needy and sinful human beings, and God the ever-present Renewer and Transformer of human life and the life of all God's creation. Whenever we read or hear anything that sets Father, Son, and Holy Spirit against each other or suggests that what one wills and does is different from what the other two will and do—then we can be sure that what we have heard is wrong. All truly Christian thinking about the ways of God in our own lives and in the world around us is thinking that remembers the inseparable connection between the triune God. For God the Father, Son, and Holy Spirit are not three different Gods willing and doing three different things. They are one God who in three different ways wills and does the same thing.

Everything that follows in this book can be understood as an attempt to think through the consequences of this fundamental rule of all genuinely Christian theology; the works of the Trinity are indivisible.

But everything we say can also be understood as an attempt to understand the consequences of a second fundamental rule to which we now turn.

THE SOCIAL TRINITY

We move now from an emphasis on what the triune God *does* to a discussion of who the triune God *is*, to the mystery of the deepest inner being of the God who is Creator and Ruler, Reconciler and Savior, Renewer and Transformer of creaturely life. It is also a move from the way both Roman Catholic and Protestant churches in the West have understood the doctrine of the Trinity to reflection on the way Eastern Orthodox churches have understood it.

Christians in the Eastern church have always been unhappy about what they believe is a one-sided Western emphasis on the unity, or oneness, of Father, Son, and Holy Spirit to the neglect of their real threeness, or the distinctions between them. In our time they have been joined by representatives of feminist, liberation, and other theologians in the West who believe that the traditional Western doctrine of the Trinity has had disastrous consequences for our understanding not only of God but also of ourselves and of our social, political, and economic life together. We must now see what we can learn from these critics.

We go straight to the heart of the issue when we look at what its critics denounce as the "monotheistic" or "monarchical" understanding of God in the West, and their quest for a genuinely *Trinitarian* understanding.[6]

Western Monotheism

One of the most common illustrations of the Trinity in the West is an equilateral triangle like figure A below: one God with three "sides" representing Father, Son, and Holy Spirit who are "equal in power and glory."

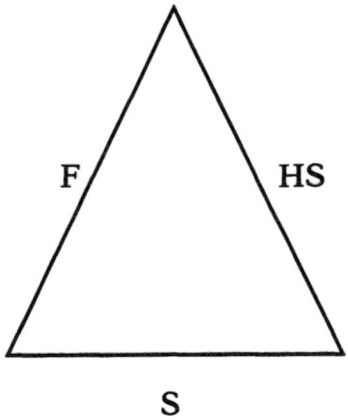

Figure A

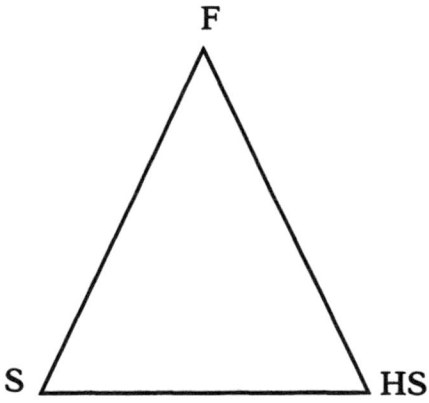

Figure B

But, say the critics of this illustration, the Western emphasis on the oneness of God tends in practice to lead us to shift to figure B.

According to our critics, when we Western monotheists say "God," we do not in actual practice think of three equal persons; we tend to think of one "top" God, the Father, and two subordinate and somehow lesser divine beings, the Son and the Spirit. When we think of *one* God, we do not think of Father, Son, and Holy Spirit together; we think of the

Father, who is the "main" God. That is not what the classical doctrine of the Trinity intended to say, but does it not sound familiar?

Consider first the consequences of the diagram in figure B for our understanding of who God is and what God is like. God the Father, the "main" God, is an isolated individual who exists in solitary loneliness "at the top of the heap," first above the Son and the Spirit, then above everything and everyone else in all creation. God is related to everyone and everything as a supreme monarch who rules with absolute authority, power, dominion, and control, unlimited by anyone or anything that could compromise the divine self-sufficiency and autonomy. Everything and everyone else are subordinate to, dependent upon, and at the mercy of this one absolute Ruler who maintains divine sovereignty and freedom by asserting it against all competing claims to power and freedom. Add to this picture our traditional way of thinking of God as a "he," and we tend to understand God as the supreme *Male* who stands with unlimited power, dominion, and control over everything and everyone below "him."

Now consider how this "hierarchical," "monarchical," "patriarchical" understanding of God is reflected in our Western understanding of what it means to live and organize our lives together as human beings in the image of God. If *God* is the supreme Individual whose selfhood is maintained and defended by "his" lonely self-sufficiency above everyone and everything that limits "him" in any way, then that is what it means to be a human being in the image of God. If *God's* freedom is freedom to do anything "he" pleases, and therefore freedom from responsibility to and for anything or anyone outside "himself," then that is what the freedom, authority, and power of human beings in the image of God means in human social, political, and economic relationships. And finally, if *God* is the great heavenly Male, then that means *male* power, authority, domination, and control in individual, familial, and social relationships.

Critics of Western monotheism argue that it supports everything that is problematical about Western society in general: extreme individualism, competitive struggle for power over other people (especially those of the opposite sex and other races, classes, and nations), resentment of anyone else's authority and power as a threat to one's own freedom and *self*-rule, exploitation of the natural world that is understood to be there to be used or misused as we see fit, and the assertion of male superiority (or female superiority in opposition to it). An individualistic, hierarchical, patriarchical, authoritarian view of God leads us to think of ourselves and others in terms of the ceaseless conflict between the superior and the inferior, the powerful and the powerless, those who dominate and control and those who are dominated and controlled. It leads us to think of freedom as freedom *from* the interference, demands, or expectations of any person or group that limits our ability to assert our own self-interest and to do anything we like with what is ours. Of course, that is not how our ideal of a democratic society teaches us to think about human relations. But is it not the way we in fact often think about the relation between racial and ethnic groups, men and women, parents and children, employers and employees, "free citizens" and "the government"?

To be sure, this analysis is a caricature of our Western understanding of God and human society. And it surely exaggerates the influence of the Christian doctrine of the Trinity on Western culture. (To the extent that there is a connection between the two, it is more likely that our self-understanding has shaped our understanding of God rather than vice versa.) But is it not true that we tend to think of God the Father as the "number one" top God with absolute sovereign power? Is it not true that we live in a society that places high value on defending the self-interest of "number one" in individual, economic, racial, political—and ecclesiastical—relations? Is it just an accident that "number one" is so important both in our understanding of God and of ourselves? There is enough truth here to make us at least interested in the possibility of another way of thinking about God and about human life in the image of God.

The Fellowship of Father, Son, and Holy Spirit

If Western Christianity's model of the Trinity has typically been a triangle, the typical model in Eastern Orthodoxy is a circle. In the religious art of Orthodox churches, Father, Son, and Holy Spirit are often pictured as three figures sitting around a table together sharing a meal (see figure C).

John of Damascus, a Greek theologian who lived in the seventh century, developed this understanding of the Trinity with a concept called *perichoresis* (perry-ko-ray'-sis). This Greek word is worth learning because it gives us a lovely picture of God. *Peri* (as in perimeter) means "around." *Choresis* means literally "dancing" (as in the choreography of a ballet). Father, Son, and Holy Spirit are like three dancers holding hands, dancing around together in harmonious, joyful freedom.

From the perspective of Western monotheism, this image of God

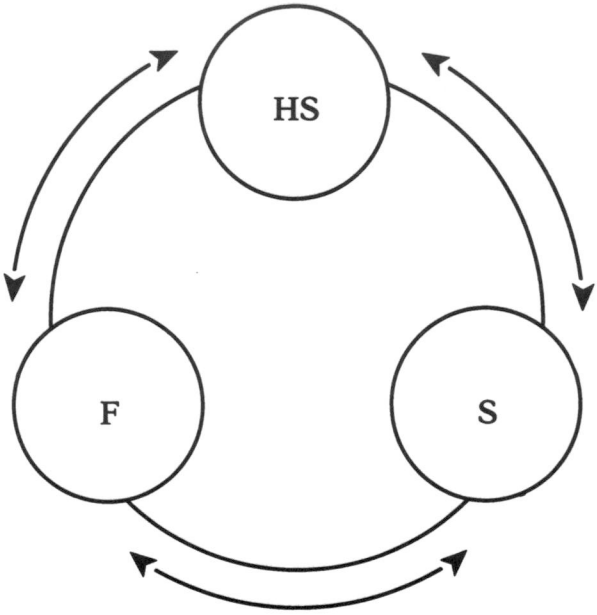

Figure C

seems to suggest not one but three personal gods. But *perichoresis* invites us to think in a new way about the very meaning of "one" and "personal." The oneness of God is not the oneness of a distinct, self-contained individual; it is the unity of a *community* of persons who love each other and live together in harmony. And "personal" means by definition *inter*-personal; one cannot be truly personal alone but only in relation to other persons. Such is the unity and personal character of God the Father, Son, and Holy Spirit. There is a deep, intimate, indissoluble unity between them. There are not three independent persons who decide to get together to form a club (or a dance group!) that might break up if the members decide to go it alone. *They are what they are* only in relationship to each other. Each exists only in this relationship and would not exist apart from it. Father, Son, and Holy Spirit live only in and with and through each other, eternally united in mutual love and shared purpose. Behind this understanding of the Trinity lies Jesus' strange statement that the Father is "in" me and I am "in the Father" (John 10:38). Father, Son, and Holy Spirit are one *social* person, for each is with and for the other so intimately that they can be said to live in and through each other.

Even with such a strong emphasis on the unity of the three, this concept of a "social Trinity" may still sound suspiciously tritheistic to us Westerners who understand Christianity as a monotheistic religion. But perhaps it is worth running the risk of being called tritheistic when we consider how our understanding of God and of ourselves changes when we think of Father, Son, and Holy Spirit according to the *perichoresis* doctrine.

Now there is no solitary person separated from the others; no above and below; no first, second, and third in importance; no ruling and controlling and being ruled and controlled; no position of privilege to be maintained over against the others; no question of conflict concerning who is in charge; no possible rivalry or competition between competing individuals; no need to assert independence and authority of one at the expense of the others. Now there is only the fellowship and community of equals who share all that they are and have in their communion with each other, each living with and for the others in mutual openness, self-giving love, and support; each free not *from* but *for* the others. That is how Father, Son, and Holy Spirit are related in the "inner circle" of the Godhead. They are one personal God in their total and unreserved fellowship and community with and for each other.

If in God's own deepest inner being God is such a community-seeking God, then that is also what God is in relation to us. Gone is the hierarchical, monarchical, patriarchical God who asserts, defends, and maintains sovereign freedom and power at the expense of God's creatures. The freedom and power of the God who is Father, Son, and Holy Spirit together is freedom and power not to dominate and control, but freedom and power to be God-with-us and for us. It is not freedom and power to do anything and everything God pleases, but freedom and power to be a loving and just covenant-making God who wills only our good. It is freedom and power exercised not to keep us dependent and powerless slaves but to set us on our feet and empower us to be God's faithful friends, companions, and partners. The freedom and power of this God, therefore, is not something we must fear, secretly resent, and rebel against because it robs us of our human dignity and freedom; it is the source of true human dignity and freedom.

Consider now the implications of this understanding of the triune God for the self-understanding and life together of human beings created in the image of God.

If the deity of God is fulfilled in the community of Father, Son, and Holy Spirit, then the true humanity of human beings created in the image of God is realized only in human community, not in the lonely self-assertion of individuals who seek to be themselves apart from and against other human beings.

If God's freedom is the freedom of God the Father, Son, and Holy Spirit to be with and for each other, then true human freedom is freedom for and not freedom from other people.

If in the divine community there is no above and below, superior and inferior, but only the free society of equals who are different from each other but live together in mutual openness, respect, and self-giving love, so it is in a truly human society of people who are sexually, racially, socially, politically, and religiously different from each other.

If in relation to us God exercises divine power not to rob us of our human freedom and dignity but to invite and enable us to be partners in God's creative, reconciling, liberating, renewing work in the world, then legitimate human power cannot be power used by some persons and groups to dominate, manipulate, and control others; it can only be power used to free and empower other individuals and groups to work together for the common good of all.

If there is equality between Father, Son, and Holy Spirit within the divine community; and if the triune God is at work in the world to break down barriers between the powerful and the powerless, superior and inferior, to create a community of equal partners who serve one another and not just themselves—then in a truly human society too there can be no room for patriarchical (or matriarchical) authoritarianism. There can only be the quest for a human society that reflects the free, open, egalitarian kind of society God the Father, Son, and Holy Spirit have with each other and will for the world.

In other words, a *perichorestic* understanding of the divine society results in a *perichorestic* understanding of human society as well.

Would we fall into the heresy of tritheism if we thought of Christian faith not as one among other monotheistic religions but as faith in the divine "society" of Father, Son, and Holy Spirit? Does this understanding of God lead to an understanding of human nature and human society that is at best unrealistic, idealistic, utopian, and at worst dangerously subversive and un-American? Or could it be that the good news of the Christian faith in a triune God is just the good news that we can give up thinking about who is number one at the top of the heap and can learn to think first of God, then of ourselves, as living in the circle of a community of free, equal partners who live joyfully and thankfully with and for one another, united in the "dance" that is God's life and genuinely human life?

TRINITARIAN THINKING ABOUT GOD, OURSELVES, AND THE WORLD

We end where we began: There is no way we can put one and three together when we think of Christian faith in one personal God who has three distinct ways of being and acting as God. We inevitably emphasize either one at the expense of three or three at the expense of one. The Trinity is a mystery to be confessed, not a mathematical problem to be solved.

Even so, everything depends for us Christians on whether we think about God, ourselves, and the world around us in light of this mystery. And in this chapter we have discussed two fundamental rules of Trinitarian thinking that enable us to do this.

1. *The works of Father, Son, and Holy Spirit are indivisible.* We may distinguish between God's work as Creator and Ruler of the world; as Reconciler, Liberator, and Savior of needy, sinful human beings; and as Renewer and Transformer of the life of human beings and all creation. But the will and work of God the Father, Son, and Holy Spirit cannot be separated or set over against each other. They can be understood only in light of each other and in their agreement with each other, for Father, Son, and Holy Spirit are one God.

2. *Perichoresis.* God the Father, Son, and Holy Spirit are one as a divine *community* who live with and for and in one another in mutual openness, freedom, and self-giving love. And this divine community is the model of all genuine human community.

You will become a *Christian* theologian as you learn to be guided by both these rules of Trinitarian thought. And you will see that everything that comes in the following chapters is simply the application of these rules in our quest to understand who God is, who we human beings are, and what it means to think and live as Christians.

FOR FURTHER REFLECTION AND STUDY

1. Look at the following passages in which Father, Son (or Lord), and Spirit are mentioned: Matt. 28:19; 2 Cor. 13:14; Eph. 4:4–6; 1 Cor. 12:4–5. What is the significance of the fact that there is no fixed

order in which the names appear? What is the significance of the fact that the three names appear together in the context of worship (baptism or prayer) or in the context of a discussion of the Christian life?

2. Creation is usually associated with the Father, reconciliation and redemption with the Son, and sanctification or newness of life with the Spirit. With whom is creation associated in John 1:1–3; Heb. 1:2; Col. 1:16? With whom is reconciliation or salvation associated in 2 Cor. 5:18–19; Titus 3:4? With whom is sanctification associated in 1 Thess. 5:23; Eph. 5:25–26; Heb. 10:10? What is the significance of this inconsistency?
3. Answer the following questions from the point of view of the doctrine of the Trinity:
   a. Would it be wrong for a parent to teach his or her child to sing "Jesus Loves Me" and then threaten the child that God will hate the child if he or she is not good?
   b. How would you respond to a friend who has lost a loved one, or whose home has been destroyed by a storm, if the friend said, "God must be against me"?
   c. What should be the attitude of a serious Christian toward such "creaturely" things as sexual pleasure, the enjoyment of good food, and play or fun in general?
   d. Should a truly "spiritual" person be interested and involved in such a "worldly" program as social welfare?
   e. Suppose you went to a church that had decided to admit only white children to its day-care program, and you heard someone say, "The Holy Spirit was certainly with us today." What would you say?
   f. How would the revelation of the will of God in Christ help us evaluate the legitimacy of "speaking in unknown tongues" as a manifestation of the presence and work of the Holy Spirit?
   g. Could the Holy Spirit be at work outside the Christian church and apart from Christians? How could we distinguish the work of the Holy Spirit from that of some other spirit when we listen to non-Christians?
   h. How should the doctrine of the Trinity influence our understanding of the legitimate power and authority of (1) a parent, (2) political leaders, (3) an employer or business executive?

6

What Is God Like?

The Doctrine of the Attributes of God

Is God dead? God's death was first announced toward the end of the last century by German philosopher Friedrich Nietzsche. For a while during the 1960s there was a much-debated "death of God" theology in North America. Some sensitive Jewish and non-Jewish thinkers still argue that since the Holocaust, when more than five million of God's chosen people were murdered in gas chambers, it is no longer possible to believe in God: the monstrous events of our century prove that if there ever was a powerful, just, compassionate God, that God is now dead.

Many of us believe that despite the casual or deeply despairing secularism of our time, the death announcement was premature. God is still alive and well. But the fact that radical doubt and practical if not theoretical atheism can be so widespread even in our "religious" nation means that we can no longer take faith in God for granted. It raises some serious questions we Christians must answer for ourselves and be prepared to answer from others when we speak about God to those who do not (perhaps cannot) share our faith in God.

It does not say anything about *God,* of course, when philosophers and even theologians announce the death of God and many ordinary people are impressed by what they say. But it does say something about *us.* The church may talk about a God who is at work in our individual lives and in the world around us. But many people experience only the distance, silence, and absence of God—like Jesus himself who cried, "My God, my God, why have you forsaken me?" Why does God seem so far away, even dead, in our time? Is it because we live in a scientific and technological age that no longer needs "God" to explain everything—or anything—that happens to us? Is it because God seems to do nothing about all the misery, suffering, and injustice in the world? Perhaps these are partial explanations. But could it be that instead of blaming science or God, we ought to ask if the fault is not in ourselves? Could it be that we have some wrong ideas about who God is and that *they* must die if we are to know and experience the reality of God in our lives? Could it be that we ought to *welcome* the announcement that "God" is dead, because only as our false conceptions of God die can we learn to know what the living and true God is really like?

God is dead. *Which* God? The god who was a great heavenly Granddaddy is dead. The god who was there to answer all our questions, solve all our problems, protect us from the hurts and hard knocks of life, make our lives warm and safe and comfortable, save us from all trouble (including the trouble we bring on ourselves). The god who made no demands of us but was there to do everything for us and give us everything we want. The god who automatically forgave us, no matter how we disobeyed that god and ignored or hurt other people. That god is dead—in fact, never was alive in the first place.

God the great heavenly (male) Tyrant is also dead—the "sovereign" god who could do anything he wanted to and proved it by arbitrarily being sometimes cruel and sometimes kind, loving some people and hating or simply ignoring others, according to the whim of the moment. The god who sneaked around spying on us, trying to catch us doing something bad so he could get us. The god whose will it was easy to know because it was always against everything that was fun and pleasant, and always demanded of us just what we did *not* like and did *not* want to do. That god is dead. We may rejoice and be thankful that he too was never alive.

Finally, that god is dead who was really only a great heavenly Idea, the god some especially educated people thought of in terms of abstract concepts: The "Supreme Being." The "Almighty." "Providence." Wisdom, Power, Justice, Goodness, and Truth. That god never did *do* anything anyway, was never a living, personal God. That god was only a Big Idea.

Which god is dead? All the gods that were really nothing but a projection of our own fears, wishes, insecurity, greed, or speculation. All the gods made in our own image. If talk about the death of God in our time exposes our idols and their inadequacy, we may welcome it. The quicker we bury and forget the gods we make for ourselves, the quicker we can learn who God really is.

Who is the living and true God? Not the great heavenly Granddaddy or Tyrant or Idea, but the self-revealing triune God we have discussed in the last two chapters—the God who came to us in Jesus of Nazareth and continues to be present and at work among us in the living Christ and his Spirit, not leaving us to guess or figure out for ourselves if "there is" a God and if so what kind of God. And what is *this* God like? That is what we must think about in this chapter—in contrast to the dead gods we have mentioned.

Even when we catch a glimpse of what this true God is like, we will not automatically solve the problem all of us sometimes have with the silence, distance, and unreality of God in our own lives, and with God's seeming absence from the world we live in. Nor will it enable us automatically to speak convincingly about God to others. But perhaps it will help us to face the difficulties of faith in God in our time as *Christians*. Perhaps it will help us at least to ask the right questions about God and not be disappointed when we do not get answers to the wrong questions!

THE LIVING, PERSONAL GOD

According to scripture, God acts, speaks, knows, wills, decides, loves, rejoices, regrets, pleads, judges, rules, suffers, triumphs. God can be angry, compassionate, jealous, merciful. All such language assumes that God is not something but someone, not just a "spiritual force" but a person. Biblical-Christian faith is faith in a *personal* God.

The Bible was written in a patriarchical society, and most of its personal images of God are masculine: God is like a father, king, husband, warrior. But scripture can also break out of this patriarchical tradition to compare God to a woman: God is like a wife giving birth (Isa. 42:14), like a mother teaching a toddler to walk and holding the child in her arms (Hos. 11:1–3), like a mother who comforts a frightened or hurt child (Isa. 66:13). Jesus can compare God's rejoicing over a repenting sinner to a woman who has found a lost coin (Luke 15:8–10).

Is not this personal language, whether the analogy is feminine or masculine, too anthropomorphic (giving human characteristics to something not human)? Is it not a very crude way of making God in the image of a human being? What gives us the right to take the concept of personality, which is clearly our experience of ourselves, and apply it to God?

In answer to this objection we ought first to admit quite frankly that we do speak anthropomorphically when we speak of God as a person.

This is especially obvious in the Old Testament, which speaks with apparently childlike unconcern of God's arm, mouth, hands, feet, eyes, and ears. We do the same thing when we ask God to watch over us, speak to us, hear our prayers, take us by the hand, and walk with us on our way.

But what alternative do we have but to speak of God in this way? In order to do justice to the transcendent mystery of God, most philosophers and many theologians have tried to speak of God in *impersonal* terms. They have usually changed personal categories expressing *action* into purely intellectual categories expressing *being:* God is the Highest Being or Being Itself. Or they think of God in terms of abstract concepts or ideals such as Love or the Good. But is an impersonal God really higher and greater than a personal one? Is a God "without passions" (Westminster Confession, 2.1) really greater than a loving God who feels with and for us? Moreover, do we really escape anthropomorphism by thinking impersonally? Is it any less anthropomorphic to apply to God our idea of being, love, or goodness than to apply to God our experience or personality? We ourselves are human, and we can think and speak only in a human way. *All* language about God, personal or impersonal, is anthropomorphic.

Having said this, we must do everything we can to guard against making God in our own image. The same Old Testament writers who seem to have spoken so naively of the parts of God's "body" lived by the command to make no idol in the form of any creaturely being (Ex. 20:4). Question 109 of the Westminster Larger Catechism is certainly correct in interpreting this commandment to prohibit also making any representation of God "inwardly in our mind." If we follow biblical teaching, we must think of God as a person, but we must also guard against picturing God, even in our minds, in any human form—that of an old man with a beard or any other such image. God is a person, but God is not a *human* person, not even a very big or very old or very perfect one.

This brings us to the last thing to be said about God's personalness. The best way of keeping our inevitable anthropomorphic thinking from getting out of hand is to interpret what we are and do in light of what God is and does, and not vice versa. We are made in the image of God, not vice versa. God is the original and authentic person. If we want to know what it means to be a real, genuine person, we must learn how God lives and acts in a personal way. *We* can be impersonal. We can depersonalize other people and be depersonalized by them. We can treat other people as objects, and to a large extent we ourselves are not the freely deciding persons we like to think we are but the product of our environment or family background. One of the primary goals of every human being is to *become* a real person. In the last analysis, then, we do not know what it means to be genuinely personal, and it would be wrong to apply our incomplete, distorted, confused ideas about personalness to God. Difficult as it is, we must be open to learn from *the* Person what it means for us to be persons and how we may become real persons. Is this an impossible task, this strange reversal in our thinking? Not if we take into account biblical-Christian faith in a God who has spoken and acted through human beings in the history of ancient Israel and above all in the one person who stands at the end of that history. Not if we let this particular person become the standard, source, and goal of our understanding both of God's and our own personalness.

THE LOVING GOD OF SOVEREIGN MAJESTY

What kind of living person is God? God is not a great heavenly Tyrant who threatens and terrifies us with arbitrary unpredictable divine power that may be for or against us. Nor is God a great heavenly Granddaddy (or Grandmother) who does everything for us and makes our lives smooth, painless, and easy, without expecting or demanding anything of us. Both these gods are dead idols. But both these figments of our imagination have an element of truth in them. The Bible does tell us two things about the living and true God. On the one hand, this God is in fact infinite, almighty, omnipresent, omniscient, beyond the greatest and highest we can imagine. On the other hand, this God is also a God who draws near to us in an intimate way as a loving parent to a child or as one who wants to be our friend and companion. God is neither heavenly Tyrant nor heavenly Grandparent, nor a combination of both. But God is in fact far above us yet with us, distant yet near, mysterious yet familiar, powerful yet loving, loving yet powerful—both at the same time.

Exodus 33:7–23 expresses this profound paradox in a delightfully simple way. God speaks to Moses "face to face, as one speaks to a friend" (v. 11). But even in this intimate relationship God remains hidden and even terrible. Moses is allowed to see only God's "back" (literally, perhaps, God's "backside") when God's "glory" passes by. In seeming contradiction to what is said at the beginning of the passage, Moses is *not* allowed to see God's face, "for no one shall see me and live" (v. 20).

(Calvin said that looking into the face of God would be like looking directly into the sun: the light would be so bright that it would blind us.)

This paradoxical nearness and distance of God is characteristic of all the Old Testament. See how it is expressed, for instance, in Isa. 55:6–9; 57:15; Hos. 11:9. God is often called the "Holy One" in the Old Testament. "Holy" means separate, totally different. But God is the Holy One *of Israel,* the God who is free and independent *above* Israel and all its claims, yet the God who graciously decides to be *Israel's* God, to dwell *in the midst* of this people.

The situation is the same in the New Testament. God is the God who "dwells in unapproachable light, whom no one has ever seen or can see" (1 Tim. 6:16). Yet Jesus can say, "Whoever has seen me has seen the Father" (John 14:9). Jesus is himself the paradox we have been talking about. In him God is both over us and with us (the doctrine of the Trinity), hidden and yet revealed (doctrine of revelation). He is just Judge and loving Savior, powerful Lord and Suffering Servant, King and Friend, almighty God and fellow human being. Not first one and then the other, not sometimes one and sometimes the other, but always both at the same time.

Perhaps we can best summarize the two sides of God with the beginning of the Lord's Prayer. We may call God "our Father," one of the most familiar, intimate relationships we know. (Remembering that scripture can also compare God with a mother, we could also call God "our Mother," also one of the most familiar, intimate relationships we know.) Yet God is our Father (or Mother) "in heaven"—above us, beyond us, foreign to us, different from us and everything and everyone we know.

If we are to think in a Christian way about what the personal God is like, we must take both sides of the paradox seriously. If we think of God only as Father or Mother, we will end up with a sweet, sentimental Grandparent who is not the God of the Bible. But if we think of God only as the God "in heaven," we will end up with an unknown, threatening Tyrant who is also not the God of the Bible.

Now, the next step we take in thinking about God is more important than it seems at first glance. In thinking of the attributes or characteristics of God, should we think first of those that describe God's nearness to us or of those that describe God's distance and difference from us? Should we begin by trying to understand God's love or God's sovereign majesty, God in relation to us or God's mysterious eternal being—God's "immanence" or God's "transcendence"?

Churches in the Reformed tradition (with Christian tradition in general) have usually thought first of the attributes that point to God's sovereign majesty, using such adjectives as infinite, unchangeable, eternal, incomprehensible, omnipotent (see the first paragraph of chapter 2 of the Westminster Confession). Then *in the second place* come the attributes of God's dealing with us: loving, gracious, merciful, patient, forgiving, just. That the first category has been considered the most important is shown by the fact that the Westminster Confession returns to it and deals exclusively with it in the second paragraph of chapter 2.

Unfortunately, we cannot follow our Reformed forebears in this approach—just because of what they themselves have taught us. It is fatally significant that they could "define" God without mentioning either biblical history or the fact that it is supremely in Christ that we learn who God is. Where did they get their information about what God is like? They surely intended to speak of no other God than the one we meet in scripture, but the fact that they begin with a very abstract description of God's divine nature rather than with a biblical description of God-with-us suggests that their concept of God actually came at least partly from another source.

The form of the attributes of God's sovereign majesty gives away what that source is. They are expressed either in *negative* or *superlative* terms that suggest either that God is what we are not (e.g., *in*finite, *un*changeable, *in*comprehensible, *im*mortal) or that God is what we are at our best but raised to perfection (e.g., *most* wise, free, holy).[1] But when we define God by comparison with ourselves (even by negative comparison), are we really talking about God or only about ourselves? If we think we can begin talking about what God is in God's innermost being, bypassing God's self-revelation in human history and experience, how can we escape making God in our own image, thus defeating our original purpose of magnifying the greatness of God?

Moreover, if we begin by thinking abstractly of the sovereign majesty of God before we speak of God's love for us in Christ, how can we avoid making God in the image of a human tyrant? Could it be that the one-sided emphasis of the traditional Reformed approach to the doctrine of God's attributes at least partly justifies the popular idea that the God of Calvinists is powerful and majestic but distant, harsh, and coldhearted?

If we are to speak of God in a biblical way, we must follow the advice of Calvin himself rather than the example of his followers who wrote many of the classical Reformed confessions. Calvin wrote:

> We know the most perfect way of seeking God, and the most suitable order, is not for us to attempt with bold curiosity to penetrate to the investigation of his essence, which we ought more to adore than meticulously to search out, but for us to contemplate him in his works whereby he renders himself near and familiar to us, and in some manner communicates himself. (*Institutes* 1.5.9)

That is, we must speak first of the God who has come to us like a mother or a father. Then, in the light of that, we can understand what it means that this God is also a God of sovereign majesty "in heaven." But we must not make a separation here as if we were speaking of two different Gods. The love of God is *sovereign* and *free* love, and the sovereign power of God is *loving* sovereignty and freedom.

GOD IN RELATION TO US

A fully developed doctrine of God would require us to investigate many attributes that describe God's fatherly-motherly approach to us. We would have to talk about God's love, mercy, pity, compassion, grace, patience, righteousness, and justice. In this brief discussion we will consider only two of these: love and justice. Love emphasizes God's kindness and care in drawing near to us. Justice emphasizes the fact that the God who draws near to us is a sovereign God who does not compromise but is faithful to God's divine freedom and integrity. The one living God is always truly loving *and* just, truly just *and* loving.

God Is Love

God *is* love (1 John 4:8). God is not sometimes loving and sometimes unloving, today loving some people and hating others, and tomorrow perhaps changing sides to love those who were previously hated and hate those who were previously loved. In *everything* God does, *always,* in dealing with *all* people, God is a *loving* God.

To say that God is love does not mean that love is God. We do not discover what God is like by analyzing and then deifying our ideas and experiences of love. Such a god would be an idol. It is not our understanding of love that defines God but God's action toward us that defines what real love is. We have only to look at God's self-revelation in biblical history and especially in Christ to see how radically different and how much better God's love is than what often passes for love among us—even among us who call ourselves Christians. As you read the following characteristics of the love of God, ask yourself these two questions: What would the church look like if its members loved each other as God loves us? How would such a church and its individual members speak and act in relation to people who follow other religious traditions or who do not believe in God at all?

God's love is universal. It seeks the welfare not just of a chosen few but of all people. It is not given to some and withheld from others; it is for everyone, for the whole world. There is no discrimination, limitation, or exclusiveness in God's love. How is this unlimited love of God expressed in John 3:16–17; 1 John 4:14; 1 Tim. 2:3–4?

God's love is unconditional. God does not say, "I will love you *if* you prove that you deserve my love and are worthy of it. I will love you *if* you first become law-abiding, God-fearing, respectable people." God does not even say, "I will love you *if* you first repent of your sins and believe." Rather: "Christ died for the ungodly. . . . God proves his love for us in that while we still were sinners Christ died for us" (Rom. 5:6–8). God's love is the love of Jesus, who was the friend not only of the moral, religious, and socially acceptable but also of the political revolutionaries (the zealots), dishonest business people (the tax collectors), the immoral (the woman caught in adultery), social outcasts (the Samaritans). There are no "ifs" or "buts," no strings attached, to God's love. God's love is unconditional.

God's love is initiating love. It does not wait for people to come asking for love and acceptance. God makes the first move, loving *before* people ask for love or even acknowledge their need for it. Long before we seek and turn to God, God seeks us out and turns to us. "For the Son of Man came to seek out and to save the *lost*" (Luke 19:10).

God's love is faithful. God never takes back God's promise to love us. Even when we are faithless, God remains faithful. We may turn away from God, but God never turns away from us. Even when God judges and disciplines us for our sinfulness, God still loves us, for God's love is "everlasting" (Jer. 31:3). Hosea went so far as to compare God's love to that of the love of a husband who still cares for and remains faithful to a wife who has become a prostitute (Hos. 3:1).

God's love is reconciling love. Jesus commanded us to love our *enemies,* not just our friends, those we find lovable and those who win our approval and support because of their admirable personal morality and social and political attitudes and actions. And that is what *God* does. God loves those who have made themselves enemies of God by their sinful rebellion and their enmity toward their fellow human beings. Even when God confronts and judges their sinfulness, it is to heal rather than to hurt, restore rather than to defeat and destroy, reclaim rather than to get even and pay back. God's love in Christ is *reconciling* love. "In Christ God was reconciling the [sinful] world to himself" (2 Cor. 5:19) in order to break down the dividing wall of hostility that separates people from God and from each other (Eph. 2:14).

God's love is costly, self-giving love. God does not say from the safe distance of divine superiority, "I love you poor people down there. Your hurt and suffering touch me deeply, and I will send help." Rather, in Christ God comes to stand with us and by us, as one of us, to *share* our hurt and suffering (including that which we bring on ourselves). The gift of God's love is not just a "care package" or this or that blessing from above; it is God's own self, the only Son (John 3:16).

God's love is helping, renewing love. It forgives and accepts us as we are, no matter what we may have done or not done. But it does not leave us as we are. God's love is not a sentimental, permissive love that allows or encourages us passively to settle down in our sinfulness with the complacent attitude that "God will forgive; that's what he's there for" (Voltaire). That kind of love would be indifference that does not care enough to take the trouble to help us renounce and move out of our self-destructive rebellion against God and alienation from other people. In contrast to that kind of pseudo-love, God's love is love that enables and empowers us to become *different* people, "new" people who realize our own true humanity as we learn to live in a right relationship with God and our fellow human beings. It is love that sets us on our feet and sets us on the way toward becoming strong, active, responsible people growing up into the "mature" humanity we see in Jesus Christ (Eph. 4:13), loving God and other people with our whole selves. This manifestation of God's love is often painful to us because it can help only as it exposes and confronts our sinful inhumanity, demanding as well as enabling change and growth in our lives. Then it becomes an aspect of God's justice.

But before we turn to what scripture teaches us about the justice of God, think again of what it teaches us about God's love. In light of our discussion of it, could it be that instead of asking as we sometimes do whether God is really a loving God, we ought rather to ask first whether we Christians are really loving people?

God Is Just

God is not only loving but also just—or "righteous," to use biblical language. God is not sometimes, with some people, loving, giving, and forgiving; and at other times, with other people, strict, demanding, and judging. God is always, with everyone, both loving and just at the same time. God's justice is loving justice, and God's love is just love. As you read what follows, ask yourself what it would mean in human relationships if we understood the relation between love and justice in God's way.

God's Loving Justice

We usually understand justice to mean fair and equal treatment of all people. When justice is done, everyone is subject to the same requirements of the law and recipient of the same benefits of the law: people get either the punishment they deserve for being "bad" and doing what the rules forbid, or the reward they get for being "good" and fulfilling what the rules require. Justice is therefore best administered by an unbiased or neutral judge who is impartial in giving people what they deserve. This understanding of justice is represented by the statue of the blindfolded woman with scales in her hand who stands at the top of the Supreme Court building in Washington, D.C. She does not see racial, sexual, class, or any other differences between people, but treats all people the same, impartially meting out what is due every person or group according to the law.

There are situations in which this concept of justice is appropriate, and a strain of it runs through the Bible (as in 2 Cor. 5:10). But it is not the predominant biblical view. According to scripture, God's justice (and therefore true human justice) differs in two ways from our common understanding of what justice means: (1) The God of scripture is not a blind judge but one who sees very clearly the difference between people—especially the difference between the rich and the poor, the powerful and the powerless, the privileged and the defenseless, oppressors and oppressed, insiders and "strangers" or aliens. And God's justice (and true human justice) is openly on the side of those who are poor, weak, threatened, and excluded. (2) God's (and truly human) justice gives people not what they *deserve* but what they *need. It is justice that gives rights to those who have no rights.* Karl Barth, the most influential Reformed theologian of this century, puts it this way:

> The people to whom God in his righteousness turns as helper and saviour is everywhere in the Old Testament the harassed and oppressed people of Israel, which, powerless in itself, has no rights, and is delivered over to the superior force of its enemies; and in Israel it is especially the poor, the widows and orphans, the weak and defenseless. . . . God always takes his stand unconditionally and passionately on this side alone: against the lofty and on behalf of the lowly; against those who enjoy right and privilege and on behalf of those who are denied it and deprived of it.[2]

In both the Old and New Testaments, this "biased" justice of God is expressed first of all in God's taking up the cause of those who are *politically* and *economically* poor and oppressed against the proud, comfortable, and secure who hold their privileged position at the expense of others. Among many passages in the Old Testament that so describe the justice that God does (and demands of God's people), see Ps. 72:1–4, 12–14; Ps. 103:6; Ps. 146:7–9; Isa. 3:13–15; Isa. 11:1–5. In the New Testament, the same understanding of justice is found in Mary's song when she is told that she is to be the mother of the promised Messiah: "He has brought down the powerful from their thrones, and lifted up the lowly; he has filled the hungry with good things, and sent the rich away empty" (Luke 1:52–53). And when in his first sermon Jesus announces who he is and what he came to do, he says (quoting Isaiah): "The Spirit of the Lord is upon me, because he has anointed me to bring good news to the poor. He has sent me to proclaim release to the captives and recovery of sight to the blind, to let the oppressed go free" (Luke 4:18).

But scripture goes beyond this political and economic aspect of God's (and truly human) justice to emphasize another dimension of it that is even more shocking. The just God of scripture is also on the side of those who are *morally* and *spiritually* poor and oppressed: poor *sinners* who are "oppressed" not just by others but also by their own sinfulness, people who are "without rights" because they deserve only condemnation for disobeying the law of God and hurting or simply not caring for their fellow human beings. Whether they are rich or poor, respectable insiders or excluded outsiders, whether they are guilty of "little" sins or the worst criminal act, God's justice means that God is for and not against sinful people, accepts rather than rejects them, seeks their restoration and salvation and not the punishment they deserve for what they have done or not done. How do we know this? Because in Jesus Christ God was the *friend* of sinners (Luke 7:34). Because God's justice is executed in the Jesus who died for the "ungodly," the "enemies" of God, so that they might be "justified" before God by God's *grace,* as a *gift* (Rom. 3:21–26; 5:6–10).

That is how different God's (and true human) justice is from that of our usual understanding of it, both when we think about it politically and economically and when we think about it ethically and theologically. That is why in the Bible God's justice is not something terrible to be avoided and dreaded but a great blessing to be hoped for and received with joy and thanksgiving (Isa. 45:8; Ps. 36:5–8; Ps. 98:7–9). That is why

Calvin can say in Question 87 of the Geneva Catechism: "We should not then fear the last judgment and have a horror of it? No, since we are not to come before any other Judge than he who is our Advocate, and who has taken our cause in hand to defend us." God's justice is not a terrible alternative to God's love; it *is* God's love.

God's Just Love

We have emphasized how completely and unreservedly God loves precisely in the exercise of divine justice. But this does not mean that God ignores all the ways we rebel against God's laws and commandments. The Bible speaks often of God as a righteous judge who will not tolerate individual lawlessness and social injustice. God's wrath burns against sinful individuals. It punishes, overthrows, tears down, condemns, and destroys sinful institutions and societies—including *religious* ones. It *is* a terrible thing to fall into the hands of an angry, righteous God. There is no point in denying this because we do not like to think of such a God. Nor is there any point in trying to argue that only the God of the Old Testament is a God of righteous anger, whereas the God of the New Testament is a God of tender love. The Old Testament speaks just as strongly of God's self-giving and forgiving love as does the New Testament, and the New Testament speaks just as strongly of God's demanding and punishing justice as does the Old Testament.

Why then does God's angry justice fall on sinful individuals and groups? Because we tend to think of God's justice in human terms, we tend to think that it must be because God is short-tempered, vengeful, and mean, or at best a heartless, legalistic judge bound to enforce the demands of the law at the expense of the human life and welfare of those who break it. But the Bible does not tell us of a revenge-seeking tyrant or of a disinterested judge trapped by responsibility to uphold an impersonal law of his own making. It tells us of a God who even in doing justice is like a loving mother or father.

That can only mean that God judges human sinfulness *just because* God loves sinful human beings (not just *us* sinners but *all* sinners, no matter how "bad" they are). God judges in order to *help,* not to pay back, get even, seek retribution, and wipe out. The very fact that God can become angry means that God really cares about us and is not willing to let us "stew in our own juice." It means that God cares enough to refuse to let us get by with the chaos and self-destruction we bring into our own lives when we rebel against God and actively cause or passively permit suffering in the lives of other people. God's law and commands were given to teach us how to live genuinely human lives as we thankfully trust and obey our Creator and live lives of compassion and justice in relation to our fellow human beings. And God condemns and punishes our disobedience in order to call us back from the godless and inhuman ways we have chosen against God, other people, and our own best interest so that we may find our own true humanity as we are reconciled to God and other people to live in community with them. God's justice, in other words, is like the tough discipline truly loving parents exercise when their children disobey rules given for their own health, safety, and growth toward social responsibility. Even when God's justice is expressed as wrath against us, this wrath is the burning of God's love for us.

How do we know that this is so? Because that is what scripture tells us about the justice of God. Speaking for God to the beloved chosen people of God, Amos said, "You only have I known of all the families of the earth; *therefore* I will punish you for all your iniquities" (Amos 3:2, emphasis added). In both the Old and New Testaments we hear that God disciplines and reproves those whom God loves (Prov. 3:12; Heb. 12:6–7; Rev. 3:19). But it is especially in the death of Christ that we see both how serious and how loving God's justice is. "The wages of sin is death" (Rom. 6:23). That is how strict God's justice is: it requires the death sentence for guilty sinners (or acknowledges the self-destruction they bring on themselves by their sin). But the death sentence is executed in such a way that it brings acquittal and life to the justly accused. The Christ who is God-with-us takes it on himself, comes to stand with and for us even in the death we bring on ourselves when we contradict God's life-giving purpose for us and all other people, and "pays the price" so that we may *go* free and *become* free—free to love God and other people as God in Christ has loved us. Later we must try to understand in more detail the meaning of Christ's death as God's judgment against us and at the same time as God's love for us. But we must point to it now as the most important clue to understanding the meaning of God's loving justice and just love.

Have we understood it? And do we believe it? Here is the test: What is the meaning of the loving justice and just love of God for our own lives when we think about all the ways we have disobeyed God, hurt other people, and compromised our own true humanity? What are the consequences of God's loving justice and just love for our understanding of criminal justice in general, and our position on capital punishment for the most serious criminal offenders? If we are guided by God's loving justice and just love, what kind of policies would we support and what kind of actions would we take in dealing with rich people or nations that exclude and oppress the poor, and with poor people or nations that turn to acts of terrorism or violent revolution to defend themselves? How would we deal with the conflict between women and men and between racial-ethnic groups in combating sexism and racism in the places where they work?

GOD IN HEAVEN

According to the Lord's Prayer, God is not only "our Father" (God in intimate relation to us) but "our Father *in heaven.*" "In heaven" does not mean "up in the sky" (see 1 Kings 8:27). It means that God is infinitely superior to us and our world, far beyond anyone or anything we know or can imagine, not to be confused with any earthly or human reality. Earlier theologians were so preoccupied with speculation about the meaning of this "transcendence" of God that they sometimes neglected what Jesus taught us about God's "fatherly" nearness to us. That is why we have spoken first about the biblical witness to God's love and justice. But scripture does also bear witness to a majestic God who is above and beyond us, and we conclude our discussion of the attributes of God by speaking of some of the big words that describe this side of God's being and work. We will do it properly if we keep in mind Calvin's advice not to speculate theoretically about the "essence" of God but "contemplate him in his works whereby he renders himself near and familiar to us." So if we have had constantly to remind ourselves that as our heavenly Father (or Mother) God is free to exercise justice and love in *God's* way, now we must keep in mind that the majestic God "in heaven" is none other than the God who in Christ is God-with-us and for us.

God is omnipotent. God is the almighty, all-powerful, sovereign Ruler of heaven and earth, unlimited by anything or anyone, absolutely free to do whatever the divine will pleases. But it is as the loving and just Ruler we come to know in scripture that God is so powerful. The sovereign power of God is not the ability to do literally anything and everything. It is not the sheer brute force of an unpredictable heavenly tyrant who may decide to be for us one day and against us the next, help today and hurt or simply ignore tomorrow. It is the sovereign power of a God who is for and not against us, whose kingdom will come and whose will for our good will be done, no matter how great the opposition may be from sinful individuals or societies. *God's omnipotence, then, means that God can do* *anything and everything that is consistent with God's goodness and love.* God *cannot* do evil, *cannot* be an arbitrary and uncaring heavenly tyrant, *cannot* act in self-contradiction to the goodness that God *is*. The power of God is the power of God's justice and love, the unlimited ability to do everything that God's justice and love allows and requires—and *only* that.

This sovereign power of God is not like that of a human king who guarantees his sovereign majesty by isolating himself from the poverty and weakness of his subjects, ruling over them from the uninvolved safe distance of the splendid comfort and invincible might of his royal throne. God can be God in weakness as well as in strength, in defeat and suffering as well as in victory, in the form of a lowly Servant as well as in the form of an exalted Lord—sharing our human condition rather than looking down on us from the safety of a heavenly throne. If we know about the accomplishment of God's sovereign will in the tragic history of the little insignificant people of ancient Israel and in a man dying on a cross as one of us, how can we think that God is powerfully at work only where we experience happiness, success, and triumph in our own lives and in the world around us? How can we limit God by thinking that God's omnipotent will for our good can be accomplished only in the good things that happen to us and not in the painful things; in deliverance from but not in the midst of pain, sorrow, and failure? Could it be that we spend too much time looking up to the heavenly heights, expecting miraculous help "from above," when we should be looking around us, ready to recognize the sovereign power of God's love and justice at work in the everyday events of our lives, even in the depths of the worst that can happen to us?

God is omnipresent, not limited by any spatial boundaries. God is everywhere, we learned as children. There is no place where God is not and cannot be present. The idea of God's omnipresence is terrifying to some people. It leads them fearfully to worry about a God whom they can never escape, a God who follows them around, spying on them and seeking to catch and punish them for doing something bad. But if we think about the omnipresence of the God we meet in the story of Israel and in Jesus Christ, the omnipresence of God becomes the greatest good news. It means that there is no place where God's love and justice cannot be and is not at work for the good of the world God created, rules, and promises to make new.

Where is God? In the church and among Christians, of course. But "the Most High does not dwell in houses made with human hands" (Acts

7:48). God is not imprisoned in the church or in the hearts of Christians. God is present and at work among non-Christians as well as Christians; with "bad" people as well as "good" people; in every other country of the world as well as in our country; with people of all races, all economic and social classes, and all cultures. God is *everywhere.* There is no place—not even hell itself—where God is not present and at work with loving justice and just love. Notice with what joy and comfort this is said in Psalm 139.

God is omniscient, a God who knows all things. Does this mean that God has known from the beginning everything that would or could happen in the history of the world and in the life of every person who ever has lived or will live? Perhaps. But when the biblical writers think of God's omniscience, they do not deal with such speculative questions. Rather, they emphasize that God knows *us.* God knows everything about us, even things we cannot admit to ourselves or talk about to others: our deepest fears and anxieties; our most ardent hopes; all the thoughts, words, and deeds we are or should be ashamed of; the good and evil desires we yield to or repress; our hurts and failures and the way we have hurt or failed others; the hunger to love and be loved that we express or are afraid to express. Everything. God's omniscience means that God is a God "unto whom all hearts are open, all desires are known, and from whom no secrets are hid."

Our vulnerability before such an omniscient God would be a terrible threat if we did not remember that the God who knows us so well is the God of Jesus Christ as scripture bears witness to him: the God who understands and cares about every one of us more than anyone else ever can; who knows us as we really are, yet loves us anyway; who knows even better than we ourselves what we need most and is eager to give us everything we need; who forgives even the worst that we have done or not done; who judges in order to help; who wills only our good. Moreover, this God who knows me and my friends and family so completely and cares for us so deeply also knows and cares in the same way for every single person in the world, including millions whom we never will and cannot know and care for. It is not just correct theology but good news that the God of biblical-Christian faith is an omniscient God.

God is eternal, not limited by time. Some Christian thinkers have thought this means that God is timeless, a God who watches the unfolding drama of human history from outside or above time as a spectator watches a play from a distant balcony, personally unaffected by and uninvolved in what is happening on the stage. But that is not the God we come to know in scripture. In the history of Israel and in the story of the life, death, resurrection, and promise of the living presence of Jesus Christ, we hear of a living God who is *in* the drama of history (the main character!). This is the God who goes with people and nations on their way in good times and in hard times, sharing their joys and sorrows, patiently sticking by them even when they least deserve it, leading them toward the final "happy ending" that is the coming of the justice, compassion, reconciliation, and peace of the kingdom of God for the sake of the whole world.

The "eternity" of God, then, means not the eternal *absence* of God *above* time, but the eternal *presence* of God *in* time. It means that at every moment in time, from beginning to end, the eternal God "has time for us." It means that there is no time—past, present, or future—when God was not, is not, and will not be powerfully present and at work in human history as the loving and just God we meet in scripture. When it is difficult to see as well as when it is easy, the rise and fall of empires and nations are in the hand of this God. Whether personal experience makes it easy or difficult, we may also calmly and joyfully confess to this God that "my times are in your hand" (Ps. 31:15). Everything else may come and go, but "the steadfast love of the Lord is from everlasting to everlasting" (Ps. 103:17). To know that is to know what it means to believe in an "eternal" God.

God is unchangeable, immutable, immovable. God is a God in whom "there is no variation or shadow due to change" (James 1:17). "For I the Lord do not change" (Mal. 3:6).

Orthodox Christian tradition sometimes taught that this means that the unchangeable God has an unchangeable plan in mind for our lives and that nothing we can say or do can alter what God has already decided will happen to us. Fearful of making God in the image of a human being whose emotions can change from moment to moment, orthodox doctrine taught that God is "without passions" (Westminster Confession, 2.1), unmoved by any feelings at all. Seeking to preserve the authority of scripture, some orthodox theologians have taught that a long time ago God spoke to give us some "eternal truths" and "absolute moral laws" by which Christians in all times and places are to live, then fell silent, leaving each person and generation after that to figure out for themselves how these general truths and ethical principles should be applied to the concrete ethical decisions they have to make in their particular time and place. In order to defend the unchanging will of God for human society, some orthodox Christians have believed that God originally ordained and continues to will the patriarchical, hierarchical, social, and political order of ancient Israel (with the ancient world in general), and that any attempt to find alternatives to such an order is to disobey the unchanging will of an unchanging God.

This cannot be what the Bible means when it speaks about an unchangeable God and the unchangeable will and plan of God. It is only persons who are literally or emotionally and mentally dead who are absolutely, rigidly unchanging and unchangeable; who are unable to say or do anything they have not already said and done in the past; who cannot hear, see, or feel anything that could move them to respond to the particular needs and problems and the specific pleas for help and guidance of people in their situation. Unlike such dead persons, the God of scripture is a living Person: a God whose mind can be changed in response to prayer (see the delightful story of Abraham's bargaining with God in Gen. 18:22–33); an ever-present God who knows and cares for each one of us and is eager to give us what we need and help us learn what we should do to be faithful in our particular individual and social situation; a God who promises to say and do surprising, new things in world history and in our individual histories (Isa. 42:9). We may be grateful that as such a living God, God *does* change.

There is also another sense in which God is indeed unchangeable. In the lives of all people, in every new time and place, in all the different things God may will for us and require of us, God is always stubbornly, consistently, dependably, faithfully the just and loving God we come to know in scripture. Whether God's specific answer to what we ask for in prayer is yes (as in the story of Abraham we mentioned) or no (as Paul reports in 2 Cor. 12:7–10), however God's specific will may be different for different people in different situations (or even the same situation), God always treats everyone with unfailing compassion and justice, and always requires of us lives that in one way or another reflect God's own justice and compassion in dealing with other people. We can never know in advance precisely what surprising, unpredictable things the living God will do and have for us to do; but we can count on the fact that whatever it is, it will always be a manifestation of the unchangeable, immutable, immovable justice and love of the living God whom we learn to know in the biblical story and in Jesus Christ—the Christ who is "the same yesterday and today and forever" (Heb. 13:8) just because he comes to every individual person and to the community of his followers with just the promises and demands of the liberating justice and love they need in their particular time, place, and situation.

We began this chapter by referring to the fact that faith in our time is difficult (was it ever easy?)—so difficult that many people can speak of the absence or even death of God. We suggested that part of the trouble may be that we have some false ideas about who God is and what God is like, ideas we need to get rid of if we are to know the true and living God. Then we spent the rest of the chapter trying to identify the God we come to know in the biblical story and above all in Jesus Christ, a God who is quite different from the great heavenly Tyrant, Grandparent, or Big Idea so many people in our time either wrongly believe in or rightly reject.

Now at the end of the chapter we return to the question with which we began. Suppose we have at least caught a glimpse of the true God. Can we modern people still believe in God—even *this* God? Or is the real problem not whether we *can* but whether we *want* to believe? The following questions are intended to help you answer for yourself.

FOR FURTHER REFLECTION AND STUDY

1. What does it mean to believe in a "personal" God? What does it *not* mean?
2. How would you try to speak of God to a child so that he or she would not picture a great big man up in the sky?
3. What are the dangers of thinking of God (1) only in terms of God's sovereign power over us or (2) only in terms of God's loving presence with and for us? How can we avoid these dangers in thinking and speaking about God?
4. What is the difference between saying "love is God" and saying "God is love"?
5. Could or should we love other people as God in Christ loves us?
6. Is it correct to say that God's justice is "biased" in favor of those who are politically and economically poor, weak, helpless, and oppressed? What about those who are poor, weak, helpless, and oppressed because of their own sinfulness?
7. What does God's just love and loving justice teach us about . . .
   a. How parents should deal with disobedient children?
   b. The Christian understanding of criminal justice?

c. What a compassionate and just social welfare system would look like?

d. How to deal with racial-ethnic conflicts and the conflict between women and men in church and society?

8. How can we recognize the presence of God in the midst of suffering, failure, and disappointment?
9. Why is it *good news* and not just theoretical information or even bad news to say that God is an all-powerful, ever-present, all-knowing, eternal, and unchangeable God?
10. Has your understanding of God changed as a result of reading this chapter? How?
11. Make a list of what you consider to be the inadequacies, mistakes, and unanswered questions in what this chapter has said about God. Save the list, and check the following chapters of this book to see if they offer help and clarification—or only make matters worse.

7

What Does God Want with Us?

The Doctrine of Predestination

"I've had the absolute conviction—it's much more real than anything one can see or touch—that God and his world exist. And everyone can enter in and find their rest. Except me. I'm infinitely far away for ever. I am alone and apart and infinitesimally small—and I can't come near."

. . . "Could there be a world, Ralph, in which God existed—but with some people in it who were never allowed to believe?"

"It would be a tragic world?" said Udal.

"Why shouldn't it be tragic," Roy cried. "Why shouldn't there be some who are rejected by God from the very beginning?"[1]

That is the problem of the doctrine of predestination, expressed in the words of a tormented man in C. P. Snow's novel *The Light and the Dark.* Is God for some people and against others? Has it been decided in advance that some are included and others excluded, some destined now and forever to life in the fullest sense and others now and forever to loneliness and death? Is it a tragic world we live in—for some people at least? In this chapter we will wrestle with this complex problem, which reaches to the heart of everything we believe about God, ourselves, and the world in which we live.

Before we begin, we need to define the problem more precisely. Contrary to a common misunderstanding, the doctrine of predestination does not say that every good or bad thing that happens to us and in the world around us is predetermined by God and that we should therefore accept everything that happens as the foreordained will of

God. It would be wrong to think of predestination, for instance, if the weather is good or bad on the day of the picnic, or if the traffic lights are for or against us on our way to work and we find or do not find a parking place when we get there. It would be wrong to think that it must have been "predestined" when someone finds or loses a job, becomes ill or recovers from illness, finds or does not find a partner in marriage. It would be wrong to think that the favorable or tragic events we read about in the paper or see on television are the working out of the predestined "plan of God" for the world. Christians do understand all the trivial or momentous events in the little history of every human being and in world history in light of God's loving and just rule over God's good creation. This aspect of Christian faith is interpreted by the doctrine of providence, which we will discuss later. (We will discover that providence too has nothing to do with a pious version of the fatalistic conviction that "what will be, will be.") However, the doctrine of predestination is not an attempt to explain how God is related to everything that happens in our own lives and in the world around us.

According to scripture (see Rom. 8:28–30 and Eph. 1:3–11), predestination has to do specifically with the question of salvation: Whom does God choose (or not choose) to love and care for in the bad as well as good things that happen to us? To whom does God choose (or not choose) to give the gift of faith that enables people to trust, count on, and live by God's love in sickness and health, in life and in death? Who is chosen (or not chosen) to be included among those to whom the "saving grace" of God is not only promised but actually given so that, whatever happens, they find wholeness of life now and forever in loving the God who loves them and in loving others as they have been loved? Who, in short, does God choose to save—or not save? That is the question the doctrine of predestination seeks to answer. In traditional theology it is called the doctrine of election: who does God "elect" to save or not save? That is the question that concerns us in this chapter.

This will be our procedure: We will investigate both the strengths and weaknesses of three ways in which Christians have answered the question of the tormented man in Snow's novel. Then we will see what conclusions we can draw for ourselves.

THREE CLASSICAL INTERPRETATIONS

There are three classical interpretations of predestination that have been offered.

Double Predestination

Some are included and some are excluded. This interpretation of predestination is often considered the one position you are supposed to believe if you are a good Presbyterian or Reformed Christian. Calvin himself taught it (see chapters 21–24 of book 3 of the *Institutes*), and it is strongly affirmed in the Westminster Confession of Faith and in the Canons of the Synod of Dort.[2] But other Reformed confessions such as Calvin's own Geneva Catechism, the Scots Confession, the Second Helvetic Confession, and the Heidelberg Catechism do not teach it. It is only one of several possible views in the Reformed tradition.

According to the Westminster Confession, "By the decree of God, for the manifestation of his glory, some men and angels are predestined to everlasting life, and others fore-ordained to everlasting death" (3.3). There is thus a "double" predestination, one negative and one positive, one to life and salvation and one to death and damnation. God is for some people (about 20 percent, Calvin once estimated) and against all the rest. According to God's eternal purpose, therefore, Christ died only for the elect. Only the elect are given the gift of faith, forgiveness for their sins, and the ability to live as children of God. The nonelect are rejected or "passed over." Christ did not die for them. God "withholds his mercy" from them. They are ordained to "dishonor and wrath for their sin" (Westminster Confession, 3.7). God has decreed to "leave them in the common misery into which they have willfully plunged themselves" (Canons of the Synod of Dort, Art. 15). It is not unjust of God to choose to be for some and against others because *all* have willfully disobeyed God's commandments and deserve God's wrath, judgment, and condemnation. If God damns the nonelect, they only get what they deserve. On the other hand, if God decides to love, help, and save the elect, it is not because they are more deserving than the nonelect but because God chooses to be gracious to them despite their sinfulness.

Several arguments can be made in favor of this interpretation of predestination:

1. It emphasizes the sovereign freedom and power of God. Like the future of the world, the future of every individual person depends finally not on what *we* are and what *we* do; it depends on who *God* is and what *God* does.

2. It emphasizes the good news of the gospel that salvation is by grace alone. We do not have to do anything to earn God's acceptance and love; they are freely given by God's sheer "generosity" and "kindness" (Calvin), without any consideration of our worthiness. Even faith that

accepts and lives by God's grace is a gift of God, not something we have to achieve for ourselves as a way of buying God's favor.

3. It tries to take seriously both God's righteousness, or justice (in condemning and judging human sinfulness), and God's merciful love (in saving sinners).

4. It seems a logical explanation of the fact that the vast majority of people do not know about, accept, and live by God's saving grace in Jesus Christ, while only a relatively few do.

5. It tries to take seriously some biblical passages that suggest a double predestination. So, for instance, according to Matt. 22:14, Jesus said, "Many are called, but few are chosen." According to John 17:9, Jesus said, "I am not asking on behalf of the world, but on behalf of those whom you gave me." And above all there is Paul's discussion in chapters 9–11 of the letter to the Romans. Paul is not thinking here about the election or rejection of individual persons but about the relation between the Jewish community and the Gentile Christian community. But he does say some things here that seem to support belief in an individual double predestination. God "loved" Jacob and "hated" Esau (Rom. 9:13). God "has mercy on whomever he chooses" and "hardens the heart of whomever he chooses" (Rom. 9:18). Does that not suggest that God graciously chooses some individuals and groups and rejects others?

On the other hand, serious questions are raised by the doctrine of double predestination (some of which you can anticipate after our discussion of the attributes of God in the last chapter):

1. It is true that the predestinating God is a "sovereign" God. But the doctrine of double predestination forgets what the Bible says about this God. Ephesians 1:3–11, another of the key passages in the New Testament dealing with the issue of predestination, tells us that the sovereign God is an unqualifiedly *gracious* God: "With all wisdom and insight he has made known to us the mystery of his will, according to his good pleasure that he set forth *in Christ*"; the God whose plan "for the fullness of time" is to "gather up all things *in him*" (emphasis added). Those who defend double predestination can talk about God's sovereignty without any reference to Christ. For them God's sovereignty is not necessarily gracious sovereignty exercised for the reconciliation of all people; it is demonstrated by God's ability either to be gracious or not to be gracious, to include or to exclude, save or damn. Is that the God we meet in Jesus Christ or a God who is the creation of our own speculation about what we think a sovereign God could or would do? Can a doctrine of predestination based on the sovereignty of a God who may or may not be

for us, be a genuinely *Christian* doctrine of predestination? (Look back to see what was said about the "omnipotence" of God in chapter 6.)

2. The doctrine of double predestination is based on an understanding of God's "eternal decrees," according to which "God from all eternity did by the most wise and holy counsel of his own will, freely and unchangeably ordain whatsoever comes to pass" (Westminster Confession, 3.1). World history and the history of every individual person then becomes the outworking of a predetermined, unchangeable "plan" of God established "from before the foundation of the earth." Does this not imply an absentee God who is simply the passive observer of a predetermined world process, a God who is not and cannot be active in our lives here and now? And does it not mean the end of all human freedom and responsibility to participate in what God is doing in our lives here and now?

According to scripture, God is a living, active God who is at work *in* the history of the world and the lives of individual people, demanding and making possible real human decisions, bringing *new* things to pass. God is indeed always "before" us, as the word "pre-destination" implies, but according to the Bible God goes before us as the cloud and pillar of fire that every new day and night went before Israel in the wilderness, leading the people to the destination God had planned for them (Ex. 13:21–22). Can a biblical-Christian doctrine of predestination, then, refer to a rigid, mechanical plan of God made "before time"? Is not double predestination based on an understanding of God's eternity and unchangeableness that is not a genuinely biblical one? (See the discussion of God's unchangeableness and eternity in chapter 6.)

3. The doctrine of double predestination properly wants to defend both the justice and the love of God. But is it right in teaching that with some people God is only just and with other people loving as well as just? Does not such a split in God's dealing with us not mean a split, or at least a lack of consistency within God? Does not scripture teach that God is always, consistently, with all people both loving and just? (See the discussion of God's justice and love in chapter 6.)

4. One argument for double predestination is that it is confirmed by experience: we can see that some people are in the church and some outside. Some people hear the Christian message and believe; others hear it and do not believe. Millions never even have a chance to hear and believe, simply because they were born in the wrong time or place. Some, like the man in Snow's novel, may desperately *want* to believe and

enter in and cannot. How can we explain that? The doctrine of double predestination jumps to the conclusion that those whom we observe to be "insiders" must be chosen and loved by God, whereas the "outsiders" must be rejected or passed over. But is that a legitimate conclusion? Is it God or we ourselves who choose and reject in this case? How do we know that those who seem to be "out" to us may not finally be "in" with God, and that some who seem to be "in" to us will not finally be "out" with God? Is it not arrogant presumption to conclude that God's choosing or rejecting corresponds to the differences we observe between people?

5. Although some biblical passages seem to support the view that God's saving grace is given only to a few but withheld from all the rest, there are also many biblical passages that say God's grace is for everyone, for the whole world. For instance: God is our Savior "who desires *everyone* to be saved and to come to the knowledge of the truth" (1 Tim. 2:4). The Lord is "patient with you, not wanting any to perish, but *all* to come to repentance" (2 Peter 3:9). "God did not send the Son into the world to condemn the world, but in order that the *world* might be saved through him" (John 3:17). Jesus is the "Lamb of God who takes away the sin of the *world*" (John 1:29). "As all die in Adam, so *all* will be made alive in Christ" (1 Cor. 15:22). "As one man's trespass led to condemnation for all, so one man's act of righteousness leads to justification and life for *all*" (Rom. 5:18). "For in him all the fullness of God was pleased to dwell, and through him God was pleased to reconcile to himself *all* things, whether on earth or in heaven" (Col. 1:19–20). "For God has imprisoned all in disobedience so that he may be merciful to *all*" (Rom. 11:32). (Emphasis has been added in all quotations.) Can a doctrine of predestination that forgets such passages as these be a really biblical and Christian doctrine?

We may summarize all these objections to the doctrine of double predestination by noting that it turns the good news of Jesus Christ into bad news at least for some people. The "mystery of God's will" of which Paul speaks with such unqualified joy and thanksgiving in Eph. 1:3–10 and Rom. 11:32–36 becomes a doctrine so gloomy and threatening that it must be treated with extreme caution (Westminster Confession, 3.8). Anyone who accepts this doctrine can speak of the good news of God's love and grace only with open or secret reservations: "God loves you—maybe. Christ died and lives for you—maybe. You may believe and have newness of life now and forever—*if* you are one of the elect."

In answer to the tortured man in Snow's novel we met at the beginning of this chapter, those who believe in double predestination would have to answer: "Yes, it is a tragic world—for some people anyway. Some are rejected from the very beginning. They cannot and never will be able to enter in and find rest. They are doomed to be infinitely far away forever. Perhaps you are one of them. But if so, you have no right to complain. God owes you nothing. You deserve the wrath of God for your sinfulness, and you will get only what you deserve."

Is that a Christian answer?

Universalism

One alternative to double predestination is the view that God loves and is gracious toward all people, chooses all, and rejects none. Everyone is included; no one is excluded. Even if some are alone and apart and cannot find rest in this life, they are destined ultimately to live in joy and peace with God, with fellow human beings, and with themselves. Salvation is universal.

Several good arguments can be made in favor of universalism:

1. Although it was condemned as heresy early in the history of the church and has never been accepted as an orthodox alternative, many biblical passages can be quoted in support of universalism. Look again at the passages we have quoted above that say God's grace is for "all" or for the "world."

2. Universalism emphasizes the sovereign power of God just as strongly as does double predestination. In fact, universalists can argue that they are even more certain of God's sovereignty than the advocates of double predestination. God's will for the salvation of all will eventually be stronger than the power of sin and unbelief in any individual person, stronger than the power of evil and injustice in the world. Christ's work for the reconciliation and salvation of the world cannot finally be ineffective and without results for anyone, anywhere. How could God be really sovereign if anyone will finally be lost to God, if Satan or the powers of rebellion against God could finally rob God of any part of the world God created, cares for, rules over, and gave the Son to restore and redeem?

3. Universalism emphasizes the biblical and Reformation insistence on "salvation by grace alone" just as strongly as does double predestination. It too emphasizes that it is only by God's grace, not by our own "free will" or "good works," that we are reconciled to God and other people. It

too understands salvation as the gift of God's freely given love, not as something we have to merit or earn for ourselves.

4. In contrast to double predestination, universalism understands predestination as glorious Good News we can joyfully and thankfully proclaim to everyone in the whole world, without any qualifying "but" or "if."

However, there are also some strong arguments against universalism:

1. If the doctrine of double predestination ignores or tends to explain away universalistic biblical texts, universalism tends to ignore or explain away those texts that speak of God's wrath and judgment. It tends to overlook those texts that warn that rebellion against God and indifference to fellow human beings have eternal consequences. Look at Matt. 25:31–46, for instance. We ought to note that Jesus' threat of "eternal punishment" here is not directed against people who have never heard of God and who are sinful, unbelieving outsiders. It is directed against those who piously claim to know and believe in God, but prove that their claim is a lie by not caring for the fellow human beings in need. That is typical of Jesus: gracious invitation and promise of new life to sinful outsiders; serious warning and threat of judgment to complacent insiders. But the warning about the separation of the "sheep" from the "goats" is there. Is not universalism unbiblically one-sided in assuming that everyone will automatically turn out to be a sheep and no one a goat?

2. If double predestination has trouble with God's unqualified *love*, universalism has trouble with God's *justice*. The one has justice without love (for some people at least); the other tends toward love without justice. In the first, God looks too much like an arbitrary tyrant; in the second, God looks too much like a permissive, sentimental grandparent. It is certainly not good news to say, "God is for you—maybe." Is it much better to say, "It doesn't matter what you are and do. God will be for you and bless you anyway"? Does that really help people trapped in their alienation from God, other people, and themselves? Does it not sound more like indifference than real love?

3. God wants a two-way relationship with us. God speaks to us and wants an answer from us. God loves us and wants to be loved in return. God commands and wants our thankful obedience. But universalism tends as much as double predestination to think one-sidedly of God's relationship with us and to do less than justice to the importance of our response. According to double predestination, some do not even have a

chance to say "yes" to God because God has said "no" to them. According to universalism, people cannot say "no" to God even if they want to. It is as if the father in the story of the prodigal son went out and forced his son to abandon his self-destructive life and go home again. Is benevolent manipulation for our own good any better than hostile manipulation? Does not good news become bad news when it says, "You *will* love God and your fellow human beings whether you want to or not"? What if there are some people (perhaps including some who call themselves Christians) who do not *want* to be reconciled to God if it means living in service of God rather than in service of their own personal self-interest or that of their particular race, class, or cultural heritage? What if some people would rather live in hell with people just like themselves than in heaven with the kind of people they fear, have contempt for, and want to have nothing to do with?

In answer to the agonizing question of Snow's character, the universalist answers: "Don't worry. You are not really alone and apart and outside. You only imagine that you live in a tragic world. God is in heaven and all is right with the world—or will be eventually. So cheer up. Sit back and relax. Everything is going to turn out fine for you, whether or not you believe and enter in; whether or not you would even want to if you knew what it would be like."

Is that what Christians have to say about predestination?

Pelagianism

If double predestination says that God chooses some and rejects others, and universalism says that God chooses all and rejects no one, this third view says that what happens to us depends on whether we choose or reject God. It is called Pelagianism because it was first formulated by a British monk named Pelagius, against whom Augustine first formulated the doctrine of double predestination in the fifth century. We will discuss two versions of it.[3]

Extreme, or "Pure," Pelagianism

This position argues that God has given us laws and commandments to tell us how we must live, and the freedom to obey or disobey them. If we choose to obey, God will be gracious to us and will help and save us; if we refuse to obey, we will get the rejection and punishment we deserve. In other words, we save (or damn) ourselves by the "good works" we do (or refuse to do).

Although Protestants often consider this to be a "Catholic" heresy, it is not unknown among Protestants themselves. It crops up every time a Presbyterian says "God helps those who help themselves" instead of "God helps those who cannot help themselves." It crops up more subtly in many ethical debates in Protestant churches today: God will love, help, and save you, your family, your church, and your society if you have the correct liberal or conservative position on abortion, homosexuality, capital punishment, the role of women in church and society, capitalism and socialism, social welfare or individual initiative. Self-salvation by good works (or at least right thinking!) is a common heresy of Catholics *and* Protestants.

It is important to emphasize that both Reformation Protestantism and Roman Catholicism reject this form of Pelagianism. Both know that it understands neither the depth of human sinfulness that makes us unable to earn God's love nor the depth of God's love that saves us despite our sinfulness. On the one hand, it does not see the ways we carefully select the laws and commandments of God we can and want to obey, and ignore those we cannot or do not want to obey. It does not see that even when we do obey some of God's laws, we often do so not because we love God and neighbor but because we love only ourselves—because we want to congratulate ourselves and be congratulated (and rewarded) by God and others for being such morally, spiritually, and ideologically superior and "correct" people. It does not see how our very goodness is sinful. On the other hand, extreme Pelagians do not really believe in the grace of God. God's grace is not given to good people who merit God's approval but to sinners who do not and cannot merit it. It is grace that does not reward people for the good they have done but enables them to do the good they cannot do. It is grace that promises salvation not as payment for credit earned but as a freely given gift.

Semi-Pelagianism

But there is a moderate form of Pelagianism that seeks to preserve a more biblical understanding of our sin and God's grace. It is this "semi-Pelagianism" that became the official doctrine of Roman Catholicism. Although Luther and Calvin and the churches of the Reformation rejected Pelagianism even in this moderate form, it has cropped up again and again in all branches of Protestantism and is still a popular (perhaps the most popular) position with many Protestants today (including many who consider themselves Presbyterian or Reformed Christians).

Simply put, this is the semi-Pelagian position: We are all unworthy, undeserving sinners. We not only leave undone many things we ought to have done; even the good we do is corrupted by sinful motives, desires, and goals. We are totally dependent on the saving grace of God in Jesus Christ for our salvation. But although it is true that we are not free and able to save ourselves by our good works, we are free and able to do one thing. We can acknowledge our *need* for God's grace and turn to God to *ask* for the deep, abiding faith, hope, and love we cannot achieve for ourselves. We can confess Christ as Lord and Savior and show our willingness to *receive* the salvation made available to us in him. We can *allow* the transforming power of God's Holy Spirit to come into our hearts. We can go to church in order to express our *desire* for the help and salvation we know comes only from God. We cannot save ourselves, but we can do that much if we really want to. And if we choose God and turn to God in this way, God will choose us, love, help, and save us. If some do not receive this saving grace, it is not because God has rejected them; it is because they have rejected God. Salvation is by God's grace alone, available to all who sincerely ask for it and want it.

It is easy to see why this semi-Pelagian position is so popular with both Catholics and Protestants. It seems to preserve what is right with both double predestination and universalism but to avoid the weaknesses of each.

1. Like double predestination and universalism (and in contrast to extreme Pelagianism), semi-Pelagianism seeks to preserve biblical hope in the saving power of God, not in our ability to save ourselves.

2. Like universalism (in opposition to double predestination), it emphasizes that the saving grace of God is available to all, not just to a select few.

3. Unlike both double predestination and universalism, it emphasizes very strongly what the Bible also emphasizes—the importance and necessity of our free decision to turn to God if we want to receive the help and salvation God offers us. Does not the New Testament teach that "everyone who calls on the name of the Lord shall be saved" (Acts 2:21)? Does it not say, "I am standing at the door, knocking; if you hear my voice and open the door, I will come in to you" (Rev. 3:20)? Do not such passages imply that although Christ achieved potential salvation for all, it becomes real only for those who freely decide to believe in him, depend on him, follow him? Does not scripture itself say that it is up to each of us to decide whether we want to accept and live by the saving grace of God, and that our salvation depends on what we decide?

Despite its appeal as an alternative to double predestination and universalism, the theology and confessions of Reformation churches (following Luther and Calvin themselves) have rejected semi-Pelagianism for the same reason they have rejected extreme Pelagianism. Their rejection can be summarized with four arguments:

1. Semi-Pelagianism overestimates our freedom to love, trust, and depend on God. Although it does not claim that we can save ourselves by being good and doing good, it does claim that we can demonstrate our willingness to *receive* God's grace and *prepare* ourselves for it by turning to God for help, accepting the salvation offered in Christ, and opening ourselves to the transforming power of the Holy Spirit. Are we really free to do even that much? There is no question that we are at least relatively free to decide and do many things. But are any of us really free to decide and do the things that matter most for our salvation? Can we simply *decide* to give up the alternate self-loathing and inordinate self-love that makes it impossible for us to love God (and other people) and let ourselves be loved in return? Can we simply *decide* not to be anxious any more about our own lives or those of our loved ones and the world around us, but to entrust our own and their future into God's care? Can we simply *decide* to "say no" to all the animosities and prejudices that sour our own lives and spoil our relationships with other people in order to "say yes" to the Christ who promises to deliver us from such self-destructive and other-hurting attitudes? Can we simply *decide* to let the transforming Spirit of God rule our lives instead of the spirit of the liberal or conservative social and political ideologies we hold most dear? Even if we do decide, can we actually *do* what we decide? We might like to think that we are free to decide to let God, Christ, or the Holy Spirit into our lives, but are we really free to do so? Is not the most agonizing problem of our lives how we who are *not* free can *become* truly free—free for God, free for other people, free to be what in our best moments we want to be? Is not the free will that semi-Pelagians believe to be the answer to the problem of predestination the very heart of the problem itself? Instead of being the means of making possible the work of God's saving grace in our lives, does not the ability to "say yes" to God, Christ, or the Holy Spirit itself depend on the work of God's grace?

2. Like extreme Pelagians, semi-Pelagians also believe in our self-salvation. Despite its talk about salvation by grace alone, for semi-Pelagians everything depends first of all and decisively not on what *God* does but on what *we* do. In our individual lives and in the world around

us, God cannot be a loving and powerful God unless and until we *acknowledge* and *ask for* God's love and power to help and save. Christ cannot be Savior and Lord unless and until we "let" him be our Savior and "make" him the Lord of our lives and the world around us. The Holy Spirit cannot change and renew unless and until we *want* change and renewal and *allow* it to happen. Unless and until we make the first move and take the first step, God can and will do nothing. The actual happening and experience of salvation is initiated and made possible not by God's turning to us but by our turning to God, not by Christ's decision for us but by our decision for him, not by the transforming work of the Spirit but by our ability to unleash the Spirit. But if God can help and save only to the extent that we permit it to happen, is not our salvation ultimately self-salvation?

3. Just because semi-Pelagianism makes salvation depend first of all and decisively on our openness to it, asking for it, and response to it, it makes our salvation uncertain. Semi-Pelagians do not have to ask, as do extreme Pelagians, "Am I *good* enough to earn my salvation?" But they do have to ask some equally terrifying questions: "Is my *faith* in God's saving grace strong enough and sure enough? Have I really and truly, without reservation, completely turned my life over to God, accepted Christ as my Lord and Savior, opened myself to God's Spirit? Have I prayed long and earnestly enough, read my Bible often and attentively enough, gone to church often enough, progressed in my spiritual development far enough to prove that I really and truly, without reservation, completely want the saving grace of God in my life and in the world? If I am a semi-Pelagian, everything depends on how I can answer such questions, because confidence in the reality and power of God's grace depends on the seriousness and completeness of my desire for it and openness to it. But who of us is not made anxiously *uncertain* about the grace of God if its reality and power depends on what we discover when we examine the depth and sincerity of our seeking God, the measure of our acceptance of Christ, the degree to which we are open to the Spirit, the extent of our spiritual development? Is not assurance of God's grace and our own and the world's salvation made just as questionable and uncertain by semi-Pelagian emphasis on our self-surrender to God as by the extreme Pelagian emphasis on our good works?

4. Behind every other fault of semi-Pelagianism is the fact that it denies both the love and the sovereign power of God. What kind of heavenly Parent (or earthly parent for that matter) is it who says, "I will

love you, come to you, be on your side and help you—*if* you first love me, come to me, ask for my help, and prove that you really want it"? What kind of Lord is it who says, "I can and will overcome all the powers of sin, evil, injustice, suffering, and death in your life and in the world around you—*if* you give me your vote of confidence and recruit enough votes of confidence from others to keep me in office"? What kind of love and power is it that is dependent on our acceptance, permission, and support before it can be effective and real?

In answer to the desperate man in Snow's novel, the Pelagian answers, "You just have to try harder. You can believe if you really want to. If you feel alone and apart, all you have to do is make up your mind to turn to God, accept Christ as your Lord and Savior, open your heart to God's Spirit. If you will just do that, God will love you, help you, save you. But you have to make the first move."

Is that the Christian answer?

THREE BASIC RULES FOR THINKING ABOUT PREDESTINATION

We have seen that each of the three main interpretations of predestination has legitimate insights into what scripture tells us about God's attitude toward us and plan for our lives. No one of them can be called *the* Christian doctrine of predestination. Nor can all three be combined into a neat system that can be called the one true Christian understanding. But although we cannot solve all the problems connected with the mystery that predestination will always be for us, there are at least some things we can say with confidence. First we will list three basic rules for approaching the doctrine of predestination as Christians.

Rule 1. We must take into account the total biblical witness, even when some passages seem to contradict others and do not fit easily into a logically consistent doctrinal system. We will never understand predestination as long as we appeal only to those passages we like and ignore or try to explain away those we do not like. This means that we must listen attentively and respectfully to those texts that can be quoted in favor of double predestination *and* universalism *and* Pelagianism.

Rule 2. Although we must not forget God's wrath and judgment and the possibility of eternal punishment, we must remember that the doctrine of predestination fundamentally proclaims good news we can gladly hear. The Bible never speaks of a plan of God before the foundation of the world to save some people and to damn all the rest. It speaks of God's plan to "gather up all things" in Jesus Christ (Eph. 1:10). In the Bible, predestination does not point to joy *and* terror, salvation *and* damnation, a Yes of God to us *and* a No. "For the Son of God, Jesus Christ . . . was not 'Yes and No'; but in him it was always 'Yes' " (2 Cor. 1:19). In Romans 9—11, perhaps the main biblical foundation for the doctrine of predestination, there seem to be many contradictions as Paul wrestles with this problem. But his final word is not yes and no but only yes: "For God has imprisoned all in disobedience so that he may be merciful to all" (Rom. 11:32). In scripture, predestination does not include what Calvin called a "horrible decree." It is the summary of the good news of Jesus Christ—for *everybody.*[4]

Rule 3. If we are to think as *Christians* about the doctrine of predestination, we must think of God's plan not only for us but for non-Christians as well in light of the biblical witness to God's will for the world revealed and fulfilled in Jesus Christ. We must think *only* in this light, not first of all or even secondarily in light of our own opinions about what God must or should or could and will do for us and for others.

These three rules will guide us as we make some concluding observations about what a genuinely Christian doctrine of predestination looks like. You will have to judge for yourself whether they consistently apply the rules.

THE FREEDOM GOD WILLS FOR ALL HUMAN BEINGS

As we have seen repeatedly, one of the persistent problems we encounter in trying to understand predestination is that it seems to force us to choose between two equally unacceptable alternatives. On the one hand, if we believe in the plan and work of a sovereign God in the history of the world and in our own lives, we seem to be forced to deny the significance of human decisions and actions. What meaning can human freedom have if God determines everything that happens? On the other hand, if we insist on the freedom of human beings to choose and determine their own destiny, we are forced to deny the sovereignty of God. What significance can a plan and purpose of God have if what God can do depends on what we will do? The sovereignty of God or human freedom—that seems to be the choice we have to make.

So long as we think theoretically and abstractly about this problem, there is no solution to it. But what if we think about it in light of what concrete human experience tells us about the kind of people we are and what scripture tells us about the kind of God the predestinating God is?

Although we may not like to admit it, honest analysis of our own experience tells us that in the deepest sense, none of us is really free. What we will and how we live is determined to a large extent by where and when we were born. We think and act with the limited point of view and biases of our particular race, cultural environment, and national heritage; with the fears and prejudices of rural, suburban, or city people; with the narrow self-interest of people who are poor, middle-class, or rich; with the advantages or disadvantages of a healthy or crippling family background. Moreover, what we want and strive for is motivated to a large extent by anxiety, pride, envy, greed, and lust. (Think of the various motives exploited by advertising and television commercials to manipulate us into buying cars and cosmetics.) Even when we are not always aware of it, we are driven and controlled by all kinds of social and psychological forces that determine our attitudes, decisions, and actions. And many of them alienate us both from God (who loves other kinds of people as much as our kind) and from other people (especially those who are different from us)—so that our enslavement to all these external and internal "powers" is what scripture calls our enslavement to *sin*. The brutal fact is that we are not nearly as free as we like to think. Attractive as it is, the Pelagian position is simply not realistic. We desperately need to *become* free.

That is just what predestination is all about. It is about the sovereign will of the God "who desires everyone to be saved and to come to the knowledge of the truth" (1 Tim. 2:4). The truth that God desires all to know is the truth about Jesus Christ, truth that makes us free (John 8:31, 36). The sovereign plan of God is not an alternative or threat to human freedom; it is the source of human freedom. Once we see predestination in the light of God's self-revelation in Jesus Christ and a realistic evaluation of the human predicament, it becomes sheer good news. For God's sovereignty is not just another power that seeks to dominate and control us at the expense of our own free human willing and doing. It is the sovereignty of God's love, God's plan to free us *from* slavery to all the internal and external, psychological and social powers that enslave and dehumanize us in order that we might be genuinely free people—people who discover and fulfill their own true humanity as they freely love God and their fellow human beings (all of them).

Predestination *or* human freedom? No. Predestination and *therefore* human freedom.

THE MEANING OF PREDESTINATION FOR NON-CHRISTIANS

We have seen that when Christians think about predestination, they think about God's plan to "unite *all* things" in Jesus Christ, to "have mercy on *all.*" For God "desires *all* to be saved and come to the knowledge of the truth" that sets people free. What does this mean when we think about the consequences of the Christian doctrine of predestination for non-Christians?

1. *God's love.* If we look at non-Christians in the light of God's plan for all in Christ, we are permitted and we are required to believe that God is for them too, desires their salvation too, works in their lives and in the world around them to enable them too to be genuinely free human beings. It may be true that they do not yet believe, or no longer believe, or only partially believe. Perhaps they will never believe. Such people do not live as those whom God chooses loves, helps, and saves. But that does not mean that we may decide that God is against them. It is not their unbelief and disobedience but the will and work of God in Jesus Christ that tells us what God's attitude toward them is and will be. We know something about them that they do not know about themselves: God wills their salvation too. Christ lived, died, rose again, and is still at work to give them too a future and a hope. How can we Christians take non-Christians' unbelief more seriously than we take what God has told us God plans and wills for them?

2. *God's judgment.* It is true that there are people (not all of them non-Christians!) who set themselves in opposition to God's promises and commandments. As long as this opposition continues, God's love can only be expressed as judgment and wrath against them, because (for their own good) God cannot and will not let them get by with the ways they destroy their own lives when they refuse to live by God's promises and requirements. This means that although we cannot believe that some are rejected by God from the very beginning (as double predestination teaches), neither can we say that God must eventually save all people (as universalism teaches). Some may not want God's love and help and the true freedom God offers. But even when we take this into account, we are neither allowed nor required to judge whether any particular person or whole groups of people will be finally saved or damned. God alone is Judge. God has not turned the decision about anyone's final destiny over to us, but is quite competent to decide without our help, opinions, or advice.

Meanwhile, we may be sure that in dealing with non-Christians as well as with Christians, God's decision will be not only just but also loving. Instead of following Calvin's example of deciding that only a few will finally be saved, we would do better to follow the example of Chapter 10 of the Second Helvetic Confession: "And although God knows who are his, and here and there mention is made of a small number of elect, yet we must hope well of all, and not rashly judge any man to be a reprobate." Or to put it in the words of the Declaration of Faith (10.5):

> We live in tension between God's warning and promises. Knowing the righteous judgment of God in Christ, we urge all people to be reconciled to God, not exempting ourselves from the warnings. Constrained by God's love in Christ, we have good hope for all people, not exempting the most unlikely from the promises. Judgment belongs to God and not to us. We are sure that God's future for every person will be both merciful and just.

3. *Christian responsibility for non-Christians.* Finally, although we are not permitted to judge for ourselves who is "in" or "out" with God, there is one clear responsibility we do have as we look at "outsiders." It is to tell them the Good News of the God who desires that they too be saved from all the internal and external forces that cut them off from God, their fellow human beings, and their own true humanity.

Why should we tell them? Not so that God may come to love them *if* they believe and obey, but so that they may hear and believe that God *does* love them. Not only so that they may go to heaven when they die, but so that they may receive the gift of freedom now. How do we tell them? Not by words only, but by demonstrating as individuals and as a Christian community the freedom for God and for fellow human beings that is the gift of God's grace.

If there are some who never "enter in," who will be responsible? Will God ask them accusingly, "Why did you not believe and obey and accept the gift of a free life?" Or will God turn to *us* and say, "Why did they not believe? Why did you not tell them? Why did you belie with your lives the truth you spoke with your lips? You who talk about the love of God for guilty, lost, helpless people, why were *you* so unloving toward them? You who talk about God's justice, why were *you* so indifferent to injustice in the world around you? You who talk about the gift of freedom for God and others, why were *you* so enslaved by anxious or greedy self-interest?" Instead of worrying theoretically about what God thinks of unbelievers or those who follow other religious traditions, could it be that we Christians ought to worry more about what God thinks of *us* when God sees people who are still outsiders because of what *we* have said and done, or not said and done?

THE MEANING OF PREDESTINATION FOR CHRISTIANS

Christians interpret the meaning of predestination also for their own lives in light of God's grace in Jesus Christ. What does that mean?

1. *If we see God's grace in Christ as the basis for our "election" to salvation, we will not dream of looking for it in ourselves and in our superiority to other people.* If we are insiders, it is not because we are better, wiser, more deserving, or even more believing than non-Christians. What failure or refusal to love and trust God and care about other people is to be found among "them" that is not still found (perhaps in more subtle and therefore more dangerous ways) among us Christians and in our church? If we do not recognize that in our own way we are just as sinful as they, do not we cut ourselves off from the love, forgiveness, and help of God that is our only hope for our own salvation? If we know that salvation is by the sheer grace of God for undeserving sinners who cannot help themselves, we will look at non-Christian outsiders without the slightest trace of smug self-congratulation, exclusive superiority, or condescending pity; we can look at them only with a feeling of compassionate solidarity. For when we look at them we see what we are too, and we know that the same saving grace of God promised to *us* sinners is promised to "those sinners" too.

2. *As the grace of God in Jesus Christ is the REASON for our election, it is also the ASSURANCE of our election.* It is important to make this point because especially Christians who believe in predestination are often anxious about whether they are included in the circle of those whom God loves, helps, and saves. And it is important because anxious, doubting Christians have often been made less rather than more certain of their election by examining themselves rather than by looking at God's grace in Christ to find the assurance that God is for and not against them.

Some people look for assurance in the external condition of their lives. They interpret sickness, trouble, and tragedy as signs that God is against them; comfort, prosperity, and success as signs that God is for them. But the Bible tells us that it is often the "wicked" who prosper, and it is often those especially beloved by God who suffer most. Our happy or unhappy experiences in themselves tell us nothing about what God thinks of us and has in mind for us. To look there for assurance is to look where real assurance is impossible. Christians are not people who are sure God is on their side if and when they *escape* "hardship, or distress, or persecution, or famine, or nakedness, or peril, or sword." They are people who know that God is with and for them in the midst of the worst that can happen, for nothing "will be able to separate us from the love of God in Christ Jesus our Lord" (Rom. 8:35, 39).

Some Reformed theologians have suggested that we may find assurance of our election in the faith and obedient life that are the result of God's grace at work in our lives. The "fruit" of God's saving grace is assuring evidence that the grace itself is present. But who of us has faith that is strong enough and lives that are pure enough to give us the assurance that we are among God's elect? Who of us can find convincing evidence of our election in the extent of our freedom from all the external and internal pressures and drives that keep us from being free for God and other people? Will not self-examination always lead us to doubt rather than to be certain that God is for us? Certainty of our election comes from hearing again and again the story of what God has done for us in Jesus Christ, not from what we can guess about God's attitude toward us by analyzing the extent of our Christian commitment and faithfulness.

On the other hand, it is true that predestination or election brings the gift of faith and freedom for a new life. Why should we not find courage and take hope when we see occasional signs that our faith is a little stronger and our lives a little freer for God and other people than once was the case? Perhaps we can sum it up this way: When faith wavers, our lives are a mess and we feel cut off from God, other people, and ourselves—then we may find assurance in Christ that despite everything God has not abandoned us. But when (perhaps only now and then) faith is strong, our lives are in order and we can see in ourselves some progress toward freedom to love and let ourselves be loved—then we may be thankful for these signs that our confidence in God's good will toward us has not been misplaced.

3. *To be among those who are chosen to receive the saving grace of God and all its benefits is to belong to the community of God's people in the world.* In order to understand the importance of this statement, we need to look at the difference between the traditional Calvinistic and the biblical understandings of predestination.

Traditional theology has usually thought that predestination has to do with isolated individuals and their personal relationship with God:

Predestination deals with the question whether God chooses, loves, helps, and saves *me,* and whether *I* receive all the blessings that come with being one of the elect. This understanding of the doctrine, with its preoccupation with "me" and what *I* get out of being a Christian, sounds strangely like what Karl Barth called "pious egocentricism." It differs from non-Christian self-centeredness only in that it seeks one's own security and happiness in God rather than in the various ways in which others seek to preserve and defend their own self-interest.

In the Bible, on the other hand, predestination has to do with the election of a *community* to be God's people. In the Old Testament it is not first of all this or that individual but the whole people of Israel whom God chooses and promises to bless; individuals are included in the promises of God as they are included in God's promises to the whole community. Jesus chooses men and women to belong to him and receive the salvation and new life he brings as they join the *company* of his disciples. The issue in Paul's great discussion of predestination in chapters 9—11 of Romans is not which individuals God chooses or rejects; it is the question of the relation between the Jewish and Gentile Christian *communities* (both of which, he concludes, are God's chosen people). When Paul speaks in Eph. 1:15–23 and in Rom. 8:28–39 about God's predestinating grace in Jesus Christ, he addresses what he has to say to Christian *churches.* According to scripture, individuals are indeed loved and chosen by God, but only as they participate in the whole community of God's people.

It is clear that if we are to understand predestination biblically, and if we are to receive the promises of God's saving grace connected with it, we have to give up the "pious egocentrism" encouraged by traditional theology. To receive the saving grace of God is to be set free *from* a private self-seeking obsession with my own present and future security and happiness. We are to expect God's saving grace where it is to be found—in a community of people who care not just about themselves but about each other; who experience the love, forgiveness, help, and salvation that is given and received in their life together.

This understanding of predestination throws more light on the problem of the assurance of our election. We cannot say that membership in the church is automatic proof that we are included among God's chosen people. But participation in the Christian community is a *sign* of our election. God is at work also outside the church for the good of all people, everywhere. Jesus Christ is loving and just Lord over and for the world as well as over and for us Christians and our church. But the church is the community of people who *acknowledge, seek, expect*, and gratefully *experience* the saving grace of God in Christ. It is the place where people are reminded over and over again of the gracious promises of God through proclamation of the good news of the life, death, and resurrection of Christ for needy, sinful human beings. It is the place where certainty that we are beloved children of God is offered and received in baptism and where the new life of Christian freedom for God and neighbor is nourished and strengthened at the Lord's Table. We will never be assured of our election as long as we try to figure out for ourselves whether we are in or out with God, or try to go it alone as Christians. But as we share in the life and worship of the Christian community, we may be assured that those promises of God are not just for someone else or for everyone in general but for us too.

4. *If we understand the meaning of predestination in light of the biblical witness to God's grace in Christ, we will understand it as both a gift and a task.* In making this point, we end our discussion by emphasizing one of the most important and most neglected emphases of the biblical understanding of predestination.

For centuries Christians have talked mostly about what a *privileged* people God's chosen people are, about the great "benefits" that come when God chooses to be for and not against us, about all the good things God will give us and do for us. All too often we have thought (and even said out loud) that we who have received the gifts of God's saving grace can congratulate ourselves that we are "in" with God, whereas others are "out"; included, whereas they are excluded; loved and helped by God, whereas they are not; saved, whereas they are damned.

That is not what predestination means in the Bible. According to scripture, it is true that God loves, protects, blesses, and saves those who are chosen to be God's people. But that is not the main thing the Bible says about them. It says that they are chosen not to be God's pets or privileged elite but to be God's *servants,* chosen not to receive and enjoy for themselves all the benefits of God's saving grace others do not have but to be instruments of God's grace so that others may receive and enjoy these benefits also.

At the very beginning of the biblical story God chooses Abraham, the father of all God's chosen people, not just so that he and his descendants may be blessed but so that through them "all the nations of the earth" may be blessed (Gen. 22:15–18).

In the Servant Songs of Isaiah (interpreted by Christians as promises of the coming of Christ), God addresses "my chosen, in whom my soul delights" as my *servant* who will never tire "until he has established justice in the earth" (Isa. 42:1–4). "I will give you as a light to the nations," God says, so "that my salvation may reach to the end of the earth" (Isa. 49:6). Throughout these songs God's chosen one or chosen people are chosen not for the sake of their own happiness and success but to be the instrument of God's love and justice for all who are poor and homeless, all who are ignored and excluded by the rich and powerful, all who are victims of oppressive political, social, and economic systems—the "outsiders" of the world.

Then there is Jesus himself, *the* chosen one of God (Luke 9:35). For him above all to be chosen by God did not mean personal security and success. It meant being God's "suffering servant" who was despised, rejected, and finally executed as a common criminal because he was the friend and advocate of *two* kinds of outsiders: poor and oppressed people excluded by an unjust social and political establishment, and godless sinners excluded by an unloving moral and religious establishment.

That is what it means for us to be the chosen people of God. We too are chosen not *instead of* but *for the sake of* the world's outsiders. We are chosen not to *escape from* a godless and godforsaken world with all its sinfulness and suffering, but to be *sent into it* and *live for it.* We are chosen not so that we can congratulate ourselves because we live in the light while everyone else gropes in the darkness, but to be a light that shines in their darkness. We are chosen so that those who are excluded from the benefits of God's loving justice and just love may be included. For we too are chosen not to be served but to serve, to take up *our* crosses as we follow the Chosen One of God who was crucified because he cared for all the wrong people.

The good news of predestination, in other words, carries with it a warning: Be careful if you want to be one of God's elect insiders. It will make your life harder, not easier. It will not give you everything you want; it will demand everything you have. It will not put you on the side of the powerful and righteous of the world but on the side of the powerless and undeserving sinners. The privilege it brings is not that of enjoying material and spiritual blessings denied others; it is the privilege of living in self-giving love for them.

On the other hand, strangely enough, it is just those who are willing to take up the costly task that goes along with the wonderful gift of being chosen to be God's elect who really receive the gift itself. "For those who want to save their life will lose it, and those who lose their life for my sake will find it" (Matt. 16:25).

FOR FURTHER REFLECTION AND STUDY

1. Read chapters 9—11 of Romans straight through. Then answer the following questions as you study this passage more carefully:
   a. Does Paul teach that the Jews are rejected by God? What is God's plan for the Jews?
   b. What is Paul's own attitude toward unbelieving Jews?
   c. What warning is given to Gentiles and what promise to Jews in Rom. 11:13–24?
   d. Do you think Paul's conclusion in Rom. 11:30–36 is consistent with the rest of his discussion?
2. Read Eph. 1:3–14 and Rom. 8:28–37. Do these passages teach universalism? Double predestination? Pelagianism?
3. Do you believe that all people have free will? Do Christians have it?
4. Why should the church and individual Christians be involved in evangelism and missions?
5. Do Christians believe that God helps those who help themselves?
6. Does God love only those who love God first?
7. How would you answer someone who asks you whether those who never heard of Christ are going to hell?
8. Are you certain that you are one of the elect? Explain your answer.
9. Dietrich Bonhoeffer, a young German theologian who was killed by the Nazis, once wrote, "When Christ calls [that is, chooses] a man, he bids him come and die."[5] What did he mean? Do you agree?
10. How would *you* answer a man who said to you what the man in Snow's novel said?

PART 3

GOD THE CREATOR AND CREATION

Christians believe in a Trinitarian God, one God who is Creator, Reconciler, and Renewer of the world and all that is in it. The Apostles' Creed, most Reformed confessions, and many Christian theologians organize their exposition of what Christians believe according to the threefold work of God. Following this traditional pattern, we come now to the first article of the creed: "I believe in God, the Father Almighty, Creator of heaven and earth."

At first glance it seems that the doctrine of creation is the easiest part of the Christian faith to understand and accept. Even people who have trouble with revelation, the Trinity, the miraculous birth and resurrection of Christ, and the "spooky" Holy Spirit find it easy to speak of God as all-powerful Creator of the world. But to say "I believe in God, the Father Almighty, Creator of heaven and earth" is just as much a confession of faith as to say "I believe in Jesus Christ, his only Son, our Lord" or "I believe in the Holy Spirit." In fact, we cannot understand and believe what Christians mean when they confess God as Creator unless we understand and believe what they confess about Christ and the Spirit. What we believe about the Creator and creation is not the result of our observations of the world around us and our speculation about where we came from. It is the result of what we know about the will and work of God in Jesus Christ and in the Spirit, who is the Spirit of the risen Christ. In other words, when we talk about God the Creator and creation, we are not talking about something that comes *before* Christian theology but about something that is *part* of Christian theology. We will see as we go along what a big difference it makes to remember this.

In this part of our study, we will deal with the following questions:

Chapter 8 (The Doctrine of Creation): What are we doing here? What does it mean to understand our lives in the world of nature and history from the perspective of our faith in God the Creator?

Chapter 9 (The Doctrine of Providence and the Problem of Evil): Why doesn't God do something about it? If it is God's world, why is there so much suffering and injustice in it?

Chapter 10 (The Doctrine of Human Beings): Who are we? What does it mean to live as creatures made in the image of God?

Chapter 11 (The Doctrine of Sin): Why don't you just be yourself? How can we understand the contradiction in ourselves between what God created us to be and the way we actually live?

8

What Are We Doing Here?

The Doctrine of Creation

The world was created about four thousand years ago. In six days God made the world with all the kinds and species of things that were ever to exist in it. God made the earth like a flat disk with all the mountains and valleys we see, and the sky like an inverted bowl over it. Below the earth and above the sky were oceans of water. God put the sun and moon and stars in the bowl. Then, somewhere in what we call the Near East, God made all the plants and animals and finally human beings. Something like that is the picture of creation and of the created world we are given in the Bible.

About four billion years ago our planetary system developed out of a disk-shaped mass of gas surrounding the sun. The earth is only one of millions of stars in a universe in which distance is measured in light years (a light year is approximately six trillion miles, and most of the stars are more than one hundred light years away from the earth). Most of the forms of life that exist on the infinitesimal speck that is our earth did not formerly exist at all, and many of those that used to exist no longer exist. The human race is at least one hundred thousand years old, though it is uncertain just how this form of life originated and developed. Although there are many theories and unanswered questions about details, something like this is the general view of the world and its origin that has emerged from the actual measurements and research of modern science.

When the contrast between the biblical and scientific understandings of the world is put this way, it is no wonder that Christians have often seen science as a threat to biblical faith, and scientifically educated people have often thought the biblical doctrine an incredibly naive relic of primitive prescientific mythology. One must choose either to "believe the Bible" or to be a modern thinker.

To compare the two views in this way, however, is like comparing apples and oranges and arguing that apples are inferior because they do not yield orange juice, or that oranges are worthless because they cannot be made into cider. The Christian doctrine of creation and the scientific description of the origin of the world answer different kinds of questions. They are not alternative truths, but different kinds of truth. Rather than being enemies, science has helped (sometimes forced) Christians to discover the real meaning of the biblical doctrine of creation; on the other hand, Christian emphasis on the world as God's good creation has made possible and encouraged the development of modern science's investigation of it.[1]

Natural sciences such as astronomy, biology, and geology ask how the world and its present forms of life came to be as they are. They ask about the observable and measurable character, structure, processes, and facts of the given world and its development in history. Scientists may speculate about but they cannot explain where it all came from and what its meaning and purpose is. To do that is the task of theologians, not scientists.

Now, included in the biblical story of creation and view of the world there is also a kind of primitive scientific explanation. It is not unique to the biblical writers. They borrowed more than one ancient myth in order to bear witness to God the Creator, and they shared many of the presuppositions of the ancient Near East in general about the structure of the world. But the purpose of the biblical writers was not to instruct their readers in astronomy or biology. The primitive science included in their message was not the message itself but only the means they used to get their message across. What they had to say was something neither ancient nor modern science can tell us. They bore witness to the God who is the ultimate source, ruler, and hope of everything that is. They spoke about the meaning and goal of human life in the world. They were not so much concerned with the question of *how* we got here as with the question of *why* we are here.

We can be grateful to modern science for forcing us to distinguish between the vehicle of the biblical doctrine of creation and its primary message, because now we can concentrate on what is really important and unique about biblical faith. The Bible is not a science textbook, and we will miss what it has to tell us if we treat it as such. We can confidently leave all our factual questions to be answered by scientific investigation. Scientists, not preachers or theologians, are the experts in answering questions about how old the universe is, what physical factors produced it, how big it is, what is "up there" in the sky, and how plant, animal, and human life on our planet has developed biologically. Christians can respect and be grateful for everything science can tell them about the mystery and greatness of God's creation.

What then is the unique content of the Christian doctrine of creation? Three truths that we can learn nowhere else will furnish the outline for our study in the rest of this chapter: (1) The God of Israel and Jesus Christ is the ultimate source and ruler of the world. (2) Therefore the world and our creaturely life in it are good. (3) We need fear nothing in the world, nor can we give ultimate loyalty to anything in the world. The truth of none of these statements is obvious. Quite the opposite, they are confessions of faith despite much evidence to the contrary. "I *believe* in God, the Father Almighty, Creator of heaven and earth."

GOD THE CREATOR

The Christian doctrine of creation does not begin with an analysis of creation itself and try to deduce from it what the Creator is like. It begins with what scripture tells us about who the Creator is and tries to understand the created world in light of that. The doctrine tells us four things about the Creator God we come to know in the Bible.

God is the Creator of the whole world. The creation story in the first chapter of Genesis says this in explicit detail: God is the Creator of day and night (and therefore of time), the earth and seas, plants and trees, sun and moon, birds and fish and animals of all kinds—and finally of human beings. (If the writers of this ancient story had known what we know about the vast expanse of the universe, they would have said, with Chapter 2.1 of the Declaration of Faith, that God is the Creator not only of our little planet but of "all the worlds that are." But following them, we will restrict our discussion to "planet earth.")

Christian tradition has always affirmed that God is the Creator—and therefore also the Ruler, Preserver, Savior, and Renewer—of all things. But it has concentrated almost exclusively on the significance of the "last day" of creation, the creation of human beings in the image of God. This focus on God's human creation is understandable, for the whole biblical story is primarily (not only!) about God and God's human creation.

Especially in our time it has become clear that such an anthropocentric (human-centered) understanding of creation is very dangerous. It has prepared the way for the fatal assumption that our natural environment is there to be exploited, abused, and even destroyed for the sake of the economic development, military and political superiority, and consumer-oriented comfort and pleasure of people who live in modern technological-industrial societies. Some have even suggested that biblical faith has actually contributed to the rape of the natural world for the sake of human power, wealth, and comfort. Does not scripture say that God commanded us to "be fruitful and multiply, and fill the earth and subdue it; and have dominion over the fish of the sea and over the birds of the air and over every living thing that moves upon the earth" (Gen. 1:28)? Does that not invite in our time a drain on the earth's limited resources through human overpopulation? Does it not give permission for human beings to do whatever they please with the rest of creation? Does it not suggest a "hierarchical" view of the world in which first God and then human beings created in the image of God have unlimited power to dominate all "subhuman" life?

It is an exaggeration to blame the Bible for the abuse of the natural world in our time. Those guilty of it have hardly been guided or restrained by the authority of scripture! Yet it may well be that a human-centered interpretation of the biblical creation story has at least indirectly contributed to the ecological crisis of our time: oil spills that pollute the oceans, killing marine and coastal wildlife; dumping of industrial waste that makes the land barren, poisons underground water, and leaves rivers and streams lifeless; clear-cutting of ancient forests that destroys whole species of birds and animal life and upsets the ecological balance of the whole planet; pollution of the air that produces acid rain and creates a greenhouse effect that turns fertile countryside into deserts; massive pollution of land, sea, and air that threatens to destroy all life on our planet, human life included.

Many contemporary Christians who have seen the ecological crisis that has been the result of a human-centered understanding of creation have joined with people of other (or no) religious convictions in our time to solve the problem with an *earth*-centered understanding. Together with other "lovers of the earth," Christians have set out to "save our planet" by emphasizing the coexistence and interdependence of human beings and their natural environment. They have supported private and governmental programs to clean up the environment, end our depletion of its resources before it is too late, and restore health to the earth that is the "mother of us all" so that our children may inherit a habitable world.

We may certainly welcome such cooperative efforts. How can Christians who know about God's good creation do anything less? But so long as such an earth-centered solution is our only response to the ecological crisis, we could leave the impression that concern for the natural environment is only a "liberal" ideology for a few impractical nature romantics who "go in for that sort of thing"—and who, for all their criticism of a human-centered understanding of the world, still think that the future of the world depends on what we human beings do. That possibility is excluded, and Christians can make a unique contribution to the environmental movement, when we seek neither a human- nor an earth- but a *God*-centered understanding of the world—a biblical doctrine of creation based on the promises and requirements of the God who is the Creator, Preserver, Savior, and Renewer of all that is. Such a new (ancient biblical) doctrine of creation will have two emphases:

First, *"The earth is the Lord's and all that is in it, the world, and those who live in it"* (Ps. 24:1). In our time these words come first of all as a warning: The land and water, fish, birds, and animals of our planet, with the air above it, do not belong to us to use and misuse as we please. They belong to God. They are God's "property." We human beings are not the lords and masters of the world; we, along with the natural environment upon which we depend for life and health, are only creatures who belong to God as God's property. Any neglect, abuse, or destruction of any part of God's creation, therefore, is not just an offense against our natural environment and a threat to the future of humankind; it is an offense against the Creator of heaven and earth. It is sin for which we are held accountable before God, with consequences just as serious as those of our sins of personal immorality and social injustice.

But the words of the psalmist are also a promise: The Creator who "owns" and rules the created world and everything in it is a God who uses the power of ownership and rule not to dominate and control but to protect, defend, and preserve. It is not well-meaning human beings but God who is first and foremost a "friend" of the earth. Therefore we do not have to take on ourselves the staggering task of "saving" our wounded and dying planet; we can count on the love and power of Creator God who alone can and will save it.

This does not mean that we can sit back and "let God do it," for there is a second thing to be said about a biblical doctrine of creation—

surprisingly enough, in favor of the very words in the Genesis creation that have been interpreted (or rather misinterpreted) as contributing to the ecological crisis of our time.

"Let us make humankind in our image, according to our likeness; and let them have dominion . . ." (Gen. 1:26, 28). Although we human beings too are only creatures who live in mutual interdependence with the rest of God's creatures, we alone are creatures made in the image of God. That does give us a privileged place in God's created world, but it is the privilege of a special responsibility and task.

Part of the privilege of being created in the image of God is that human beings do indeed have a godlike power over the rest of creation. No other creatures have the power we have to affect our natural environment and all life in it for good or ill. No other creatures can do as much damage on such a massive scale, and no other creatures can (within limits) undo it.

To be uniquely created in the image of God means that we also have a responsibility no other creatures have. It means that as God uses God's power not to lord it over but to befriend and help God's created world, so we creatures in the image of God are created to use our unique power over our fellow creatures. It means that what we have to "have dominion" over and "subdue" is first of all our own lust for power, wealth, and comfort that makes us the enemies rather than the friends of our fellow creatures. It means, to use some traditional Christian language, that of all the other creatures we alone are created to be the "stewards" of God who "manage" God's property in the interest of the Creator's good will for the *whole* created world and *all* its creatures. God can and will defend and preserve God's creation without our cooperation and, if necessary, despite our refusal to cooperate. But in inviting and commanding us to be stewards of it, God has graciously invited and commanded us to participate in God's own creative work in and for the world. The God who has given us this unique gift and task will also hold us responsible for the faithful fulfillment of it.

Everything else we say about God the Creator and God's created world must be consistent with such an "ecological" doctrine of creation.[2]

God creates in the beginning. To say that God creates in the beginning suggests to most of us that God's creative activity took place in the distant past, back there at the beginning of time when the world came to be. This interpretation is certainly included in what Genesis 1:1ff. and John 1:1ff. tell us happened "in the beginning." We need not try to say *how* the creative process took place. And there is no point in trying to answer the impossible question where God was and what God was doing before the beginning. We cannot even imagine "before time" or "outside space." But Christians do believe that whenever and however it took place, and however God existed before then, God the Creator is the original source of all that is.

However, we would miss the full meaning of "in the beginning" if we thought that it means only "back there and back then." The Bible says not only that God *was* but that God *is* and *will be* Creator. God's creative activity is not limited to the distant past, as if a long time ago God did everything God planned to do, then retired from the scene to let the world run by itself according to its own built-in laws (a view called Deism). Even now God "gives life to the dead and calls into existence the things that do not exist" (Rom. 4:17). Even now God makes us to be new creatures in Christ (2 Cor. 5:17). And one day God will create a whole new heaven and earth (Rev. 21:1). In confessing that God *is* Creator, Christians confess that God is *continuously* making new beginnings, opening up new possibilities, initiating new events.

This biblical idea of the Creator's continuous creative activity helps us interpret theologically the discovery of modern science that our world did not come into existence in its present form all at once, but developed gradually, with inexplicable gaps and the emergence of brand new forms of life over countless years. We will not be surprised or shocked to learn this if we know that the living Creator is constantly at work creating afresh. We may in fact *expect* new things from such a God.

The biblical idea of the Creator's continuous creative activity also tells us something about ourselves and other human beings. God is *our* Creator, a God who continues to do new things in *our* lives. The psalmist did not say that a long time ago God created Adam and Eve, from whom we are all descended; he says, "You knit *me* together in my mother's womb" (Ps. 139:13, emphasis added). The whole of Christian tradition has agreed with Luther, who wrote in his Small Catechism that to believe in God, the Father Almighty, Creator of heaven and earth, is to believe that God created *me*. The psalmist and Luther knew the "facts of life" about "where babies come from." But they also knew that the sexual process of procreation and its circumstances do not tell us the whole truth about where we came from, who we are, and what we can become. Without explaining how it is so, Christians believe that God the Creator stands at the beginning of every individual human life, gives it unique value and dignity of its own, goes with every one of us on our way, opens up the possibility of new beginnings even when the circumstances of our birth and environment seem to trap and paralyze us. Faith in the God who is also *our* Creator, in other words, gives us hope that things can be different in our own lives and in the lives of other people and groups no matter how hopeless our or their lives may seem.

There is only one God, who alone is Creator and Ruler of everything that is. The affirmation of biblical faith in God the Creator is a protest against all forms of the "dualism" that was characteristic of most ancient religions and is not unknown even among people in our own time (including some who call themselves Christians).

One popular form of dualism asserts that there are two eternal powers at work in the world: the power of a god of light, truth, order, and goodness; and the power of a god or gods of darkness, lies, chaos, and evil. The history of every human being and the history of the world is the story of the battle between these rival gods for control of the world. It is uncertain whether one will finally defeat the other or whether they will "divide the spoils" between them, each side claiming victory over some people and parts of the world.

Another form of dualism teaches that there is a similar battle between a good divine Spirit in opposition to inferior or evil physical and material reality that is unspiritual. The history of every human being and the history of the world is the story of a war between our spiritual-soulful-rational side that comes from God and our physical-bodily-sensual side that is the enemy of God. And again, it is uncertain which side will finally win.

Classical Christian theology formulated the doctrine of God's good creation "out of nothing" (*ex nihilo*) in opposition to both forms of dualism.[3] According to this doctrine, before the world was created there was nothing except God—no other eternal realities and powers alongside this one God; no resistant "matter" to be rejected and overcome if the "spiritual" life God wills was to prevail. Only God. This one God alone is the source and ruler of everything that is, spiritual *and* material, human souls *and* bodies.

Biblical-Christian faith is realistic about the power of evil at work in the world to resist God and corrupt God's good creation. But it insists that evil cannot come from a rival god or gods, for there are no such things. Nor can it come from a "lower" physical-material-bodily reality that must be rejected and overcome if the "higher" spiritual life God wills is to prevail, for everything that is physical, material, and bodily is

God's good creation. Evil can then only come in some way from rebellious creatures who refuse to acknowledge and serve God and who misuse God's good creation.

Everything we will have to say in the next chapter about the problem of evil and everything we will have to say later in this chapter about human life in God's good creation depends on this rejection of all forms of dualism from the very beginning—even "before" the very beginning!

The Creator is powerfully above and independent of the created world but also lovingly present and at work in it. We have seen repeatedly that biblical-Christian faith emphasizes both the sovereign power of a "transcendent" God *over* all created reality and the nearness of an "immanent" God *in* and *for* all created reality. One of the most difficult problems of a Christian doctrine of creation is the problem of maintaining a proper balance between these two emphases. Every attempt to talk about the relation between Creator and creation tends to defend one at the expense of the other. As we look now at the three main ways in which Christians in our time talk about how God is related to the world, which seems to you to do the best job of preserving both the transcendence and the immanence of God?

1. *Theism.* The word *theism* comes from the Greek word *theos*, "God." A theist, then, is a religious person (philosopher or theologian, Christian or not) who believes in the ultimate reality of God—as opposed to an a-theist who does not. The traditional Christian doctrine of creation is based on a Christian version of theistic thinking in general.

According to Christian tradition, God, who from all eternity was the only "being" there was (no dualism!), decided to give being to a second reality outside God's own being. So for God's own glory and good pleasure (not out of any need within God), by a sheer act of will, God created the world a real and good but inferior reality that is at every moment dependent upon and ruled by the Creator as a people and land are dependent upon and ruled by a king (see figure D).

From a biblical point of view, the strength of Christian theism is its clear insistence on the great distance and difference between Creator and creation, and on the absolute power of the Creator over creation. Its weakness is that it is not so clear about the loving presence of God with and for God's creatures. It is true that in confessing God as "God, the *Father* Almighty," the church has traditionally confessed the love as well as the power of the Creator. But the love of God as theism conceives it is that of a superior condescending to "look down on" and help inferior

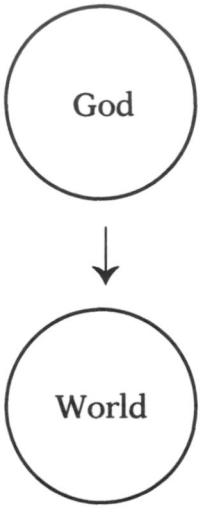

Figure D

creatures from the heavenly heights, safely removed from intimate personal involvement in their need, hurt, and pain. According to Christian theism, God sent Jesus to share all the weakness and suffering of human life and to pay the cost of self-giving love for sinful human beings even to the extent of dying for them. But God himself cannot and does not do that, cannot and does not suffer and experience what it is like to die. Theists know that God is the world's powerful Lord and Ruler, but they have trouble understanding how God can be the world's faithful Friend and Companion whose unfailing and constant loving presence we can count on even in the depths of the worst that can happen to us as creatures and sinners.

Is the God of theism the God we meet in the Old Testament story of God's faithful covenantal relationship with Israel, the God who shares the humiliation of the defeats and failures of God's people, as well as giving them victory and success, the God who sticks with them even in their constantly repeated sinful rebellion? Is the God of theism the God we meet in the story of a human creature who is called "God-*with*-us"? Is it the God who promises by God's Spirit to dwell *in* us? It is not surprising that, just because they want to be biblical thinkers and not just "theists," some Christians in our time have looked for other models to think about the relation between Creator and creation.

2. *Pantheism.* The word *pantheism* is a combination of the Greek

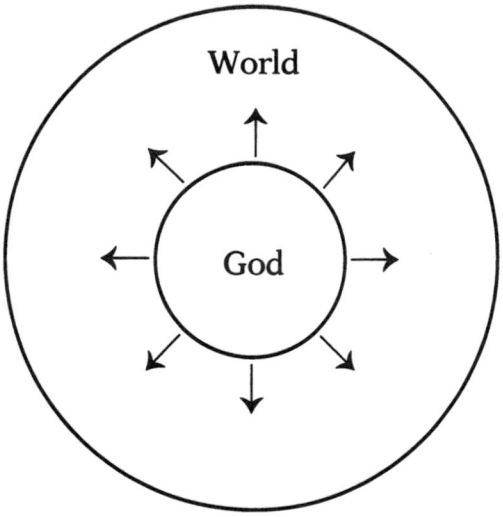

Figure E

words *pan,* which means "all," and *theos.* In contrast to various forms of theism that say that everything comes *from* God, pantheism says that everything *is* God. A common way of describing it is to say that Creator and creation are related as soul and body are related in a human being: the world is "God's body," the external self-expression of the internal reality and life-giving presence of God (see figure E).[4]

Pantheism, long rejected as a heresy by Christian tradition, has gained advocates, especially among some contemporary Christians concerned about the ecological crisis of our time, because they believe that it makes unmistakably clear the fact that our offenses against our natural environment are offenses against God—an attack on God's own body, as they put it.

Pantheism has also gained followers among feminists and others who reject the hierarchical, monarchical, patriarchical character of traditional Christian theism and its consequences for the way we think about the structure of human society and human relationships in it. These Christians find in pantheism a much-needed alternative to theism's predominant image of God as a father who first engenders life outside himself, then exercises authority over it as "head of the family." Pantheistic thinking enables us to think of God as more like a mother who so identifies her own life with that of her child that neither has a life apart from the other; her life *is* the life of her child, and the child's life *is* her life.

From a biblical-Christian point of view, the strength of pantheism is that it emphasizes as theism does not, the *nearness* of God to God's creation, God's *sharing* the life of all creatures, God's constant presence *with* and *for* us, God's making the welfare of creation a matter of God's own deepest self-interest. But it also sacrifices theism's emphasis on the difference between Creator and creation. The God of pantheists is not just *present* in the created world but *confused* with it. As a result, worship of the Creator becomes (as with some ecologically concerned people in our time) worship of creation—the world of nature itself. From a biblical perspective, that is the sin of idolatry, the sin that lies behind all other sins. On the other hand, pantheism makes the Creator as dependent on creation as creation is on the Creator. This leads to the strange idea in our time that because the world is God's body, those who give themselves to "save the planet" must also save *God*—as if instead of our needing to be saved by God, God needs to be saved by us! Instead of hoping in the power of *God's* love and justice and *God's* ability and promise to make all things new, Christian pantheists are prone to place their hope in what we can and must do to save the world and ourselves.

We may welcome the concern of Christian pantheism to find an alternative to the dangers of the hierarchical, monarchical, male-oriented thinking of Christian theism. But are not the consequences of pantheism's *confusion* of Creator and creation just as disastrous as the consequences of theism's *separation* of God and creation?

3. *Panentheism.* Pan-en-theism says that everything that exists is *in* God. The world is in God and God is in the world (see figure F).

Of several possible versions of panentheism, the version proposed by contemporary Reformed theologian Jürgen Moltmann is perhaps the most impressive attempt to find a way for Christian thinking about the relation between Creator and creation that preserves the strengths and avoids the weaknesses both of theism's emphasis on God's transcendent existence *apart from* the world, and of pantheism's emphasis on the immanent presence of God *in* the world.[5] According to Moltmann, God who is "all in all," the only reality there is, made and continues to make room *within God's self* for life different from God. This means, as theism insists, that the world is always dependent on God and can never be confused with God. But it also means, as pantheism insists, that God is never separated from the world but always, at every moment, dwells within it as the source of its life. The best analogy for this understanding of the relation between Creator and creation, Moltmann suggests, is not

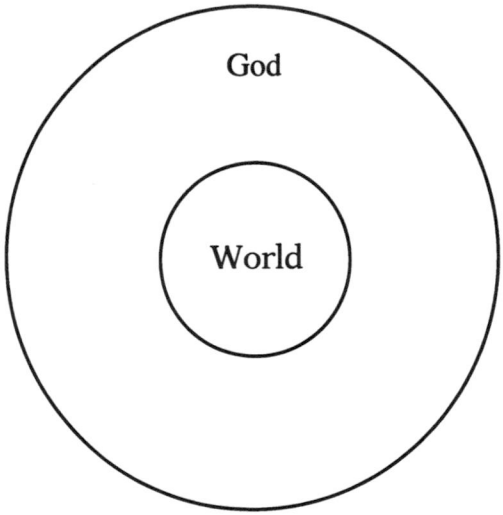

Figure F

the creative power of a father who engenders and rules over life outside himself but that of a mother who makes room for and nourishes new life within her own body. The life of the child she bears is at once totally dependent on her yet has an independent life of its own.

This Christian panentheism may sound strange to those of us who have learned to think theistically about the relation between God and the world. But does not scripture itself teach that all life comes from the gift and indwelling of God's Spirit? Does it not teach, speaking specifically about the God who comes to us in Jesus Christ, that "*in* him all things in heaven and on earth were created" (Col. 1:16, emphasis added)? Did not Paul say that it is "in" God that we live and move and have our being (Acts 17:28)? Does not the whole of scripture tell us that we are never *separated* from the love of God?

Christian panentheism is one way of proclaiming the good news that our God really is "omnipresent" and "ever-present." It is also one way of proclaiming good news about our own lives: God is behind *and* above *and* under *and* in front of us. We come from God. As we go on our way, God "looks down" on us with a kindly eye, God "upholds" us with a protecting and helping hand, and God's life-giving Spirit dwells within us. And we go to meet God. At every moment—past, present, and future—we are "surrounded" by God. We live not only from but in God.

In the last analysis, neither theism nor pantheism nor panentheism can explain the mystery of the relation between the Creator and the Creator's good creation. Each of these theories or models says some important things and leaves other important things unsaid. What is important is that we criticize and learn from each of them in light of biblical witness to a Creator who always, with all creatures, is a transcendent God powerfully independent of the created world and everything in it, yet also an immanent God who in self-giving love is present and at work in the created world and everything in it.

GOD'S GOOD CREATION

"God saw everything that he had made, and indeed, it was very good" (Gen. 1:31). The created world is good and life in it is good. They are good because a good God made them, continues to give them life, and promises them new life. We have already emphasized as strongly as possible that *all* that God created is good—not just human beings but also the world of our natural environment and all life in it. And we have emphasized that this means that we are to respect, value, protect, and work for the welfare of the whole created world. Now we will concentrate on what it means for us to recognize specifically human life as God's good creation.

It is true that we human beings (like no other creatures as far as we know) rebel against our Creator, misuse God's good creation, and make ourselves and others miserable because of our rebellion. Immediately after the creation story comes the beginning of the long story (that still continues) of human sin and its consequences. But neither the Bible nor genuinely Christian theology says that God's good creation has become a bad creation. The evil that invades God's good creation is not stronger than the Creator. It cannot change the essential goodness of what God creates. So before we try to understand the evil that is an "intruder" in God's world, we must try to understand what it means to believe that despite everything that spoils and corrupts it, we live in a *good* world, and it is *good* to be alive in it.

It means in general that, unlike some other religions and unlike some common perversions of Christianity, the Christian faith is a world-affirming and not a world-denying faith. Christians do not affirm the world because they are optimistic about the world as such and unrealistic about all the suffering and injustice in it. They affirm it because God created it and says yes to it. Even when evil invaded it and seemed to gain control over it, God did not abandon and turn against the creatures who had turned against their Creator. In the life and death of Jesus God entered into the "fallen" world to suffer with and for it. In the resurrection of Jesus God reclaimed what already belonged to God and asserted again God's powerful and loving lordship over the world, for the world. In the future God promises not only a new heaven but a new earth. Christians, then, are world-affirming because they believe in a world-affirming God. To seek escape from worldly life and worldly responsibilities and pleasures is to seek escape from *God.* Otherworldly spirituality may seem very pious, but it is not Christian. It is pious rebellion against God, the Creator of heaven and earth and everything in them.

Let us look more specifically at two of the characteristics of the "worldly" Christianity that follow from the Christian doctrine of creation.

Bodily-physical life is good. Dualistic religions and a falsely spiritual Christianity have always been suspicious of the body, even to the point of finding the origin of sin there. They understand religious life as denial of and escape from physical needs and desires. In contrast, a biblically oriented faith is shockingly "materialistic."

Part of what God made and pronounced very good is human sexuality. Maleness and femaleness are in fact connected directly with our being created in the image of God (Gen. 1:27). Scripture knows very well that we may rebel against God, hurt other people, and destroy ourselves with the misuse of our sexuality. But nowhere does it suggest that sex itself is "not nice." On the contrary, our sexuality is to be thankfully and joyfully received (and responsibly used) as a good gift of the Creator.

Again, the creation story tells us that the plants and trees were created by God to provide the food that sustains our bodily lives. In the Lord's Prayer Jesus instructed us to pray for "our daily bread." In his Small Catechism, Luther interprets this to be a petition not only for bread but for "everything required to satisfy our bodily needs"—food, clothing, shelter, money, property, family, good government, health, education, honor. Desire for all these earthly goods may lead to greed, envy, pride, and the other seven deadly sins. But if God invites us to pray for them, then they are not sinful in themselves, and it is God's will that we be concerned about them, work for them, and enjoy them.

Some Christians have thought that it is legitimate to be concerned about creaturely *necessities* but not to enjoy creaturely *pleasures*. Sex is all right for the propagation of the race but not for fun. We should eat only the simplest foods needed to nourish our bodies. In general, we ought to give up every luxury we can do without. But this austere view is, in the words of Calvin, "far too severe," for it would "fetter consciences more tightly than does the Word of the Lord—a very dangerous thing."[6] The Creator gives us not only water to quench our thirst but "wine to gladden the human heart" ("to make us merry," Calvin says in his commentary on these words from Ps. 104:15). Jesus was not ascetic, but went to parties (John 2:1ff.) and came "eating and drinking" so that he was accused of being a "glutton and a drunkard" (Matt. 11:19). The Song of Solomon certainly does not suggest sexual love only to propagate the race. In the passage just quoted and in other places, Calvin also mentions among the good gifts of God such things as fragrances, colors, music, and beauty in general, none of which are useful *for* anything. It is not necessarily true that Christians identify virtue with ugliness and sin with anything that is pleasant and fun!

Everything we have said about satisfying our creaturely necessities and enjoying creaturely pleasures is true only to the extent that we remember that God is not only our Creator but the Creator of *all* human beings, and that God's good gifts are given not just to us and our kind of people but to *all* people. To deny these gifts (necessities *and* pleasures) to any person or group, or to support any political or economic system that does so, is rebellion against the Creator who said that the physical-bodily life of every human being is good.

Temporal life is good. Life in time has always been a problem for human beings. Some ancient Greeks thought that the life of every person and the history of the world are meaningless, hopeless repetitions of the cycle of birth, decay, suffering, and death. There is no point in being concerned about life in this world either for myself or for others, for it is at best fleeting and doomed sooner or later to come to an end. Serenity and meaning can be found only by being indifferent to what happens in the world, stoically accepting the futility of historical existence, contemplating only eternal truths now, and hoping to escape to a better world when we die.

Into this pessimistic Greek world came the Hebrew Christian faith declaring the good news that the history of the world and of every individual *does* have meaning. It is true that all human beings are born, grow old, suffer, and die—or suffer and die before they have a chance to grow old. It is true that empires and nations rise and fall. But it is also true that there is a loving and powerful Creator who stands at the beginning and at the end of the history of the world and of every human being in it, and who works out the Creator's purpose for their good *in* their history. The Creator of the world not only was and will be but *is* at work in the world to overcome evil and establish justice, care for the sick and dying, empower the powerless, free those who are enslaved. God's good will for God's creation will finally be fulfilled only at the end of history (when there will be no more injustice, suffering, and dying for anyone, anywhere); but already now, *within* history, God is at work for our good. Therefore, despite all the forces in the world that sour, torment, and destroy human lives, Christians confidently and courageously live by the truth that life here and now is good. They do not run and hide or try to escape from historical existence. They thankfully and creatively receive life in time as the good gift of God the Creator.

This biblical view of time has shaped the whole of Western civilization. Confidence that history is "going somewhere" and that progress is possible in our individual lives and in the world around us—this is the legacy of the Judeo-Christian tradition. It is true that the Western world has forgotten the original reason for this confidence. It has come to have confidence not in the Creator's but in "man's" wisdom, virtue, and power, and therefore in progress as such. The result has been a new wave of deep hopelessness and despair in our time. The consequence of our faith in "man" and in "progress" is the brutality of modern warfare, the suffering of oppressed racial and ethnic minorities, the rape of our natural environment, the ever-widening gap in our own country and around the world between the few rich and comfortable and the many poor and destitute, the driven lives of some people who want more and more, and the hopeless lives of others who can expect less and less.

What shall we do in this situation? The Christian answer is not to give up on life in this world, to withdraw from it and look for personal comfort in otherworldly religions. The Christian answer is, "I believe in the God who is the Creator, Preserver, Ruler, and Renewer of heaven and earth." To believe in *this God* is to give ourselves with confidence and hope to the struggle for the improvement of human life in *this world*. We can do it and we must do it, because the struggle against poverty, ignorance, disease, injustice, war, and oppression is not our fight alone. It is the fight of a loving and powerful God who not only saves us at the end of time but invites and commands us to participate in God's creating and recreating work here and now, in "secular" history, for the good of all people everywhere.

GOOD BUT NOT GOD

We have stressed as strongly as possible the goodness of everything God has made. The doctrine of creation makes us free for a thankful, joyful, responsible *worldly* life. We do not qualify but only underline what we have said when we now emphasize just as strongly that although the created world is good, it is not God. This seemingly obvious statement has two very important consequences that are not so obvious.

Nothing in the world is to be feared. Because the whole world and everything in it depends on God for its very existence, nothing in all creation can have absolute and undefeatable control over us. We see what good news this is when we consider the fact that the Christian tradition has interpreted God's creation of "heaven and earth" to mean God's creation of all things "visible and invisible."

There are many "visible" things in the world that though good in themselves can be perverted so that instead of being good gifts of the Creator they become terrible threats. Political authority, ordained by God to preserve justice and peace, can become an instrument of terror and oppression. Wine, given to "make us merry," can become a cruel tyrant that makes us haunted slaves. So also food, sex, money, possessions, and the achievements of science and technology can become things that use us instead of good gifts to be used by us. But to believe that God is the Creator and Ruler of "all things visible" means that we do not have to surrender hopelessly to the tyrannical power of any of these things over our own lives or over the lives of others. We can resist and fight for liberation from every form of tyranny that enslaves and destroys human lives, for the Creator who understands and shares the suffering of enslaved people, and is on their side, is at work to set them free. How can any creature finally be stronger than the Creator?

The same is true of the "invisible" world. When the Bible and the ancient church confessed that God is Creator of the "heavens," they did not mean only the sky. For them the heavens were the realm of all kinds of unseen demonic powers that controlled the destiny of human beings. In confessing that God is Creator and Ruler of this realm also, the early church denied that any of them have final and absolute control over our lives. All these "rulers, dominions, and powers" are only creatures, not rival gods. The risen Christ has power over them too (Rom. 8:38; Eph. 1:21; Col. 1:16).

Now whether or not we modern people believe with Luther that this is a world "with devils filled," the church's ancient confession still has meaning for us. It means the end of all talk about the unseen power of fate ("It's written in the cards." "A bullet with my name on it." "What's your sign?"). It means the end of all superstitious belief in good or bad "luck," all fear of ghosts or the supernatural, all anxious seeking of guidance from a horoscope. It also means that, without denying their reality, we do not have to surrender hopelessly to all the unseen powers the modern scientific world has taught us to dread—the psychological power of the unconscious or subconscious, the biological power of heredity, the sociological power of environment. Powerful though they may be, even these unseen powers of our modern world do not have the last word about what we are and may become.

Faith in the God who is the Creator and Lord of heaven and earth means the end of paralyzing fear of all the very real seen *and* unseen tyrannies that have invaded God's good creation. The Creator is against them and more powerful than they, so we may confidently do battle against them too—whether they be the tyranny of political oppression, alcohol, drugs, sex, possessions, psychological depressions and compulsions, hereditary and environmental handicaps, or any other tyranny.

Nothing in the world is to be worshiped. The doctrine of creation is a great warning and battle cry against all forms of idolatry. Idolatry is by definition giving absolute loyalty to something that is only a creature rather than to the Creator. When the good gifts of God are made substitutes for God, they become demonic, enslaving and destroying even as they promise to help, fulfill, and save. We see how this happens when we think of the gods modern people worship as absurdly as ancient people worshiped images of woods or gold.

National identity, which is good in itself, becomes demonic when a nation becomes a god demanding total, unquestioning loyalty and obedience. International wars and domestic tyranny and oppression are the inevitable result. Faith in God the Creator means that "we must obey God rather than any human authority" (Acts 5:29)—even if it means passive resistance or active rebellion against "the law of the land." This faith, by its protest against national arrogance abroad and injustice at home, helps to restore a nation to its proper role as servant rather than god of the people.

Sexual, racial, and cultural differences are not bad in themselves; in fact, they contribute to the richness and variety of life in God's good creation. But they become demonic when people make a god of their particular sex, race, and cultural tradition. The result is sexism, racism, and classism that ignore, exclude, despise, seek to humiliate and subjugate—or in our "enlightened" modern world even wipe out—anyone who is not like "me" and "my kind of people." Equally demonic is commitment to any "politically correct" ideology that leads people to ignore, exclude, despise, humiliate, and seek to defeat or wipe out those who disagree with their particular remedies for racism, sexism, and classism! To believe in God who created human beings in God's own image is to protest against all the gods made in the image of any human being of any race, sex, or class. It is also to protest against the god made in the image of any liberal or conservative ideology. It is to serve the Creator who is at work to free both ourselves and others from the arrogance, fear, bitterness, and inhumanity that result from serving any of these idols.

So it is with other creaturely realities that are more commonly recognized idols of our time. Money and possessions; physical or intellectual pleasure of all kinds; personal happiness, security, and success—none of these is to be given absolute priority in our lives. We rebel against the Creator and hurt both ourselves and other people when we make gods of any of them. To say that we must love and serve God above all is not to deny and reject the creaturely world with all its various needs and pleasures. On the contrary, by insisting that everything in it is only the gift of God and not a substitute for God, we make possible the real fulfillment of every legitimate creaturely need and desire.

"I believe in God, the Father Almighty, Creator of heaven and earth." That means at once freedom *from* the world (as the home of all enslaving idols) and freedom *for* the world (as God's good creation).

FOR FURTHER REFLECTION AND STUDY

1. Many people believe that it is impossible to be both a "Bible-believing Christian" and a modern scientifically educated person. Do you agree? Why? Why not?
2. To what extent do you think we have the right or responsibility to "subdue" and "have dominion" over our natural environment?
3. If a child should ask you, "Where did I come from?" how could you answer in a way that is both honest about the biological facts of life and faithful to what Christians believe about God the Creator of all life?

4. Read John 1:1–3; Col. 1:15–16; and Heb. 1:1–2. What difference does it make to know that the world was created in, through, and for Jesus Christ?
5. What are the strengths and weaknesses of a theistic, pantheistic, and panentheistic understanding of the relation between God and the world? Which do you prefer?
6. Read through the whole book of the Song of Solomon. Do you think teenagers should be encouraged to read this part of the word of God?
7. Is money the root of all evil?
8. Read the following passages in the Gospel of Luke (sometimes called the Gospel of the poor) and Acts (a continuation of Luke's Gospel): Luke 1:51–53; 6:20–25; 8:1–3; 18:18–25; 19:1–10; Acts 2:44–45; 9:36; 10:2. Must we be poor to be a Christian? Is it sinful to have money and possessions?
9. Do Christians believe in progress?
10. How would you answer someone who argues that either heredity or environment, or a combination of both, determines what every person is and can become?
11. Does a Christian doctrine of creation lead to a liberal or conservative social ethic?
12. List what you believe are the most popular idols that are worshiped and served in our time. Now make a list of the idols *you* are most tempted to worship and serve.

9

Why Doesn't God Do Something about It?

The Doctrine of Providence and the Problem of Evil

The doctrine of providence is an extension of the doctrine of creation. It says that the loving, just, and powerful God who first made heaven and earth continues to uphold, protect, rule over, take care of—provide for—God's good creation and each one of us.

Everything we have said about the Creator and what we have to say now about God the "provider" sounds very nice—for children in Sunday School, preachers and theologians, and people standing up to confess their faith in quiet sanctuaries with stained glass windows they can't see through to see what life in the world is really like. That world is a world plagued by cancer, the torments of mental illness, battered women and children, bloody wars, millions of homeless and starving people around the world, the spread of the deadly AIDS virus, suffering and injustice of all kinds everywhere. How can Christians be so naive and sentimental in their glib talk about a powerful God of love and justice at work in the world? Given the kind of world we really live in, must we not conclude that if there is a God at all, that God must be either loving and just but not powerful enough to do anything about it, or powerful but not loving and just enough to do anything about it? A God who is either willing to prevent evil but not able, or able but not willing—is that not our alternative if we believe in God at all?[1]

That is the problem we will consider in this chapter. First we will acknowledge the reality of evil that challenges everything Christians believe about God. Then, following a distinction philosophers and theologians of all traditions make between two kinds of evil, we will consider how Christians understand the nature and origin of "the dark side of creation" (natural evil) and "the powers of darkness" (moral evil). Finally, we will discuss "the light shining in the darkness," the Christian doctrine of providence and its implications for our lives.

THE REALITY OF EVIL

Because the fact of evil is such a threat to what Christians affirm about God and God's good creation, we might expect that the Bible and Christian theology would try to solve the problem by trying in one way or another to explain away its terrible reality.

Some people try to deal with the evil around them and in their own lives by pretending that it isn't there at all, or at least is not as bad as it seems. They cheerfully remember that April showers bring May flowers. When the dog bites and the bee stings, they think of their favorite things. They promise themselves that the sun will come out tomorrow. In one way or another they practice the "power of positive thinking." Sometimes such Pollyanna sentimentality has crept into the church, but the main stream of Christian tradition has rejected it. Some of the worst injustice and suffering in the world is the result of "good" people simply refusing to acknowledge that evil exists and therefore doing nothing to challenge it.

Another solution to the problem is the "omelet" theory: Eggs have to be broken if you want to make an omelet. If we look far enough ahead, we can see that evil contributes to good and so is not really evil at all. A war that slaughters millions of people can bring peace. If a church refuses to welcome and minister to some objectionable people who would drive its members away, it can grow financially and numerically and thus increase its influence in society. Political and economic policies that hurt some people can contribute to the welfare of most people. But even if some good does sometimes come from evil, does that make evil good? What kind of God would create a world in which wrong and the infliction of suffering is the law of progress toward right? Christians cannot dispose of the problem of evil as easily as that.

Against all attempts to explain evil away in one way or another, Christian faith is uncompromisingly realistic. Immediately following the biblical story of the good God and God's good creation comes the story of the Tempter and his satanic work. According to Jesus, the evil that was unleashed at the very beginning of history and has been at work through all history will be there until the very end. Until the end of history there will be wars and rumors of wars, nation against nation, famine, earthquakes, suffering, false leaders, injustice, hatred, persecution of the righteous (Matt. 24:3–14). History is not the story of gradual human progress in which there is less and less evil and more and more good; it is the story of the past, present, and future power of evil that threatens to spoil and destroy God's good creation.

This unflinching realism about the reality of evil becomes even more intense at the event that stands at the center of all history—the cross of the Jesus whom Christians believe is God-with-us. Evil is so strong that it seems not just the enemy of God but the victor over God. Good is defeated and evil triumphs. Hatred overcomes love. Justice loses and injustice wins. God's world becomes Satan's world. That is not the end of the story of Jesus, of course, but it is an inescapable part of it. The same cross that is the symbol of Christian faith in the powerful love and justice of God is also the symbol of the terrible reality and power of evil.

If, then, we talk about the problem of evil as Christians gathered around the cross, no trivial, easy answers will do. Christian faith is not an escape from the problem of evil; it raises the problem to the nth degree.

THE DARK SIDE OF CREATION

It will help us to get to the heart of the problem if we discuss first what is usually called "natural" evil, evil that comes from natural causes not influenced by human motives, decisions, and actions—suffering that results from what Karl Barth has called the "dark" or "shadow" side of God's good creation.

A woman develops cancer and, after a long agonizing illness, dies, leaving a family without wife and mother. A storm rips through a city leaving demolished homes, mangled bodies, and hunger and disease in its wake. Parents who have eagerly awaited their first child take her home from the hospital knowing that she is hopelessly deformed physically or mentally. A large part of a whole continent becomes a desert after years of unrelieved drought, and millions of men, women, and children die of malnutrition. And we ask, "If there *is* a God, why did God let this happen—or did God actually *make* it happen?"

Four things can be said that help us understand such misfortunes (though nothing can be said to take the hurt away).

Human Finitude

Some hard and painful experiences in our lives are simply the result of our being finite creatures. It is part of our creaturely existence that there is decay as well as growth, age as well as youth, loss as well as gain, pain as well as pleasure, sickness as well as health, death as well as birth. Creaturely life at best is fragile, vulnerable, and temporary. Scripture is quite honest about this. Human beings are like the flowers of the field that blossom, live for a while, then wither and die (Ps. 103:15; Isa. 40:6–7). Some suffering and death is the result of our own or others' sinfulness, but according to scripture, suffering and death as such are not evil. They only mean that we are creatures and not God. Unlike the Creator, we creatures do not live forever.

Real evil enters the picture when we refuse to accept the finitude of human life or try to play God with our own or others' lives. Death, for instance, is not evil in itself. But terror in face of death or frantically clutching our own or others' lives at all costs—that is evil. What is evil is not the fact that the life of every creature comes to an end. It is our worship of youth, terror of old age, refusal to admit that people do actually die (instead of "passing away"), desperate use of every possible medical technique to prevent life from coming to an end and to "torture people to life"—or on the other hand, using "human finitude" as an excuse for not doing what we can to protect and preserve the limited but good gift of life God wills for us and for all other human beings.

The first thing to be said about natural evil, then, is that we must honestly acknowledge that there *is* a dark side to God's good creation. The vulnerability and mortality of our lives are painful and hard to bear—especially when life seems to end too soon or to drag on too long, or when the possibility of a full and meaningful life is severely threatened by tragic sickness or disabling handicaps. But the shadow side of life is an absolutely intolerable problem only for those who cannot accept the fact that they are creatures and not gods, who do not know what a compassionate and just God can do within and despite the limitations of our lives, and who do not know that God's will for our good will finally be stronger than the worst that can happen to us, including death itself.

Natural Law

Modern science has learned that the "laws of nature" are not as mechanically fixed and absolute as we once thought. Nevertheless, part of the goodness of creation is that our world is not an unpredictable chaos but at least a relatively ordered, intelligible system of interrelated parts that function in a relatively consistent way we can count on. All the advances of modern science and technology in making human life in the world safer, healthier, and more productive are the result of the dependability of the laws of physics, biology, and the like. But the very regularity of nature that usually helps human life can also hurt it. Given certain conditions, living cells that grow according to their dynamic structure as cells can become malignant cancers. Under certain conditions, the meteorological forces that make our weather predictable and usually favorable to human life can also bring tornadoes, destruction, famine, and death.[2] "Mother Nature" is neither our friend nor our enemy. She operates by her own rules that are sometimes beneficial and sometimes harmful to us.

Is God responsible for the suffering that results from natural causes? Yes and no. Yes, in the sense that God willed and created the orderly structure of the world, gave it a relatively independent existence of its own, and does not constantly interfere with it. No, in the sense that God is not directly responsible when that same structure works to our disadvantage.

At this point most modern Christians disagree with earlier Christian tradition in two ways:

1. Earlier Christians tended to believe that God is directly responsible for everything that happens to us, good or bad. They knew about what we call the "natural" causes of things that happen (they called them "second" causes), but they still believed that they happen because God willed them. For instance, Question 26 of the Heidelberg Catechism speaks of the "evil he sends upon me in this troubled life." There are still Christians who ask when a hurricane comes why God "sent" it; or when a baby dies, why God "took" it. When tragedy strikes, they try to comfort themselves and others by saying that "we must accept the will of God." But most modern Christians who watch television know that God does not aim storms at any particular place; they are the result of global systems of high and low atmospheric pressure. When sickness comes, even the most committed Christians go first to a medical doctor to deal with the infection, virus, or other physical factors that caused it. If a baby dies or is born with a severe handicap, we know that it is not because God willed it but because something went wrong during the pregnancy or delivery, or perhaps because of the genetic structure of the father and mother. Christians in our time too believe that God is at work in our lives and in the world around us. But we do not blame God for all the bad things that happen because we know that God did not "make" them happen. We look for and expect God's presence and work indi-

rectly *in* and *through*—and sometimes *despite*—the natural processes that affect our lives favorably or unfavorably.

2. But it is not just modern science; it is scripture itself that leads us to think differently from earlier Christian tradition about the way God is at work in the world. That tradition tended to understand the relation between God and what happens in the world with a cause-effect explanation. This way of thinking led Calvin, for instance, to believe that everything that happens is determined (caused) by the will of God, and that nothing happens that is not the will of God.[3] Sometimes scripture also speaks of God's "causing" things to happen. But, unlike classical Christian theology, the Bible does not think of God as an impersonal "First Cause" that mechanically determines and programs everything. The God of scripture is a living, personal God who is present and at work in our lives to lead the way, set free, judge, forgive, help, and save—not just cause, program, and determine everything that happens from above. Christians guided by scripture, then, seek to understand what God wills for their lives and is doing in their lives by listening to what the Bible tells us about who God is and what God does, not by trying to figure it out for ourselves by assuming that God is the hidden cause behind everything that happens.

Painful and tragic things sometimes happen to us because we live in a world that operates according to the natural laws and processes God has built into it. But they hurt less when we know that God does not will and cause them to happen, but is God with and for us in hard times as well as in good times, in failure and sorrow as well as in success and happiness, in sickness and suffering as well as in health and prosperity, when death comes as well as when life is spared. Question 28 of the Heidelberg Catechism puts it beautifully when it says concerning what the doctrines of creation and providence teach us: "We learn that we are to be patient in adversity, grateful in the midst of blessing, and to trust our faithful God and Father for the future, assured that no creature shall separate us from his love, since all creatures are so completely in his hand that without his will they cannot even move."

Human Responsibility and Negligence

Many natural evils are at least partly the result of our neglect or refusal to take advantage of the ability God has "provided" us to care for our own and others' safety and welfare. If a plane crashes, should we ask why God let it happen or why safety measures were not enforced? If millions of people around the world are hungry and homeless, should we ask why God allows it to happen or why we do? If I get sick, is it because God has not taken care of me or because I have disregarded the rules of health that enable me to take care of myself? If there is so much sickness, disease, and suffering in the world around us, is it because *God* doesn't care or because *we* don't? If a hurricane brings death and destruction to people who live (or have summer homes) along a beach, should we ask why God created a world in which hurricanes can happen or why we build homes (sometimes flimsily built ones) in hurricane-prone areas? Human negligence, selfishness, and unconcern cause many forms of evil we like to blame God for. And human intelligence and good will can remedy many forms of evil we think God ought to do something about.

Tragedy and suffering come that no one could prevent and no one is responsible for. We do not have to torment ourselves by assuming that misfortune is always our own fault, anxiously asking, "What did I do to deserve this?" And it is cruel to allow or encourage others to torment themselves with the suggestion that their misfortune is always their own fault, the consequence of something they have done or not done. Nothing is more unfair than blaming the victim. Nevertheless, *sometimes* misfortune and suffering are clearly the consequence of our neglect or refusal to provide for our own or others' welfare, and it does not help to ignore or deny it. Even in such cases, however, Christians can remind themselves and others of a God who does not hold grudges and seek vengeance but loves and forgives sinners, a God who promises to be with and for us even in the consequences of our sinfulness.

Unanswered Questions

What we have said about human finitude, the laws of nature, and human responsibility may have helped us understand a little better the pain, suffering, and death that are the consequences of the "natural evil" that is the dark side of God's good creation. But our discussion has left two very important questions unanswered.

First, granted that suffering, pain, and death are part of every human life, why do they come when, where, and how they do? Why do some people suffer more than others? Why do some have more tragedy in their lives than anyone should have to bear? Why do "good" people who don't deserve it sometimes suffer more than "bad" people do? Why the debilitating disease, the tragic accident, or the death of a child or young person whose life is just beginning? Why is a family deprived of the support and care of a father or mother it desperately needs? Why must an older person have to suffer so long? Why is a nation or business deprived of a leader upon whom so much and so many depend? Or more concretely: Why me? Why my child, my mother or father, my husband or wife, my friend? Why them and not me? Why all those other people around the world whom God loves just as much as God loves us? Why them and not us? The questions are endless.

And the answer? We don't know why. What we know about human finitude, the laws of nature, human responsibility, and the consequences of irresponsibility can sometimes give us partial answers, but in the last analysis we just do not know, should not pretend that we do, and do not have to feel guilty because we don't. We can do what we can to relieve our own and others' suffering. We can stand by one another to share one another's suffering and grief to make it a little easier. But the one thing we cannot do and should not try to do is explain why—especially with glib talk about the "will of God" or speculation about what people do or do not deserve. There is a dark side of creation that is simply a mystery to us.

What we can do is what we have in fact already begun to do in our discussion of the dark side of God's good creation. Without even trying to explain why it invades our lives when, where, and how it does, we can remind ourselves and others of the light that shines in the darkness: the light of a loving God who understands and shares the depths of our suffering and dying; the light of a powerful God whose will for our good will not be defeated, who is stronger than death itself, who makes the dead live again.

But how do we know that this kind of God-talk is not just whistling in the dark, the wishful thinking of those who try to make themselves feel better when the shadow of the dark side of creation falls across their lives? Unlike the "why" question, Christians do have an answer to this question. But before we talk about it, we need to talk about another kind of evil that makes faith in God even more difficult—and more important.

THE POWERS OF DARKNESS

Terrible as it can be, the worst form of evil is manifested not in natural misfortune that happens to us but in what we human beings do to each other. It appears not in pain, suffering, and death as such, but in the pain, suffering, and death we inflict on each other.

The evil we do to each other has three dimensions. It is always rebellion against God and the order of God's good creation. It is always indifference or enmity toward our fellow human beings. And it is always the self-destructive contradiction of what we ourselves were created to be. The worst form of evil, in other words, is "moral" evil that expresses itself as sin.

But evil is more than sin. When we sin, we come under the spell of a power greater than ourselves and our ability to resist, a power from which we cannot free ourselves no matter how hard we try. We *do* evil, but when we do we are trapped and controlled *by* evil. It dwells in us yet somehow has an existence of its own outside us.

I may decide that I will entrust my life into God's care and not be anxious about the future. I may decide to be more understanding, more open, more patient as I live with other members of my family, with friends, and with business associates. I may decide that my position on economic, political, and social issues will be determined by consideration of the common good of all people, not by my own self-interest or that of my particular sex, race, class, or nation. But I find over and over again that I cannot do what I decide but do what I do not want to do. I cannot blame anyone else for my sin (not even the devil) because *I* do it. Yet I can't *help* doing it. "Something gets into me" and "takes over" my feelings and actions that makes me the kind of person I do not want to be and makes me do the kind of things I do not want to do. That "something" is the dark power of evil in my life. (How does Paul talk about this in Rom. 7:14–25?)

Even when we do set out to combat the power of evil, we find that we are mastered by it. Parents fight the temptation to think of their own comfort and security, and sacrifice for the good of their child—only to find that it is not really the children's good but their own ambition or concern about "what other people will think" that actually determines their parenting. A nation fights tyranny in another nation in order to free its citizens from injustice and suffering—and finds that to do so it must cause horrible pain, suffering, and death. A community establishes a program of urban renewal so that poor people may have decent homes—but in tearing down slums, deprives some poor people of any home at all. We fight evil and discover that we are its instruments.

When we ask about evil, we ask about this mysterious, enslaving power that takes possession even of decent people, and perverts even the good they want to do. We ask *why* even well-meaning people sin, *why* we cannot avoid sin even when we try, *why* even our efforts to destroy evil perpetuate rebellion against God, enmity against neighbor, and self-destruction. Where does this evil come from that "gets into us"? What is the nature of this dark power that has invaded God's good creation? We will look at several answers that have been given to this universal problem and evaluate them from a biblical point of view.

An Evil God?

One of the most ancient explanations of the existence and power of evil is to say that besides the good God there is an evil god—an eternal principle of Evil that opposes an eternal principle of Good. We have already encountered—and rejected—this "dualism" in our study of the doctrine of creation. We may acknowledge that there is a kind of *relative* dualism in scripture. Against God there is also Satan, who can be described as "the god of this world" (2 Cor. 4:4) or the "ruler of this world" (John 12:31; 14:30; 16:11). But in the last analysis the Bible and Christian tradition reject the dualistic explanation of evil. God would not be God if there were another god who could finally thwart God's will and work. Before the world was, there was only the one true God. We do not have to look forward to a dreary, never-ending battle between a god of light and a god of darkness. Whatever Satan is, he is not really a second god. (Notice how the passages in John we have just quoted all speak of the defeat and destruction of this "pretender to the throne.") Christians do not believe in a powerless or only partly powerful God. We believe in the one true and living God who *alone* is God and who *alone* will be triumphant in and over the world.

God "Himself"?

We could logically reason that if God is the Creator and Ruler of all that is, then God must be the source of "moral" evil too. This answer has always been rejected by Christian theology—and most vigorously by Calvinistic thinkers who could be most easily tempted by it (and who have always been accused of implying it) because of their insistence on the sovereign "will" or "plan" of God that lies behind everything that happens. The Bible teaches uncompromisingly that God is against evil. How could God will or cause resistance and opposition to God when the Creator created human beings precisely for the purpose of having *fellowship* with us, when Christ who is God-with-us came to *overcome* human resistance and opposition in order to *reconcile* us to God? How could God will or cause human indifference, enmity, and injustice in human relationships when God created us to love, help, and do justice in our life together; when Christ came to fulfill God's plan to reconcile us not only to God but to each other? How could God will or cause our self-destroying inhumanity when God created us to be genuinely human as we love God and neighbor, when God sent Christ and gives us the gift of God's Spirit to transform our sinful inhumanity so that we might become again what we were created to be? We will see that God is powerful enough to make good come out of evil. But we cannot say that God is the author of evil. *Evil is by definition what God does not will and does not do.* There is no secret identity between God and the devil.

Human Bodily Existence?

Many philosophers and theologians have concluded that if evil does not come from God or from a second god, then it must come in one way or another from human beings. One such explanation comes from the ancient Greeks before Christianity came on the scene. They believed that the root of evil is in human sensuality. The needs and especially the pleasures of the body are a "drag" on our "higher" nature, and they cause us to give in to the evil influence of our "baser" instincts and lusts. Despite the fact that this theory of the origin of evil crept very early into the Christian church and has probably influenced all of us, it is unbiblical and unchristian.

This explanation is wrong first because it traces evil to something God has willed and created, and thus makes the Creator the source of evil. Bodily needs, desires, and pleasures may of course be the instrument of all sorts of evil, but nowhere does the Bible suggest that they are evil in themselves or the source of evil.

Second, this explanation is inadequate because it implies that evil can be overcome if we develop our own and others' rational capacity to subdue and control our bodily desires. (A modern version of this argument is that personal immorality and social injustice can be overcome if we can just "educate" people to understand that they are "inappropriate" or "antisocial" or "self-defeating" or "against your own self-interest.") But reason too can become evil and the servant of evil. The rational person is not necessarily the good person. Coldly rational, calculating people can in fact do far more harm than people driven only by their passions, for they are more imaginative in devising destructive forms of evil. It was not sensual, lusting, "animal-like" people, but highly educated, reasonable people who developed and used nuclear weapons! The point is not that reason in itself is any more evil than the body (and ignorance is certainly not the same thing as innocence or virtue). Reason is also a good gift of the Creator. The point is that we must look deeper than either body or mind to discover the origin and nature of evil, which can possess both but arises from neither.

Social Influences?

A modern explanation of evil is that it comes from a bad family background or from an unjust social system or political structure.[4] There is obviously something right about this argument. Parents who batter children were often battered children themselves. A deprived or dysfunctional family can be the breeding ground for juvenile delinquents and criminals. Alcoholics often had an alcoholic parent or parents. A racist society nourishes and passes on racism from one generation to another. A patriarchical society can produce both women and men who believe that women are inferior. Some forms of capitalism, based on the premise that all have the same opportunity to work and provide for themselves and their families, in fact favor the rich, powerful, and advantaged at the expense of the poor, powerless, and disadvantaged. Bureaucratic socialism can be more concerned to enforce the rules and regulations of well-meant social programs than to meet the real needs of the people they are supposed to serve.

Important as it is to take the social context of evil into consideration, social explanations do not get to the heart of the problem of evil. They do not explain how or why social structures themselves become evil. Moreover, instead of solving the problem, blaming a familial or social system for evil can make it worse. We do not have to take responsibility for our own lives, nor will we be able to do so, so long as we can blame our parents or someone else for our faults and problems. We cannot encourage and help others to take responsibility for their own lives or to challenge a repressive social system so long as we allow them to continue blaming family background or "the system" for their faults and problems. On the other hand, those who believe that evil can be overcome by changing a particular social, economic, or political system forget that when the oppressed who have no power get enough power, then the oppressed usually become the oppressors, doing unto others what has been done to them. Evil does not end; it only changes managers and forms of expression.

Could it be that evil does not reside in any one sex, class, party, group, or institution, but that it is a power at work in *all* of us: men *and* women; rich, poor, *and* middle class; conservatives *and* liberals; "foreigners" *and* our own people; black *and* white and every color in between?

Free Will?

Perhaps the most common way of explaining the origin of evil is to say that it comes from the God-given ability all human beings have to choose between good and evil. How could we choose good if evil were not an alternative? Evil comes into our lives and in the world around us because we freely choose evil rather than good.

But logical as it sounds at first glance, this explanation is neither experientially realistic nor biblical, and it intensifies rather than solves the problem of the origin of evil.

Are we in fact really free to choose either good or evil? We may be free to choose to be moral or immoral, be law-abiding or lawless, go to church or stay home, do all kinds of "good works" or not. But the good God requires of us and wills for us more than just morality, piety, and good deeds. We are to love, trust, and obey God with glad thanksgiving in all that we do. We are to love and help, and let ourselves be loved and helped, by other people (not just some of them, when it serves our self-interest; but all of them, even when it seems against our self-interest). We find our own true humanity as we live in a right relationship with God and other people. Are we free to choose and do that? Are we not in fact driven and controlled by all sorts of fears, anxieties, doubts, suspicions, hostilities, and rebellion that keep us from loving God and other people and letting ourselves be loved by them? Is not the most fundamental problem of our lives how we who are *not* free can *become* truly free—free for God and our fellow human beings, and therefore to be the kind of people God created us to be? Do not both our own experience and scripture teach us that instead of being free to choose either to sin or not sin, we are "slaves" of sin and need to be set free from it? (See our earlier discussion of "free will" when we dealt with semi-Pelagianism in chapter 7.)

If this is the situation in which we find ourselves, then the evil we choose does not come from our ability to choose as such. It comes from the rebellious, hostile, self-destructive thoughts, attitudes, and desires that are in our hearts *before* we choose, whose influence over us is so powerful that it is they and not our "free" wills that determine how and what we choose. The problem of evil is precisely where these thoughts, attitudes, and desires come from that enslave our wills.

The argument that finds the origin of evil in the human will, in other words, only forces us to look deeper than that to find the true origin of evil.

Fallen Angels?

Evil cannot come from God, for what God wills and does is good. It cannot come from an evil god who is the rival of the good God, for there is only one God. Nor can it come in any of the ways we have discussed from human beings. Our bodies, minds, hearts, and wills, and our social environment may be *instruments* but they are not the *source* of evil. Where then does it come from? According to scripture, it comes from the "Tempter"—Satan. He was already there in the form of the serpent at the very beginning of human history before human beings did anything. It was this already existing Evil One who put evil desires into the heart, mind, and will of the first human beings (the representatives of all humanity ever since) and tempted them to choose to rebel against the Creator. It was this Tempter who led them to deny and contradict their own humanity in the image of God as they broke fellowship with God and then inevitably also with fellow human beings. Satan does not play an important role in the rest of the Old Testament, but in the New Testament he is often mentioned as the source of opposition to God and God's reconciling work in Christ, in the Christian community, and in the world.

Who is Satan? According to ancient Christian tradition, he is a creature of God—not a human creature but an angelic creature of some kind. He, and perhaps other angelic creatures with him, rebelled against God and then became the source of the corruption of God's good creation. This understanding of Satan is hinted at in 2 Peter 2:4 and Jude 6, though, in general, scripture itself shows no interest in where he came from.

How shall we modern Christians understand the reality and power of this Evil One? There are two possible ways: a literal interpretation and a symbolic one. Which seems best to you?

A Literal Interpretation

Some Christians today believe that if we are faithful to scripture, we must believe in the literal existence of a personal devil and in invisible demonic powers at work in our own lives and in the world around us. We may grant that this is a possible interpretation under three conditions:

1. Christians do not "believe in" the devil. We confess our faith in "God, the Father Almighty" and in "Jesus Christ, his only Son, our Lord" and in the "Holy Spirit." No Christian creed contains a profession of

faith in Satan. That would not be strict orthodoxy, as some have thought; it would be idolatry—*worship* of evil. Christians believe not *in* but *against* the power of darkness in God's good creation.

2. Our interest in the devil and demons must not become so central and intense that their reality becomes more important to us than the reality and power of God. Whenever Satan and his demons appear in scripture, it is always the story of God's power over them and of their defeat and destruction. The devil and his demons are by definition those powers that God in Jesus Christ has *already* opposed and defeated (Luke 10:18; Matt. 12:28; Mark 3:22; John 12:31; Col. 1:13). Even *now* they are limited and controlled by the risen Christ (Rom. 8:37–39; Eph. 1:19–23; Col. 1:13). And finally he *will* utterly crush and destroy them (Matt. 25:41; 1 Cor. 15:24–28; Rev. 17:14; 20:10). We cannot for a moment entertain the possibility that the power of Satan might be greater than the power of God. This means that although we must take the powers of darkness seriously, we can never make them the center of our thought, thinking too long and talking too much about them. That gives them too much honor and suggests that Christians are more interested in the destructive power of sin and evil than in the saving power of God. Christians make theology, not demonology. It is the power of God *over* sin and evil, not sin and evil as such, that interests us and is the most important thing we have to talk about.

3. If we listen to what scripture tells us about Satan and his powers of darkness, we will not look for their work only where there is obvious filth, obscenity, and godlessness in the world around us; we will look at ourselves and at the Christian community! It was not the prostitutes, social outcasts, dishonest business people, and political subversives, but God-fearing, law-abiding Pharisees whom Jesus called sons of Satan (John 8:44). It was not his enemies but one of his closest friends, Peter, whom he called "Satan" (Mark 8:33). Satan is most dangerous when he "disguises himself as an angel of light" and when his servants "disguise themselves as ministers of righteousness" (2 Cor. 11:14 and 15). So let us take warning when we talk about the reality of a personal devil. It is not only in those godless, unchristian people "out there" that Satan is at work. He is also at work especially where pious people try to use God to maintain their own personal or social security, prosperity, and power instead of serving God. He is at work not only where people hurt other people and destroy themselves by lust, drunkenness, and immorality of various kinds, but especially where morality, respectability, and law-

abiding piety become more important than the needs of other people and an excuse to reject or ignore them.

Symbolic Interpretation

Some modern Christians believe that we can no longer believe in the reality of a personal Satan and personal demonic forces. Biblical talk about them, they argue, is only a primitive way of expressing the truth that in God's world there is not only order but also chaos, not only humanity but also inhumanity, not only good but also evil. We may still believe everything the Bible tells us about the reality and power of evil without thinking literally of demons and devils running around getting into people. Even without that, we can speak in all loyalty to biblical truth about the "demonic" or "Satanic" power that can take possession not only of individuals but of whole societies and institutions, changing ordinarily decent people into brutal, bloodthirsty mobs or simply into people who are coldly indifferent to injustice and the needs and suffering of others.

One advantage of thinking this way is that it enables us to think of impersonal as well as personal forces of evil at work in and among us. Many people who have never experienced or witnessed demon possession understand what it means to be "possessed" by the power of greed, fear, lust, prejudice, and hatred. Why should not such a "demythologized" interpretation of Satan be legitimate so long as (a) it is not secretly an attempt to explain away but faithfully to interpret for our time the ancient biblical way of talking about evil, and (b) we remember that the power of God is also more powerful than all the impersonal demonic or satanic forces that oppose God and corrupt God's good creation?

Neither the literal nor the symbolic interpretation of Satan explains the origin of evil. Even if we think literally of a rebellion of angels that took place before creation, we only push the problem back one step and leave unanswered all the objections we have raised to attributing evil to any creature of God. How could *any* of God's creatures rebel against their God when *all* that God creates is good?

Just when we are driven finally to biblical statements about Satan, we are driven to the conclusion that there *is* no explanation for the origin and reality of evil in God's world. The Genesis story is very profound in its simplicity at this point. It makes no attempt to explain where the Tempter came from or how he could exist at all in God's world. Satan is a hideous intruder who does not belong in the picture but is nevertheless there. Logically, evil is impossible in a world created and ruled by God, for it is just what God did *not* create and does *not* will. That is the parasitical power of evil. It is not the truth about what we are and what the world is like; it is a *lie*, a *contradiction* and *denial* of the truth. That is why it is so dangerous. Evil is the lie that leads us to the futile, self-destructive attempt to live without and against God, when the truth is that we can be truly human only as we trust and obey God. It is the lie that leads us to the futile, self-destructive attempt to live without and against our fellow human beings, when in fact we can be ourselves only when we live with them in mutual interdependence. Evil is the Big Lie that is so destructive and terrible just because it convinces us that the truth about God, God's world, and life in it is not the truth.

The real problem of evil is not how we can explain its origin. It is whether and how the death grip this lie has on all of us can be broken. That is what we must think about next.

THE LIGHT THAT SHINES IN THE DARKNESS

We have tried to be honest about the pain, suffering, and death that is part of our lives as creatures and that we inflict on ourselves and each other because of the evil that has invaded and corrupts our creaturely lives. Now we come back again to what the Christian doctrine of providence tells us about the love, justice, and power of God that shines in the darkness. From the very beginning of our discussion, we have not been able to talk as Christians about the darkness in which we live without catching a glimpse of the love of God that comes to us in it and the power of God over it. Now we have to bring into the foreground what so far has been in the background, and at the same time try to answer some of the unanswered questions we have raised.

When things go well with us and in the world around us, it is not hard to believe in a loving, just, and powerful God who "provides" for God's good creation. But when we experience tragic suffering in our own lives and see so much tragic suffering in the world, we wonder whether all talk about a loving and just God is not in fact the wishful thinking or whistling in the dark we mentioned earlier—talk by people who are not courageous enough to face up to the fact that we live in a godless and godforsaken world.

So long as we try to figure out for ourselves whether and how God is at work among us, our faith will always be uncertain and confused. But the Christian doctrine of providence is not based on what we can figure out for ourselves from our own experience or observation of the world, balancing evidence for and against faith in God. It is a *Christian* doctrine based on what scripture tells us about the presence and work of God in the story of ancient Israel and above all in Jesus Christ. That story, of course, is not proof that there is a God who comes to be with and for us in our suffering and triumphs over it. It is a confession of faith. But it is not a confession of faith based on wishful thinking of people who could not face up to the brutal facts of life as it really is and the bleak finality of suffering and death. It is a confession based on what Israel and the first Christians remembered that God had actually done in their personal experience and in the history of their people, and what they therefore hoped that God would continue to do in the future. Christians too may *begin* with all the questions and doubts about God anyone else has when they look at the darkness that invades their lives, but we *end* by interpreting our own and the world's history in light of the memory and hope of those ancient Jews and first Christians. Their memory and hope is our memory and hope too—and the basis of a Christian doctrine of providence.

The Memory and Hope of Israel

When we look at the story of the people of God in the Old Testament, we discover that sometimes God's providential care meant that God gave individuals and the people as a whole the life, health, and happiness they wanted and God promised to give them. But by and large the story of Israel is not the story of people whose lives were trouble-free, painless, and victorious because a powerful God loved and cared for them. Even their great God-chosen leaders experienced the same disappointments, failures, hardships, suffering, and death that other human beings experience. As a nation they were for brief periods of time powerful, prosperous, and victorious over their enemies; but for the most part theirs is a story of defeat and suffering of a people who were at the mercy of more powerful nations around them, a people who ended up homeless refugees or the victims of foreign powers that occupied their land.

The Old Testament writers are very realistic about the contradiction between what their life was really like and what they believed about the God who chose and promised to help them. The psalmist expresses it most clearly. Over and over again throughout the Psalms he complains about the distance, silence, absence, and hiddenness of God: Why have you abandoned me and your chosen people? Why have you gone to sleep on us? Why don't you wake up and do what you are supposed to do? Why don't you answer our prayers for help? Why do you let the rich and powerful oppress the poor and defenseless? Why do you let bad things happen to good people and good things to bad people? We find in the Psalms not orthodox confession of the "omnipresence" of God, but heretical confession of the omni-absence of God. Not triumphant confession of the "omnipotence" of God, but confession of the omnipotence of those who rape, oppress, and destroy the innocent, weak, and needy. Not confession of the saving love of God, but confession of a God who refuses help just when it is needed most. Not comforting assurance that God answers prayers, but bitter complaint that God refuses to answer prayers. Not "resting on the promises of God," but the hostile charge that God has not kept God's promises. In short, "My God, my God, why have you forsaken me?" (Ps. 22:1)—a shockingly honest acknowledgment of the experience of godlessness and godforsakenness in a suffering world.

Yet after the psalmist has given full vent to his frustration, anger, pain, and despair at the silence, absence, and hiddenness of God in his present experience, over and over again he remembers what God had done in his own past and in the past of his people. For instance: "I consider the days of old, and remember the years of long ago. . . . I will call to mind the deeds of the Lord; I will remember your wonders of old" (Ps. 77:5, 11). Repeatedly throughout the Psalms, the psalmist remembers and tells the story of times when God *was* present, *did* answer prayers, *did* act to help and save. And above all, he remembers and tells the story of how God liberated the people from the oppressor Pharaoh, fed and defended them when they wandered in the wilderness, gave them a land of their own and laws to guide and protect their life together.

Remembering the past gives hope for the future. Again and again the psalmist expresses his confidence that the God who *has* been present to help, protect, liberate, and save will do it again. The memory of the powerful love and justice of God in the *past* brings hope for the powerful love and justice of God in the *future*.

As a result, even in the godless and godforsaken present the psalmist can confess that the absent, silent, hidden God is nevertheless near and on the side of the brokenhearted, the crushed in spirit, the poor and those who have no helper, the weak and the needy (Psalms 34 and 72). Then he commits himself obediently to serve the loving and just God from whom he comes and toward whom he goes, the God who even now is present with him and his people. Memory of what God has done in the past and hope for what God will do in the future lead him to active service of God in anticipation of the liberation, justice, and peace that may not be here yet but are surely on the way.

That is the way it has always been with faithful Jews, even in our time when they have experienced the utter godlessness and godforsakenness of concentration camps and gas chambers. Some Jews (and some Christians) have concluded that since the Holocaust, when more than five million of God's chosen people were slaughtered, it is no longer possible to believe in God. Godlessness and godforsakenness and the utter despair that goes with them are all there is. But some who remember the ancient story of God's presence and work in the ancient story of "our people" still believe in God despite the Holocaust and keep on working for the justice and healing of the God who *has* liberated and who they are sure *will* liberate.

The Memory and Hope of the First Christians

The first Christians remembered Jesus. They remembered how he healed the sick, ministered to the brokenhearted, defended the cause of the poor and oppressed, forgave sinners, and announced the coming of the rule of God's justice and compassion in the world. But they also remembered that people did not want him—not even the good, law-abiding, pious people who were offended because he proclaimed and demonstrated the love of God not only for good people and insiders but also for unworthy sinners and outsiders, and because he proclaimed and demonstrated the justice of God that seeks not to punish and wipe out but to reconcile the enemies of God and God's people. They remembered how he was deserted by his friends, defeated by his enemies, the victim of all the powers of darkness and evil he came to combat. They remembered how the one they believed was God's representative on earth suffered and died on a criminal's cross with the despairing cry of the psalmist on his lips, "My God, my God, why have you forsaken me?" (Mark 15:34). They remembered how the kingdom of God he promised did *not* come and how the will of God was *not* done on earth as it is in heaven.

How then could these Christians nevertheless continue to believe in God and in the Jesus who came from God? They remembered not only Jesus' godforsaken death but the power of God that raised him from the dead, victorious over all the worst that the powers of evil, sin, injustice, and death could do against him. Jesus Christ is risen! Good Friday is not the last word about ourselves and the world we live in. The Christ who was the victim of evil is also the victor over evil. Easter Sunday means that God "has rescued us from the power of darkness and transferred us into the kingdom of his beloved Son" (Col. 1:13), one who has "disarmed the rulers and authorities and made a public example of them, triumphing over them" (Col. 2:15).

As a weak, despised, persecuted community who followed a crucified Messiah, the first Christians knew all too well in their own experience that after Easter Sunday the powers of darkness were still at work in and around them. But because they remembered the power of God that raised Jesus from the dead and made him to be not only their Lord but the Lord of the whole world, they were sure that however powerful the forces of evil may be, however much damage they may still do, they are doomed to failure in their attempt to take a throne that does not belong to them. These Christians, therefore, looked forward to the future with the absolute certainty that the justice and love of God that *had* been victorious *would* finally be victorious both in their own lives and in the world around them.

Even in their present experience they could see signs that their hope for the future was not in vain. The Spirit of the living Christ dwelt among them already here and now, reconciling men and women, rich and poor, Jew and Gentile, transforming enemies of God into friends of God, enabling them to lead joyful lives in the service of God. It was only a small beginning, but they were confident that what was happening among them was a "foretaste" of the whole new humanity in a whole new world that is surely on the way because the risen Christ who *will* be the Lord of the world is *already* its Lord.

The early Christians' memory of Jesus' resurrection also led them to remember the cross of Christ in a new way. It became for them a sign not only of Jesus' (and God's) powerlessness in the face of evil but also a sign of the love of Jesus (and God), which was so great that he (and the God who sent him) was willing to suffer and even die for needy, suffering, sinful people. If the memory of Jesus' resurrection meant confidence in God's liberating power over the powers of evil, the memory of Jesus' cross meant confidence in the self-giving, suffering love of a Christ (and God) who was present with them even in the depths of their suffering and dying. It meant that nothing could separate us from the "love of God in Christ Jesus our Lord" (Rom. 8:38–39).

Our Memory and Hope

We conclude this chapter by summarizing what a Christian doctrine of providence looks like that makes our own the memory and hope of God's people in scripture.

1. A Christian doctrine of providence based on the biblical story makes no cheap promises that if we will just trust in God, we will be spared the hardship, pain, and suffering that are the "dark side" of our creaturely existence and the result of the powers of darkness that have invaded God's good creation. Its confession of a loving and just God who cares about us and cares for us raises all the "why" questions that come when we face tragedy in our own lives, try to comfort loved ones and friends in their suffering, and look at the staggering power of evil and injustice in the world around us. It invites the honest acknowledgment of our experience of the silence, distance, and hiddenness of God. It does not try to silence but encourages us to ask with the psalmist and Jesus himself, "My God, my God, why have you forsaken me?"

2. A Christian doctrine of providence based on the witness of scripture to *the self-giving, suffering love* of God expects and recognizes the presence of God in the depths of tragedy and suffering, not just when we escape them.[5] God's sovereign power is not only God's willingness to save us from the hurts and hardships of life; it is God's willingness to share them with us. It is God's willingness to take our deserved and undeserved suffering into God's own life, suffering with and for us as our friend and companion in suffering, walking with us through the "valley of the shadow of death" to comfort and give us strength and courage to endure what must be endured. Could it be that sometimes God seems so far away because we look for God's presence only when things go well, when problems are solved and questions answered; and do not look for it where God also promises to be present with us—where everything falls apart in our own lives and in the world around us? (Think of the astounding confidence in God's love and justice expressed by some desperately poor and oppressed Christians in Latin America, Africa, and the United States—in contrast to the doubt expressed by some Christians whose lives are far more prosperous and comfortable.)

3. A Christian doctrine of providence based on the memory of God's self-giving love expects and recognizes God's presence in people who love enough to risk their own comfort and security to sit at the side of the sick and dying, befriend the friendless, accept the unacceptable, help those who cannot help themselves, defend the cause of the victims of injustices. This means that we can recognize God's presence when other

people minister to *us* in this way. It also means that in our turn we are invited to be instruments of God's providential care by our willingness to minister to other people in this way. We must be aware of the consequences of such a statement, however. It is the invitation not to escape but deliberately to accept suffering on our part—the suffering that inevitably comes when we stand with and by and for others who suffer. But when that kind of suffering comes to us, it is not grounds for doubting the love of God but for thanksgiving that we are given the great honor and privilege of bearing witness to it. That kind of suffering and hardship is not a sign of the distance, silence, and indifference of God but precisely of the presence of God in our godless and godforsaken world. (Was the suffering and death of Martin Luther King Jr. for the sake of racial justice a sign of God's absence or of God's presence in the world?)

4. A Christian doctrine of providence based on biblical witness to the liberating power of God's love that delivered Israel from bondage and raised Jesus from the dead knows that God is so powerful that evil must finally serve God's good will for our sake. God does not will evil; evil is what God does *not* will. Nevertheless God's power is so great that it can make good come out of evil.

In the Old Testament we see this most clearly perhaps in the story of Joseph and his brothers. Against everything God wills for family relationships, they sold their own brother into slavery. Yet their act of inhuman rebellion against God and their hostility toward him made it possible for Joseph to become a ruler in Egypt who could save them when famine came. "You meant evil against me," Joseph said, "but God meant it for good" (Gen. 50:20, RSV). This is a good example of how God's providential care works both *through* and *despite* free human action.

The same point is made even more clearly in the death and resurrection of Christ. God did not will the sin and injustice that led the political and religious leaders, and in their own way even Jesus' own disciples, to reject Jesus and the kingdom of God's love and justice he served. Yet it was precisely their rejection that made possible the salvation of the world through the Christ whom God raised from the dead. Just where evil seemed to triumph most completely, just there it served the powerful, liberating love of God.

This does not mean that evil is secretly good. It does not mean that we may do evil in order that good may come from it. It does not mean that we ought to try to comfort ourselves and others too quickly and piously by assuring ourselves and them that the tragedy, suffering, and injustice are not really so bad after all because it is for our own good. But it does mean that God's love is so powerful that when all is said and done even the worst manifestations of evil must finally serve God's good will for us and for the world that was and is and will be *God's* world.

5. A doctrine of providence based on the memory of the biblical story of the suffering love and liberating power of God enables us to live in hope for the future even when present experience seems to offer no hope. For all of us sometimes and for many people around the world most of the time, present experience seems to point only to the absence, silence, and distance of God—if there is a God. For all of us sometimes and for many people most of the time, present experience seems to bear indisputable evidence that we live in a godless and godforsaken world. But faith in a loving and just God is not based either on good or on bad experience in the present. It is based on what God has done—sometimes in our own little personal histories and above all in the history of God's people. It is that memory of God that enables us to hope, despite all evidence to the contrary, that the God who *has* been at work in self-giving love and liberating power in our lives and in the world *will* be at work in self-giving love and liberating power.

6. Remembering what God has done in the past and promises to do in the future, a biblical doctrine of providence recognizes signs *here* and *now* of God's presence and work in our lives and the world around us. The final victory of God over the powers of darkness and evil is yet to come, but even in our present experience there are little, provisional, temporary victories that announce and anticipate the big final victory that is coming. Here and now, once in a while, now and then, here and there, sickness is healed, life is spared, justice triumphs over injustice, war gives way to peace, people who are suspicious of each other and hate each other are reconciled—light breaks into our darkness. These little victories are signs that our memory and hope for the love and justice of God are not just wishful thinking. They are *experienced* indications that our memory is true and that our hope is not in vain. They are *experienced* promises of more to come.

7. These little victories, provisional and temporary though they may be, give us courage and confidence despite all the opposition and setbacks, failures and defeat we experience in a godless and godforsaken world, to keep up our struggle for the rule of God's love and justice that

has come, *is* coming, and is already *on the way* in our individual lives and in the lives of all people everywhere. Chapter 10.5 of the Declaration of Faith puts it this way:

> We know that our efforts cannot bring in God's kingdom.
> But hope plunges us into the struggle
> for victories over evil that are possible now
> in the world, the church, and our individual lives.
> Hope gives us courage and energy
> to contend against all opposition,
> however invincible it may seem,
> for the world and the new humanity that are surely coming.

We do live in a dark world. But there is a light shining in the darkness, and the darkness will not be able to overcome it. How do we know? Because even in the darkest days and years we remember the God from whom we come; therefore hope in the God toward whom we go; and therefore, despite everything, can recognize and serve the God who goes with us on our way.

FOR FURTHER REFLECTION AND STUDY

1. Is death evil?
2. How would you answer a friend or loved one dying of cancer who asked you, "Why does God let this happen to me?"
3. What would you say to someone whose response to his or her own or another's suffering is, "We must accept the will of God"?
4. Having looked at the various explanations for the "origin" of evil, where do *you* think evil comes from?
5. Should Christians believe in a personal devil? Do you?
6. How do you think we should respond to Jews and Christians who agree with those who say that since the Holocaust it is impossible to believe in God?
7. The whole book of Job wrestles with the problem of suffering and especially why God allows good people to suffer. Finally, after hearing all Job's complaints and questions, God answers him (chapters 38–41). What is God's answer? What is Job's response? Do you think this is a satisfactory answer to Job's question?
8. Does a good end justify evil means (a) in the case of a war to bring peace? (b) in the case of excluding some people for the sake of peace and the numerical and financial security of a church? (c) in

the case of lying on income tax reports for the sake of my family's welfare?

9. As you look at your own life and at the world around you, would you say that there is more experiential evidence for or against the existence of a loving, just, and powerful God?
10. Many theologians today are arguing that the Christian answer to the problem of evil lies in "memory and hope." Do you find this a satisfactory answer?

10

Who Are We?

The Doctrine of Human Beings

Suppose you were a long way from home, got involved in a conversation with a total stranger whom you instinctively liked, and he or she suddenly asked, "Who are you, anyway?" Stop now and make a list of ten or more things you would say to identify yourself. (Why is it easier to be honest about ourselves with people we never expect to see again?)

When you have finished, ask yourself more directly, "Who am I?" Add to the list those things too "close to home" to tell even a stranger.

After you have finished your whole list, go through it and underline what you think are the most important facts or characteristics.

Now analyze your list with the following questions:

1. Do the most important things come first? last? What is the significance of their place on the list?

2. How many items on your list identify your public and private image of yourself in terms of personal relationships (married, single, parents, children, friends, associates)? How many items are not relational (purely intellectual or physical)?

3. Which of the following categories are emphasized and which are left out: *politics* (nationality, party, conservative or liberal convictions), *economics* (business or profession, indications of financial status and needs), *religion* (church affiliation, reference to God), *physiology* (sex, state of health, physical characteristics, age) *culture* (racial or ethnic identity, degree of education, artistic tastes, leisure time activities), *psychology* (expressions of happiness or unhappiness, loneliness, fears and anxieties, likes and dislikes)? What is the significance of your emphases and omissions?

4. Are there contradictions in your list—items that express not so much what you are as what you *wish* you were, think you *ought* to be, want other people to *think* you are?

5. Which of the items would you say are essential to your basic humanity? Which are incidental? Which are destructive of your basic humanity?

If you were honest (or at least if you are like all the rest of us), the analysis of your list probably yields two basic conclusions:

First, all of us tend to understand ourselves primarily in terms of a few areas of our lives and to forget or ignore the very important influence of other areas. That means we have a dangerously limited understanding of ourselves. Moreover, it is very difficult to fit even the various facts about ourselves we *are* aware of into a unified picture. In fact, the more different factors we take into consideration, the harder it is to know who we really are.

Second, as soon as we try to explain to others or to ourselves who we are, we run into some disturbing self-contradictions. Why can't we *be* what we know we are? Why is there such a gap between what we know about ourselves deep down and the way we actually live?

We will deal with the first of these problems in this chapter and with the second in the next chapter. Meanwhile, save your list to see whether you would change it when you have finished these two chapters.

Our questions now are these: What does it mean to be a "human" being? What were we talking about in previous chapters when we spoke about "true," or "genuine," humanity? More directly, Who *are* we? Who am I?

Before we begin discussing the Christian doctrine of human beings, we need to say something about how it is related to what we can learn from all the various sciences that study human nature and behavior. Experts in such modern disciplines as biology, sociology, cultural anthropology, and political and economic sciences can tell us some important things about ourselves that the ancient biblical writers did not know and that modern preachers and theologians cannot tell us. If we know that all truth comes from God, we need not be afraid to learn everything these "secular" disciplines have to teach us. But the task of a Christian doctrine of human beings is to do two things they cannot do:

1. Each of the sciences we have mentioned gives us a one-sided, fragmentary, partial, and therefore distorted understanding of human life from one particular perspective. The task of Christian theology is to fit all the pieces of information they give us about various aspects

("phenomena") of human life into a unified total view of what it means to be a human being. But how can we do that?

2. The sciences understand what it means to be human without reference to God. Christians believe that in entering into human life and history, God revealed not only who *God* is but also who *we* are. Although our faith does not replace (but in fact needs) all we can learn about ourselves from all kinds of other sources, it does add a dimension to our self-understanding we can discover no place else. The task of Christian theology is to interpret everything we know—or think we know—about ourselves from other sources in light of what the will and work of the God we come to know in scripture tells us about the meaning and purpose of our lives.

Our study in this chapter will be guided by this twofold understanding of the unique task of a Christian doctrine of human beings.

CREATURES IN THE IMAGE OF GOD

Like all other animals, human beings are born, eat, sleep, procreate, struggle for survival in an indifferent or hostile environment, fight a losing battle with death, and return to dust. What is it that makes us distinctively *human,* different from other animals? Traditional Christian theology answers that we are created "in the image of God" (Gen. 1:27). But different Christians in different times and situations have had very different ideas about what that means. Very often, instead of asking how scripture understands this concept, they have simply understood it in light of the self-understanding they had before they opened the Bible, then read into the Bible what they already thought about what it means to be human. We will look first at some of the more popular of these "inserted" views of the image of God and then at what most contemporary theologians believe the Bible itself means by it.

Rationality?

Western civilization in general has followed the ancient Greek belief that it is the capacity to reason that makes human beings human and like God. It is not surprising, then, that Western Christianity assumed for centuries that "image of God" means ability to reason and act in accordance with what is reasonable and rational. (Whatever you may think theoretically about this, did it occur to you to say "I am a rational animal" when asked who you are?) But although the Bible does not deny that we are thinking beings and shows no contempt for the intellect, nowhere does it suggest that this is the key to our humanity. On the contrary, it knows what modern psychology has also taught us—that a person may be quite rational and logical, yet diabolically or pathetically inhuman.

The Soul?

Another understanding of the image of God is that it is the "spiritual" side of human nature or the soul. This view also comes from the ancient Greeks, who believed that the human soul is divine (of the same "essence" as God) and that the body is only the "house" or even the "prison" in which the human (basically divine) self lives. (Did it occur to you to say "I am an immortal soul" when asked who you are?) But popular as this view has been in the church, it is not biblical. The creation story (like scripture in general) does make a distinction between body and soul. Genesis 2:7 says that the Lord "formed man from the dust of the ground and breathed into his nostrils the breath of life" so that the man became a "living being," or "living soul." But in this passage (and in scripture as a whole) the soul is not the inward, "divine" part of human beings; it is simply the "breath of life" that makes us living creatures. All the birds and beasts have this "breath of life" too (Gen. 1:30). Nor does this passage (or scripture as a whole) imply that the bodily side of human life is an inferior part of our being. This passage must be read along with Genesis 1:27, which identifies the image of God precisely with the *physical* life of human beings as male and female. In short, we cannot understand the biblical doctrine of the image of God in terms of a body-soul split. In the Bible human beings are not essentially spiritual *or* physical. Whatever our basic humanity is, it has to do with our *whole* being, spiritual *and* physical, body *and* soul in their inseparable interrelatedness. It is as *embodied* souls (or life) and *besouled* (or living) bodies that we are created in the image of God. (We will return to the relation between soul and body in the last chapter when we discuss Christian hope for the future as hope for the "resurrection of the body" rather than as hope for the "immortality of the soul." Meanwhile you may want to look up *soul* in a biblical or theological dictionary.)

Moral Capacity?

Still another possibility is to identify the distinctive character of a human being, and thus what makes a human being like God, as the human capacity to make moral judgments and the freedom to live by them. Sometimes this is the interpretation given to the statements in

Reformed confessions that identify the image of God with the godlike "righteousness" or "holiness" human beings originally possessed (see Heidelberg Catechism, Q. 6; Second Helvetic Confession, 8; Westminster Confession, 4.2). We will have to return presently to what this "original righteousness" does mean. Now it is important to say that in the Bible it does not refer to an independent moral capacity of human beings to know right and wrong and to act accordingly. On the contrary, the first human beings were forbidden to eat of "the tree of the knowledge of good and evil" (Gen. 2:17). It is the temptation of Satan and rebellion against God to desire to be good and know the good for ourselves (Gen. 3:5). To want a righteousness of one's own is to be ignorant of the true righteousness that comes from God (Rom. 10:2–4). Like Paul when he was still the persecutor of the church and of Christ himself, one can be "blameless under the law" and still be the enemy of God. The legally moral person is not necessarily genuinely human and godlike. Sometimes it is just the most moral people who are the most inhumanly unforgiving, unloving, insensitive to the needs of others, and unwilling or unable to let themselves be loved and forgiven. To be a morally responsible agent does not in itself make a person to be a truly human person in the image of God.

Power and Dominion?

A very modern (and very ancient) interpretation holds that it is will-to-power that is the most essential characteristic of human beings and that makes them godlike—their ability to exercise dominion and power over other creatures. As we have already seen in chapter 8, some have thought they found biblical justification for this interpretation in God's commandment that human beings created in God's image should "subdue the earth" and "have dominion" over all other creatures (Gen. 1:28). Some have also quoted Gen. 3:16 to argue that God also created men to "rule over" women. This interpretation has resulted in a hierarchical understanding of human life in the world: As God rules over the world, so human beings are to dominate other creatures, and men are the masters of women. The relation between all individuals and groups is understood as the assertion of power of "superiors" over "inferiors." This is a fatal misunderstanding both of God's power and of the power God gives to human beings created in God's image. God exercises divine power not to dominate and control but to protect, help, and defend all God's creatures. God gives power to human beings created in God's image not to dominate and control their natural environment but to care for it; not to dominate and control any of their fellow human beings but to live together with them as friends and partners. (Genesis 3:16 does not describe the relation God intends for men and women; that passage describes their relation as fallen, sinful creatures who are no longer the "partners" God originally intended them to be according to Gen. 2:18.) Power in itself does not make us to be human beings in the image of God; power may be an expression of rebellion against what God created us to be and do.

A Biblical Understanding

Suppose we gave up the attempt to tell ourselves what it means to be human beings in the image of God by analyzing ourselves and identifying it with this or that capacity, quality, or endowment we find in ourselves. Suppose we remembered that what we find when we analyze ourselves is not the human beings God created us to be but *sinful* human beings for whom rationality, spirituality, moral consciousness, power, or other characteristics of the human species become instruments for our self-contradictory, self-destructive refusal and inability to be what God created us to be. Suppose that instead of interpreting what scripture says about our creation in the image of God to confirm the self-understanding we already have, we read the Bible to give us a *new* self-understanding. What would a genuinely biblical understanding of human life in the image of God look like?

Jesus as True Human Being in God's Image

If we want to see what it means to be human beings in God's image, we cannot look first at the story of Adam and Eve in Genesis. Theirs is the story of people who from the very beginning, with the very first act we hear about, refused to be what God created them to be. They are the prime example for all time of what human life in the image of God does *not* look like. To find what we are looking for, we must go to the New Testament. There we hear about a "Second Adam" who was what Adam and Eve (and every man and woman since) were unwilling and unable to be (Rom. 5:15–21; 1 Cor. 15:45–49). *He* is the human being who is "the image of the invisible God" (Col. 1:15), "the likeness of God" (2 Cor. 4:4, RSV), "in the form of God" (Phil. 2:6). Jesus Christ is the true human being, the one who in everything he said and did lived out a truly human life in God's image, the one in whom we learn what it means for us to be true human beings in the image of God.

What is the true humanity we see in Jesus? Not his wisdom or rationality. Those who saw him only as a wise man and teacher missed the point completely. Not his otherworldly spirituality, religious piety, or even morality. He went to parties, was accused of being a glutton and drunkard, was the friend of prostitutes and dishonest business men and political revolutionaries, broke the laws of Sabbath observance, and was completely unconcerned about what good, pious, law-abiding people thought about him (Mark 2:15–27). And certainly it was not his use of power to dominate and control. He came not to lord it over others but to give himself for them; not to rule but to serve.

What made Jesus the unique person he was? Not any of the internal, self-contained personal attributes or qualities traditionally identified with human life in the image of God. It was the way he lived. He was the one person who lived completely for God and in thankful obedience to God, and completely for fellow human beings and for their good. This does not mean that he was the weak, passive, "selfless" man we often think of him as being. On the contrary, he was a strong, self-assertive man who let nothing and no one keep him from loving God and loving his fellow human beings (not just some of them, but all of them, especially those who were despised, rejected, and oppressed). Neither the political and religious authorities nor Satan could force or scare or bribe him into turning away from the life of God-serving and other-serving justice and compassion he was committed to.

What we learn from Jesus, then, is that to be truly human in the image of God is not to possess some intellectual, moral, or spiritual capacity *within* ourselves; it is realized only in relatedness, community, or fellowship with others *outside* ourselves. We cannot be human by ourselves in independent, self-sufficient loneliness. Only as we discover the meaning of our very existence in relatedness to God and fellow human beings can we be truly human. And just then we discover that this means not the sacrifice but the realization of true human selfhood.

The Creation of Human Beings in the Image of God

If we give up the attempt to read our own self-understanding into what the Old Testament stories tell us about the meaning of our creation in God's image and listen to what they actually say, we discover that they confirm what we learn by looking at Jesus' humanity. Genesis 2:18 says, "It is not good that the man should be alone; I will make him a helper as his partner." So, according to Gen. 1:27, "God created humankind in his own image, . . . *male* and *female* he created them" (emphasis added). Nothing is said about how human beings are different from and superior to other creatures because they are intellectually, morally, or spiritually gifted in a unique way. On the contrary, to be human beings in God's image is first of all to have something *in common* with all other animals—sexuality! What in the world does the sex and sexuality of human males and females have to do with God and the image of God?

In order to understand this connection, we have to remember what we have learned about who the God is in whose image we are created. The God of the Bible does not dwell in lonely, self-sufficient sovereign power. This God is a covenant-making God who creates human beings in order to have fellowship with them, a God who seeks to be with and for them as their friend, companion, and helper. (Even within God's own being, we have learned, God is not a lonely "I" but a Trinitarian community of "persons" who are distinct from each other yet united in mutual love.)

It is because God is a God who seeks community with us and wills that we live in community with each other that God created us as male and female. To be male or female means that we cannot find our humanity in isolated, autonomous individuality. We can find it only in fellowship with an "other" and with "others" outside of and different from ourselves. Human beings differ from other animals (when they *are* different!) in that this orientation toward others is not purely instinctive or automatic but freely chosen and personal. It is first of all a personal relation between human creatures and their Creator in which there is mutual openness to speak and listen, ask questions and give answers, love and receive love in return. And it is a similar relation between human creatures themselves. As God is spontaneously and freely with and for us, so we are created to be spontaneously and freely with and for one another.

The humanity we see fulfilled in Jesus, in other words, is the same humanity God originally intended and still intends for all human beings. It is a humanity that uses whatever intellectual, spiritual, moral, or physical powers we possess in and for the sake of fellowship with God and our fellow human beings. In the rest of this chapter we will investigate in more detail what such a humanity in God's image looks like.

FELLOWSHIP WITH GOD

Truly human community among human beings is a fellowship of equal partners. But human community with God is a partnership of *unequal* partners, a "superior" Creator and "inferior" creatures. Some have believed that we can assert human dignity and freedom only if we rebel against this "above-below" relationship and assert our independence from God. But let us look at what it means when we remember what it means for us to be creatures in the image of God.

Creatures of God: Our Total Dependence on God

To say that we are God's creatures is to emphasize our total dependence on God. The doctrine of creation is a constant warning against all human arrogance. None of us is or can be a self-sufficient, independent, "self-made" person. Everything we have comes from God, even the breath of life itself. God has authority over us and gives us commands to tell us how we should live, and whether it goes well or ill with us depends on whether we recognize God's authority and obey God's commands. If God were a different kind of God, our dependence on God would indeed be a threat to our "life, liberty, and pursuit of happiness." If God were concerned only about God's own majesty and power over us, we might still have to admit our dependence because God is bigger than we are, but we would do it only grudgingly and resentfully. But the God upon whom we are dependent is a God who is *for* us, who promises to give us everything we need to achieve true life, liberty, and happiness; a God who exercises authority and gives commands precisely to set us free for genuinely human lives. Dependence on *this* God, therefore, is not reason for resentment but for thanksgiving. Acknowledgment of total dependence—with thanksgiving—is the first characteristic of a right relationship with God.

Creatures in God's Image: Partnership with God

Faith in God is not just a matter of depending on God for everything we need. Nor is it a matter of obeying God's commands because they turn out to be in our own best interests. A dog has that kind of relationship with its owner! By emphasizing too exclusively our total dependence on God, the church has sometimes given the impression that to believe in God is to be a weak, passive pet waiting to be fed. By talking too exclusively about why people "need" God, we have encouraged the whining or hostile question "What can God (or the church) do for me?" or "What do I get out of believing in God (or going to church)?" We have nourished the attitude that being a Christian means going to church only to ask God for what we need, and to thank God for what God has given us and done for us. No wonder strong, healthy people are bored with such a religion and rebel against a God who treats us as if we were pet dogs!

To acknowledge God as our Creator and ourselves as God's creatures does remind us of our dependence on God. But human beings are not only creatures of God; they are creatures uniquely created in God's own image. We are creatures God has equipped and empowered to be God's partners to participate in God's own work in and for the world. We are "junior partners," to be sure, but nonetheless true partners whom God has invited and commanded to join God's "business" of preserving and caring for the world of nature, doing justice and showing compassion in human society, sharing the suffering of those who suffer, and using power to free those who are enslaved and oppressed by their own or others' sinfulness. The humanity of those created in God's image is anything but purely passive. It is the active, aggressive humanity of people who are given and accept responsibility for the cause of God in the world. To talk about our relationship with God only in terms of dependence is not a mark of genuine piety. It is to reject the very God upon whom we are dependent and to reject our own true humanity in God's image.

It is of course as dangerous to overemphasize our partnership with God as to overemphasize our dependence upon God. We are in fact only junior partners. God has not turned God's business over to us to run as we see fit, according to our own agenda. It is *God's* will and *God's* work, not our own or the church's, that creatures in God's image are created and empowered to do. We do not need to resent this "inferior" status "under" God. On the contrary, we may be grateful for it. It means that we do not have to take on ourselves the terrible burden of figuring out for ourselves how we and other people ought to live. Nor are we left alone to defend the cause of God by ourselves, with our own resources. We can count on the guidance and support of a superior Power who is infinitely wiser, more loving and just, and more concerned about our own and others' welfare than we will ever be.

A right relationship with the God who has created us in God's own image involves thankful dependence on a God who wills and enables us to be free human beings, *and* it involves obedient commitment to serve a God whose help we must but also can always depend on. Dependence on God and human freedom/responsibility are not contradictions. They are two sides of the same coin.

HUMAN LIFE IN COMMUNITY

To be a human being in God's image is to live in fellowship not only with God but also with our fellow human beings. People who seek escape from life in community into a life of safe independence and self-sufficiency seek to escape their own humanity. True humanity is by definition co-humanity.[1]

In order to grasp what this means, let us go back to the question we raised earlier: What is the significance of the fact that Gen. 1:27 identifies creation in the image of God with the creation of human beings as male and female? We can best understand what it means in contrast to what it does *not* mean.

1. It does not mean that because human beings in the image of God are either male or female, God must be one or the other or have the attributes of both. As we have already emphasized in chapter 5, God is neither male nor female nor a combination of the two. It is the *kind of relationship* God intended between human beings, not sexuality as such, that is the meaning of our creation in God's image as male and female.

2. Our creation as male or female does not mean that only married or "sexually active" people are fully human, and that therefore "sexually inactive" people who never marry or who are divorced or widowed (not to mention children!) are somehow less than human. Jesus, *the* true human being and our example of true humanity in the image of God, was not married, nor so far as we know was he sexually active. It is not marriage or sexual intercourse as such but what our creation as male or female tells us about how God intends us to live with and for one another that is the clue to the meaning of our being in the image of God.

3. Our creation as male or female does not mean that only relationships between people of the opposite sex are genuinely human. Scripture is full of stories of friends, companions, and fellow-workers of the same sex who commit themselves to each other in faithful, loving relationships: David and Jonathan, Naomi and Ruth, Jesus and his disciples, for instance. Such relationships should not be interpreted to mean that scripture blesses same-sex or homosexual love (in fact, scripture sometimes expressly condemns it). But they do raise the question whether the key issue in evaluating both homosexual *and* heterosexual relationships might not be whether they are marked by faithfulness or promiscuity, commitment to one another or simply using one another for self-gratification or self-fulfillment, affirmation or denial of the maleness or femaleness of the other.

4. Our creation in God's image as male and female does not bless any of the ancient or modern stereotypes of the proper role of males and females. It does not imply, for instance, that males are the rational, aggressive, strong, superior sex whose role is to go out and conquer the world; whereas females are the emotional, passive, weak, inferior sex whose role is to stay home, decorate the house, cook, and care for the children. Nor does it say, as some do who protest traditional patriarchical social patterns, that women are more personal, sharing, relation-oriented, cooperative, caring, and gentle; whereas men are more impersonal, self-centered, unfeeling, competitive, and insensitive to the needs of others. The creation story says nothing about just how men and women are to live together except that God intended them to love and care for each other as "partners" who support and help each other, neither superior to the other. (Paul, a first-century Jew for whom the patriarchical arrangement of society seemed normal, did not always remember this. But in Galatians 3:28 he says that the above-below distinction between Jew and Gentile, slave and free, male and female is overcome in Christ.)[2]

5. Finally, our creation in the image of God as male and female does not mean that our humanity is fulfilled only in individual personal relationships. The biblical story is not just the story of how God created and enabled individual men and women to fulfill themselves in private interpersonal relationship with each other. It is the story of how God called them into the larger community of God's people Israel and the church. It is the story of how, as individuals and as a community, their humanity in the image of God was fulfilled (or more often, *not* fulfilled) in just and compassionate social, political, and economic relationships. The kind of relationship God intended for male and female, in other words, is a basic model, or prototype, for the kind of relationship God wills also for groups of people of different races, classes, cultures, and nations.

In criticizing false ideas of the connection between the image of God and our existence as male and female, we have already suggested what the true connection is. Humanity in the image of God is realized not just in human relatedness in general but in the relatedness of individuals and groups who are *different* from each other—as different as male and female. It is safer, easier, and more comfortable to seek the company of others who are just like us—same sex, same race, same cultural background, same political ideology, same national heritage. We are disturbed, frightened, suspicious of, and threatened by people who are not "like us," not "our kind of people." They are "the enemy." But when we are willing to associate with, befriend, and love only other people who are a mirror image of ourselves, we run from genuine human relatedness in order to be alone with ourselves. It is only when we risk life together precisely with those who are *not* like us, *not* our kind of people, that we discover who we ourselves are and what it means to be human beings created in the image of the Creator who chose to be with and for us creatures, and created *us* for community with others who are different from us.

We can make this togetherness-in-difference clearer by discussing some of the most fundamental ways in which it happens in both our personal and social relationships.

WAYS HUMAN BEINGS RELATE TO EACH OTHER

In the following discussion we will consider the ways in which people most commonly relate to one another. It is important to emphasize that people who are more or less limited in their ability to communicate with one another in these usual ways can be just as human, sometimes *more* human, than others who are more fortunate. Blind people can sometimes "see" more clearly, and be more willing to let themselves be seen as they are, than some others with 20/20 vision. People who cannot speak can sometimes "say" more than others who speak all too easily, quickly, and often. People who cannot hear are sometimes more sensitive to what is really being said and what is really going on than others who hear every word. People with physical disabilities sometimes help others in ways that go far beyond ordinary means of helping. They remind us that every one of us is "handicapped" and in need of help in one way or another. Some of them set an example for all of us in their ability graciously and thankfully to receive help.

Seeing and Being Seen

The most basic form of human encounter is looking one another in the eye. How can we be with or for one another if we do not first *see* one another? There are many ways we deny our own and others' humanity by not seeing. Sometimes we do not bother even to look (as when we cannot remember which waiter in a restaurant is ours, though we have spoken with him). Sometimes we deliberately avoid seeing (as when we carefully do not see the people in the slum section we drive through to work every day). Sometimes we do not see real people but only abstract categories: "Jews," "Catholics," "foreigners," "conservatives" or "liberals," "women" or "men," or people of this or that race. "They're all alike, you know."

Just as dehumanizing as not seeing is not letting ourselves *be* seen. Instead of being open enough to let other people see us as who we really are, we "act like" the Business Man, the Business Woman, the Mother, the Father, the Conservative or the Liberal—whatever role we assume and image we try to project. We all have functions to fulfill, but when we use the function as a mask to hide behind, we make it impossible really to do what our function requires just because we avoid genuinely interpersonal human relationships.

To see and let ourselves be seen can be painful. We have to risk involvement with others' needs and problems. We have to admit our own fallibility and vulnerability. It is easier and safer to have eyes but not to see and to retreat behind our masks. But we do so at the great price of our own and others' humanity.

Speaking and Listening

Important as they are, looks can be deceiving. To know others by sight alone is not yet really to know them. To judge by appearance alone is often to gain a false impression. Real human encounter does not take place until speaking and listening are added to seeing and being seen. When we speak to each other, we are saying, "Let me explain to you who I am, and let me tell you who I think you are. Let me tell you something you don't know but need to know about me and my impression of you." We take each other seriously enough to share ourselves and to try to understand one another. "I have nothing to say to her" or "We are not speaking" means a deliberate denial of the very thing that makes us human beings.

Speaking is useless without listening. Willingness to listen to what others are saying (not just waiting for them to stop talking so I can talk) says, "I do not really know you, but I want to. I want to give you a chance to correct the false impression I may have of you. I believe that you have something to tell me I need to learn." Listening is perhaps even more important than speaking as a way of taking another person seriously. "He has nothing to say that could possibly interest me" or "I wasn't listening" or "Shut up!" means the refusal to accept another person as a human being—and therefore also the denial of our own humanity.

Words, of course, may be dishonest words, empty words, or mere propaganda. They can prevent as well as establish real communication. But there can be no communication *without* words. "Human relations" means willingness to *speak* (with the intention of clarifying and not concealing the truth) and to *listen* (with openness to change my mind as a result of what I hear). Speaking and listening are an absolute prerequisite for all genuine human community between individuals (husbands and wives, children and parents, friends and enemies, fellow workers) and between groups of people who are "strangers" to each other because of differences of religion, race, class, culture, political ideology, or national identity. It is no accident that the one person who has ever lived out a genuinely human life in the image of God was called "the Word."

Helping and Being Helped

We have not really seen or heard each other in a human way until we understand and respond to our encounter as a mutual call for assistance. When we recognize one another's humanity, we learn that to be human is to depend not only on God but on one another. As human beings we need each other's help.

All helping is not human. Sometimes when we help others we are only playing God. We go to our neighbors in need as superior to inferior, wise to foolish, strong to weak, good to sinful. We think we are competent to give them good advice and tell them what they ought to do so that they can become as wise, strong, and virtuous as we are. Then we are offended because they are not properly grateful for the patronizing help they know we have offered only to justify ourselves and control them!

Sometimes we are kind to other people only to put them in our debt so that we can make them pay off in one way or another for services rendered, or manipulate them into being and doing what we want. ("How can you act that way, after all I have done for you?")

At other times, we are only salving our own guilty consciences when we help others. What is really important to us is not their need but our own peace of mind and the warm glow we get from having done a good deed. ("I couldn't live with myself or be happy unless I helped others.")

There are two prerequisites for genuinely human help of one another. First, we must recognize that the help we can give anyone is very limited. We cannot heal the deepest hurts, relieve the torments and consequences of guilt, wipe out the crippling effects of wrongs suffered and inflicted. Most of the time we do not really know ourselves what is good for others. The most we can do is stand by them in their need, giving them what support we can, aware that we are only fellow human beings, not their saviors.

Second, our help of others will be genuinely human when we acknowledge that we need *their* help as much as they need ours. It is especially difficult for people who write and read books like this one to grasp this truth. When we deal with people who are different from us, we are often more aware of their need for us than of our need for them. But if some people need our love and forgiveness because they are guilty of sins we do not commit, perhaps we need their love and forgiveness for the self-righteousness we demonstrate when we condescend to offer them our love and forgiveness. If we think those who stridently protest racism and sexism in church and society need to learn from us how to work for change in a decent and orderly way, perhaps we need to learn from them what it means to have a passionate, uncompromising commitment to justice. Perhaps some of the people on welfare rolls we want to teach to be more responsible in caring for themselves and their families can teach us that it is equally important not to be so busy accumulating wealth and possessions that we have no time left to give our families the love and attention they need more than anything else. Perhaps some of the people we care for in our shelters for the homeless can teach us how to face hardship and suffering with dignity, courage, and faith. In our own way all of us need to be helped by others. Only when we are not too blind or too proud to acknowledge the help *we* need will we be able to give others the help *they* need.

"Then the Lord God said, 'It is not good that the man should be alone; I will make him a helper as his partner,' " (Gen. 2:18). To be a human being in the image of God means to help and let ourselves be helped, recognizing our mutual dependence on one another.

ME, MYSELF, AND I

We have emphasized as strongly as possible that human life in the image of God is life in community with God and fellow human beings. This means that Christians must stand firmly against all "rugged individualism." The individualistic desire to be independent, self-sufficient, and self-centered is inhuman.

Having said that, now we must add finally that the doctrine of creation in the image of God preserves *individuality* just as strongly as it condemns *individualism.* A genuine relationship between ourselves and others is possible only when there is a distinction between us in which we remain who we are and others remain who they are. To attempt to do away with our own or others' unique individuality is to make a real relationship between us impossible, and is just as inhuman as individualism. There is a kind of Christian talk about self-denial, self-sacrifice, and tolerance that is profoundly inhuman and unchristian. And there is a kind of self-assertion, often regarded by Christians with suspicion, that is genuinely human and Christian.

Think first of our relation to God. There is a kind of spirituality in which people seek such complete unity with God that they literally try to "lose" themselves in God. In giving themselves totally to prayer, meditation, and devotional exercises they seek so completely to deny themselves that there is no longer any self-awareness but only God-awareness. But such spirituality means not only that they have abandoned their fellow human beings in their exclusive (and paradoxically self-centered) concern for unity with God, but that any real relationship with God is impossible. It is far better, like Job or Jeremiah or the psalmist, to "get mad" at God, argue or even fight with God, than to be so "spiritual" that no dialogue or confrontation is possible either from God's side or from mine, because I have in fact withdrawn myself from God by trying to pretend that there is no difference between us, who we are, and what we think and want.

Or take the husband-wife relationship. Sometimes a husband or wife thinks that to love the partner means to sacrifice all one's own desires, likes and dislikes, interests and concerns, for the sake of the other. ("Whatever you say, dear.") One simply dissolves himself or herself into the other, becoming a carbon copy of the other. ("They've been married so long you can't tell them apart.") Such a relationship may make for "peace" in a marriage, but it is not love. It really means that one partner has so withdrawn from the other or has been so absorbed into the other that real loving and being loved are impossible. How can one love and be loved if he or she is not even there any more? It takes two individual, self-affirming persons to make a marriage. There can be no "we" unless there are two "I's."

A political or social community that tramples individual rights (including the right not to conform to prevailing conservative *or* liberal "correct thinking") is no more a genuine community than one in which the insistence on individual rights is really an excuse for social irresponsibility and anarchy. As individuals exist only in social relationships, so societies can endure only when the variety and uniqueness of individuals are not only allowed but protected and encouraged. There are no individual rights without civil rights, and no civil rights without individual rights.

Interreligious dialogue between representatives of different Christian traditions or between Christians and followers of other religious traditions is not dialogue at all when the two parties are so "tolerant" of each other and so eager to make peace between the two camps that they cover over, ignore, or deny the real theological and ethical differences between them. When that happens, how can either side have anything interesting to say to the other or learn anything new from the other? Might not unquestioning agreement with whatever others say actually mean *indifference* toward them, a sign that we do not want to be bothered by the difficulty of a serious conversation with them? And might we not show that we really care about them and respect what they believe just when we take the time and trouble to lay out for them who we are and why we believe what we do, invite them to do the same for us, and then have a friendly but honest debate about our differences? So long as both sides demonstrate a genuine openness to listen and learn as well as eagerness to speak and instruct, cannot self-asserting opposition be a sign of a genuine other-affirming conversation?

The problem of finding a right balance between an emphasis on human individuality and an emphasis on human community is a fundamental problem that confronts us in all our personal and social relationships. There are no easy or final solutions to it. But we suggest two guidelines for dealing with it:

1. As human beings created in the image of God, we can realize our distinctive individuality only in and for the sake of community with God and other people; and we can live in true community with them only as we respect, preserve, and defend our own unique individuality and that of other people. True individuality and true community cannot be separated; each has to be understood in inseparable connection with the other. So if what is most important to you is the dignity, freedom, and rights of the individual, remember this: individual life that ignores or destroys life in community with God and other people (especially people who are different from you) is inhuman. And if what is most important for you is the solidarity and unity of life in community, remember this: life in community with God and others that ignores or destroys the dignity, freedom, and rights of individuals (especially those who are different from you) is inhuman.

2. Because it is human life in the image of God we seek to understand

and realize as we struggle to relate legitimate self-assertion and life in community, we may expect to find help with our struggle as we continually ponder afresh the story of how the God in whose image we are created, and how Jesus the faithful human being in God's image, did it. According to scripture, how was God faithful both to God's own "personal integrity" and freedom, and to God's will for community with God's (sinful!) people? How did Jesus uncompromisingly live his own life and fulfill his own particular task in such a way that he lived at the same time totally and unreservedly for God and for other people? Every chapter in this book could be read as one answer to these questions. What is your answer?

Who are we? Who am I? We are human beings created in the image of God. And what does that mean? We can summarize everything we have said in this chapter and everything we say in this whole book by saying, "You shall love the Lord your God with all your heart, and with all your soul, and with all your mind. . . . You shall love your neighbor as yourself" (Matt. 22:37–39).

FOR FURTHER REFLECTION AND STUDY

1. Is an educated person more likely to be a genuinely human person than an uneducated one?
2. Much of modern thought understands human beings primarily in terms of the satisfaction of their bodily needs and pleasures—hence its materialistic emphasis on economic production and consumption. Some Christians say that a materialistic concern about bodily needs and pleasures and the economic programs that influence their satisfaction are unimportant; as Christians we are concerned only about the soul and its eternal destiny. Which view is more accurate in light of the biblical doctrine of human beings in the image of God?
3. In what ways can morality be a contradiction of what it means to be human beings in the image of God?
4. How should Christians respond to a person who says he or she wants to be a "self-made" person who asks no favors from anyone, owes nobody anything, and "makes it on my own"?
5. How would you explain the meaning of the statement in Gen. 1:27 that to be created in the image of God is to be male and female?
6. Friedrich Schleiermacher, perhaps the greatest theologian of the

nineteenth century, believed that true piety is a feeling of "absolute dependence" on God. Do you agree? Why or why not?

7. In what ways do we often show by our dealing with the following that we do not really see people as persons but only as categories: (a) Jews, (b) "foreigners" who live among us, (c) men or women in church or in society, and (d) conservatives or liberals?
8. Can you think of some ways homeless people who walk the streets of our inner cities might "help" people who live in middle-class suburbs?
9. What is the difference between individualism and respect for individuality?
10. What is the relation between individual rights and civil rights?
11. How would you respond to someone who says (a) all religions are saying the same thing in different ways and (b) religion is just a matter of personal preference, and one is as good and true as another so long as it is sincerely believed?
12. Look at the list you made at the beginning of your study of this chapter. Would you make any changes in it now?

11

Why Don't You Just Be Yourself?

The Doctrine of Sin

"I'm sorry. I didn't mean to say that. I'm just not myself today."
"She's not really a bad girl. She's just trying to find herself."
"Why don't you stop pretending you are something you aren't and just be yourself?"
"He's not even human; he's just an animal."
"You'll go to pieces if you don't pull yourself together."
"That guy thinks he's God Almighty."

All these everyday expressions we use to talk about ourselves and other people acknowledge the self-contradiction that plagues all our lives. "I am not myself" says illogically but realistically, "I am not what I am." Trying to "find" or "be" or "get hold of" myself is admitting the illogical but true predicament we are all in: I am somehow separated from my inmost, truest self. A human being by definition is not and cannot be an animal or God, yet all of us sometimes act as if we were what we are not and cannot be.

This self-contradiction that makes life so hard to understand and live is the symptom of what Christian theology calls *sin.* That is what we are going to consider in this chapter.

We have already indirectly defined what sin is. In the last chapter we learned that to be a human being means to be created in the image of God. That means: (1) life received from and lived for God in a relationship of thankful dependence and active obedience; (2) life with and for our fellow human beings in a relationship of mutual openness and help; (3) life that is self-affirming and self-fulfilling when we live in community with God and other people. But the more concrete we become about what it means to live as human beings in the image of God, the clearer it becomes that no one (with one exception) has ever lived such a life. In various ways all of us try to live without or against God and our fellow human beings, and in so doing deny our own humanity. That is what lies behind the self-contradiction expressed in our daily recognition that we need to "be" or "find" or "get hold of" ourselves. Our basic problem, to use the strong language of the Heidelberg Catechism (Q. 5), is that though we are our true selves only in community with them we are prone to *hate* God and our neighbor.

Why do we have such trouble being ourselves—or even knowing for sure what we would be if we were? *Why* do we so stupidly keep trying to get loose from God and other people when our own humanity depends on living in community with them? *Why* do we sometimes try to live as if we were animals or to play God? These are the specific questions that concern us now.

Before we begin, we must be clear about where we stand when we speak of sin from a Christian point of view. We must take sin very seriously, but not too seriously. Contrary to the impression we are sometimes given, sin is not the main theme and central emphasis of the Christian faith. We see this both when we look at the doctrine of human beings in the image of God and when we look at the doctrine of Christ.

In the first place, from the point of view of the doctrine of human beings, we must talk with dead seriousness about ourselves as sinners, but we must not suggest that our sinfulness is the basic truth about what we are. The basic truth is not that we are sinners but that we are human beings created in God's image. Sin distorts, twists, corrupts, and contradicts this truth, but it does not change us into something other than what God created us to be. Sin is not stronger than God. In the Bible, even sinful people are still recognized as people in the image of God (Gen. 9:6; James 3:9). We may disobey God and turn against other people, but we cannot really escape them. By our very nature we are dependent upon and responsible to them. We may refuse to acknowledge, but we cannot escape, the relatedness of our lives as human beings. Sin may become "second nature" to us, but it is never really "natural." What we are "naturally" is what God created us to be. All of us are sinners, but our sinfulness is something *unnatural.*[1] That is why it is such a problem. We keep trying to be what we are not, but we can never bring it off. No matter how hard we try, no matter how we ruin our own and others' lives in the attempt, we can no more really live without God and our neighbor than a chicken can turn itself into a duck and learn to swim. We may kill ourselves (and other people) trying, but we cannot turn ourselves from the human beings God made us into animals or substitute gods.

We can express the same thing by pointing out that in the Bible the word *sin* itself has only a negative meaning. It means departure from what is normal, to miss the real and true way, to get lost or miss the goal. Dangerous and destructive as it is, sin is not the truth about us but the distortion or denial of the truth. (It would be helpful here to look up the word *sin* in one of the theological word books.) Humanity and not inhumanity, the meaning and realization of a *right* relationship with God and fellow human beings—that is what Christians are primarily interested in.

We see the same thing from the point of view of Christian faith in Christ. It is no accident that when we confess our faith in the Apostles' Creed, sin is mentioned only when we say that we believe in the *forgiveness* of sin. Although he certainly reckoned with its reality, Jesus himself never speculated about sin as such or even explained what he understood by it. And the followers of Jesus do not "believe in" sin; we believe that "Christ died for our sins" (1 Cor. 15:3). Paul did not come preaching the bad news of sin but the good news of the Christ who loves and helps sinners (1 Cor. 2:2). We must talk about sin in order to understand the forgiveness of sin, Christ's death for our sins, and the good news that in him God was and is at work in the world to overcome and free us from sin. But sin itself is neither the first nor the last nor the most important word about who we are. We give sin too much honor when we give it such a central place in our thinking.

So if we have to talk about sin now, we do it only "in passing"—in passing from the humanity God gave us in creation to the new humanity God is restoring in us; in passing from the work of God the Creator who made us in God's own image to the work of God the Reconciler and Giver of new life who renews that image in us (Col. 3:10).

THREE BASIC FORMS OF SIN

We can best understand the meaning of sin as self-destructive breaking of relationship with God and other people by looking at some of the forms in which it appears.

Sin as Disobedience

Most Reformed confessions, following one emphasis in biblical thought, define sin as disobedience to the law of God. If we are correctly to understand sin as disobedience, however, we must be very careful to understand the law of God in the radical sense in which Jesus interpreted it and not in the way moralistic, legalistic thinkers since the Pharisees have always understood it. What God's law requires is *ourselves* (our "hearts," to use the biblical terminology), not just certain external actions. And what it forbids is the withholding of ourselves from God and other people, not just the doing of certain bad things. The intention of the whole law and of every part of it, in other words, is the commandment that we love God with our whole being and our neighbor as ourselves. Doing things that in themselves may be quite proper but doing them without love, or *not* doing what love requires—this is disobedience to the law of God.

In relation to God, sin as disobedience is not just being irreligious or breaking the Ten Commandments. Disobedience can also take very pious, religious forms. It is obeying all the commandments, perhaps very strictly, not because we love and trust God but to get something out of God. It is treating our relation to God as a business deal, trying to use God for personal success and happiness (tithing because you get a good return on your investment), or seeking only to save ourselves when we die (see Matt. 16:25).

Sin is not just making graven images of wood or gold but making God into the image of a person of our own particular race, sex, or class and thus worshiping ourselves even as we pretend to worship God.

Sin is taking the Lord's name in vain not only by cursing but also by making it trivial. It is using "God" or "the will of God" only to justify our own personal, social, or national prejudices and ambitions—or, on the other hand, claiming to be Christians whose lives belong to God, but saying that religion has nothing to do with practical matters.

Sin as disobedience in relation to other people is not only the external act of adultery; it is *wanting* to commit adultery (Matt. 5:27–28). It is living in a legally faithful marriage without love and compassion for the partner. It is being legally faithful while in fact only using the partner to satisfy one's own needs, pleasures, comfort, desire for social status, or quest for security.

Sin is not just killing people; it is having contempt for any human being (Matt. 5:21–22). It is not only murdering other people but simply letting them starve to death physically or emotionally because we decide that social welfare and foreign aid are "money down a rathole."

Sin is not just robbing banks. It is also stealing other people's money by false advertising. It is not just waylaying people and leaving them lying in a ditch; it is also "passing by on the other side" when we see people in inner city ghettos helplessly at the mercy of unscrupulous landlords and indifferent politicians.

Sin, to sum it all up, *is* disobedience to the law of God. But it is not just something those immoral, unbelieving outsiders do. It is something *we* do. More than that, they and we do not just *do* sinful things; we *are* sinners—"in our hearts." Sin as disobedience means that we as well as they must confess, "I am by nature prone to hate God and my neighbor." Whoever cannot say that honestly has not yet learned what disobedience to the law of God is.

Sin as Sensuality

When most of us hear the word *sin,* we think first of "worldly" or "fleshly" sins connected with bodily needs, desires, and pleasures. Although the Bible indicates that sin may express itself in this form, it is by no means the center of the biblical doctrine of sin. Why then do we automatically think first of all along these lines? There are probably two reasons.

First, such sins as sexual immorality, drunkenness, and gluttony are "safe" sins to talk about. Everyone already knows they are wrong. They are often more prevalent (or at least more visible) among people outside the church, and no one is offended so long as we are talking about other people's sins. It is safer and easier to talk about personal immorality than about social injustice, which is emphasized far more strongly in the Bible.

Second, the emphasis on sin as sensuality enables us to blame sin on our bodies, telling ourselves that though the "flesh" tempts us to do bad things, our "heart is in the right place" or we "mean well." We may *do* sinful things, but we are not "basically" sinful. Once again we run into the classical Greek idea that our "lower" (evil) physical selves are a drag on our "higher" (good) spiritual nature.

We can learn the true meaning of sin connected with our sensual appetites under three conditions:

1. We must not forget that this is only *one* form sin can take. If I am better off than some others in this respect, that does not mean that I am less sinful than they. It would be hard to argue that the moral, law-abiding Pharisees were less sinful than the prostitutes and tax collectors—especially in light of Matt. 21:31–32 and Luke 18:10–14 (not to mention the part the Pharisees played in the crucifixion of Jesus).

2. We can think correctly of sinful sensuality only when we remember that the source of *all* sin is the "heart." We must look for the root of such sins as sexual immorality, drunkenness, and gluttony not in the body but in the *self.* When Paul speaks of sinful "flesh" (Rom. 8:3) or living "according to the flesh" (Rom. 8:12), he is not referring to sins of the body alone but to the whole personality of sinful people. Thus the "works of the flesh," according to Gal. 5:19–21, include physical sins: immorality, impurity, licentiousness, drunkenness, carousing, and the like. But "works of the flesh" are also such nonsensual sins as idolatry, enmity, strife, jealousy, anger, selfishness, dissension, party spirit, and envy. Paul does not suggest that one kind of "fleshly" sin is worse than the other. The point is that the body is no more sinful in itself than the heart, soul, or spirit; and the heart, soul, and spirit are no less sinful than the body. *I* am sinful—not just my body.

3. Finally, it follows from what we have just said that we can understand the sinfulness of physical immorality only when we think about it in *personal* terms.

The act of stuffing too much food (or only the finest gourmet-approved foods) into the stomach is not in itself sinful. Nor is drinking too much cheap (or expensive) alcohol. Sin comes into the picture only when we ask *why* people become gluttons or drunkards. Do they eat and drink too much because they make themselves into gods through inordinate self-love—or because they make themselves into animals by thinking only of physical pleasure? *Why* do they want to escape their own true humanity in one way or the other? Is it wrong self-love or self-hatred? How does their eating or drinking affect their relationship with wife or husband or children, with friends and associates? Food and drink are not sinful—*people* are.

Illicit sexual intercourse is not sinful just because two bodies are joined—just as "legal" sexual union is not necessarily free from sin. Whether within or outside a legal marriage relationship, we cannot know whether and how a sexual relationship is sinful without asking such questions as these: Is it a genuine giving and receiving human relationship based on faithfulness and love? Is it a distorted self-love that leads one partner only to use the other for his or her own self-gratification or self-fulfillment? Is it idolatry that makes a god not out of the self but of the other? ("He worships the ground she walks on." "She adores him.") What kind of personal relationship with God and the partner is expressed in this sexual togetherness?

Sin does express itself in sensual ways. But we will never understand it (or learn how it can be overcome) until we ask who the *people* are and what kind of *personal relationship* they have with God and other people in the use of their bodies and the physical things and activities that meet their needs and give them pleasure.

Sin as the Desire to Be Good

Christian theology understands the story of the sin of the first man and woman in the garden to be the clue to the meaning of the sinfulness of all men and women in all times and places. Stop now and read the story in Gen. 3:1–13.

What is the sin of Adam and Eve—and our sin? It is an indication of how profound this ancient story is that several answers can be given, two of which we have already discussed.

We could say that the root of all human sin is disobedience. It is doing what God commands us not to do.

Perhaps we could find an indirect connection between sin and *sensuality and sexuality.* It is a very indirect connection, for the story shows none of the preoccupation with this form of sin that has obsessed the church through the centuries. But the text does say that the woman "saw that the tree was good for food, and that it was a delight to the eyes" (Gen. 3:6). And it does say that the result (not the cause) of sin is shame and guilt that comes with the awareness of nakedness.

According to the most emphasized interpretation in the history of the church, the fundamental sin of Adam and Eve and of all human beings since is *pride.* Sin is the desire to be "like God" (or more accurately to be like what we *think* God is and would be if *we* were God). Our sin is that we are not content to be dependent on God, let ourselves be loved and cared for by God, love and serve God. We want to be self-sufficient and autonomous; able to do anything we please; unlimited by anyone or anything outside ourselves; with power to exert absolute control over our own lives, over the lives of other people, and over the natural world around us.

Contemporary feminist and liberation theologians have argued that the sin of Adam and Eve and our sin is not so much arrogant self-assertion as *passive self-denial* and *servility.* Like Eve (who let the serpent control her life) and Adam (who let Eve control his), we cave in to the temptation to give up asserting ourselves as the free, mature, responsible human beings God created us to be as we live in faithful service of God and partnership with one another. Perhaps some of us (especially men and people who have positions of power?) may sin by pridefully playing God as we seek to dominate everything and everyone outside ourselves. But many of us (especially women and those who are the victims of unjust and oppressive social structures?) sin by subserviently allowing others to tell us who we are and what we can and cannot become, what we can and cannot do—even if it means surrendering our value and dignity as human beings created in God's own image and our responsibility under God to defend the value and dignity of other people who are also created in God's image. Our sin is that we think not too much but too little of ourselves and what God created and empowers us to be and do.[2]

Still another interpretation of the story of Adam and Eve is to say that the root and essence of their and our sin is *lack of faith.* We do not believe that we are safe under the care and command of God, so we try to take care of ourselves and tell ourselves how to live. Pride and unbelief go hand in hand.

All these interpretations may be legitimate, but they ignore the significance of the literal words of the text itself: "*The Lord God* commanded the man, 'You may freely eat of every tree of the garden; but of the tree of the knowledge of good and evil you shall not eat, for in the day that you eat of it you shall die' " (Gen. 2:16–17, emphasis added). But the *serpent* said, "You will not die; for God knows that when you eat of it your eyes will be opened, and you will be like God, knowing good and evil" (Gen. 3:4–5, emphasis added). What is the root and essence of sin? It is the *desire to know good and evil!*

How can that be true? Is not the whole point in going to church, reading the Bible, praying, and trying to live a Christian life precisely to learn the difference between good and evil so that we can be good and not evil? No wonder that some thinkers have said that the "fall" of Adam and Eve was a fall *upward!* Does not all progress in individual human development and in human history depend on learning to distinguish between what is good and what is evil? But it is no accident that the story of Adam and Eve traces the desire to be like God in this way to the temptation of the devil. Those who first told the story knew that this desire is the fundamental sin that lies behind all three of the basic forms sin may take.

1. The desire to know good and evil is rebellion against God. God alone is good, and God alone knows what is good and not good. To want to know and be good by ourselves (to establish our own righteousness, as Romans 10:3 puts it) means that we do not want to learn afresh from God every day, in every new decision and situation, what is good and

how we ought to live; we want to know for ourselves without having to depend on God's guidance and help. But once we think that we do know, then we feel competent not only to be our own moral instructors and judges, and not only to be the instructors and judges of other people, but even to say what *God* must say and do if *God* is really good (according to *our* standards). We no longer need to be instructed, judged, and corrected by God; on the contrary, God is instructed, judged, and corrected by us. For it is not God but we who are the infallible judges of good and evil. That is the sin of "good" people—the sin of people who in their very pious and "ethical" desire to know the good that only God knows rebel *against* God.

2. The desire to be like God knowing good and evil is enmity against our fellow human beings. Who are more dangerous than people who are sure that they know both for themselves and for everyone else what is good and what is not good? Who are more inhuman than those who are sure that they are in a position to instruct and judge others but do not need themselves to be judged and corrected? What crimes against their fellow human beings have been committed by "good" people who are sure of their own superior wisdom and virtue, and are therefore sure that anyone different from them is foolish and evil and must therefore be "helped" to be good like themselves—by force, if necessary? How demonic are people who think they are like God, knowing good and evil!

3. The desire to be like God knowing good and evil is self-destructive. People who are sure that they know what is good and not good for themselves, for other people, and even for God cut themselves off from the relationship with God and fellow human beings in which their own humanity is realized. They think that they will be free if they no longer have to learn from God and others, if they can tell themselves, what they should do and how they should live. But they do not become free. They become slaves of their own self-deception, self-deifying arrogance and inhumanity. They do not become like God; they become like Satan. People dehumanized by their presumed knowledge of good and evil may be worse off than people dehumanized by addiction to liquor or drugs, or by sexual immorality, because they do not even know that they have destroyed themselves and are desperately in need of forgiveness and help.

We can sum up everything we have been trying to say about what sin is by going back to what we said at the beginning of our discussion. Whether expressed in terms of disobedience, sensuality, pride, passive acquiescence, or self-righteousness, sin always means broken relationships. It means unwillingness to be what we are as human beings in the image of God, human beings who are ourselves only as we live in community with God and our fellow human beings. In short, sin is not loving and not being willing to let ourselves be loved. Only when we understand this, and get beyond thinking of sin as immorality or irreligiousness, can we know and mean what we are saying when we confess in church that "there is no health in us." Only when we learn that however moral, law-abiding, and religious we are, we are still "miserable sinners"—only then will we understand the power of sin in our lives.

ORIGINAL SIN

A mother says to herself at the breakfast table, "I'm going to do better today. I won't be as impatient with the children as I was yesterday." But when she goes to bed that night, she feels guilty, knowing that despite her good intentions, today was yesterday all over again.

"I'll be more understanding, more forgiving and open, more courageous in standing up for what I know is right—more Christian." Who of us has not decided that over and over again in dealing with members of our families, with friends and people we work with, with strangers who wait on us in stores—only to discover over and over again that we should but can't or could but don't?

What we are up against is "original sin." The problem lies in two apparently contradictory truths: (1) Sin is universal and inevitable. All people, everywhere, always, have lived in self-contradiction to their true being in the image of God (Rom. 3:10–11). But if *all* are sinners, then *everyone* must be a sinner. There is no one who can *not* sin. (2) Nevertheless, every person is responsible for his or her sinfulness. No one forces me not to love God and other people. It is *I* who sin and I know that *I* am guilty, even if I do not want to do it. All of us, in other words, are caught in the trap William Faulkner describes when he has a wise person in *Requiem for a Nun* say paradoxically about sin: "You ain't *got* to. You can't help it."[3]

Christian theology has tried to understand the predicament of our inevitable but responsible guilt by following Paul, who in Rom. 5:12–21 and 1 Cor. 15:21–22 connects it with the "original sin" of Adam. (It is interesting that although the biblical story of sin's entrance into human history is the story of Adam *and* Eve, Paul and Christian tradition make Adam alone the center of discussion about the connection between the sin of the first human beings and that of all those who come after them.

In our discussion we will follow this tradition, remembering that "Adam"—which in Hebrew means simply "man"—now becomes the prototype, or model, for the sinfulness of all human beings, both men and women.) We will consider two ways in which the relation between Adam and "all" has been interpreted in the Reformed tradition.

Inherited Sin

The traditional Christian explanation of why all people are sinners and cannot *not* be sinners was first formulated by Augustine. Most of the older Reformed confessions follow him. The first man, Adam, sinned, and his "sinful nature" has been passed down to all other people as a "hereditary disease, wherewith infants themselves are infected even in their mother's womb" (Belgic Confession, Art. 15). We are connected with Adam and his sin by our biological descent from him.

This explanation has some things in its favor: (1) It seems logical and even "scientific." We know that some characteristics are inherited. Why not sinfulness also? (2) This explanation seems to have a biblical foundation. Did not Paul say that sin came into the world through one man and spread to all other people from him? Does not Ps. 51:5 say, "Indeed, I was born guilty, a sinner when my mother conceived me"? (3) This explanation seems to establish a clear historical connection through the generations between Adam and us.

However, the explanation of original sin as inherited sin can also be criticized for several reasons:

1. If this view is correct, how can people be held any more responsible for their sinful nature and sinful acts than for the fact that they inherited blue eyes or physical handicaps? The doctrine of inherited sin is not consistent with the biblical view that every person is accountable for his or her own sin. The Bible does teach "You can't help it." But it also teaches "You ain't *got* to."

2. In the background of the doctrine of inherited sin is the unbiblical idea that sex is the root of all sin and that sexual intercourse is responsible for the spread of sin from parents to children. Medieval theologian Peter Lombard, for instance, taught that lust stains the semen in the act of procreation, and the stain defiles the soul when it is united with the body. (That is why classical Roman Catholic theology said that if Christ was to be sinless, his mother had to be a virgin.) But nowhere does scripture make such a connection between sex and the origin of sin.

3. Although the Bible does connect the sinfulness of all people with Adam, it says nothing at all about a cause-and-effect hereditary connection. Even Ps. 51:5 means only that I have been a sinner since my birth. In the Bible sin has to do with personal relationships. It is not a medical problem of genes and chromosomes, semen and prenatal development.

4. Finally, the biological explanation of the connection between Adam and us distracts attention from the one way in which sin and guilt *are* transmitted from person to person, generation to generation—not by sexual intercourse but by social influence. Racially prejudiced parents, for example, pass on their prejudice to their children. A society that deprives some people of economic, political, and educational opportunities is partly responsible if some of these people turn to crime. This social solidarity and interconnectedness of sinful people is far more biblical than the strangely mechanical view that the connection is only biological, because the social view understands human beings not just as biologically determined animals but as creatures in the image of God who are what they are for better or worse as a result of the communities in which they live.

Adam as Our Representative

Another interpretation of the connection between Adam and all people works not with biological but juridical, or legal, images. It says, in the language of classical theology, that Adam is the "federal head" of the human race and that God "imputes" his sin to us (see Westminster Confession, 6.3). Expressed in contemporary language, this view says that Adam is not just the first man at the beginning of all history. The story of Adam is the story of *every* person. What Adam did, everyone does. What he was, we all are. The character of all history, including our own, is exposed in his history, for people in all times simply repeat over and over again Adam's "original" sin, with the same consequences. If I want to understand who I am and what I am like, I have to look at him. I *am* "Adam" (even if I am a woman!).

There are several advantages to this interpretation:

1. It avoids the fatalistic, deterministic view of the doctrine of hereditary sin. According to this view, Adam has not poisoned the human race or passed down an inescapable disease or infection. No one *has* to be Adam. "You ain't got to!" All people do repeat Adam's sin, but they do so on their own responsibility, by their own choice. Sin is not a fate forced on us; it is what *we* are and do.

2. This interpretation understands sin personally. It is an interpretation of Adam's and our relation to God and other people. It is the truth about *us*, not about an impersonal disease or defect.

3. This interpretation is also biblical. It maintains Paul's understanding of all people in connection with Adam without looking for an artificial, nonbiblical connection between us in terms of heredity. Moreover, we can accept this "representative" interpretation whether we think of Adam literally as the first man in history or as a parable about all human beings.

From one point of view, of course, the representative view of Adam has a big disadvantage. It does not explain, as does the biological view, *how* or *why* it is that all people, everywhere, always, do what Adam did. It simply states that this is the predicament we are all in: "You ain't *got* to. You can't help it." We can't blame Adam or anyone else for the fact that over and over again, in all the many variations we have discussed, we rebel against God, turn against our fellow human beings, and contradict our own true humanity. No one forces us to be Adam. But on the other hand, we can't help it. No matter how good our intentions, how often we "turn over a new leaf," we cannot love God with our whole being and our neighbor as ourselves, not even when we believe that it is the key to real self-fulfillment. As soon as we overcome sin in one form (immorality, for instance), it crops up in another (a self-righteous, unforgiving attitude toward those who are not as "good" as we).

"You ain't *got* to. You can't help it." That is an illogical, contradictory, impossible statement. But that's the way life is. That's the trap we are in. And the real problem is not how we can explain the intellectual puzzle of our responsibility for sin that is inevitable. The real problem is whether and how we can get out of this trap.

THE CONSEQUENCES OF SIN

We can summarize the results of this chapter and catch a glimpse of where we go from here by discussing two consequences of Adam's (our) sin: total depravity and death.

Total Depravity

According to the Reformed confessions, people who "fall" from their humanity in the image of God are "unable to do good, and prone to evil" (Heidelberg Catechism, Q. 7). They are "wicked, perverse and corrupt" in all their ways (Belgic Confession, Art. 14). They no longer have the "free will" to do good but have become "slaves of sin" (Second Helvetic Confession, 9; Belgic Confession, Art. 14; Westminster Confession, 11). They are "utterly indisposed, disabled, and made opposite to all good, and wholly inclined to all evil" (Westminster Confession, 6).

We must be very careful how we interpret such statements about this "total depravity" if we are not to confirm the idea of many people that Christians (especially Calvinists) are cynical, sour people who believe in sin more than in anything else, refuse to see any good anywhere, always look around suspiciously for the real evil under every apparent good, and especially denounce any good that non-Christians accomplish.

All people (including those who are moral and religious) are sinners. But that does not mean that there is no difference between a Martin Luther King Jr. or a Gandhi and an Adolf Hitler. It would be absurd to say that because according to Jesus a person who lusts is guilty of adultery, there is no difference between someone who fantasizes about it and someone who actually commits it, or that there is no difference between a man who is angry with his neighbor and a man who murders him. The extreme statements in the confessions or in Jesus' teaching do not mean that all people are monsters or devils, or that they are all equally "bad."

Nor do such statements about the inability of sinful people to do any good mean that there is no progress in history and that it is useless for Christians to cooperate with attempts to make the world a better place to live in. The abolition of slavery, the gradual realization that women are human beings and not property, the achievement of democratic forms of government, reforms to make treatment of prisoners and the mentally ill more humane—such achievements are certainly progress. Sometimes progress is made by unbelievers and "mere humanists" without the help, even despite the opposition, of Christians who said that nothing good can be accomplished in this hopelessly sinful world!

Total depravity, correctly understood, means that although both Christians *and* non-Christians can do much good, nothing we do is free from the corruption of sinful self-interest. It means that although there may be all kinds of progress in history, human beings themselves are monotonously the same, repeating over and over again the little drama in the garden of Eden. (We are no longer savages who throw hundreds of our enemies to the crocodiles. Now we are savages who neatly kill hundreds of thousands with weapons developed through scientific "progress.")

We are obviously "free" to do many things: to go to church or stay home, to be honest or dishonest in our business relations, to be moral or immoral in our sexual relations, to be just or unjust in our social and political relations. And it makes a great deal of difference how we use this freedom. But "total depravity" means that we are *not* free wholeheartedly, without reservation or qualification, to love and let ourselves be loved by God and the people with whom we live. In this sense, good and bad people alike, Christians and non-Christians, we are "slaves to sin"—slaves trapped by the anxiety, division within ourselves, and self-contradictions that result from the twisted relationships in which we all live. This is a trap from which we cannot free ourselves, no matter how hard we try.

Death

Death is the second consequence of sin. "In the day that you eat of it you shall die" (Gen. 2:17). "The wages of sin is death" (Rom. 6:23). What is meant here is not just physical death, which in itself is only a sign of the fact that we are finite creatures who do not live forever. It is the death Paul speaks of when he speaks of being "dead through trespasses and sins" (Eph. 2:1). It is the death John refers to when he says, "Whoever does not love abides in death" (1 John 3:14). Sinful human beings—that is, human beings who do not and cannot love—are *dead*. They are dead even though they may still be walking around and acting as if they were alive. They are "dead inside," as we express it in everyday language.

To say that sinners are dead in their sins is to say that just as dead people cannot make themselves alive again, neither can we help ourselves out of our self-contradictory inability to live in real community with God, our families, our associates, and people of other races, classes, and cultural heritages.

The point of saying that the "wages of sin" is death is not so much a warning about what God will do to us, as it is a warning about the self-destruction we bring on ourselves when we contradict our humanity in God's image. Moreover, the whole Bible bears witness to the truth that God still loves and is still faithful even to people who do not love and are not faithful to God. The Bible does not end with the Genesis story of sin and the death it brings. That is only the beginning!

Proneness by nature to hate, slavery to sin, separation and alienation, living death, inhumanity—such topics have been the main theme of this chapter. But this theme is not the main theme either of the Bible or of the Christian faith. The main theme is the story of the God who brings love, freedom, righteousness, real community—genuine *humanity*—

precisely to people who are dead in and as a consequence of their sinfulness. We cannot understand the joyful main theme apart from the tragic secondary theme. But we must not peer too long into the darkness, lest we come to love darkness rather than light. It is time now that we turn again to the light that shines in our darkness.

FOR FURTHER REFLECTION AND STUDY

1. Is sin "doing what comes naturally"?
2. Read Ex. 20:1–17. Stop after you read each commandment and ask yourself whether you could honestly respond with the words of the Heidelberg Catechism, "By nature I am prone to hate God and my neighbor" (Q. 5).
3. Is it legitimate to be a Christian because it "pays off" in happiness, success, and peace of mind?
4. "My husband has been a Methodist all his life, but if it comes to choosing between being a Methodist and an American, he'll be an American every time."[4] Do you consider this a sinful statement? Why? Why not?
5. Is a loveless marriage as sinful as adultery?
6. Read Rom. 14:1–23 and 1 Cor. 8:1–13. Do these passages give us any guidance about how Christians should deal with the problem of drinking? What about sex ethics?
7. Remembering the basic meaning of sin, do you think hard work motivated by greed is less sinful than laziness motivated by irresponsibility?
8. "Hell is the home of honor, duty, justice, and the rest of the seven deadly virtues. All the wickedness on earth is done in their name."[5] Do you agree with George Bernard Shaw?
9. "You ain't *got* to. You can't help it." Do you think these words of Faulkner about sin are an accurate description of the human predicament?
10. Do you think it is proper to speak of "inherited" sin? Does Paul teach it in Rom. 5:12–21?
11. Is "total depravity" a misleading description of humankind's sinfulness? Why? Why not?
12. Read 1 John 3:14–18. How would you explain John's statement "Whoever does not love abides in death"?

PART 4

GOD IN CHRIST AND RECONCILIATION

"And in Jesus Christ, his only Son, our Lord . . . conceived . . . born . . . suffered . . . crucified . . . died . . . was buried . . . descended . . . rose again . . . ascended . . . is seated at the right hand . . . will come again . . ." These words from the second article of the Apostles' Creed suggest four things we must keep in mind as we begin our study of the work of God in Jesus Christ.

1. When we come to this part of Christian theology, we do not come to just one doctrine among others. It is no accident that the part of the creed dealing with Christ is the longest part. This one doctrine gives meaning and content to all the others. All the doctrines of the Christian faith are related to Christ as spokes to the hub of a wheel. We could not talk about who God is, how we know God, what God is like, and what God wants with us without talking about God's self-disclosure in Christ. Nor could we talk about what it means to be human beings in the image of God and sinners who contradict their own humanity without talking about Jesus. We will see that the same holds true in the parts of the Christian faith that are still before us. It is only by looking at Christ that we know who the Holy Spirit is, what the church and Christian life are all about, and what will happen to us and the world in the future. We stand now at the very center of the Christian faith. Everything else Christians believe stands or falls with what they believe about Jesus.

That means that we must proceed very carefully here—and very modestly. For now we come to a mystery no one can grasp and master. Those who think they understand everything here, who have it neatly wrapped up in a neat system and no longer need to listen and be open to correction, only prove that they understand nothing. This does not mean that we must not try to understand as best we can who Jesus Christ is and what he means for us. But it does mean that we never reach the end of our attempt to understand. When you have finished this part of our study, you will have been successful if you can say, "Now I understand a *little* better and see a *little* more clearly."

2. What do we believe? When the church confesses its faith, it does not say, "I believe in the virgin birth, the substitutionary atonement, the empty tomb, and the second coming." We believe in a person—"Jesus Christ, his only Son, our Lord." The doctrines dealing with his birth, life, death, and resurrection are necessary if we are to articulate our faith. But they are not themselves the object of our faith. Our trust, hope, and confidence are in Jesus and him alone. We must take doctrines *about* him very seriously, but we must never confuse even the most orthodox doctrine with genuine Christian faith. We may in fact be comforted by the fact that faith in him can be real even though our ability to express that faith in words is always inadequate. As we begin our study of "Christology" (the doctrine of Christ), we must keep constantly in mind that our main concern is with Jesus himself, not with our own or the church's ideas about him—not even the ideas we think are right.

3. Who is this person who stands at the center of Christian faith? It is significant that the Apostles' Creed speaks of Jesus with verbs: born, crucified, rose, ascended, and so on. It does not give us an explanation or analysis of his "deity" and "humanity" and how they are related. It simply tells his story. That is also how the New Testament talks about him. It too gives us no theoretical discussion of the "two natures." It tells us who Jesus is by telling and interpreting the story of what he said and did. He is one who speaks with authority, heals, serves, loves, obeys, commands, forgives, judges, prays, suffers, gives up his life, lives, triumphs, rules. Consider the meaning of these *actions,* the New Testament tells us, and you will learn the secret of who he *is*. Therefore, if we follow the Bible and the Apostles' Creed, we cannot separate the "person" of Jesus from his "work," as theologians have often done in the past. We can only learn who the person is *from* and *in* his work. As we go about our study of Christology, we must keep in mind that it is not an intellectual or metaphysical puzzle we are working at but an interpretation of history.

4. Both the Apostles' Creed and the New Testament talk about who Jesus is by telling his story, but there is one big difference between the ways they do it. The creed jumps from the story of Jesus' birth to the

story of his death, from "conceived" and "born" to "suffered under Pontius Pilate . . . crucified, died, and was buried." It is as if the whole story of Jesus between his birth and death were not important; as if we could understand who Jesus is without hearing and obeying his invitation to join the company of his disciples. (A weakness of the Apostles' Creed as a whole is that it says nothing about Christian life, suggesting that it is possible to think like a Christian without living like a Christian.) Unfortunately, traditional Christian theology followed this bad example. In our study we will continue to follow the outline of the creed, but in agreement with most theologians today we will pay attention to the *whole* story of Jesus. We will try to understand the meaning of his birth, death, and resurrection in light of the story of his earthly ministry. Moreover, we will keep in mind that faith in Jesus is possible and becomes real only for those who obediently follow and serve him as Lord and Savior.

The question before us, then, is this: Who is this person who stands at the beginning, middle, and end of everything Christians believe, whom we come to know in the whole story of his life? We will try to answer this one question by dealing with three different questions:

Chapter 12: "Where Is God?" Christians answer this question by affirming that God is "God-with-us" (see Matt. 1:23) and by trying to say what this means with the doctrine of the incarnation.

Chapter 13: "Is God against Us?" Christians answer that "in Christ God was reconciling the world to himself" (2 Cor. 5:19) and try to explain what this means with the doctrine of the atonement.

Chapter 14: "Who's in Charge Here?" Christians answer, "God has made him both Lord and Messiah, this Jesus whom you crucified" (Acts 2:36), and try to explain this with the doctrine of the resurrection.

12

Where Is God?

The Doctrine of the Incarnation

"He was conceived by the power of the Holy Spirit and born of the virgin Mary."
"Round yon virgin mother and child."

We say and sing these words in church. Once a year we even blast the words of the carol over loudspeakers in drugstores and supermarkets. Non-Christians shake their heads in amusement or amazement over this "primitive mythology." Christians, especially theologians and preachers, sometimes fight bitterly over it. But what does it mean? Why all the fuss? In this chapter we are going to talk about who Jesus is and what the incarnation means from the perspective of the Christmas stories in Matthew and Luke and the church's doctrine of the virgin birth, which depends on them. This is not the only way we could do it. We will see in a moment that other biblical writers can talk about who Jesus is without mentioning his miraculous birth. However, we will take this as our point of reference because the classical creeds and confessions of all churches confess it, because it is important that we know what we are saying when we repeat the creed, and because both those who defend and those who reject the virgin birth often do so for the wrong reasons.

Some Christians in all sincerity confess, "I believe in Jesus Christ, his only Son, our Lord," but do not think it necessary to confess that he was "conceived by the power of the Holy Spirit and born of the virgin Mary." They point out that the story of Jesus' birth is recorded only in Matthew and Luke. It is not mentioned in Mark or John. Paul never mentions it in any of his letters; nor do any of the other New Testament writings. It is not mentioned in the earliest summaries of the Christian gospel and of the first Christian preaching in 1 Cor. 15:3–4 or Acts 2:22–36. (What *is* mentioned in these texts as the center of the Christian faith?) Does this not indicate that many of the first Christians, including Paul himself, could be real Christians without talking about (perhaps without even knowing about) the story of Jesus' miraculous birth? Were not the birth stories of Matthew and Luke added later to try to explain how or prove that Jesus is really the Son of God? And do they not fail to prove what they are supposed to prove, for they both trace the genealogy of Jesus to Joseph rather than to Mary?

Other Christians defend the birth narratives by suggesting that they could have been such common knowledge that it was unnecessary for the other biblical writers to mention them. Is it not significant that after the birth stories, Joseph is very seldom mentioned, whereas Mary is mentioned fairly often? It could be argued that the genealogies intend only to show that through Joseph Jesus had a legal but not a natural connection with the line of David.

After we have listened to all the arguments on both sides, it is hard to argue that one cannot be a real Christian without believing in the virgin birth. Why could not a person, without knowing about or accepting the birth narratives, believe that in his life, death, and resurrection Jesus is really God-with-us, our Lord and Savior? What concerns us now, however, is not to argue this point but to ask about the *meaning* of these stories. Some Christians have trouble with them because they do not understand what Matthew and Luke, and Christian tradition following them, really meant to say. Other Christians, as we have already said, vigorously defend the virgin birth for the wrong reasons. In what follows we will try to understand what we are saying when we confess "conceived by the power of the Holy Spirit and born of the virgin Mary." Our purpose, remember, is not to understand the doctrine for its own sake but to learn from it who Jesus is.[1]

REAL GOD AND REAL HUMAN BEING

Whatever else they may mean, the birth stories of Jesus emphasize that the Christian belief that "God is with us" (Matt. 1:23) is not just a beautiful idea or an abstract theological truth. It *happened*! John also tells us that it happened when he says that the "Word" (God's self-communication, the Word that *was* God) "became flesh and lived among us" (John 1:1–14). But Matthew and Luke tell us more specifically that it happened at a particular time, in a particular place, in connection with a particular mother: "In the days of Herod the king," "when Quirinius was governor of Syria," in Bethlehem, of Mary. When we speak about God's presence and activity in the world, we are not talking only about a "spiritual presence," or a "feeling" of God's nearness, or God "in our hearts." We are talking about *geography*: He was born in Palestine. We are talking about *politics*: He was born when a census was being taken, when there was danger of political revolution, and he himself was expected to be a political revolutionary (Luke 1:51–53; Matt. 2:3–5, 16). We are talking about *economics*: He was poor, born in a barn, and he came to help the poor (Luke 1:53; 6:20–26). In short, we are not just talking about religious ideas and doctrines; we are talking about *history*.

It is obviously a history that cannot be proved or verified. In the first place, not only the birth stories but the story of *all* Jesus' life is preserved for us not by objective historians but by people who believed in him and who wrote in order to convince other people to share their faith. They were "prejudiced" witnesses who did not just stick to the facts but interpreted what they had heard and seen in the light of their faith. Even if some unbiased newspaper reporters with television cameras and tape recorders had been there at his birth and during his life, we still could not prove that God was present and at work in this helpless baby, this itinerant preacher, this dying man. Even if we had a medical report, not just the word of believing witnesses, to prove that he really died and lived again, we still would not have proved that God raised him and made him Lord over all things.

Nevertheless, the stories of the birth of Jesus (to limit ourselves now to this part of the history) tell us that it is into the real world of flesh-and-blood human beings that God comes—whether it can be proved and verified or not. The Christmas story is anything but the sentimental, harmless, once-a-year occasion for a "Christmas spirit" that lasts only a few days before we return to the "facts" of the "real world." Christmas is the story of a radical invasion of God into the kind of real world where we live all year long—a world where there is political unrest and injustice, poverty, hatred, jealousy, and both the fear and the longing that things could be different. John tells us that when Jesus comes "the light shines in the darkness" (John 1:5). Matthew and Luke tell us just what the darkness is into which the light shines. It is the same darkness in which *we* live. John tells us that the "Word became flesh." Matthew and Luke emphasize that it is the same flesh we know—that of a human being who came into the world the same way and lived under the same threatening conditions we do. John says it happened. Matthew and Luke say that it did not happen only in sermons or in Christmas plays at church; it happened also *outside* the church, in the *world.*

The incarnation of God in the man Jesus does not mean that Jesus is half God and half man. To put it bluntly, "conceived by the power of the Holy Spirit" does not mean that the Holy Spirit is a substitute for the human male in the conception and birth of Jesus. The church has never held that the Spirit is the "father" of Jesus. There are many pagan mythologies about gods having intercourse with human females, producing half-breed offspring that are a combination of both. But the biblical accounts of the virgin birth are not examples of such mythology. Neither Matthew nor Luke tells us about a Jesus who is somehow superhuman but less than God, a combination or mixture neither quite human nor quite divine.

Some people who insist on the importance of the virgin birth do so because they have this pagan, mythological understanding of Jesus. Probably the most common idea of his deity and humanity in our time is that he had a human body but a divine "soul." "Outside" he was a man, but "inside" he was God. This kind of half-and-half Jesus is not the Jesus of the Bible or of Christian theology. This understanding of him, sometimes mistakenly considered orthodox, is a heresy (Apollinarianism) condemned by the church long ago in the fourth century.

"Conceived by the power of the Holy Spirit" really means not that the Spirit is the father of Jesus, but that according to his human existence Jesus had no father at all. This phrase is not a biological explanation of Jesus' "two natures." It means that there *is* no explanation, that the Word became flesh purely by the will and word of God. God spoke, and Mary heard and responded, "Let it be with me according to your word" (Luke 1:38). The proper analogy here is not the physical process of procreation but God's original creation of all things "out of nothing" when God simply spoke and it was done.

Karl Barth has noted that the exclusion of a human father in Jesus' miraculous birth tells us something about ourselves as well as about God. Human history as we have told it has usually been the story of human males, the story of the power and accomplishments (often in the name of God) of statesmen, warriors, explorers, entrepreneurs, philosophers, and so on. But now in the most important event of all history the mighty male is excluded! It is a *woman* who is the agent of God's work in the world and gives us the first and prime example of the proper role of human beings in relation to God and God's work. Mary's modest "Let it be done with me according to your word" tells all of us, male and female alike, that our task is to bear witness to God's and not our own greatness, to be the servants and not the sponsors of God in the world.[2]

In any case, those Christians who cannot in honesty accept the stories of Jesus' miraculous birth should acknowledge that the church has never understood the doctrine of the virgin birth to be an *explanation* (much less a proof) of what happened and how it happened when God came to us in a human being. The doctrine is only a way of stating the mystery that it did in fact happen. On the other hand, those Christians who do accept the doctrine must be careful that they do not interpret it to mean a half-and-half Jesus who is neither really one of us nor really God in our midst. Of what interest or help could such a half-breed be?

A REAL HUMAN BEING

Christians most eager to defend the virgin birth often do so primarily in order to insist on the deity of Jesus. We will see presently that this is proper in itself. However, it can be done correctly only when we first understand how this doctrine preserves the real *humanity* of Jesus. Those who do not understand this invariably use the doctrine to support the very heresy it was used to defeat in the early church. We will first describe the heresy and then see how the doctrine of the virgin birth guards against it.

The heresy is called "docetism," from the Greek verb that means "to seem." It is a heresy that threatened to destroy the Christian faith almost as soon as it was born and is just as popular and dangerous in the twentieth century as it was in the first. Docetism asserts very strongly that Jesus was divine but denies that he was really human. He only "seemed" to be a human being. Actually he was God *disguised* as a man. His human nature was only a mask or costume behind which his true divine self was concealed. Jesus was not a truly human being but a spiritual being who was not really subject to all the limitations and problems of earthly human existence. In him God was only pretending to be with us in the midst of our sinful, suffering, creaturely existence. His purpose was not to help us *in* the world but to help us escape *from* the world.

Already in the New Testament period the church began a two thousand–year struggle against this spiritualizing heresy. Its apparently very pious insistence on the deity of Jesus was really a denial of the very good news that makes the Christian faith Christian, the good news that in him God was really *with us.* John 1:1–14, for instance, was written precisely to protest against docetism.

Another way the early church fought this faithless spirituality, with its contempt for bodily existence, was to insist that Jesus was "born of a woman" (Gal. 4:4), flesh and blood of his mother. In this respect he was just like every other human being. He—God-with-us!—was born as we all are. He was once a helpless baby who had to be fed, whose diapers had to be changed, who had to develop and mature slowly. The Apostles' Creed asserts that Jesus was "born of the virgin Mary" not only to emphasize that he came from God but to insist that he came into the world in the same way every other human being does. He did not just appear out of nowhere like a ghost, a "heavenly body," or an alien from outer space. The creed emphasizes Jesus' real humanity by putting his birth in line with other marks of real human existence: born, suffered, died, and was buried.

The birth stories, then, are just as important to protect Jesus' real humanity as to protect his real deity. What is this "real humanity"? To answer this question we have to read the whole story of this man "born of a woman," Mary's baby, as it is told by Matthew, Luke, and the rest of the books in the New Testament.

Jesus was a Jew. Jesus was not a heavenly ideal man, not a human being in the abstract. He was a *Jewish* human being—one of that group of people who from the first century to the present have been laughed at and joked about, excluded and persecuted and (especially in our "enlightened" time) slaughtered by the millions, sometimes by people who called themselves Christians. Although the New Testament shows no interest in what Jesus looked like, we may be sure that he was not the blond, blue-eyed, pink-complexioned figure of much Western religious art and Hollywood productions. Men of the Near East look neither like Anglo-Saxons with long hair nor like All-American boys. It is important to underline Jesus' Jewishness for several reasons: (1) It emphasizes the fact that like all real human beings Jesus belonged to a particular group of people. (2) It tells us that the God he came to serve is a God who is especially on the side of people who are left out, rejected, and despised. (3) It reminds us of the continuity between the Old and New Testaments: The God whom we come to know in Jesus is none other than the God of Abraham, Isaac, and Jacob. (4) It reminds us that anti-Semitism always implies the rejection of the one whom Christians call Lord and Savior, and the rejection of the God he came to proclaim and represent.

Jesus was a male. Real human beings are normally either male or female. Jesus was a male; he was, like all Jewish boys, circumcised on the eighth day. We ought not to make too much of Jesus' masculinity. It does not mean that because Jesus was also God-with-us, God is male. "God is a Spirit and hath not a body like man" (Child's Catechism). God is not made in the image of any earthly creature, male or female (Ex. 20:4). Nor does the fact that God's representative on earth was male mean that men are the superior sex, born to rule and dominate in church, home, and society. Jesus came not to lord it over others (women or men) but to serve and give his life for them. The New Testament makes nothing of Jesus' masculinity as such—and certainly not in terms of our stereotypical view of a "man's man" who goes out to compete, conquer, and rule so that he can be "on top." It is Jesus' *humanity,* not his masculinity, that the New Testament writers are interested in, a humanity shared equally by women and men (both of them created in God's image), a humanity that is the model for the true humanity of *all* human beings. The significance of the fact that Jesus was male is only that he was a real flesh-and-blood human being, nothing more than that.

Jesus experienced every human need and limitation. He was completely human in *all* aspects of his life. We have learned to accept this with respect to his physical life. It is no longer offensive as it once was to think that the man who was God-with-us could be hungry and thirsty, need food and rest, suffer, and die. But many Christians are still hesitant to accept Jesus' humanity with respect to his inner mental and spiritual life.

Like any other real human being, Jesus was limited in his knowledge. He had to *grow* in wisdom as well as in stature (Luke 2:52). He himself confessed that he did not know everything (Mark 13:32). He was not just God pretending to be a human being. He was a real human being, a man of the first century who knew no more than any other person in his time—a man, for instance, who shared the prescientific worldview of everyone else in his society. According to the Gospels, he could sometimes know things others did not know. But when that happened, it was the result of wisdom given him by the Holy Spirit in order to fulfill the work he came to do, not the result of his being superhuman or of his divine omniscience.

The same real humanity characterized Jesus' spiritual life. We often hear that he prayed, without any suggestion that he was only talking to himself. When he knew he was about to die, we hear of his inner struggle with himself and with God. Like any human being, he did not want to die. Then in his prayer on the cross we hear that he felt completely separated from his God, doubting God's presence with him. There is no stronger proof of Jesus' genuine, total humanity than those agonizing words of Matt. 27:46.

Physically *and* intellectually *and* emotionally *and* spiritually, Jesus lived the same life we all live. He hurt. He played and went to parties. He had to learn. He could be afraid as well as self-confident. He could feel lonely and abandoned by God and his friends. He was one of us—a human being.

Like every other human being, Jesus was tempted to sin. According to the amazingly strong words in Heb. 4:15 (RSV), he was "one who in every respect has been tempted as we are." What are *your* everyday temptations—the ones so shameful you never speak about them to anyone and hardly admit them to yourself? Jesus faced the same kind of temptations. He was not just God pretending to be a human being. He was subject to all the same pressures, doubts, fears, and desires we are. If he was not, how could he be God-with-*us*? How could he "sympathize with *our* weaknesses" (Heb. 4:15)?

Unlike every other human being, Jesus was without sin. He was tempted in every respect as we are, "yet without sin" (Heb. 4:15). Could he still be really human if he did not sin? Yes, because, as we have already learned, sin is not a part of what it means to be human. It is the corruption or contradiction of true humanity. It is not "natural" but unnatural. Jesus was a real human being not only in the sense that he shared our human condition in every respect, but also in the sense that he was a human being who perfectly fulfilled his humanity.

In what sense was he sinless? How should we understand his sinlessness? In the present context, when we are asking about the significance of the stories of Jesus' virgin birth, we need to say first of all what it does not mean. Protestant theology does *not* teach that the explanation or cause of his sinlessness was the fact that his mother was a virgin. Behind this view is the unbiblical idea that sexuality as such is sinful and the source of sin. In the background also is the unbiblical view that "original sin" is "inherited sin," so that the biological connection between Adam and all people must be broken if the stain of sin is to be removed. Once one accepts this idea, the logical consequence is the doctrine of Mary's "immaculate conception," which says that Mary too had to be born in a miraculous way so that she too was not corrupted by inherited sin and could not pass it on to the child. We must reject from the very beginning any biological explanation of Jesus' sinlessness, and that means that we cannot trace it to the virginity of his mother.

How then should we understand what it means to say that this human being was without sin? The key lies in what we said at the beginning of this chapter about how the New Testament writers try to understand who Jesus is—not in terms of his nature or essence but in terms of his actions. He was sinless, not because he escaped a biological defect everyone else has, but because he *lived* without sin. And to understand what that means, we must go back to what we learned in chapters 10 and 11. Jesus was sinless because, unlike Adam and Eve and all other human beings, he fulfilled his true humanity in the image of God. He lived always, without exception, in perfect love for God and other people.

How did he live this life of perfect relatedness and therefore sinlessness? *He was sinless because he was the friend of sinners!* "This fellow welcomes sinners and eats with them" (Luke 15:2). Jesus' sinlessness was anything but obvious. The sign of it was not heroic moral purity but a life that called his purity into question. His friends and associates were not the good church people of his day. *They* were his enemies, not because he rejected them but because they rejected him. His friends were political revolutionaries (the Zealots), dishonest business people who were also traitors to their nation (the tax collectors), immoral women (the woman caught in adultery), social outcasts, and half-breeds (the Samaritans). People in his day said just what they say now: "A person is known by the company he or she keeps." "Birds of a feather flock together." It was precisely this morally suspicious life that was the sign of Jesus' sinlessness. In this way he was for his fellow human beings as they really are—guilty, needing forgiveness, acceptance, and help. In this way he was obedient to God and fulfilled the task God had given him to do—not to minister to well people who do not need a doctor but to sick people who do; not to call the righteous but sinners (Matt. 9:12–13). His sinlessness was his willingness to be sent "in the likeness of sinful flesh" (Rom. 8:3–4) in order to overcome the broken relationship between God and humanity and between human beings themselves. It was the willingness of the one who "knew no sin" to be made sin for our sake (2 Cor. 5:21). Jesus was sinless because, in perfect obedience to God and perfect love for his fellow human beings, he was willing to risk his good name and his "moral integrity" to be with and for undeserving, unworthy, *sinful* people.

Jesus was a dangerous human being. What we have said about Jesus' sinlessness leads us to say one more thing about the real humanity of the child born of Mary on the first Christmas. This sweet little baby lying in a manger with shepherds and angels gathered around him grew up to be a radical subversive preacher who was all the more dangerous because he claimed that what *he* said and did is what *God* says and does.

Jesus was not only the friend of sinners; he dared to *forgive* their sins, claiming to be able to do what only God has the right to do. He taught that the righteous who are sure that they have obeyed God's law will be excluded, judged, and condemned when the kingdom of God comes; whereas undeserving sinners who have obviously not obeyed God's law will be included, forgiven, and saved. And the religious leaders condemned this heretical preacher as a blasphemer.

Jesus was also the friend of the wrong people socially and politically. He was the friend of women whom no decent and respectable man of his time would have anything to do with unless they were members of his own family. He violated social morality and convention by openly speaking to strange women in public (John 4:7–26), having women friends (Luke 10:38–41), and including women among his disciples (Luke 8:1–3). Moreover, he was the friend of all who were poor and oppressed, and had harsh words to say against the rich who oppressed them. He claimed that he was anointed by God's Spirit to bring good news to poor people, proclaim release to captives, and liberate the oppressed (Luke 4:18–19). "Blessed are you who are poor, for yours is the kingdom of God . . . , but woe to you who are rich, for you have received your consolation" (Luke 6:20–24). "It is easier for a camel to go through the eye of a needle than for someone who is rich to enter the kingdom of God" (Luke 18:25). And the political leaders accused him of being a rabble-rouser and revolutionary who disturbed the peace and destroyed law and order.

Yet the "little people" and their defenders who longed for liberation from oppression did not like him either. They hoped that he would be a Messiah who would start a holy war to wipe out their enemies, but he refused to use violence to achieve the justice he proclaimed. He taught and practiced *love* for the enemy. They finally joined the religious and political leaders in wanting to get rid of him: "Crucify him!"

Even his own disciples were disappointed in him. They had hoped that following him would bring personal power, influence, privilege, and success (Mark 8:35–38). But he told them that it would bring only rejection, suffering, persecution, and death like his own. When they saw that this was true, they too deserted him.

This was a very offensive man socially, politically, morally, and religiously. In the end *everyone* (except for a few women!) rejected him—rich *and* poor, conservative *and* liberal *and* revolutionary, pious *and* impious, enemies *and* friends. Jesus was not the sweet, harmless "mythological" figure of many Sunday school lessons and sermons. He was a real historical human being—a very dangerous one.

In the first century (as in the twentieth), it was not easy to recognize this shockingly human man who was the son of Mary as one who is also the Son of God, God-with-us.[3]

GOD-WITH-US

In this real flesh-and-blood man, Jesus of Nazareth, God was uniquely present in the world. This man was not just a great teacher of profound truths about God and the secret of a happy, successful life. He was not just a revolutionary political leader with a vision of a more human and just society. He was not just a great moral hero for us to imitate as best we can. He was not just a very godlike personality, the model of a truly spiritual life. Nor was he just the founder of a religious club later called the church, where religious people with a common interest in him come together to admire him and admire themselves for admiring him. To know this man is not just to know a very great, very good, very wise, very spiritual human being. It is to know *God.* His very name is "Jesus," which in Hebrew means "God helps" or "God saves" (Matt. 1:21). He is the "Christ," the "Messiah," the "Anointed One" of God. He is the "Son of God" (Mark 1:1). His miraculous birth is a sign of the fact that where he comes from, who he is, and what he does cannot be explained in terms of the ordinary process of human life and history. This man comes from God. What *he* says and does is *God's* word and action. He is "Emmanuel," God-with-us (Matt. 1:23).

Before we try to understand what this confession means, we must speak of the connection between it and the Christmas story of Jesus' virgin birth. Jesus' virgin birth did not make or prove him to be God-with-us. Even if it could be proved that his mother was a virgin, that would only prove that his birth was a medical anomaly. Christians do not believe that Jesus was God-with-us because he was born of a virgin.

On the contrary, because they have already come to believe that he was God-with-us, they listen to the stories of his miraculous birth. The way goes from faith in Jesus to the virgin birth, not vice versa.

This is the way it is in the New Testament itself. When Jesus spoke during his life, people did not say, "Here is the Son of God who was born in such a miraculous way. We'd better listen to what he has to say." They said, "Is not this Jesus, the son of Joseph, whose father and mother we know?" (John 6:42). Even those who followed him did not follow him because they first knew the secret of his origin. Only after they had lived in his company, listened to what he said, watched what he did, and especially after they had seen his death and experienced his presence as the Risen One—only then did they understand who he was. For the earliest Christians, then, "suffered under Pontius Pilate, was crucified, died, was buried, and rose again" came before a true understanding of "Jesus Christ, his only Son, our Lord." Their deepest faith came not by looking at the beginning but by looking at the end of Jesus' life on earth. Had they not experienced his presence as the living risen Christ, they would simply have dismissed him as another martyred prophet and never have understood who he was and where he came from.

Is not this the way faith comes also to modern people? How many people first believe that Jesus is "divine," born in a miraculous way, then decide to become Christians who place their lives in his hands and follow him? Is it not so that also today people are confronted first of all with the man Jesus—his teaching, his deeds, his suffering, and his living presence—and *then* confess him as God-with-us? What does this have to say about the way we ought to present Jesus to non-Christians? Is *talk* enough? Will people believe what Christians say about Jesus unless they see some evidence of the truth and way of Jesus in the lives of those who talk about him?

What we have been suggesting is the same thing we said at the beginning of this chapter and later with reference to the sinlessness of Jesus: People do not come to believe in Jesus by speculating about his divine and/or human nature. Faith comes by seeing, hearing, and experiencing what he *does*. In our present context this means that we come to recognize Jesus as God-with-us not first of all by speculating about the meaning of his birth but by listening to the story of his life *after* his birth. He is God-with-us because throughout his life he did what God does.

In the light of these considerations, then, what does it mean to say that

Jesus is God-with-us? We will answer this question by reflecting on the meaning of the New Testament confession that Jesus is the "Son of God."

In the first place, "Son of God" is obviously a title of majesty. Before his birth, the angel said to Mary, "He will be great, and will be called the Son of the Most High . . . and of his kingdom there will be no end" (Luke 1:32–33). Fulfilling this prophecy, the man Jesus spoke with godlike authority and acted with godlike power. He dared to correct the word of God in scripture: "You have heard it said . . . but I say to you" (Matt. 5:21–22). He did what only God has the right to do when he forgave sins (Mark 2:5–7). He performed miraculous works demonstrating divine power over evil, sickness, and death. How do we know that this man Jesus is the Son of God, God-with-us? Because he speaks with the authority of God and does mighty works that are God's works.

However, we do not see what is unique about Jesus if we think only of his majestic power. "Son of God" was a common title in the ancient oriental world. Many ancient rulers were called "son of God" because their majesty and power supposedly proved that they were the offspring of the gods. In the New Testament period, one could meet everywhere men who called themselves "son of God" because they claimed that they had miraculous divine powers. Some of them called themselves "savior" for this reason. Perhaps we meet such people in Acts 8:9–11. The fact that Jesus was a miracle worker and spoke with authority was not in itself unique. If he had only been a son of God or savior on the basis of the miraculous powers he demonstrated, he would have been nothing unusual, certainly not *the* Son of God.

The unique thing about *this* Son of God, that which set him apart from all the many "sons of God" and set the Christian religion apart from other ancient religions, was not first of all his strength but his weakness, not his majestic power but his suffering, not his authority and rule but his obedience and service. He was a *lowly* Son of God. We see this at several critical points in the life of Jesus.

Think first of the birth stories. An insignificant little colony of the Roman empire. A stable. The wife of a common laborer. A child of poor people. Who would expect the appearance of the Son of God under these circumstances? What an inappropriate way for God Almighty to come to us!

In the temptation story in Matthew 4:1–11, the Tempter says, "*If* you are the Son of God . . ." Jesus' temptation is that he should use his divine power to care for his own need, gain popularity by miraculous deeds, and become a great world leader. Jesus proves himself to be the true Son of God by refusing to be what other "sons of God" wanted or claimed to be. He came not to fulfill his own needs, desires, and ambitions but to serve the compassion and justice of God in the world.

In Matthew 16:13–20, Peter confesses that Jesus is the "Son of the living God." But when Jesus begins to teach the disciples that as such he must suffer and be killed, Peter protests. And Jesus says to him, "Get behind me, Satan!" (16:23). The idea that the Son of God is to be great and powerful on earth and lord it over people is the idea of the devil. He came not for his own benefit but for that of others, even to the extent of giving up his life for the sake of those who rejected him.

Finally, it is when the centurion sees Jesus dying on the cross between two criminals that he confesses, "Truly this man was God's Son!" (Mark 15:39). It is in Jesus' weakness, failure, and defeat that God's presence and work in him becomes recognizable.

What is the meaning of such texts that contradict what "Son of God" meant to everyone in Jesus' time—and to many Christians in our time? How can we reconcile texts that speak of Jesus as a lowly, suffering Son of God with those that speak of his majestic divine power as the Son of God? The traditional answer is that passages that speak of his weakness and suffering point to his *humanity,* whereas those that speak of his great wisdom, authority, and power point to his *deity.* If that were the case, we would learn nothing new either about God or human life from the story of Jesus. We do not need Jesus to tell us that God is big, strong, and powerful, and that human beings in comparison with God are little, weak, and powerless. Everyone already thinks that the relation between the "divine" and the "human" is the relation between above and below, superior and inferior, master and servant. Some especially pious people have even said that to be truly religious is to think that God is "everything" and we poor sinful human beings are "nothing." (No wonder that others have thought that if we want to defend the value, dignity, freedom, and responsibility of human beings, we must reject faith in God!)

However, the story of the Son of God born on the first Christmas does not just confirm what we already know. It is the amazing good news of the shocking *reversal* of what most people have always thought about God, human beings, and the relation between them. The story of *this* Son of God is not the story of "big God" and "little human beings," the story of a God who asserts divine greatness and power in contrast to human weakness and powerlessness. It is the story of a *God* who becomes little, weak, and powerless so that *human life* may be affirmed, protected, and defended.

Another way to talk about the great reversal that takes place in Jesus is to use language from traditional Christian theology that speaks of his "humiliation" and "exaltation." Christian tradition has usually thought that the humiliation of Jesus is his human life of weakness, suffering, and death; and his exaltation is his divine power over human weakness, suffering, and death. But the great reversal we are suggesting is that in the story of Jesus Christ, Son of God, the Word become flesh, God-with-us, we see the self-humiliation of God and the exaltation (making great) of humanity.[4] *That* is the meaning of the Christmas story, which has been the main theme of this chapter and tells us from the very beginning the meaning of the whole story of Jesus.

The Exaltation of Humanity

In Jesus Christ God came to us in a human being and put God's stamp of approval on human life. Christmas means that what God wills and accomplishes in the world is not the creation of religious people but the creation of *human* people; not just the salvation of our souls but the renewal of our flesh-and-blood humanity; not the ability to escape from our human existence but the ability thankfully to accept and courageously to live an authentically human life both now in this world and in the new heaven and earth to come. God's coming to us in a human being means that God supports and participates in every religious *and* secular movement that enables human life to be more fully human and frees people from all the forces within them and around them that enslave and dehumanize them. Ever since the first Christmas, whoever is against *human beings* (*any* of them) is against *God*, for in Jesus God took up the cause of humanity to make it God's own cause.

The Self-Humiliation of God

If Christmas means that God affirms and exalts the cause of human beings in the world, it also means that God is not too high and mighty, too good, too holy, or too proud to "come down" to our level to participate in earthly human life. God does not sacrifice but exercises divine power, goodness, and holiness in doing this. Christmas means that God is not the prisoner of God's own spirituality, unable to be God in the realm of the unspiritual. It means that unlike all false gods the true God can accomplish the divine will in weakness as well as in might, in self-sacrifice as well as in self-assertion, in the nonreligious as well as in the religious sphere. It means that in taking up the cause of sinful human beings God does not compromise God's justice and holiness; God's good will toward them and for them *is* God's justice and holiness. Christmas means the self-humiliation of the Creator to share the life of the creature. It means the self-humiliation of the Righteous One to stand with and for the unrighteous. Whoever will have God only in heaven, in church, and in religious affairs, or only where there is personal and collective success and happiness; whoever will not look for God in the everyday world, among ordinary human beings, participating in secular human affairs, present also in human failure and suffering—that person will never know God at all. For God is the God who comes to us in the man Jesus, who was born in a stable, grew up to be the friend of sinners and advocate of all who are poor and oppressed, and was (therefore) tried and condemned in a courtroom and executed at public execution grounds.

If you want to know what it means to be a genuinely human being and to stand for the cause of humanity—look at Jesus Christ. If you want to know who God is and what God is doing in the world—look at Jesus Christ. That is what we confess when we say, "I believe in Jesus Christ, his only Son, our Lord. He was conceived by the power of the Holy Spirit and born of the virgin Mary." *How* it is that in this one person we meet both an authentic human being and "God, the Father Almighty" the church has never been able to explain. All attempts to explain it have finally only affirmed *that* it is so. He is at once true human being and true God—God-with-*us* and *God*-with-us.

FOR FURTHER REFLECTION AND STUDY

1. Read the Christmas stories in Matt. 1:18–2:23; Luke 1:26–56; 2:1–20. Make a list of all the names or titles given to Jesus. What information do the two stories have in common? What information is peculiar to each? Do you find contradictions between them? In what sense do you think these stories are history?
2. How would you answer someone who said that the story of Jesus' birth is just another example of the many myths in ancient religions about gods coming miraculously to earth in human form?
3. John of Damascus, a theologian of the eighth century, said that Mary's ear was the bodily organ of the miraculous conception of Christ. What did he mean? Do you agree?

4. Do you think Jesus could have thought that the earth is flat?
5. In what sense, if any, could we say that when Jesus died, God died?
6. The great Greek writer Nikos Kazantzakis wrote a novel, *The Last Temptation of Christ,* in which he suggested that Jesus was troubled by sexual temptations. Do you think the book should be condemned?
7. Do you agree that Jesus was sinless just in being the friend of sinners? How would it influence our daily lives if we followed him? How would it influence the life of the church?
8. If Christians are successful in their business, is that a sign that God has blessed them? If their business is a failure, does that mean that God has not been with them?
9. Read the Magnificat, Mary's song before the birth of Jesus, in Luke 1:46–55. Does this explain why some people have called Christmas a dangerous revolution?
10. We sometimes speak of Christianity as God-centered or Christ-centered. In the light of Christmas, is there a sense in which we ought to say that it is human-centered?
11. In the light of the Christmas story, what is the relation between "secular" and "religious"?
12. If you had to explain who Jesus is to someone who had never heard of him at all, how would you begin?

13

Is God against Us?

The Doctrine of the Atonement

Once upon a time a boy went to a revival meeting. He had grown up in a Christian home and in the church, but he heard something that night he had never heard before.

The preacher held up a dirty glass. "See this glass? That's you. Filthy, stained with sin, inside and outside."

He picked up a hammer. "This hammer is the righteousness of God. It is the instrument of God's wrath against sinners. God's justice can be satisfied only by punishing and destroying people whose lives are filled with vileness and corruption."

The preacher put the glass on the pulpit and slowly, deliberately drew back the hammer, took deadly aim, and with all his might let the blow fall.

But a miracle happened! At the last moment he covered the glass with a pan. The hammer struck with a crash that echoed through the hushed church. He held up the untouched glass with one hand and the mangled pan with the other.

"Jesus Christ died for your sins. He took the punishment that ought to have fallen on you. He satisfied the righteousness of God so that you might go free if you believe in him."

When the boy went to bed that night, he could not sleep. Meditating on what he had seen and heard, he decided that he was terribly *afraid* of God. But could he *love* such a God? He could love Jesus, who had sacrificed himself for him. But how could he love a God who wanted to "get" everyone and was only kept from doing it because Jesus got in the way? The thought crossed the boy's mind that he could only hate such a hammer-swinging God who had to be bought off at such a terrible price. But he quickly dismissed the thought. That very God might read his mind and punish him.

Some other thoughts also troubled the boy. Despite what the preacher said about the righteousness of God, is it really right to punish one person for what other people do? And granted that he was a pretty bad boy sometimes, was he really all that bad? Did he really deserve to *die*? Was he really so sinful that God had to *kill* Jesus to make up for what he had done?

Finally, he wondered what good it had all done in the end. The glass had escaped being smashed to bits, but nothing had really changed. After the drama was over, it was still just as dirty as it was before. Even if Jesus did save him from God, how did Jesus' sacrifice help him to be a different person?

Most of us suspect that there is something wrong with the theology illustrated by the preacher's object lesson. But what? Our purpose in this chapter is to discover the true meaning of Jesus' death for us, to bring back into focus the popular but distorted doctrine of the atonement we have described, and to answer as best we can the questions we have raised.

We do not approach this problem as something brand new, of course. The work of God in the death of Christ has shaped what we have said about the nature of God and human beings, the relationship between them, and the meaning of God-with-us in the birth and life of Jesus. We do not really take up a new topic now but only concentrate on a topic that has run through everything we have been saying from the beginning of our study.

First we will look at the various biblical images that describe the meaning of Jesus' death. Then we will try to understand the underlying truth these images seek to describe in different ways.

THE BIBLICAL IMAGES

When Jesus died, a dream died in the hearts of his followers. They had hoped that he was the Messiah, the chosen one of God who would free their country from the rule of a totalitarian foreign government and establish it not only as a free nation but as one that would be the center of power, virtue, wisdom, and glory in the whole world. They expected to be rewarded for their loyalty to him by receiving positions of honor and authority in the new government. But Jesus was a failure. He did not defeat his enemies; he was defeated by them. He did not free his nation; he was executed as another of many unsuccessful revolutionaries. Following him meant following a loser, not a winner. His death meant nothing but disappointed expectations and unfulfilled hopes—the end.

Only after Easter morning and their experience of the presence of the risen Christ did the first followers of Jesus begin to understand that his death was good news and not just a tragedy. In order to interpret its positive meaning, they used various images or analogies already at their disposal from everyday life. If we are to understand their significance, we need to remember two things about them.

First, the images do not describe a "theory of the atonement" or "plan of salvation" that explains what God must do and what must happen to Jesus if God wants to save the world. The first Christians had been forced to give up all their theories and plans, because God did not act according to their calculations and expectations. They used these images not to explain what God *must* do in order to save us but to interpret what God actually *did* do.

Second, it is no accident that in the New Testament several images are used to interpret the meaning of Jesus' death. No one of them is adequate by itself. Every one of them has its limitations and needs the emphasis of the others for a grasp of the total picture.

The images serve the event, not the event the images. No one image can say everything that needs to be said. We must remember both things if we are not to fall into the error of taking one or another of them too literally and too exclusively, thus forcing the death of Jesus to fit our theories rather than letting our theories be corrected by what actually happened.

Although they often overlap and run into each other, we can distinguish four main images used in the New Testament to interpret the meaning of the first Good Friday.

The Financial Image

The scene is a slave market or prison camp. There sit captives who have lost their freedom. But a man steps up and pays the price (or gives the ransom money) to purchase their freedom (or redeem them). We are the slaves or prisoners. Jesus is our Redeemer. The ransom price is high—his life for ours. But he pays it gladly for our sake.

This image is used frequently in the New Testament. We find it, for instance, in Mark 10:45; Rom. 3:24; 1 Cor. 6:20; 7:23; Gal. 3:13; Titus

2:14; 1 Peter 1:18. It is not the main image used in the confessions of the Reformed tradition, but it does appear in them—as when the Westminster Confession (8.8) says that Christ has "purchased redemption" for us.

Throughout the history of the church, theologians have struggled with a difficult question raised by this image: To whom is the ransom paid to "redeem" us? Some thinkers in the ancient church believed that we are captives of the devil and that Jesus is God's payment to him to buy our freedom. It is a strange idea that God owes the devil anything or would do business with him! Others have believed that it is *God* to whom the ransom is paid. Because of our sinfulness God has become our enemy and Jesus pays the price (death!) demanded by God to save us from God's righteous hostility. But did not Jesus come precisely to fulfill his Father's gracious will for our salvation? Is he himself not God-with-us? Does not the death of Jesus mean that we are saved *by* rather than *from* God?

In a moving way this image describes us as trapped people who cannot free ourselves from the captivity of our sinfulness. It describes Jesus as one who at great cost to himself sets us free. But we ought not try to make the image to say any more than this. We push it too far when we ask to whom the ransom is paid, for there the analogy breaks down.

The Military Image

The scene is a battlefield. God and the devil are at war for possession of people whom the devil has stolen from the kingdom of God and carried off to his kingdom of darkness. A warrior from God invades the territory ruled by Satan to bring these people home again where they belong. It is a deadly, real battle. On Good Friday God's warrior is killed and the powers of darkness seem to be victorious. But on Easter morning he triumphs over them and frees the captives. Jesus is the "Victor" who delivers us from Satan's realm of darkness and death to bring us into God's realm of light and life.

This military image appears, among other places, in Col. 1:13; 2:15; 1 Cor. 15:24–28. It has never been especially popular in the Reformed tradition, but the Eastern Orthodox church and the Lutherans have often used it. (A vivid example is Luther's hymn "A Mighty Fortress.") It is also an image presupposed by various versions of contemporary political and liberation theologies.

To many people in our time the idea of a "cosmic battle" between God and the devil seems too mythological. Moreover, the very idea of God or Jesus as "warrior" is offensive to many in a time when we have seen the devastating consequences of modern warfare, and when we have become aware of the danger of what is called "triumphalism" in the church (the arrogant assumption that as representatives of God Christians are called to defeat and if necessary destroy "evil" people and groups of people who do not think and live as we do). Yet, why should not this "mythological" military imagery still make sense so long as we remember that it is not to be taken literally but precisely as imagery, and so long as we remember that the battle between God and the powers of darkness is not one between "us good people" and "those bad people" who are different from us, but one that goes on in the heart of every one of us, and in the church as well as in the world outside the church?

This dramatic image of the work of God in Christ emphasizes the seriousness both of our predicament and of God's love. We cannot free ourselves from the evil forces that dominate us, but God cares enough about us to enter into a costly struggle to rescue us from them. The disadvantage of this image and of the financial image is that they make us only a prize to be bought or fought over. The battle and ransom imagery explain the difference in our *status* as a result of the work of Christ, but they say nothing of a change in *us*. The sin to which we are slaves or prisoners is not only something *outside* us but something *in* us. Are we ourselves any different just because we are moved from one place to another or from the possession of one person to that of another? How are we any freer for God and for other people because of the work of Christ? Other images are necessary to deal with this question left unanswered by the ransom and battle images.

The Sacrificial Image

The scene is now a place of worship with a bloody altar where sacrifices are offered. There stand guilty people who deserve God's wrathful punishment. A priest comes forward who is the mediator between God and the people. He makes a sacrifice to atone for the people's sin. Blood is shed. A life is offered up. It is a sign of the people's sorrow for their disobedience, their offering of their own lives to God, and cleansing from the stain of their sin. But this priest is different from all other priests in that what he sacrifices is not the life of an animal or a bird but his own life. He lets his own blood be shed to make peace again between the people and God. He is himself the "lamb that is slain." He suffers as the representative of sinful people so that they may be reconciled with God.

This imagery occurs throughout the New Testament (see, e.g., Mark

14:22–24; John 1:29; Rom. 3:25; 1 Cor. 5:7). It is the dominant imagery in the letter to the Hebrews (see chaps. 8–10), where Christ's work is interpreted as that our "Great High Priest." The image of Christ's work as a sacrifice occurs often in all Christian traditions. A good example in the Reformed tradition is chapter 9 of the Scots Confession.

When the New Testament was written, the sacrifice of animals was a familiar part of worship, so it was natural to interpret the death of Jesus as the shedding of blood to atone for our sins. We no longer worship in this way, and it is hard for us to understand what the sacrificial system meant to the people who practiced it. Many people in our time are repulsed by a "blood" theology. That is perhaps the main disadvantage of this imagery for us. But if we can overcome our aversion to the bloody rituals of the ancient Jews, we can see that this imagery says something very important. It points to our guilt and need for forgiveness, our estrangement from God and need for reconciliation. The shed blood of Jesus emphasizes in a shockingly realistic way his unlimited love for us and the cost he was willing to pay to help and heal us.

One danger of using sacrificial imagery to speak of the significance of Jesus' death is that it can easily be corrupted in a way similar to the way the sacrificial system in ancient Israel was corrupted. The prophets warned the people of Israel that God was sick and tired of their sacrifices and would not listen to their prayers so long as the reconciliation to God promised in their religious rites did not find an echo in their life together (see Isa. 1:10–31; Amos 5:22–24; Hos. 6:6; Micah 6:6–8). This warning also applies to Christians who think that Christ's sacrificial death for us is permission complacently to settle down in our personal and social sinfulness, confident that God will automatically forgive because "Jesus paid it all." All talk about sacrifice—even Jesus' self-sacrifice for us—is empty religiosity if we do not cease to do evil, learn to do good, seek justice, rescue the oppressed, and care for those who like orphans and widows cannot help themselves (Isa. 1:17). What would the prophets say to modern Christians who divide up sides to support *either* a church that sticks to proclamation of salvation through the sacrificial death of Christ *or* a church concerned with issues of social justice?

The Legal Image

The scene is now a courtroom. God, the just Judge, sits behind the desk, and people who have broken the law stand in front of it to be tried. They hear the verdict: Guilty. They receive the sentence: Death. But a righteous man who has obeyed the law perfectly comes and stands beside the accused, takes the death penalty on himself, and suffers the consequences of their guilt in their place. Those who were enemies of the law (and thus of the Judge also) are now acquitted and reconciled. Order is restored. They no longer have to fear the Judge but are free to go out to begin a new life.

This legal imagery is especially characteristic of Paul (see Rom. 5:6–11; 2 Cor. 5:16–21; Col. 1:19–20). (According to these texts, is God reconciled to us or are we reconciled to God? Who does the reconciling?) This imagery is used more than any other in the confessions of the Reformed tradition.

What is said with the legal image is basically the same thing said with other images the New Testament uses to speak of the meaning of Christ's death for us. It too describes our desperate situation before God and the unreserved love of Christ for us. But unlike some of the other imagery we have discussed, this imagery has the advantage of being immediately understandable to us. Concepts like judge, law, guilt, verdict, sentence, justice, and reconciliation are all part of our everyday vocabulary and experience.

On the other hand, the legal image raises difficult questions similar to those raised by the other images (and by the preacher's object lesson with which we began this chapter). Does Christ's "taking the rap" for us mean that we are now free to go on living however we please? Can the guilt of some people be transferred to another? Is it fair for God to punish Christ for our sins? If, according to the New Testament, the Father and the Son will and do the same thing, how can we understand the Son's self-giving love in opposition to the Father's wrathful justice? The very familiarity of legal imagery makes it all the more difficult to understand the meaning of Christ's death for us.

Now that we have the atonement images of the New Testament in mind and have seen something of their strengths and weaknesses, we will try to understand the one gospel they all seek to proclaim.

GOD VERSUS THE GODS

One way to get at the meaning of the doctrine of the atonement in biblical religion is to contrast it with what atonement, or reconciliation, meant in other ancient religions (and still means in some modern versions of them).

People in the ancient world lived in terror before gods who were easily offended by disrespect and disobedience, and quick to seek revenge and retribution. In order to live in peace and prosperity, people had to do what they could to appease, placate, or satisfy the angry gods. Prayers, good deeds, and above all sacrifices were the means by which they sought to ease their guilty consciences, atone for their sins, and win the approval of the gods. These religious rituals and moral achievements were also ways of manipulating the gods into giving people supernatural help. What their gods thought of them and how their gods acted toward them depended upon what the people (or a priestly representative) did to "butter them up" and "buy them off." Sometimes this cost people a great deal, but with their piety and sacrifices *they* paid the price and *they* won the salvation. It was basically "do it yourself" religion.

The situation of estrangement and need for reconciliation we have described is not strange to us. That is why biblical religion can be so easily twisted into superstitious "primitive" paganism in our time too. But the God of the Bible is different from the gods, and the Christian doctrine of atonement is different from what we have just described. We see the difference when we look at the character of the God we meet in the history of Israel and above all in Jesus Christ. Or to put it in terms of the church's doctrine of the Trinity, we see the difference when we remember the Trinitarian rule that the works of the Father, Son, and Holy Spirit cannot be separated or set in opposition to each other, for what one wills and does is what the others will and do also (see chapter 5).

The Love of God

Christians also know that sinful human beings are alienated from God. It is our fault. We have disobeyed God's commandments. Even worse, we have ignored or rejected God's love. But strangely enough, it is not the guilty but the *injured* party who acts to restore the broken relationship. God does not demand that we first do something to make up for what we have done or not done before God reluctantly agrees to forgive and love us again. God makes the first move. Exactly the opposite of the procedure in pagan religions, it is not God who is reconciled to us but we who are reconciled to God. It is not we who make peace with God but God who makes peace with us. That is what the death of Jesus is all about.

It is especially important to emphasize this point, because it is called into question by one classical view of the work of Christ that has strongly influenced all Christian traditions, including the Reformed tradition (Westminster Confession, 8.5). We refer to the view of Anselm (A.D.

1033–1109), who reasoned that our sin has offended God's honor and righteousness. God cannot be reconciled to us until something is done to make reparation for our insulting the divine dignity and to pay for the sins we have committed. By his perfect obedience and sacrifice Jesus fulfilled this requirement and made it possible for God to accept us. Jesus thus changed God's mind toward us and purchased God's love for us. This is called the "satisfaction" theory of the atonement.

Despite the great influence of Anselm's view, it is unbiblical. Nowhere does scripture use the word *satisfaction.* It tells us that Jesus came to *express,* not to *change,* God's mind. It says that reconciliation is the work *of* God, not that it is purchased *from* God. What Jesus does is not done *over against* God; his work *is* God's work, for he himself is God-with-us.

The Bible does not teach that *if* certain conditions are fulfilled with, by, or for us, *then* God will love us. Nor does it say that *if* our sins are atoned for in one way or another, *then* God will forgive and save us. What kind of love or forgiveness is it that has to be bought or wrung out of another? What the Bible does teach is that "God proves his love for us in that *while we still were sinners* Christ died for us" (Rom. 5:8, emphasis added). It teaches that "We love because he first loved us" (1 John 4:19). Jesus died not so that the God who did not love us could begin to love us, but because he already loved us. Quoting Augustine, Calvin put it this way:

> For it was not after we were reconciled to him through the blood of his Son that he began to love us. Rather, he has loved us before the world was created, that we also might be his sons along with his only-begotten Son—before we became anything at all. The fact that we were reconciled through Christ's death must not be understood as if his Son reconciled us to him that he might now begin to love those whom he had hated. Rather, we have already been reconciled to him who loves us, with whom we were enemies on account of sin. (*Institutes* 2.16.4)

This change from pagan concern to reconcile the gods to us to Christian faith in the God who was in Christ reconciling us to God obviously affects the meaning of all the images that describe the work in Christ in the New Testament.

The *financial* image does not mean that God is bought off by Jesus. What Jesus "purchases" is sinful humanity (1 Cor. 6:20; 7:23)—not *from* but *for* and *by* God. To be "redeemed" is not to be saved from an angry God seeking revenge. It is to be saved or redeemed from the sin that separates us from the God who loves us and wills only our good even when we live in self-destructive, sinful alienation from God.

The *sacrificial* imagery does not describe Jesus' self-sacrifice as something that God needs but something that we need. The New Testament never suggests that it was necessary to "satisfy" God's justice or change God's attitude toward us. On the contrary, the New Testament speaks of its effect on those for whom the sacrifice was made (Heb. 9:9, 14; 10:10, 14; 13:12).[1] Even in the Old Testament, sacrifice is not something that comes from the people to pacify a reluctant God; it is given by God because God desires reconciliation with them (Lev. 17:11). In a much debated statement, Rom. 3:25 says that Jesus' blood is a "sacrifice of atonement" (earlier translations say "propitiation" or "expiation"), but even there it is explicitly said that *God* "put forward" Jesus. A sacrifice is made to set things right between a righteous God and sinful human beings. But if Jesus is himself God-with-us, it is God who makes the sacrifice. Jesus' self-sacrifice is also God's self-sacrifice: The "Son" loves us so much that he gave up his life for us, and the "Father" loves us so much that he gave up his only dearly beloved Son for us.[2] Jesus' sacrifice is not a way of manipulating God to be on our side; it is God's way of winning us to God's side.

The *legal* imagery of the New Testament says the same thing. Jesus does take the deserved punishment for sin upon himself, but not to satisfy the justice of a Judge who is against us. Jesus is himself the Judge (2 Cor. 5:10; Acts 10:42). If he is judged and condemned for us, then that means that the Judge gives *himself* to be judged for us, in our place. If we speak of "satisfaction" at all, we must say that in Jesus God satisfied God's just judgment against us by taking it on God's own self. Calvin expresses this beautifully in Question 87 of the Geneva Catechism: "We should not then fear the last judgment and have a horror of it? No, since we are not to come before any other Judge than he who is our Advocate, and who has taken our cause in hand to defend us."

In summary: In contrast to ancient (and modern) paganism and Anselm's legalistic view, the biblical doctrine of the atonement teaches that it is *God* who initiates and fulfills the reconciliation between sinful humanity and God. God is the subject, not the object, of what happened on Good Friday. God's desire is not to crush us "dirty glasses" with the hammer of God's wrath so that we have to turn to Jesus to keep God from doing what God would like to do to us. Jesus is himself the coming of "God our Savior, who desires everyone to be saved" (1 Tim. 2:3–4). The death of Jesus for us is God's own action to fulfill that desire. "All this is from God, who reconciled us to himself through Christ (2 Cor. 5:18). The doctrine of the atonement should awaken in us first of all not terror of God's wrath but joyful thanksgiving for God's love.

Costly Love

If God already loves and forgives us, why atonement at all? Why did Jesus have to die to reconcile us to God? Why did not God just say, "I forgive you," and let it go at that?

We can catch a glimpse of the answer with an analogy in human relationships.[3] Suppose that I have done something that betrays a friendship and hurts a friend. Suppose that I go to her to tell her how sorry I am and how bad I feel about it, and she says to me, "That's OK. It doesn't make any difference. Forget it." Has she forgiven me? What she has really said is, "I don't care enough about you to be bothered by anything you say or do. You are not that important to me." She also leaves me alone with the pain of my guilt, refusing to help me deal with it, put it behind me, and make a fresh beginning with her.

Good-natured indulgence and casual acceptance are not forgiveness and love but an expression of indifference and sometimes hostility. Real love and forgiveness mean caring enough to be hurt, caring enough to put ourselves in others' shoes and sharing their guilt as if it were our own. Real love and forgiveness are costly—not in the sense that the guilty party must squeeze them out of the injured party but in the sense that the injured party genuinely sympathizes with the guilty and shares his or her pain.

Why did Jesus have to die? Why atonement? Because God cares for us too much to dismiss our sin and guilt with a flippant "It doesn't matter." Because words were not enough: *action* was necessary to prove that God's love and forgiveness are genuine. Because God wanted to stand with us in the loneliness and alienation we bring on ourselves when we separate ourselves from God and other people. Because it is just when God comes to our side in our loneliness, alienation, and guilt that they are overcome. In the cross God says to us, "Yes, it is true. You *have* hurt and offended me. But I still love you. Therefore I will make your guilt and its consequences my own. I will suffer with you—*for* you—to make things right between us again."

The Wrath of God

Only in light of the love of God so unqualified that God is willing to pay the cost of loving can we understand what the Bible means when it speaks of the wrath of God (see, e.g., Rom. 1:18; 5:9; Eph. 5:6; Col. 3:5–6). In pagan religions the wrath of the gods is an *alternative* to love. Their hostility can be changed to acceptance and love only after those who have offended them have been made to pay for their offenses. But if the God of Christian faith *is* love, then this God's wrath cannot be an alternative to love; it must be an *expression* of love. The death of Jesus for our sin shows us how this is true in at least three ways:

1. The very fact that God can be angry with us means that God is interested in us and cares enough to be offended and hurt by us. We have just seen that simply to ignore or shrug off sin would mean not love but indifference. God's relationship with us is not like that of a husband and wife who never fight with one another because they live together as politely uninvolved strangers. Nor is it like that of a parent who does not care enough about a child to become angry when the child "acts up." God can be angry with us *because* God loves us. In this sense the wrath of God that demands the atoning death of Jesus is a part of the gospel: God *cares* about us!

2. God's wrath is an expression of God's love because it means that God cares enough to refuse to let us get by with our sin. When we refuse to love God and our neighbors as ourselves, we not only sin against God; we deny our own humanity and hurt ourselves. God's wrath burns against us in order to call us back to order again for our own good. The cross of Christ who died for our sins means that God judges and disciplines in order to help, to put an end to the inhuman, self-destructive path we have chosen, and to set us on the right path again. God's wrath is God's *loving* wrath.

3. God's wrath is an expression of God's love because in the death of Christ *God* bears the painful consequences of our sin. This brings us full circle to our beginning point. The wrathful Judge looks over the desk and pronounces the death sentence, but the death of Christ for us means that the Judge then goes around to the other side of the desk to accept the sentence on behalf of those who deserve it. The Judge rules with harsh, uncompromising justice that the debt to law and order must be paid—then the *Judge* pays the fine. The holy God thunders that a sacrifice must be made to atone for human sin—then makes a *self-sacrifice.* If the object lesson with which we began this chapter were to be similar in any way to what really happened, the preacher would have to put his own hand over the dirty glass to receive the blow of the hammer. He would hurt himself, of course, but that is just how God executes God's wrathful judgment.

Must we talk about the wrath of God? Yes. But God's wrath is not like that of the gods. It is the wrath of the God who was in Christ reconciling the world to God's self. We cannot understand the depth of the love of God without talking about God's wrath. But neither can we understand God's wrath without talking about God's self-giving love.

WERE YOU THERE?

We have been thinking about what the death of Jesus means from God's side—God's taking the initiative to reconcile us to God. But it takes two parties for reconciliation to happen, those who need to be reconciled as well as the one who reconciles. If we are to understand the meaning of the cross, then, we have to ask how *we* are affected by what happened on Good Friday. To believe that Jesus died for us is not only to have a radical new understanding of God but to have a radical new understanding of ourselves. More than that, it means to *be* different. But *how* are we different?

In a sense, all the rest of this book will be an attempt to answer this question, but we must begin to answer it now. In doing so, we will pick up the questions we have kept raising about our involvement in the atonement: Are we really so bad that only Jesus' death could make things right between ourselves and God? Is it fair for another to "take the rap" for us? Does it really help? Are we not still the same old "dirty glasses" we were before? Words are inadequate to express what Christians experience and believe at this point. But we can list at least four things the cross tells us about ourselves and does for and to us.

The cross convicts us of our sinfulness. "Were you there when they crucified my Lord?" Yes, we were there. What they did then, we still do. The cross of two thousand years ago exposes the kind of people *we* are.

We were there with *Judas* who sold out, probably because Jesus refused to serve Judas's military and political goals for his nation. If it comes to a choice between the justice of the kingdom of God for all people and the self-interest of our own people, it is clear which we must choose.

We were there with the *disciples* who deserted him and fled when they discovered that loyalty to him meant being rejected by both the political and religious authorities, thrown in jail, and perhaps killed. Why be a Christian if it does not pay off? Who wants to follow a loser—especially one who gets us into trouble with the authorities?

We were there with the pious *leaders of the religious establishment* who were out to get him because he did not act as they thought one sent from God ought to act. He criticized good law-abiding people and made friends with guilty sinful people. He thought human beings were more important than moral and religious rules and conventions. Who can tolerate such a threat to the moral and religious foundations of our society?

We were there with *Peter* when he denied him. When it is safe and words are cheap, we too confess, "You are the Messiah, the Son of the living God." But when we are among outsiders, we too are afraid to be different. It is better to be silent, and if necessary deny him, than to get into trouble by having convictions and attitudes that only make people mad and turn against you.

We were there with *Pilate* when he made the decision to let the mob have Jesus, although he knew the defendant was innocent. It is better to sacrifice Jesus than to go against the will of the majority of the people. What can you do when the choice is between justice that threatens and injustice that preserves your own comfort, power, and wealth?

We were there with the *soldiers* who played games while he died. While many of us enjoy all the pleasures of American affluence, within a few blocks of where we live (not to mention across the world) children go to bed hungry at night, "strangers" are excluded not only from the benefits of our civil society but also from our churches, sick people are untended, lonely elderly people are forgotten or ignored, prisoners sit alone in darkness. According to Jesus himself, when they suffer he suffers too. What we do or leave undone with them, we do or leave undone with him.

We were there. The cross of Jesus exposes not just "their" sin back then and there but *our* sin here and now. When we read about them, we read about ourselves. Those of us who are willing to let ourselves be told this will not even think of going on with defensive questions and arguments about whether we are as bad as some other people or so bad that the atoning death of Christ was really necessary. We can only ask how we can be changed from the kind of people we are to become new and different people. Is it possible that only the *death* of what we are can make a new life possible?

The cross enables us to live as forgiven sinners. Is it fair for one person to suffer for what another has done? No, of course it is not fair. In one sense it is not even possible. If I had committed a crime, no court would allow an innocent person to go to jail or be put to death in my place. Even if another did receive the punishment I deserve, I would still be guilty for the crime I have committed. Guilt is not transferable. My guilt cannot be removed or made up for by anyone else.

However, the legal and sacrificial imagery of the Bible does not intend to picture a kind of legalistic transaction in which our guilt is transferred to Christ. The unheard-of act in which the Judge takes the sentence on himself or the Priest sacrifices his own life moves far beyond what is merely fair or necessary if justice is to be done. When we talk about *this* Judge and Priest, we have to do not so much with the legal demand that debts must be paid as with love that forgives debts. Jesus taught us to pray, "Forgive us our debts." The cross says to us, "Your debts are forgiven." What does that mean?

It means the recognition that we are still debtors, still guilty. Everything has not been stamped "paid" so that the books are in order and we can complacently go on our way. We *have* worshiped and served ourselves rather than God. In all kinds of ways we *have* hurt other people, or by our silence and inactivity *let* them be hurt. We *have* contradicted our own humanity. Christ does not take away our guilt so that all the damage we have done to others and to ourselves is magically undone. We *are* guilty sinners. We have just seen how the cross of Christ exposes our guilt.

But to know that we are *forgiven* debtors means that we do not have to circle round and round ourselves, arrogantly defending or anxiously condemning ourselves, or trying to think up excuses to make our guilt seem less than it is and easier to bear. We have been forgiven! God forgives us. We no longer have to spend our lives with tormented consciences, desperately trying to work off our guilt, desperately trying to convince ourselves that we are not so bad after all, or desperately trying to justify ourselves by arguing that at least we are not as bad as some others we could name. To be forgiven means to be free to put behind us what we have been and done, or what we have *not* been and *not* done. It means to be free for a new beginning with God, other people, and ourselves. If God has forgiven us, without demanding that we "pay up," then we can forgive ourselves. We can forget what lies behind and press on to what lies ahead.

A legalistic view of the death of Christ that says he has paid God off makes us complacent in our sinfulness: because he has satisfied the Judge, we can go on living as we please. Or it makes us miserable, because we know that in truth we are still the same old sinful people we were even if we do escape the wrath of God. But to believe that Christ died "for us" and "in our place" means that we can honestly acknowledge what we have been and still are but that we may live as *forgiven* sinners, free both from self-hating preoccupation with our guilt and from defensive attempts to deny it, free *from* the past and free *for* a new future.

The cross means the death of sinners. We have said that we were there on Good Friday with all the people around the cross because we do the same things they did. But the New Testament teaches that we were there also in another sense. We were there *on* the cross. What happened to Christ has also happened to us. When he died for us sinners, we were put to death with him. See how this is said in Rom. 6:1–14; 2 Cor. 5:14–15; and Gal. 2:20.

Here we encounter a way of thinking that was familiar to the ancient Semitic mind but is very strange to us. In our time, probably only those with the very deepest Christian faith and experience can understand it—and even they cannot explain it to those who have not shared the experience. What can it possibly mean to say that "one has died, therefore all have died," and more directly, "I have been crucified with Christ"?

The ancient Jews believed that one person could represent, or "stand for," other people so completely that what happened to that person actually happened to them too. It did not happen to him *instead* of to them. Rather, his experience *was* their experience. Perhaps we can get a vague idea of this complete identity from some of our own experiences. A mother can love a child so much that when the child is hurt the mother hurts too. A wife can love her husband so much that when he dies, she can say, "Something in me died with him." Some people can be so totally committed to a political or social cause that its victory or defeat is a matter of life or death to them personally. More superficially, some people can be so involved with football players who represent them on the field that the defeat or victory of the team is a bitter loss or a triumphant gain for them also. Something like this losing and finding our own existence in someone or something outside ourselves is meant by the biblical concept of representation.

Even if these examples dimly echo the kind of identity Paul says Christians have with Jesus, there is still the big difference that Jesus lived a long time ago. How can we say that what happened to him back then happened also to us? Following is an attempt to answer this difficult question.

To believe in Jesus is to believe that when I hear about him, at the same time I learn who I am. He is one who lived a truly human life and reveals to me what my own true humanity is. Yet the contrast between us exposes the fact that I have not (cannot) fulfill that humanity. I have denied it by not loving God with my whole being and my neighbor as myself. But then I hear that Jesus was the *friend* of sinners—people like me who are alienated from God, from other people, and therefore also from themselves. He stood with and for us so completely that he suffered the death that is the consequence of *our* sin. From him I learn that in order to achieve true humanity in community with God and my fellow human beings, my self-destructive inhumanity must be put out of the way. I do not learn this only intellectually; I learn it in my own experience. This Jesus who lived so long ago is so much a part of me and the way I understand myself, and I am so closely connected with him, that when I hear about his dying, I die too. My old self is "crucified" with him. I experience the new and genuine humanity that he represents and that I receive in his company.

How does Jesus' death affect me? Not just as something that happened to him instead of me, but as something that happens to me too. On that Good Friday so long ago was revealed the truth about *all* people in *all* times and places, including me in my time and place. As I believe in and follow the one who died then, what he was and did and what happened to him shape my own life. I discover, in short, that "I have been crucified with Christ; and it is no longer I who live, but it is Christ who lives in me. And the life I now live in the flesh I live by faith in the Son of God, who loved me and gave himself for me" (Gal. 2:19–20).

Is this putting to death of our "old" inhuman selves and the birth of "new" truly human selves through our identity with Christ even conceivable for us today? Can we give ourselves so completely to him? These are questions that the doctrine of the atonement itself does not answer. The answer lies in the doctrines of the Holy Spirit, justification, and sanctification that still lie ahead of us.

For the present, it is enough to say that when we begin to wrestle with this way of looking at the meaning of Jesus' death, we are a long way from the tin pan crushed instead of a dirty glass. From our present point of view, the cross means that we dirty glasses *are* destroyed when we meet God in Christ. To be a Christian is not to escape from this shattering encounter. Escape would mean only escape into the hell of continued existence in lonely separation from him, from other people, and from our own true selves. The Christian way is not the way of escape so that we can keep on the way we are; it is the death of what we are. For only as our old inhumanity is painfully given up can we hope for a genuinely human life. "For those who want to save their life will lose it, and those who lose their life for my sake will save it" (Luke 9:24).

The cross changes our relationship with other people. Our emphasis until now has been on how the death of Jesus affects our relationship with God. But our discussion would not be complete if we did not emphasize finally how it affects our relationship with other people. If this is the last thing we say about the significance of the atonement, it is also the test of whether everything else we have said is only pious talk.

If the cross really enables us to understand and live by the good news that our debts are forgiven, and if it means that our old selves are really killed in order that new selves may be born, then we will be reconciled not only with God but also with fellow human beings. At the same time that Christ breaks down the walls of hostility between us and God, he also breaks them down between us and other people (Eph. 2:14). To believe that God has loved us at such great cost is to know ourselves called to love one another (1 John 4:11). If we follow Jesus, who took the form of a servant, "humbled himself and became obedient to the point of death," then we will have the "mind of Christ," looking not only to our own interests but to the interests of others (Phil. 2:3–8). The New Testament makes this unmistakably clear: *There is no such thing as reconciliation with God without reconciliation with our fellow human beings.* Hostility and ill will toward them—*any* of them—is also hostility and ill will toward God. Peace with God always means peace also with them—*all* of them.

Moreover, the way reconciliation with God takes place determines *how* reconciliation with other people happens. The *offended* takes the initiative (not just with words but with action) to go to the side of the other. There can be no question of "*If* you pay for what you have done, *if* you make up for your offenses and prove yourself worthy, *then* I will forgive you." There will be no suggestion that our acceptance, forgiveness, and love have to be earned, bought, or squeezed out of us. This does not mean that Christians are sweet, passive doormats who excuse all offenses and injustices with a gentle, suffering smile. It does not mean, for instance, that we should simply suffer in silence when others have hurt us, or that parents should not discipline disobedient children, or that society should not punish criminals. Nor does it mean that victims of social injustice should accept the way things are for the sake of "peace and order." Instead of commitment to reconciliation, that would mean ignoring, covering over the *need* for reconciliation, both on the part of those who have caused or allowed others to be hurt and on the part of those who have been hurt. There is such a thing as legitimate anger at offenses to ourselves, lawlessness that destroys human community, and especially at social injustice. Such anger is the honest acknowledgment of the hostility, alienation, and wrong that in fact exist and must be exposed, opposed, and corrected if genuine reconciliation is to be achieved. But legitimate anger (that is, anger that reflects the wrath of God) will not express itself in a vindictive desire to get even, pay back, and destroy "the enemy." It will express itself in the search for ways to heal broken relationships, restore order, and liberate the oppressed for the good of everyone on both sides or all sides.[4]

We will consider later how such reconciliation is achieved when we think about what faithful Christian life looks like. The point to be made now is simply that to believe that "God was in Christ reconciling the world to himself" means inevitably and inescapably to take the initiative to do what is necessary to achieve genuine reconciliation in all the human relationships in which we live—reconciliation between children and parents, husbands and wives, women and men in church and society, homosexual and heterosexual people, Christians and non-Christians, people of all races, classes, and national heritages.

Here we learn at the very heart of the Christian faith, at the cross of Christ, what we have seen at every other point in our study: Christian faith never has to do only with the "religious" sphere of life and our "spiritual" relationship with God. It always includes *every* dimension of our lives, secular as well as religious, social and political as well as personal and familial, life in the world as well as life in the church.

FOR FURTHER REFLECTION AND STUDY

1. Which of the biblical images describing the atonement is most helpful to you? Which would be most helpful in expressing the meaning of Christ's death to a non-Christian?
2. Ancient people believed they could pacify their gods and buy their support by sacrificing animals. How do modern people try to pacify God and win God's approval and help?
3. Do you agree with the position defended in this book that God does not need to be reconciled to sinful people but that they need to be reconciled to God? Support your answer with scripture.
4. Can forgiveness and love be earned?
5. Is it harder to forgive or to accept forgiveness?

6. What is the difference between tolerance and love?
7. In what way should parents let a disobedient child know that they are not against but for the child?
8. How could a husband or wife or friend show genuine forgiveness by sharing the guilt of a partner who has been unfaithful?
9. Would the most healthy marriage or friendship be one in which the partners never expressed anger toward each other?
10. How would you answer the question regarding how the death of Christ two thousand years ago affects us today?
11. There are three major theories about the purpose of punishing criminals: protection of society by preventing further crimes, retribution or expiation for the crime, and rehabilitation. In light of the doctrine of the atonement, which of these do you think Christians should support? Does the doctrine of the atonement help us decide whether Christians should support capital punishment?
12. Is there a conflict between seeking *reconciliation* or seeking *justice* in the relations between (1) people of different races, (2) men and women in business and professions?
13. Read Matt. 18:23–35. What light does this parable throw on the connection between reconciliation with God and reconciliation with other people?

14

Who's in Charge Here?

The Doctrine of the Resurrection

"The third day he rose again from the dead. By this he declared himself the conqueror of death and sin, for by his resurrection he swallowed up death, broke the fetters of the devil, and destroyed all his power." That is what Calvin said in Question 73 of his Geneva Catechism. That is what the Bible says. That is what we sing with full organ and trumpets at Easter: "Hallelujah! The Lord God omnipotent reigneth. . . . The kingdom of this world is become the kingdom of our Lord and of his Christ, and he shall reign for ever and ever."

But that is not what the newspapers and television say. Rather, they report another devastating earthquake, hurricane, drought, or flood. The cold war between the great superpowers ended only to give rise to regional wars around the world (strangely enough, in our "secularized" world, to defend "true" Christianity, Judaism, Islam, or Buddhism). Hundreds of thousands of refugees are driven from their homes with no place to go because no one will take them in. Another forty thousand people have been fired by another big company because computers and machines are replacing workers in modern business and industry. Statistics show that the few rich in the world are still growing richer while the many poor are growing poorer. There are reports of squalor, misery, crime, and riots in inner cities everywhere. Racism persists despite pious talk. AIDS. Drugs. Cancer. Abused women and children. Inefficient and corrupt government. Stories of churches that can offer no guidance and help because they are split into the same warring ideological factions as the society in which they live.

By the time you read this the specific details will be different, but it will be the same old story. Death, sin, and the devil will *not* be overcome. They still will be making the headlines—or be hidden in the back pages or not mentioned at all, depending on whose death, whose sin, and which works of the devil seem newsworthy.

Is Easter only for people who close their eyes to the facts of life and seek escape in fairy stories, baby bunnies, spring flowers, and loud music? Is there any connection between the news and the Good News, between the "kingdom of this world" and "the kingdom of our Lord and of his Christ"? That is what we have to discuss in this chapter as realistically and as faithfully as we can. First we will look at the New Testament stories of the resurrection and ascension of Jesus. Then we will begin the task of trying to understand what that event in ancient history means for us today.

ON THE THIRD DAY

If it could be said that the whole of the Christian faith stands or falls with any one claim, the claim that God raised the crucified Jesus from the dead is that claim. Without faith in a risen and living Christ there would be no Christianity. It was not Jesus' ethical teachings and example or his noble death that gave birth to the Christian church and made it spread; it was the news of his resurrection. We have seen that it was only because they first believed in a risen Christ that the first Christians looked back to ask about the meaning of his birth, life, and death. Paul wrote: "If Christ has not been raised, your faith is futile and you are still in your sins. . . . [W]e are of all people most to be pitied" (1 Cor. 15:17–19). The earliest Christian confession summarizing everything the first Christians believed was "Jesus is Lord"—a title conferred on him because of his resurrection.

In the past the church often made the cross the center of its faith. Calvin and the Westminster Confession, for instance, gave careful attention to the meaning of Jesus' reconciling death for us, but only very briefly discussed the resurrection. Having for a time rejected such a one-sided emphasis on Jesus' death, contemporary theology has "rediscovered" a theology of the cross and found new meaning in it. In face of the tragic suffering of so many people in the modern world, especially those who are poor and oppressed, the gospel is the good news of a suffering, crucified Jesus—and therefore a suffering, crucified *God*—who is present in self-giving love with suffering people to stand with and for and by them in their suffering.[1] Both the classical and contemporary emphases on the significance of Jesus' suffering and death are indispensable for a genuinely biblical and realistic understanding of the Christian faith. But the cross is an appropriate symbol for Christians only if it is an *empty* cross. The foundation, center, and goal of Christian faith is not suffering and death but new life, not tragedy but victory beyond tragedy. Christian faith is faith in a Suffering Servant who is and will be risen Lord. The God we meet in Christ is indeed a God of self-giving, suffering love, but also a God of powerful, liberating love. To be a Christian is not just to experience the forgiving grace of God for sinful people; it is to experience the renewing grace of God that empowers them to get up and move out of their sinfulness into active, joyful service of God and fellow human beings. To be a Christian is not just to expect the *presence* of God in the depths of our own and others' suffering; it is to expect the active *work* of God in our individual lives, in the church, and in the world to create a new humanity in a new world in which the life, justice, and peace of the kingdom of God will finally triumph over the powers of sin, evil, suffering, injustice, and death. Why is this so? He is risen! That is the first and last word about what it means to believe and live as Christians. The resurrection of Christ is the one event in history that gives meaning to all of history, including our own.

But can we believe it? What is actually supposed to have happened, and what evidence is there that it really did happen? Let us look at the story. We find five different versions of it: Matt. 28:1–20; Mark 16:1–19; Luke 24:1–51; John 20:1–21, 25–27; 1 Cor. 15:3–8. A comparative study of these accounts yields the following conclusions.

Emphasis on the Risen Christ

Many people witnessed the crucifixion, but no one witnessed the resurrection. No one was there when it happened, and no attempt is made in the New Testament to describe it. The resurrection stories are not really accounts of the resurrection itself but accounts of the appearances of the risen Jesus. This ought to warn us against any speculation about what happened in the tomb and how a dead man came to life again. Strictly speaking, Christian faith is faith in the risen Christ, not faith in the empty tomb or in the resurrection as such.

Faith, Not Proof

There is no proof that Jesus rose from the dead. Even an empty tomb does not prove it. In light of what both personal experience and scientific possibility or probability teach us (dead people stay dead!), is it not more likely that Jesus was not really dead in the first place but only in a coma? Or that his disciples stole the body (see Matt. 28:13)? Moreover, even if there were medical reports to confirm it, they still would not prove that *God* raised him or that his resurrection meant his victory over all the powers of sin and evil. It would only prove that a medical wonder happened. The empty tomb, in short, is no proof of anything.

Critics have argued further that the different accounts of the resurrection do not jibe. The sequence of events on the first Easter Sunday and the following days is different from one story to the next. The accounts differ in reporting to whom he appeared and when. They contradict each other in details. How many angels were there, for instance, and where were they? It is very difficult, if not impossible, to harmonize the various resurrection stories. Does not their conflicting witness throw doubt on the truth of what they are supposed to report?

Finally, it has also been pointed out that only *believers* ever saw the risen Christ. Is it not significant that no unbiased observer ever saw him? Were not the appearances of the risen Jesus in fact only hallucinations of those who could not accept the fact that he was really dead? Is it not possible that they simply made up the stories to try to convince other people that they had not been wrong in believing Jesus to be the Messiah?

The criticisms we have mentioned can be partially answered. We have already pointed out that the faith of the first Christians was not founded on arguments about the empty tomb but on their encounter with the risen Christ. It was not from the tomb but from *him* that they learned the meaning of his resurrection.

Second, it is true that the reports cannot be harmonized in detail. Why should we be surprised, considering the fact that they were first written down a generation or more after the event? Besides that, however they differ in details about *how* it all took place, they are all agreed on the essential point *that* the same Jesus who died on Good Friday lived again and appeared to his followers.

Again, it is true that only believers saw him. But all the reports emphasize that the women and the disciples did not expect to discover that he lived and were anything but eager to believe it. They were worried, afraid, skeptical even after they saw him. See Matt. 28:17; Mark 16:8, 11, 13; Luke 24:11, 36–39; John 20:24–28. It was not just a matter of convincing others; their own unbelief had to be overcome. It was not a matter of wishful thinking and wanting to pretend to themselves that he was alive; their own certainty that he was dead, buried, and gone from them forever had to be overcome. They were *reluctant* believers.

These answers do not prove that the reports are true, of course. There *is* no proof. Doubts and questions about the whole thing are inevitable. Jesus' own closest disciples, people who were there when it happened, had trouble believing it. Yet faith does not come only where there is proof without doubt or question. It comes in the midst of doubt and questioning. For us that means we must listen, without any proof at all, to what we are told about this absolutely unique "unscientific" event. Why should we listen? We do so, not so that we may believe the witnesses as such, but so that we may know the risen, living Christ to whom they bear witness. We listen, not so that we may believe that it really happened, but so that we may know him to whom it happened and, knowing him, share with him a new life.

The Nature of the Resurrection

Before we move on to ask what the resurrection means, there are two aspects of these stories that can help us to avoid wrong paths some Christians have taken in trying to understand it.

First, it is important to note that according to the New Testament *God* raised Jesus from the dead (Rom. 8:11; Phil. 2:9). He did not raise himself. The New Testament does not speak of the resurrection as the result of an inner divine power within Jesus that survived death and enabled him to live again. He really was dead—*totally* dead. The resurrection is the story of God's giving life to a dead man, not of the immortality this man possessed in himself.

This must be emphasized, because Easter is often understood after the analogy of trees and plants that "come to life" again every spring after passing through the "death" of winter. This analogy of death and an afterlife is common in pagan mythologies. But the story of the resurrection is not such a myth. It does not describe the potential we have in ourselves to survive or revive after death, an automatic "immortality of the soul." The New Testament does not teach that either about Jesus or about us. It is much more realistic and serious about death than that. Jesus' death and our own deaths are not just a "passing over" to a new and higher form of life. Rather than being the sentimental (and false) assurance that death is not so bad after all because our inmost selves do not really die but live on forever, the good news of the resurrection is that *God* is stronger than death. It is the assurance that God can and will give us the eternal life we do not have in ourselves. It means hope in a

God who raises the dead, not in the immortality of human beings who do not really die.

We will return to this point in the last chapter when we speak about our own death and eternal life. But it is important now as we speak of Jesus' resurrection that we do not let it become a kind of cheap happy ending that takes neither his real death nor his real resurrection seriously. The resurrection means far more than a doctrine of immortality that many people have believed without even knowing about or believing in Jesus.

The second aspect of the resurrection stories that can keep us from a distorted doctrine of the resurrection is the emphasis the New Testament places on the *physical, worldly* reality of the risen Jesus. It is true that there was a mysterious difference between the Jesus the disciples had known before the crucifixion and the risen Jesus (John 20:14–17; Luke 24:13–16, 30–31). Nevertheless, the biblical writers go out of their way to emphasize that the risen Jesus is the same Jesus they had known before. He walks, talks, eats, and can be touched. The risen Jesus is no ghost or phantom. He is a real flesh-and-blood human being. We will consider later what it means for us to believe in the resurrection of the *body*. Now the important point is that we must not spiritualize the resurrection so that it has only an otherworldly significance for the next life. The resurrection happened in *this* world. For Jesus himself and for us it means the renewal of human life, not escape from it. The resurrection, in other words, does not have to do only with the significance of Jesus for us after we die and leave this world. It has to do also with our lives here and now.

THE LORD AND HIS KINGDOM

According to the New Testament, the resurrection of Jesus meant that he who gave himself as the Suffering Servant of God is now revealed to be the triumphant Lord. He who came preaching the kingdom of God is now seen to be the sovereign King of the kingdom. Lord, king, kingdom, victory, rule, authority, sovereignty—these are concepts that characterize biblical faith in the risen Jesus. These are the concepts we must try to understand.

We begin with some comments about the terminology of resurrection theology. Words like lord, ruler, king, and kingdom sound strange to us. They sound so archaic, so undemocratic—and so *male!* Should we not translate this outdated hierarchical, "sexist" language taken from the environment of the ancient world into language that makes more sense in our time and is less likely to give ammunition to those who want to defend the superiority of men and the inferiority of women? Several things need to be said in answer to this legitimate question.

First, it is no accident that the New Testament uses political images to speak of the meaning of the resurrection. We will see that this is not just a matter of language but of essential content. Any translation we made, then, would have to be made into appropriate political imagery.

Second, the meaning of the resurrection *is* undemocratic. Jesus is not Lord by our permission or because he has won enough votes to get into office. *God* made him Lord and Christ, without any support or cooperation from the side of his followers—in fact, despite their unwillingness and hostility (Acts 2:36). Like the sovereignty of God, the lordship of Christ has nothing to do with the will of the people. So any modern imagery we might choose cannot come from the democratic form of government. The risen Christ is not president, chairperson of the board, or elected representative to whom *we* give power and from whom *we* can take it away.

What political imagery do we have to express this absolute authority of Jesus? Tyrant? Dictator? Boss? Chief Executive Officer? None of them will do because they suggest the possibility of unjust or arbitrary power. The good news about the power of the risen Jesus is that, unlike all other unlimited power we know, his sovereign power is the power of self-giving love. He is the Lord who gave his very life for us. He exercises his power in such a way that it does not dominate or control, does not rob us of our freedom and destroy our human dignity, but rather gives and nourishes genuine free human life for all of us—people of both sexes, of all races, classes, cultures, and nations. He became Lord without our approval or support, but as Lord he is for us and not against us. He is not for us in a paternalistic, condescending way as a master cares for a dog, an owner cares for a slave, or the traditional "head of the house" cares for "his" woman. His goal is not to keep us weak and dependent and passive. Rather, he is for us as one who shared and still shares the human existence of every one of us and wants every one of us to grow into strong, free maturity of our own.

What title or name is appropriate for such an authority? There is no political office and no political officer comparable to what he does and what he is. Even "lordship" and "Lord" are really inappropriate. This language was originally borrowed partly from ancient Jewish religion and partly from ancient pagan emperor worship. In the first century it was loaded with heathen connotations. Who Jesus is and what he does are so unique that he cannot be fit into *any* of our thought patterns, ancient or modern. If we stick with such archaic terminology as "Lord" and "lordship," then, it is not because this language is especially sacred in itself, but because precisely in our time when it sounds so strange it may suggest the uniqueness of this political figure and his government over against all the (female and male) politicians and forms of government that are part of our daily experience.

If we do use this ancient language, however, we must take special care to see how the risen Christ touches our lives in the world today. This brings us back to the question with which we began this chapter. What does the good news of Easter have to do with the real world we read about in the newspapers? In light of the way life really is, how can we seriously confess that Jesus is the Lord who rules over the world with absolute power and at the same time with freeing, humanizing love? In order to answer this question, we will look at the various ways Christian thinkers have tried to understand the meaning of his lordship and the kingdom of God that challenge and defeat the powers of sin, suffering, injustice, and death at work in all the kingdoms of this world.

The Kingdom as an Ideal to Be Realized

One way of dealing with the contradiction between Christian claims about the lordship of the risen Christ and the kind of world we actually live in is to say that Jesus brought not the reality but the *ideal* of God's kingdom of justice, love, freedom, and true humanity. To be a Christian is to get to work to make the ideal a reality. By our commitment to Christ and by our Christian obedience, we may hope gradually to overcome the forces of evil in the world and "bring in" the kingdom of God. This hope may take either a "liberal" or a "conservative" form: If the church and individual Christians will just commit themselves to the battle against racism, sexism, homelessness and poverty, militarism, ecological irresponsibility and other social evils, then we may hope for the coming of God's kingdom on earth. Or we may hope for the coming of the kingdom if individual Christians and the church join in the battle against such evils as pornography, the erosion of traditional family values, the moral relativism and permissiveness rampant at every level of modern society. However different their strategies, such liberal or conservative positions have in common the belief that the kingdom of God is a yet unrealized goal toward which we must strive.

This is probably the most common idea of the lordship of Christ and the kingdom of God in our time. We speak of "letting" Christ be the Lord of the church and our individual lives, or of "making" him Lord. Especially when we take up the offering, we pray that our money will be used to "spread" the kingdom. We speak of "applying" Christian "principles" or Christian "ideals" to our family, business, or social life. All these expressions are ways of saying that Christ is not Lord but *ought* to be, that the kingdom of God is not a reality but a goal to work toward, and that it is up to us to realize the ideal.

This way of thinking has the advantage of taking into account the great gap between life in the world as we experience it and faith in the lordship of the risen Christ. It can point to some passages in the New Testament itself that speak of the rule of God over all things as a future hope. It also sees that faith in the lordship of Christ requires active obedience on our part.

However, the idealistic answer is not the biblical solution to the problem. It subtly changes the kingdom of God into the kingdom of Christians or the church and makes them the real ruler instead of Christ. If Christ can be Lord only insofar as we let him be or make him Lord, who really is in control? If the kingdom can become a reality only insofar as *we* bring it in or make it spread, whose kingdom is it really? Suppose we did collect enough money to build churches everywhere and expand the church's program beyond our wildest dreams—would a successful rule of the church be the same as the kingdom of God? Suppose Christians (especially those who think like I think and want the same things I want) did get in control of everything—would our rule be the same as the rule of God? What about the sinful self-interest and hostility toward others who think and live differently from us *within* the church and *in* us Christians, whether our position is left, right, or middle of the road? Could it be that there is so much "burnout" and despair among ministers and church members today precisely because we have taken on ourselves the terrible burden (along with the terrible arrogance) of assuming that the kingdom of God cannot come unless *we* make it happen?

According to the New Testament, it is God and God alone who makes Christ to be Lord and who brings in the kingdom. Although Christ invites and commands us to acknowledge and participate in his kingdom, it in no way depends upon our help and cooperation, nor is it identical with our efforts and achievements. What bad news it would be if we had to think that the kingdom of God could be real only to the extent that we Christians and our church really believe in it and work for it! How terrible it would be if God's justice and love were no greater or more effective than ours!

To relate the kingdom of the world and the kingdom of God as reality versus ideal is a denial of the truth of the resurrection. The resurrection means that the hope of the world is in *Christ,* not in us Christians. It means that the reality of the kingdom of God depends not on what *we* may one day succeed in doing if we try hard enough and work at it long enough, but on what *God* has done, is doing, and will do.

The Kingdom as Hope in the Future Coming of Christ

Another solution to the contradiction between the kind of world in which we live and the claims of the Easter message is to push the kingdom of God or the lordship of Christ into the future in another way: Christ may not yet be the Victor and Ruler, but he will be when he comes again. The kingdom of God has not yet replaced the kingdom of this world, but it *will* do so at the end of this age. Easter is the proclamation not of a present reality but of a future hope.

This solution is like the idealistic one in that it understands the kingdom as a future reality. It differs in that it believes that it is not Christians but God who will "realize" it, and that this will happen not by a gradual process of improving the world but by a sudden catastrophic judgment and destruction of the world as we know it.

This apocalyptic understanding of the rule of God in Christ has some biblical justification. During his life Jesus himself sometimes spoke as if, far from becoming gradually better, the world will become worse and worse until finally at the "last day" God will step in and set things right. See, for instance, Matt. 24:3–35; Mark 13:1–37; Luke 21:5–36. (When do these passages suggest that the end will come?)

There is also some justification for the futuristic understanding of the lordship of Christ in the New Testament's interpretation of the resurrection of Jesus. Throughout the letters of the New Testament we find the expectancy that the risen Christ will come again to judge, save, and claim the world that belongs to him. Some passages interpret the time between the resurrection and the end of the world as being for Christ himself as well as for us a time of waiting until his enemies are defeated. See 1 Cor. 15:25 and Heb. 10:13.

It is clear, then, that there is indeed a futuristic aspect of Christian faith in the lordship of Christ and the kingdom of God. If that were all there is to it, the problem we are considering in this chapter would be solved. Or rather, we would deny that there is any problem. We may expect injustice, hatred, godlessness, suffering, and inhumanity in this world. This world does belong to sin, death, and the devil. There is nothing we can do about it, and there is no point in trying. All we can do is sit, wait, hope, and pray for the "second coming" of Christ at the end of the world when the kingdom will come and Jesus will be Lord.

This position has led some Christians who accept it to say to the victims of injustice and evil, "There is no use complaining or trying to better your condition. That's the way it is in this evil old world. Just be patient and believe, and someday you will be saved." Hope for the coming kingdom becomes a pious excuse for Christians not to participate themselves, and to criticize those who do participate, in efforts to create a more just and more human world. Occasionally it can even lead to a perverse rejoicing at the triumph of evil: the greater the evil and misery around us, the more people will give up confidence in all optimistic worldly "do-goodism" and "turn to Christ." It was just this kind of Christianity that Karl Marx called an "opiate" distributed by privileged and powerful people to maintain the political and social status quo and to keep the victims of injustice passive and submissive.

A purely futuristic way of understanding the lordship of Christ does see one side of biblical teaching, and it does take seriously the power of sin and evil in the world. But it conveniently listens only to one aspect of biblical teaching and ignores another, and in so doing finally denies the good news of Easter. According to the Gospels, the earthly Jesus who spoke of the future coming of the kingdom could also say that with his coming the kingdom *has* come (Matt. 12:28; 28:18; Luke 10:17). After his resurrection the first Christians still looked forward to the final victory of Christ at the end, but they did not believe only that Christ *will* one day triumph over sin, evil, and death; they believed that on Easter morning he *did* triumph over them. The New Testament does not teach that sometime in the future Christ *will* be Lord; it says that he *is* Lord (see, e.g., Acts 2:36; Phil. 2:9–11; Rev. 17:14).

If this is true, then we do not *have* to nor are we *allowed* to sit and wait, doing nothing until the end of the world. To do that would be to say in effect that Easter is not true, Christ is not risen, the power of God in Christ is not really stronger than the power of sin and evil. If we believe that all the "principalities and powers" are *already* subject to the risen Christ, then we can and we must confidently throw ourselves into the fight against evil in our own lives and in the world around us, knowing that we do not fight alone but with the one who is stronger than all the forces of evil within and without. If we believe that all authority has already been given to him, then it is faithless and disobedient to tell others and ourselves that nothing can be done about unjust social structures, economic systems, and political regimes because the world is hopelessly ruled by sin, death, and the devil.

We will return presently to what is legitimate in the futuristic view of the Lord and his kingdom. But taken by itself it cannot be accepted as the Christian solution to the problem of the conflict between the kingdom of God and the kingdom of the world.

The Kingdom Here and Now

The idealistic and futuristic interpretations of the lordship of Christ try to solve the problem of the contradiction between the facts of life in the world and the claims of the Easter message by pushing the kingdom of God into the future, either as a goal to be gradually realized by us or as a goal to be suddenly realized by God. Both solutions deny the Easter claim that in Christ God has *already* triumphed over the powers of injustice, suffering, and death.

Now we come to a third position that emphasizes just this missing element in the first two positions we have discussed. Instead of an "idealistic" or "futuristic" eschatology, it defends a "realized" eschatology. (Eschatology is the study of "last," or "end," things, and is the theological name for a consideration of when, how, and where God's intentions for the world are fulfilled.) Realized eschatology holds that the coming of Jesus and especially his resurrection means that the long hoped-for kingdom of God is a *present* reality, *here* and *now*. The Gospels tell us that during his earthly ministry Jesus fed the hungry, defended the cause of the poor and outcast, healed the sick, raised the dead, comforted the sorrowing, forgave sinners and gave them a new start in life, demonstrated his power over evil spirits that "possessed" and destroyed the bodies, minds, and souls of people. For the first Christians, Jesus' compassion for "outsiders" and his miracles were more than signs of his care for needy individuals; they were signs that the loving and just rule of God on earth was not just something to be expected in the distant or even near future but something that was happening before the very eyes of those who encountered him. Jesus' death and resurrection, then, were only the final confirmation of his kingdom-bringing life. In the earthly and risen Jesus, God's will *was* and *is being* done on earth as it is in heaven. In him God's kingdom has *already* come and is a present reality for all who "have eyes to see and ears to hear."

This position is a much-needed corrective to the one-sidedness of the other views we have discussed. But it too can be criticized. It neglects the New Testament texts that tell us that the final victory of Christ over the powers of evil does indeed lie in the future. If futuristic eschatology must be criticized by realized eschatology, the reverse is also true. Can we really do without the expectant hope that the kingdom of God will one day triumph once and for all over the kingdoms of this world? This question becomes all the more acute when we look at the way realized eschatology in its turn also sidesteps the obvious contradiction between what human life in the world is actually like and the Easter claim about the lordship of Christ.

Those who defend this position are not so unrealistic that they deny the fact of evil in the world. In order to be realistic about the world and at the same time hold that the risen Christ has already triumphed over sin, death, and the devil, they tend to narrow the extent of Christ's lordship and the kingdom of God. The resurrection means that Christ rules *in the hearts and lives of individual believers* or *in the church.* The world at large may still be gripped by the powers of darkness, but their power is broken in believers who place their trust in Christ and acknowledge his lordship in their lives. They experience the present reality of the freedom, love, joy, reconciliation, and new life of the kingdom of God.

Now the New Testament does, of course, teach that the risen Christ is the Lord of individual Christians and the church, and that his renewing power and help is especially at work among them. But even if we could claim that the faith and life of Christians and the Christian community actually do manifest the healing presence and powerful rule of Christ (insiders as well as outsiders may have their doubts!), it will not do to limit Christ's authority and work to individual believers and the "spiritual" realm. To do so is to deny what the New Testament explicitly teaches about the meaning of the resurrection: "*All* authority in heaven *and* on earth has been given to me" (Matt. 28:18, emphasis added). God has put him "far above *all* rule and authority and power and dominion, and above *every* name that is named" (Eph. 1:21, emphasis added). He is Lord over *all* lords, king over *all* kings (Rev. 17:14). According to the New Testament, to confess that Jesus is Lord is to confess that he is Lord not only in the lives of individual believers and not only Lord of the church but Lord over the whole world, including the secular forces and political authorities of the world.

Narrowing the lordship of Christ as it does, realized eschatology tends to make obedience to the Lord only a matter of individual ethics and religious observance. But if Easter is really true, if Christ is really Lord over all, then we cannot exclude *any* area of our lives from responsibility to him. Resurrection faith means that we are called to bring the claim of his lordship to bear on our own *and* others' individual *and* social-political lives, spiritual-psychological *and* material-physical needs, religious *and* secular interests and commitments. For all their emphasis on the lordship of Christ here and now, the adherents of realized eschatology, with their tendency toward individualism and spiritualizing, tend to become as passive and irresponsible as the adherents of a futuristic eschatology when it comes to confident, obedient service of the risen Christ in and for the world.

Like the other two views of the kingdom of God we have considered, the view of realized eschatology is partially true. But it also is too one-sided to do justice either to the Easter confession that Jesus is Lord over all things or to answer the question of how we can believe in his loving power and powerful love in the kind of world we actually live in.

The Kingdom "Between the Times"

We come now to a view of the lordship of Christ and the kingdom of God that tries to put together all the partial truths of the other views we have discussed. It is probably fair to say that it is the view shared by most contemporary biblical interpreters and theologians, Roman Catholic and Protestant alike, though they interpret it in different ways.[2] According to this position, just what seems to be the greatest problem in the New Testament teaching about Jesus and the kingdom is itself the answer.

This is the problem: The New Testament takes so seriously the powers of sin, suffering, injustice, and death that it expects them to be about their destructive work among us as long as the world exists. Christ's final victory over these "enemies" will not come until the history of the world itself ends. On the other hand, the New Testament also takes so seriously the victory of Christ over these enemies in his life, death, and resurrection that it confidently asserts that they are already defeated and doomed. In other words, both things are said to be true: the rule of God in and for the world is *not yet* here but it is *already* here. Christ is *not yet* but *already* Lord. Is it not an outright contradiction to say both things? Must it not be *either* "already" *or* "not yet," *either* the kingdom of God as a future hope *or* the kingdom as a present reality? No, say those who want to take both claims of the New Testament seriously, the whole truth of the gospel of Jesus Christ is precisely that *both* are true. But how can this be possible?

The biblical interpreters and theologians who first sought to defend this "dialectical" understanding of Christ's lordship and God's kingdom worked it out in the 1940s and 1950s, and illustrated it with what has become a familiar analogy from the end of World War II. When the Allied forces landed in Normandy, the decisive battle of the whole war was fought. After that it was certain that Nazi Germany was going to lose. Between D-Day (the day of the invasion) and V-Day (the day the Allies' victory was finally declared) the Germans fought a number of desperate fall-back battles across Europe. Many lives were lost and much damage done before they finally surrendered. But after the decisive battle in Normandy, it was clear how the war was going to turn out. The war was already won even if it was not yet over.

The decisive battle of all human history was fought when in the life, death, and resurrection of Jesus, God "invaded" a world ruled and tormented by the dark powers of evil. But the final victory of God over them will come only with final triumph of the risen Christ at the end of history. "Between the times" (between Easter and the end), the deadly battle between God and the powers of darkness still goes on, but the victory of Christ that has been won is the guarantee of the final victory that is surely on the way. So both things are true: In Jesus Christ the kingdom of God *has* come and *is* coming. Jesus *will* be victorious Lord because he is *already* victorious Lord. It is true that we live in a "twilight zone" in which the light of God's compassion and justice is still at war with the powers of darkness, but because we *remember what God has done* in Christ and can therefore have *hope for what God will do,* we may be certain that it is not the twilight that comes before darkness overcomes the light but the twilight that is the dawn of a new day when light will overcome darkness. (See what we said in chapter 9 about Christian life as life lived between memory and hope.)

Let us look at some of the concrete implications of this view of the lordship of Christ and the kingdom of God for our lives as Christians "between the times."

1. *We must take evil seriously.* The view we have described is no sentimental, optimistic one that piously explains away evil or cheerfully pretends that things are not so bad after all. It realistically confesses that godless injustice, suffering, and inhumanity do and will continue to ravage our individual lives and our world. There is no naive confidence that human wisdom, virtue, and power will gradually triumph over

them, or that Christians can bring in the kingdom of God if they work at it long and hard enough. Evil is so powerful that no human beings in history but only Christ at the end of history will finally overcome it. Until then Christ himself is often not present in the world as a triumphant Lord who overcomes all the oppressive, death-bringing powers of evil that threaten God's good creation and human life in it. Rather, he is often present as a despised, rejected, crucified Lord who suffers with and for all who are the victims of these powers.

2. *We must not take evil more seriously than we do God.* If faith in the lordship of Christ "between the times" is not optimistic, neither is it pessimistic. It is true that this is a world in which there is and will be evil of all kinds. But Jesus Christ is risen! Evil may be stronger than even the best of us (even us Christians), but it is not stronger than God. It does not and will not have the last word. Christ's resurrection means that God has already challenged the powers of darkness and even now is at work in the world and in our individual lives to bring reconciliation where there is hostility, freedom where there are all kinds of slavery, life where there is death, humanity where there is inhumanity. Knowing the power of evil, Christians are not surprised or disillusioned when they see it cropping up over and over again in ever new ways and places—also in the church and among Christians. But knowing the resurrection victory of God in Christ, Christians cannot be ultimately pessimistic and gloomy about the world, the church, and themselves. No matter how hopeless the situation may seem, they know of a power at work *here and now* greater than the power of evil, a power that keeps breaking into our godless and godforsaken world to heal old wounds, make new beginnings, and (if only now and then, here and there) give us a glimpse of the final victory of God's compassion and justice that are on the way.

3. *We can and must fight against evil.* We saw in our criticism of a purely futuristic eschatology that Christians who believe that Jesus is Lord cannot sit around wringing their hands over how evil the world is, passively waiting for God to do something about it. Now we can see more clearly why this is true.

All of us could be tempted simply to give up in despair when we take a hard look at the world around us and the mess we make of our own lives. The hostility between people who are sexually, racially, and politically different from each other; never-ending national and international conflicts with the threat of nuclear war that will never go away; the misery and suffering of the ever-increasing number of the world's poor; the depersonalization, manipulation, and exploitation of human beings in and by modern technological societies; the steady destruction of our natural environment; the inadequacy of the church; the conflicts in our personal and family relationships; the anxiety and insecurity that in one way or another seems to master all of us—in the face of all that, what use is it even to try to do anything? But if we believe that since Easter the powers of evil are fighting a losing battle and that the one who has already conquered them is still at work to finish what he began, then we can take heart nevertheless to keep fighting, however powerful the enemy without and within may seem.

On the other hand, if the past victory of Christ makes it possible for us to keep struggling, the fact that the final victory has not yet been won makes it necessary. There is still work to be done. The goal has not yet been reached. The confession that Jesus is Lord does not mean that we can sit back with a sigh of relief and tell ourselves that everything is all right now. The powers of evil around us and within us have not yet admitted defeat. The risen Lord is still finishing the work he began, and to call him Lord means to throw ourselves into the battle with him. The Declaration of Faith (10.5) puts it this way:

> The people of God have often misused God's promises as excuses for doing nothing about present evils.
> But in Christ the new world has already broken in and the old can no longer be tolerated.
>
> We know our efforts cannot bring in God's kingdom.
> But hope plunges us into the struggle for victories over evil that are possible now in the world, the church and our individual lives.
> Hope gives us courage and energy to contend against all opposition, however invincible it may seem, for the new world and the new humanity that are surely coming.
>
> Jesus is Lord!
> He has been Lord from the beginning.
> He will be Lord at the end.
> Even now he is Lord.

Some difficult questions still remain even after we have begun to understand the meaning of the lordship of Christ "between the times" and the kingdom that is "already" but "not yet" here: How and where is this Lord present and at work in the world between the times? How can we have such faith in the truth of the Easter message that we actually live by it with the confidence, joy, and freedom we have so easily claimed that Christians have. If the risen Christ is Lord over the world as well as over the church, what is the difference between church and world, between those who acknowledge and accept his lordship and those who do not even know about it or refuse to accept it? Our task for the rest of this book will be to answer these questions.

Meanwhile, we conclude this chapter by pointing out that the very fact that we will have to spend so much time dealing with such questions is proof of how central to the Christian faith are the resurrection doctrines of the lordship of Christ and the kingdom of God. The earliest Christians knew what they were doing when they summarized the whole of their faith with the apparently simple confession "Jesus is Lord." Everything Christians believe depends on our learning what it means that individual Christians, the church, and the whole world are on the way between "the third day he rose again" (a historical event in the past) and "he will come again to judge the living and the dead" (a historical event in the future). The clue to what is going on between the times is the confession that the one who died on Good Friday, rose on Easter Sunday, and will come again as the "Lord" who even now has all the authority of one who has "ascended into heaven" and "is seated at the right hand of the Father" (the meaning of history in the present).[3]

FOR FURTHER REFLECTION AND STUDY

1. Compare the versions of the Easter story in Matt. 28:1–20; Mark 16:1–19; Luke 24:1–51; John 20:1–21, 25–27; and 1 Cor. 15:3–8:
   a. What is the sequence of events in each story?
   b. How many angels were at the tomb, and where were they?
   c. Who saw the risen Jesus first? In what order did others see him?
   d. What were the reactions of those who saw him?
   e. What material is unique in each account?
   f. What conclusions would you draw from a comparison of these accounts if you were not a Christian? What are your conclusions as a Christian?
2. Is it important to believe that the resurrection happened literally? Would it be enough to believe that Jesus lived on in the memory of his followers or continued to be very real in their hearts?
3. Why is it wrong to make an analogy between the resurrection and the rebirth of the natural world at springtime?
4. Do you agree that the archaic title "Lord" is a meaningful way of talking about Jesus in our time? If you had to translate this title into modern terminology, how would you do it?
5. Is your church a democracy? Should it be?

6. Which of the four views of the kingdom of God best describes what you thought about the lordship of Christ before you read this chapter? Have you changed your mind?
7. Was Jesus mistaken in his predictions in Mark 9:1 and 13:30?
8. How would you answer Karl Marx's charge that religion is the opiate of the people?
9. On the basis of the New Testament understanding of the lordship of Christ and the kingdom of God, defend or criticize the following statements:
   a. We ought to make Christ the Lord of our lives.
   b. Christians ought to give their money and their talents to help bring in the kingdom of God.
   c. It is useless for us to try to correct social and political injustice because the world is controlled by Satan.
   d. We cannot hope for a better society and world until individuals are converted and turn to Christ.
   e. It will make people lazy and irresponsible if we say that Christ is already Lord of the whole world.
   f. The kingdom of God is present in the hearts of believers.
   g. Considering the way the world really is, it is absurd to say that all authority in heaven and on earth has been given to Christ.
   h. When we accept Christ as Lord, the inner turmoil and struggle of our lives will be overcome.
10. What do we mean in the Lord's Prayer when we pray, "Thy kingdom come," and then end by saying, "For thine *is* the kingdom, and the power, and the glory"?

PART 5

GOD THE HOLY SPIRIT AND NEW LIFE

"I believe in the Holy Spirit." The repetition of "I believe" when we come to this part of the creed suggests that we have come to a turning point. Something new is about to be said. The new thing is that we begin to confess something about *ourselves.* "I believe in God, the Father Almighty" confesses God *over* us. "I believe in Jesus Christ, his only Son, our Lord" confesses God *with* and *for* us. But "I believe in the Holy Spirit" confesses God *in* and *among* us. We now reach the purpose and goal of everything else we have said to this point. "I will be your God" is what the first two articles on God's work of creation and reconciliation tell us. But why does God want to be our God? The third article tells us that it is so that "you shall be my people." The first two articles speak of God in relation to us. Now the third speaks of us in relation to God.

Another way of describing the significance of all the statements connected with the Holy Spirit in the creed is to say that they are the "subjective" part of our confession of faith that follows the "objective" part. The first two articles speak primarily of who God is and what God does. Now we come to speak about ourselves—the community of *us Christians,* the forgiveness of our sins, the resurrection of our bodies, our everlasting life. How do we come to say not only God but *my* God, not only Lord but *our* Lord? How does what God did "back there" touch *us* and affect *our* lives? How do *we* fit into the picture—we who live "between the times," after the reconciling death and victorious resurrection of Christ but before his final victory over all the forces of alienation, hostility, slavery, and death around us and in us? These questions have concerned us all the way along in our study, of course, but now they become the central theme when we begin to speak of the work of God the Holy Spirit.

In chapter 15 we will think about who the Holy Spirit is—about how and where God is at work in our lives "between the times." There is no better way of doing this than to ask, "What's New?"

In chapters 16 and 17 we will consider how Christian *individuals* enter into and live in the kingdom "between the times." Christian theology has traditionally spoken of justification and sanctification to deal with this question. We will consider these doctrines under the title "Are You a Christian?"

In chapter 18 we will examine the Christian *church* and its task in the world "between the times." In our time, the body of Christ is in such trouble that we will talk about it under the title "Living or Dead?"

Finally, in chapter 19 we will ask, "What's Going to Happen to Us?" Here we will deal with the question of the future of individuals, the church, and the world as we look forward to the final victory of the Lord at the end.

15

What's New?

The Doctrine of the Holy Spirit

We live in a time when there is a widespread hunger for a "new spirituality" or "spiritual renewal." Outside the church it is expressed in the popularity of the "new age" movement. Among Christians it is expressed in the growth of pentecostal and charismatic movements within and outside traditional churches, and in the popular demand (also among "ordinary" Christians) for literature and study groups dealing with "spiritual development."

However differently these insiders and outsiders seek to satisfy their spiritual hunger, they all talk about it in the same way. They feel oppressive boredom, meaninglessness, stagnation, burnout, hopelessness—deadness—in their individual lives, in their personal relationships, in their work (even "good works" in the service of justice and peace), in the political and social structures that shape their lives—and in churches that conduct business as usual while everything is falling apart in the lives of their own members and in the world around them. These people hunger for new freedom, joy, enthusiasm, and energy that make them "feel alive" again and enable them to hope that things can be different in their own lives and in the world. Their hunger for a new spirituality is hunger for new life in the midst of all the deadness in and around them. Whatever words they use to talk about it, they hunger for the Holy Spirit who is the Lord and Giver of new life.

Different people (including different Christians), however, have different ideas about what this new spirituality or new life would look like, and different ideas about the renewing spiritual power that is the source of it. In this chapter we will first seek to learn from scripture who the

Holy Spirit is who is the true source of the new life for which we all hunger. Then we will consider the meaning of authentic Christian spirituality that is based on the presence and work of this Spirit. Finally, we will discuss the "gifts" of the Spirit that enable us to experience and live by such a spirituality.

WHO IS THE HOLY SPIRIT?

According to the Bible, the Holy Spirit is the presence and work of the living God here and now in our individual lives, in the church, and in the world. In this section we will look at some of the implications of this one simple (not so simple!) statement.

A Personal Spirit

A common error is to speak of the Spirit as a neuter: "When *it* works in our lives" or "When *it* controls what we feel and say and do." We have a tendency to think of the Spirit as an impersonal divine power or energy that somehow gets into people. A frequent but badly mistaken analogy is to think of the Spirit as something like electricity: If we can somehow be "plugged in" to God, a "power" will flow into us that makes the light shine in our hearts or "recharges our batteries." Such an analogy depersonalizes the Holy Spirit, and it depersonalizes human beings. The Spirit is not some magical "something" that gets into us but *Someone* who comes to dwell in and among us. Nor are human beings objects like light bulbs or batteries to be "turned on" and controlled by some outside force; they are thinking, willing, feeling persons. We can avoid all kinds of superstitious ideas about the Holy Spirit if we think of the Spirit's relationship with us as a personal relationship between God and ourselves.

What kind of person is the Holy Spirit? When we discussed the doctrine of the Trinity in chapter 5, we considered the suggestion that we should think of the Spirit as the feminine side of God. There is good reason to take this suggestion seriously. In the Hebrew language of the Old Testament, the word for spirit (*ruach*) is feminine. In the New Testament, the beginning of Christian life is described as "birth" of the Spirit (John 3:4–6), and the comforting role of the Spirit (Acts 9:31) reminds us of the God who cares for us as a mother comforts her child (Isa. 66:13). Moreover, a theology of the "maternity" of the Spirit could counterbalance male imagery of God as "Father" and "Son." So there is no reason why we should not, and good reason why we could, use feminine as well as masculine imagery in thinking and talking about God and the Spirit of God. But "the Triune God is neither an exclusive fraternity nor a company composed of two males and a female."[1] God (especially God as "Spirit") is beyond all our gender distinctions. All our language about God is analogical or metaphorical language used to talk about God's relation to us. In order to keep this in mind, we will avoid speaking of the Holy Spirit as "she" just as we have avoided speaking of God as "he."

Who, then, is the God who is present in and among us here and now as personal Spirit? The Trinitarian God we learn to know in the scriptures of both the Old and the New Testaments.

The Spirit of the God of Israel[2]

The Old Testament tells us several things about the Spirit of God that Christians who think exclusively of the Holy Spirit in the New Testament are prone to forget.

1. The Spirit is at work in God's creation and preservation of the world and human life in it (Gen. 1:2; 2:7; Ps. 104:30). In both the Old and New Testaments the word *spirit* means literally "wind," then "breath of life" (the wind we breathe in and out in order to stay alive), and finally simply "life." It is no accident that the Nicene Creed calls the Holy Spirit "the Lord, the Giver of Life." God's Spirit is the source and "livingness" of all life—first of all simply physical, creaturely life. Wherever there is life instead of death in the world (in human beings and in the natural environment of human beings) and wherever life is respected, preserved, and defended—there we may recognize the creative, life-giving Spirit of God at work.

2. In the Old Testament the Spirit of God is the source of all human culture, art, creativity, and wisdom (Ex. 31:1–6; 35:31; Job 32:8; Dan. 1:17). Perhaps we can recognize an echo of this "worldly" work of the Spirit in Phil. 4:8–9, where Paul tells the Christians in Philippi to "think about" a list of virtues that were the highest virtues of ancient "pagan" Greek culture. We may recognize all such "nonreligious" gifts as gifts of God's Spirit wherever we see them outside or inside the circle of believers.

3. Finally, the Spirit is the Spirit of the God who is on the side of all who are helpless, poor, wretched, and oppressed because they have been forgotten or excluded by the rich and powerful (Ps. 103:6 and Ps. 146). The Spirit of the Lord is therefore present in (or "upon") leaders and prophets who demand and promise political, economic, and social

justice for the victims of injustice (Isa. 11:1–5; 42:1–4; 61:1–4). Wherever such justice is done in the world (even if it is by those who do not know God), there the Spirit of the Lord is at work. And wherever such justice is *not* done (even if those who allow or cause it are pious believers), there the Spirit of the Lord is absent.

In the New Testament the Spirit is present and at work primarily in individual Christians and in the Christian community. But the New Testament itself tells us that the "wind" (Spirit) blows where it will (John 3:8). And the Old Testament tells us specifically that this means also in the world *outside* the circle of believers however and by whomever natural and physical human life is maintained; wherever there is wisdom, beauty, and creativity; wherever justice is done for the sake of the poor and oppressed. The Holy Spirit does not belong to us Christians and is not trapped in our hearts or in our church. The Holy Spirit is the Spirit of a God who is Creator, Preserver, and Defender of the life of *all* God's creation and *all* God's creatures.

The Spirit Who Was Present in and Sent by Jesus Christ

According to the New Testament, if we want to know who the Holy Spirit is, we have to look first at Jesus of Nazareth. The New Testament connects the Spirit and Jesus in two ways: Jesus is one who *received* and *bore* the Spirit, and one who *promised* and *sent* the Spirit.

The Old Testament prophets spoke of a coming Messiah who would be filled with the Spirit (Isa. 11:1–2; 42:1; 61:1). The Gospels tell us that their prophecies were fulfilled in the coming of Jesus. He was conceived by the Spirit (Matt. 1:20). At his baptism the Spirit of God descended upon him like a dove (Matt. 3:16). By the power of the Spirit he healed the sick, cast out demonic forces that destroyed people's minds and bodies (Matt. 12:28), and brought the kingdom of God to the poor (Luke 4:18). Peter later summed up his whole story by proclaiming Jesus as one whom God anointed "with the Holy Spirit and with power" (Acts 10:38).

At this point we do not have to think of Jesus specifically as the Son of God or God-with-us. The Gospels teach us to think of him also as a human being who at every point in his life, in everything he said and did, was filled, led, inspired, and empowered by God's Holy Spirit. Look at Jesus, they tell us, if you want to know what it means to have the Holy Spirit dwell within you. He is our prime example of what it means to be a Spirit-filled person.

What kind of life is that? It is not the kind of life people in his time (as in our time?) expected of a "spiritual" person. Rather, it was the life of a person who went to parties, ate and drank, had a good time. He talked more about what people did with their money than about their sexual purity and was as interested in the health of their bodies as in their souls. Jesus was the friend and companion not just of the morally pure and pious but of immoral, unbelieving sinners. He defended the cause of those who were rejected and despised by polite society and the religious and political establishment. He believed that human need takes precedence over strict conformity to the law. He came to serve other people, not to assert his moral and religious superiority over them. He loved his enemies and did good to those who hated him. He trusted and served the God he called Father even when it did not pay off in personal success and happiness, even when it meant giving up his own life for unworthy, no-good sinners. His life was the life of one who prayed even when everything he had worked and hoped for was denied him and he felt forsaken by God. That is the kind of life that is the result of God's Holy Spirit coming to dwell in a person.

Jesus was not only filled with the Spirit himself; he promised the coming of the (his) Spirit to his followers. In his "farewell speeches" in John 14—15, Jesus spoke about an "Advocate," the Holy Spirit, who will come after he is gone. Here we learn several new things about who the Spirit is and what the Spirit does: (a) The Holy Spirit comes in Jesus' name (John 14:26), is in fact Jesus himself with his followers in a new way (John 14:16). To put it in Paul's language, the Holy Spirit is none other than the risen Christ himself, continuing the work that the earthly Christ began. (b) The coming Spirit will be a "teacher," the "Spirit of truth," who will remind Jesus' followers of what he taught them in the past and who will have *new* things to say to them (John 14:26; 16:12). (c) The Spirit is promised to the *community* of Jesus' disciples. This promise was fulfilled at Pentecost when the Spirit came when "they were all together in one place" (Acts 2:1). The promise of the Spirit, in other words, is first of all a promise made not to isolated individuals but to the *church*—not just for its own sake but for the sake of its service of the kingdom of God in the world. We will return later to the significance of the last two of these points. Right now it is the first that interests us: If we want to know who the Holy Spirit is and what the Spirit does, and if we want to know what a Spirit-filled person looks like, we have to look first at the story of Jesus. The Spirit is by definition the Spirit who dwelt in Jesus, comes from him, and continues the work he began.

The Unique Work of the Holy Spirit

We have said that the Spirit is the Spirit of God the Creator, the Lord of Israel, and the Spirit of Jesus Christ. But the Spirit is not just the agent or instrument of God the Father and God the Son. According to the New Testament, the Spirit does something that is the Spirit's own unique work. It can be summarized with the word *new*. The Holy Spirit brings new creaturely life that is stronger than sickness and even death itself; gives new beginnings to people whose lives seem to be at a dead end; brings new wisdom and guidance from God; calls, holds together, and sends out a new reconciled and reconciling community called the church; works in the world to create a whole new humanity and a whole new creation. When the Spirit breaks in, old ways of thinking and living are left behind and new ways of thinking and living begin to take over. Old boring, oppressive, and dead social structures and institutions are transformed into exciting new, liberating ones. It may not happen all at once, but when the Holy Spirit comes there is the dawn of a new day, hope for a new and different future, and courage and strength to move toward it.

People who like things the way they are, who benefit from the status quo, who therefore value stability, permanence, and order above all else—they are suspicious and afraid of the Holy Spirit, and too much talk about the Spirit makes them nervous and defensive. But people who suffer and see no way out of suffering, who are enslaved and oppressed by their own or others' sinfulness and injustice—they yearn for the coming of the Holy Spirit and cannot talk enough about it. For the Spirit is not just the Lord and Giver of Life but the Lord and Giver of *new* life—to individuals, to churches, to the natural environment, to political, social, and economic structures.

Discerning the Spirit and Testing the Spirits

Not every new thing is the work of the Holy Spirit—not every shattering emotional experience that changes a person's life, not every new insight into the meaning and purpose of life, not every new vision and plan for correcting what is wrong with the church and the world. Moreover, *some* established ways of thinking and living that have become familiar to us may be the result of the renewing work of the Spirit that began before we came along. (Protestants, for instance, believe this about the new insights and goals of the Reformation.) But if any and every new thing does not automatically indicate the presence and work of God's

Spirit, and if everything that seems "old" to us does not indicate the absence of the Spirit, how can we recognize the Spirit's word and work among us?

The question is made even more difficult because the Spirit works inwardly in human hearts and minds, and there is therefore the danger that we will confuse the Spirit's inspiration with our own ideas and opinions, and the Spirit's guidance and empowerment with the fulfillment of our own personal or collective wishes, desires, and ambitions. Psychologists (confirmed by the history of religion) have shown that the ecstasy of religious experience is sometimes only thinly veiled sexual ecstasy. Social analysts have noted ironically how strange it is that both Christians who defend and those who protest against the present situation in church and society are sure that the "Holy Spirit" supports the self-interest of their particular gender, race, class, nation, and religious group. Church members are not always wrong in suspecting that their leaders sometimes claim to be "led by the Spirit" when they are simply defending their own conservative or liberal ideological biases, just as church leaders are not always wrong in suspecting that church members can do the same thing.

The Holy Spirit, in other words, is not the only spirit at work in and among us. There are also other spirits: our own individual spirits, the spirit of the times, the spirit of this or that particular interest group. There are also the spirits of envy, revenge, malice, greed, lust for power, and other *evil* spirits (at work in Christians inside the church as well as in non-Christians outside the church!).

Scripture tells us not to "believe every spirit" but to "test the spirits to see whether they are from God" (1 John 4:1). How can we do that? Both a negative and positive answer can be given. The negative answer is that the Holy Spirit is not to be confused with any feeling, thought, or desire within us, or with any liberal or conservative movement in the church or in the world outside the church. That does not mean that the Spirit is the Spirit of an unknown God whose will and work we have to figure out for ourselves from our own personal experience or from an analysis of the world around us. For (and this is the positive answer to the question) the Holy Spirit is the Spirit of the God we know from the pages of the Old and New Testaments—the God of Israel, the God who was uniquely present and at work in the life, death, and resurrection of Jesus and continues to be present and at work in the risen Jesus and the community gathered to bear witness to him. The Holy Spirit may—will!—say and do unanticipated things that are new to all of us (conservatives and liberals alike), but they will always be new and surprising things that are the will and work of *this* God.

To know who the Spirit is does not automatically solve the problem of deciding what we will think and do if we are Spirit-filled Christians. Nor does it automatically tell us what the church should say and do if it is a Spirit-filled church. But if we know what kind of personal and communal life is willed and created by the triune God we come to know in scripture, then we will know where we have to look to find the answers.

CHRISTIAN SPIRITUALITY

Having spoken about who the Holy Spirit is and having established the criteria for testing the spirits and discerning the Spirit, we now return to the hunger for a new spirituality or for spiritual renewal we spoke about at the beginning of this chapter. What would a Christian spirituality that comes from the life-renewing Spirit of God look like? We will answer this question first by describing some general characteristics of an authentic Christian spirituality.

Christian spirituality begins by looking outside, not inside, ourselves. A very long tradition that began in classical Roman Catholicism and has continued to be popular with many Protestants assumes that spiritual renewal begins by looking deep within our own souls and our private religious experience. Behind this assumption is the belief of the ancient Greeks that the human soul is a "little piece of divinity" in us, so that to get in touch with ourselves at the deepest level is to get in touch with God or the Spirit of God. It is true that God's Spirit comes to dwell within us. But we have just seen that it is not necessarily the presence of the Holy Spirit we discover when we analyze and meditate on our inner selves and the religious significance of our personal experience. It may be only our own finite and often sinful human feelings, wishes, longings, and ambitions. If we want to distinguish between God's Spirit and our own spirits, we said, we have to look at what scripture tells us about who the Spirit is and what the Spirit does. This means (in direct contrast to a common approach in spiritual development programs today) that if we want to recognize and experience the presence of God's life-renewing Spirit *in* us, we must be willing first to look *away* from ourselves, *outside* ourselves, *beyond* our personal experience.

If I want to know what God is doing and promises to do in my life, I cannot just analyze and tell *my* little story (or listen to the little stories of others); I must interpret my story (and theirs) in light of *God's* story with ancient Israel and the first Christian community. If I want to know what it would mean for me to be a truly spiritual person, I must first of all look at the life of Jesus Christ and the kind of person he was, not at my own life and the kind of person I would like to be. If it is really God's agenda in our lives and not our own that we are interested in, and if it is a genuinely Christian spirituality and not just some kind of self-concocted spirituality we want, we must first follow Calvin's advice to "get out of ourselves," "forget ourselves," stop circling round and round our own personal feelings, needs, problems, fears, and hopes, even our own "spiritual journey" (*Institutes* 3.7.1–5). We must first let ourselves be told something we cannot tell ourselves about the work of the Spirit of the God of the Bible who does indeed come *to* us but not *from* us. We will see later that this happens as we come together with fellow Christians in the church who gather week after week to understand their individual lives in light of the story of the God who has been at work in the world long before they came along and will still be at work in the world long after they are gone; and in light of the story of the Christ who is not just "my" Lord or the church's Lord but Lord of the world.

The first thing to be said, then, about Christian spirituality in distinction from other forms of spirituality is that it is not self-centered but God-centered and Christ-centered. We need not be afraid that we will be left out if we forget ourselves (at least for a little while) and focus on what the Bible tells us about the Spirit and the Spirit's work. For the Spirit is the Spirit of a God who cares for each of us, knows better than we ourselves what we need most, and promises to be present and at work in our hearts and lives with renewing power just as we give up a self-centered preoccupation with ourselves to think about the Holy Spirit of God who comes not from inside but from outside us.

Christian spirituality is this-worldly, not otherworldly. Some Christians think that to be "born again" of the Spirit means to experience renewal that is purely private and religious. Spiritual life has to do with prayer, seeking personal inspiration from Bible-reading, and feeling the presence of God when we withdraw from the world to commune with God in the company of a few like-minded Christians. Spirituality has nothing to do with such "unspiritual" things as bodily needs and pleasures, how we make and spend money, or the social arrangements that shape our public lives. Again and again in this book we have run into this kind of spirituality that identifies Christian life with indifference toward or contempt for everything that is physical and this-worldly, and longs to escape into the higher and purer life of the soul. Now we have to criticize this false spirituality in order to take seriously what the Bible tells us precisely about the presence and work of God's Holy Spirit.

We have seen that the Spirit we meet in scripture is the Spirit of a this-worldly God—a God who (1) created, blesses, protects, and defends the physical life of all God's creatures; (2) is at work to establish just social conditions that provide for the welfare especially of those who are most unable to care for themselves; (3) came to us in a flesh-and-blood human being who was the friend of worldly sinners and gave his life to reconcile all kinds of people to each other as well as to God; (4) called together the Christian community not just to enjoy fellowship with each other but to be empowered to serve the world God loves; (5) promises not only a new heaven but a whole new earth.

The Holy Spirit of this God enables people not to escape *from* the world but to live *in* it in such a way that not only their personal lives but also the world around them begins to be made new. Truly spiritual people, therefore, are not recognized by how suspicious they are of physical needs and pleasures but by how joyfully, thankfully, and responsibly they acknowledge them as good gifts of God. They are recognized not just by how much they pray but by how much they pray for the world. They are recognized not just by how much they "praise the Lord" for what "the Lord has done for me" but by how sensitive their praise makes them to the needs and hurts of other people and the protection of the natural environment in which they live. They are recognized not just by how much they read the Bible, but by how their Bible reading influences their business practices, political commitments, and social relationships. They are not recognized just by their testimonies to how God befriended and came to their aid when they were lost in sin, but by the way they befriend and come to the aid of other lost sinners.

A spirituality that retreats from the world into the self-serving safety of a private religious life (either alone or in the company of other religious people) is a false spirituality that *flees* the Spirit of God. True Christian spirituality cheerfully and confidently plunges into the life of this world, for there is where we meet the Spirit of the God of the Bible who is at work not to save us from but in and for the sake of the world.

Christian spirituality recognizes the presence and work of the Holy Spirit as much in ordinary as in extraordinary events. Some Christians expect and find evidences of the Spirit's work only when they see (often through the agency of Christians of great faith and charismatic power) miraculous restoration to health when the doctors have said there is no hope, or astonishing deliverance from trouble and hardship when all human wisdom and resources have been exhausted. God's powerful Spirit can, of course, work in such inexplicable, miraculous ways. Why should there not be some Christians with "faith that can move mountains"? But Christians who know the Spirit of the God of the Bible also expect and find the work of the Spirit in ordinary, everyday human experience when there seems to be no supernatural intervention. They recognize and thank God for the life-giving power of God's Spirit when health is restored and life is saved in a hospital by the scientific knowledge and technical skill of doctors and nurses who may or may not be Christians. They recognize and thank God for the justice-bringing work of God's Spirit when they see justice done by a "secular" court of law or governmental body (sometimes despite the indifference or opposition of some very "spiritual" Christians and churches). They recognize and thank God for the work of the Spirit of the risen Christ when alienated marriage partners are reconciled through the mediation of an agnostic therapist. Knowing the great Spirit of the great God who is free to "blow where it will," Christians expect and recognize the work of God's Spirit wherever, by whomever they see life preserved, justice done, hostile individuals and groups reconciled, new beginnings and new life. It does not matter to them whether they, the church, or even God "get credit" for it. They rejoice and their faith is strengthened wherever in the world they see evidences of God's life-renewing Spirit at work, and they gladly join hands to cooperate also with non-Christians or questionable Christians through whom they see their God at work, grateful that everything does not depend on us Christians and our church.

It is a sign of *false* spirituality and *weak* faith when people are unwilling or unable to recognize the work of the Spirit in ordinary processes of everyday life as well as in miraculous interruptions of it, through people who do not even know by whose Spirit it is that they know what they know and do what they do, as well as through Christians of great faith.

Christian spirituality recognizes the presence and work of the Holy Spirit in bad as well as in good times. The spirituality of some Christians is based on their experience of how God has helped them to solve insoluble problems, saved them from sickness or trouble, or given them what they prayed for. Their faith is strong so long as they can bear witness to such experiences, but without them their faith crumbles. Spirituality that depends on "success stories" is shallow and short-lived. Genuine Christian spirituality, on the other hand, is that of Christians who are indeed grateful for concrete, visible signs of the life-giving work of the Spirit but whose faith does not depend on these signs. It is spirituality like that of Jesus who trusted God and entrusted his life to God even as he suffered and died feeling totally godforsaken. It is spirituality like that of the apostle Paul and countless Christians through the centuries like him who understand that no more than their crucified Lord are they spared the hardship, suffering, and dying that is the lot of all finite creatures; who understand in fact that for them as for him *added* hardship and suffering come to those who serve the unqualified compassion and the unrelenting demand for justice of the kingdom of God that breaks into a hostile world. True spirituality is that of Christians who know that "in the suffering of this present age" (between the times), the Spirit does not always save us *from* our weakness but helps "*in* our weakness" to give us the comfort, help, courage, and strength to endure and entrust our lives to God, knowing that "neither death, nor life, nor angels, nor rulers, nor things present, nor things to come, nor powers, nor height, nor depth, nor anything else in all creation, will be able to separate us from the love of God in Christ Jesus our Lord" (Rom. 8:18, 38).

True Christian spirituality is not based on and does not depend on present experience of the power of God's Spirit over sickness, suffering, and death. It is based on and lives by Christians' memory of what the God who raised Jesus from the dead has done in the past, and therefore is their sure hope for what this God will do in the future—for them and for all people, everywhere.

When we speak of faith and hope like that, we have already begun to speak about the gifts of the Spirit that are the source and norm of all the aspects of genuine Christian spirituality. These gifts make true spirituality possible, and they tell us how it is concretely expressed in the everyday life of Spirit-filled Christians.

THE GIFTS OF THE SPIRIT

The New Testament mentions a large variety of the Spirit's gifts.[3] Not all of them are given to every Christian, but even those that are given only to a few are given for the sake of three gifts promised to all: new life, new truth, and new community. These three gifts always go together. Each of them is a test of whether we have truly received and understand the other two. As we consider them, we will also ask what we can do if we want to receive them.

The Gift of New Life

In 1 Corinthians 12—14, Paul mentions such sensational spiritual gifts as the ability to speak in unknown tongues, work miracles, heal, and impart supernatural wisdom from God—gifts that some Christians consider the highest and most impressive evidence of the working of the Spirit. But then Paul says there are still "greater gifts" than these, "a more excellent way." What could be greater than those extraordinary gifts that so obviously set some Christians apart from others? Love! Not just love as a sentimental feeling but the kind of no-strings-attached, no-one-excluded, no-cost-too-great love of God in Jesus Christ. That is the theme of 1 Corinthians 13. Without love like that, speaking even the language of angels (the greatest ecstatic religious experience) is just plain noise. Without such love, the most profound knowledge of all the mysteries of God (the greatest spiritual wisdom) is nothing. Without such love, the most committed service of other people and the most heroic self-sacrifice (even for the cause of the justice and peace of the kingdom of God) are worthless. The gift of love, Paul says, is even greater than the gifts of faith and hope (though, as we have seen, they too are indispensable parts of the new life of Christians).

What does it mean for the Spirit of God to break into our lives? Perhaps it does mean a tremendous emotional experience for some. And why should it be inconceivable that the Spirit should enable some to accomplish miracles or know what no one else knows? But even more important than that, the presence of the Spirit means a new relationship with God that is expressed in a new kind of relationship with other people. What greater miracle and what greater healing is there than the ability to put away "all bitterness and wrath and anger and wrangling and slander, together with all malice," and to be "kind to one another, tenderhearted, forgiving one another, as God in Christ has forgiven you" (Eph. 4:31–32)? What greater "fruits of the Spirit" can be imagined than "love, joy, peace, patience, kindness, generosity, faithfulness, gentleness, and self-control" (Gal. 5:22–23)?

Perhaps the best way to "test the spirits" and to discern a true spirituality in our own lives and in the lives of others is to ask whether our personal and corporate worship, our religious feelings and experiences, and our faith and hope in God are accompanied by openness and sensitivity to all the people we encounter every day. No matter how intensely pious or moral or orthodox we are, we have not yet known the presence of the life-giving Spirit of God in our lives until the love the Spirit brings shapes the relationship between employers and employees, rich and poor, educated and uneducated, family members and strangers, people like us and people different from us. According to Gal. 5:19–21, to be really spiritual people means that along with immorality, impurity, licentiousness, drunkenness, and carousing, also other "works of the flesh" such as strife, jealousy, anger, quarrels, dissension, factions, and envy begin to disappear in all areas of Christians' lives—including the church community, which is not immune from these works of the flesh!

How, then, can we have this new life of love that is perhaps the clearest and most important sign of the genuine spirituality of Spirit-filled Christians?

First, if such a new life is a gift of the Spirit, we cannot give it to ourselves. Not only the New Testament but also our own experience tells us that we cannot simply decide to love other people with the same unqualified love with which God has loved us. Sometimes when we most desperately want to, we find that we simply cannot.

Second, there is nothing we can do to force the Holy Spirit to come to us and give us this (or any other) gift. We cannot manipulate the Spirit to work according to our desires and schedule. There is no more guarantee that the Spirit will come with renewing power if we turn off the lights and sit in the dark than if we sit in broad daylight. The Spirit is no more bound to come in a church sanctuary or home prayer group than in a restaurant or in the work place. The Spirit is no more summoned by sentimental spiritual songs and highly emotional preaching than by sixteenth-century chorales and colorless preaching—or vice versa. The Spirit is free to work when, where, and how the *Spirit* chooses.

That does not mean we can do anything we please or nothing at all, excusing our unloving attitudes and actions by complaining that the Spirit has not chosen to come to us to enable us to love. Although we cannot control the Spirit's coming and going, we can place ourselves in situations in which we open ourselves to the possibility of the new life of love promised by the Spirit.

Perhaps we do not and cannot love people who are different from us, who seem undeserving and unworthy of our love, whose way of thinking seems so wrongheaded and way of living so unacceptable to us. But we can take the initiative to seek out their company and invite them into our company (including the church), sit down in the same room with them, and talk and listen to them. Who knows how the Holy Spirit might open our closed minds and warm our cold hearts if we were willing to do that? How can we ever learn to love others if we refuse to have anything to do with them, if we only look at them from a safe distance?

Perhaps even when we do care about others, we are reluctant to get involved with them because their problems and suffering are so great that we are afraid we will not be able to give them the help they need, because we are afraid that we will say or do the wrong thing, or because we know that it will be too painful to expose ourselves to their pain. But despite all the good or bad reasons we can find to hold back, we can go to them, put ourselves in their presence, and share their needs and hurts even when we cannot "fix it" with our prayers, good advice, or help. How will we ever learn what the Holy Spirit can enable us to do if we are afraid to plow into difficult situations in which we might find out?

We cannot force the Spirit to empower us with the ability to love, but we can risk the threat and cost of putting ourselves into situations in which we are in a position to receive the Spirit's gift of love. If we are unwilling or afraid to do that, is the problem that the Spirit has abandoned us or that we have abandoned the Spirit whose gift of love we say we want?

The Gift of New Truth

We saw earlier that the Holy Spirit is the Spirit of the Creator who is the source of all true wisdom and truth in the world, and the "teacher," or "Spirit of truth," whom Jesus promised he would send to his followers not only to remind them of what he had taught them but to lead them to new truth (John 14:26; 16:13). When we think of the gifts of the Spirit, then, we must speak of the gift of wisdom and understanding, the gift of truth.

There are Christians who believe that true spirituality has only to do with feeling the presence of the Holy Spirit in our hearts. It is to experience and bear witness to the overwhelming joy, peace, comfort, security, and assurance of salvation we feel when the Spirit touches our lives. To *think* too much about the Christian faith, on the other hand, is dangerous because a "cold intellectual approach" destroys people's personal relationship with God and leads them to doubt their personal experience of God's saving grace. It is in feeling not thinking, emotions not the mind, that people are receptive to and actually experience the work of the Holy Spirit in their lives. True Christian fellowship, therefore, is one in which people have had the same life-changing religious experience and share it with one another, not one in which people argue and fight about the truth of the Christian faith.

It is true that when the Holy Spirit comes into our lives, "our hearts are strangely warmed" by the assurance of God's saving grace (Wesley). It is also true that there is a kind of sterile intellectualism (dead orthodoxy or arrogant liberalism) that can "quench" the Spirit and destroy Christian fellowship. But the Holy Spirit is the Spirit of truth that enlightens our minds as well as warms our hearts, enables us to understand and live by God's truth as well as feel God's presence, gives the Christian community a common mind to serve God and God's world as well as a common religious experience to share with each other. To be Spirit-filled Christians, then, is to love God with our whole mind as well as with our whole heart and soul. True Christian spirituality is more than a matter of bearing witness to the *personal experience* of God's grace in our own lives; it is also a matter of seeking to understand and witness to the *truth* of God's grace that was already at work in and for the world before we experienced it, and continues to be at work in and for the world even in times when we do not experience and recognize it.

If the Holy Spirit is the Spirit of truth, then we seek and claim the gift of the Spirit when we study together as well as when we pray together, when we share our thoughts as well as when we share our feelings, when we work together to understand the truth of God and what it means for our lives in the world as well as when we share our personal experience of God's grace. Our talk about the truth of the Christian faith will be unconvincing to ourselves and to other people if we cannot talk about how it has touched our hearts. But it will also be unconvincing if we cannot talk about it in a way that makes sense. If we are afraid to examine our personal Christian experience in light of the truth of the Christian faith, how can we know whether our faith is anything more than a self-deceiving, self-serving spirituality based only on our own subjective feelings and emotions? How can we open ourselves to the Holy Spirit who is the Spirit of truth if we are unwilling or afraid to ask and talk about what the truth is that is the gift of the Spirit?

What can we do, then, to receive the Spirit's gift of truth? As with the gift of love, we cannot give it to ourselves. Personal experience can tell us how we *feel* about God's presence in our lives. Rational analysis of our own lives and the world around us can tell us what we *think* about God.

But only God can tell us the truth "for sure." That does not mean, however, that we can sit around waiting for God to reveal that truth "out of the blue." Although we cannot tell ourselves the truth, we can open our minds to learn the truth God has already given us in the scriptures of the Old and New Testaments.

But reading the Bible in itself is not enough. Unless the Holy Spirit enlightens our minds, we cannot understand the truth contained in this ancient book and how it helps us make decisions about our lives here and now. Are we once again left hopelessly waiting for a gift we cannot give ourselves? No. Although we cannot force the Spirit to come to us, even when we read the Bible, we can do at least three things to open ourselves to recognize and receive the Spirit's gift of truth to guide and help us.

1. In reading the Bible, we can ask ourselves constantly whether we really want to hear the truth it offers. Do we want to find there only confirmation and support for the opinions, prejudices, and desires we already have? Are we willing to let scripture change and correct what we want and what we think we already know? If we use the Bible only to justify our liberal or conservative opinions, we do not really want the guidance of the Spirit, nor can we expect it. If, on the other hand, we go to the Bible and listen to it preached with a sincere willingness to learn, change our minds, and be corrected, then we will be open to hear what God's Spirit has to say to us.

2. We can remind ourselves of what the Bible tells us about the truth that is the gift of God's Spirit. It is truth we recognize outside as well as inside the circle of believers wherever we see the Creator God we come to know in scripture at work to maintain the life, health, and welfare of all God's creatures, especially those who are poor, excluded, and oppressed. It is truth that we recognize outside as well as inside the Christian circle when we see the love of God in the risen Christ at work reconciling all kinds of people to each other (including people who are not "our kind" of people in what they think and how they live). It is the truth that we recognize outside as well as inside the Christian circle when the new life, new love, new justice, and truth that are the transforming work of God's creative and reconciling Spirit become visible in the lives of individuals and human society.

Indeed, if we really want the Spirit's gift of truth, we will not be afraid of truth from *any* source that echoes and points in the direction of the will and work of the triune God of scripture—whether it comes from Christians or non-Christians, religious people or "secular" scientists, psychologists, or sociologists. If, as Calvin taught us (*Institutes* 2.2.15), the Spirit of God is the source of all truth, we will recognize the Spirit's truth wherever it might appear. If we are unwilling or afraid to do that, then we do not really want the guidance that comes from the Spirit of God to whom scripture bears witness, nor should we be surprised that we do not receive it.

3. Finally, if it is really the Holy Spirit's gift of truth we seek when we read the Bible and seek to discern the will and work of the Spirit in the world around us, if it is not just support for our own personal and social self-interest, then we will seek the truth in the company of other Christians. We will not seek it alone, depending on our own experience and insights. Nor will we seek it only in the company of a few other Christians whose religious experience is the same as our own; whose race, class, and political convictions are the same as ours. We will do it in the company of other Christians who are different from us. They have their biases and limited vision too. But if we read the Bible and seek the truth together, then we show our willingness mutually to correct each other's biases and limitations so that it really is God's truth and not just "our" truth we seek. If we are unwilling or afraid to risk the disagreement, conflict, and possibility of change it takes to do that, then once again we do not really want the guidance that comes from God's Holy Spirit, nor should we be surprised that we do not receive it.

Even when we do everything we can genuinely to open ourselves to receive the Spirit's gift of truth, there is no guarantee that we will truly and accurately perceive it. But insofar as we remain willing to recognize that "we know only in part" and that we "now . . . see in a mirror, dimly" (1 Cor. 13:9, 12); insofar as we are willing to admit that all the truth may not be on our side (even on the side of us Christians); insofar as we recognize that we are not the only ones seeking the truth of God and that others may have learned from God's Spirit some things we need to learn too—to that extent we may count on the faithfulness of the Christ who *promised* to send us the Spirit of truth to enlighten our minds and guide us in our individual lives, in the church, and in the world where we are called to love and serve the truth—*God's* truth.

The Gift of New Community

We have seen that Jesus promised to send the Holy Spirit to the community of his followers, not just to isolated individuals. The Spirit first came when "they were all together in one place" (Acts 2:1). The gifts of the Spirit are given to individual Christians not just for their own personal benefit and enjoyment but "for the common good" (1 Cor. 12:7), to "build up the church"(1 Cor. 14:4), "for the work of ministry, for building up the body of Christ" (Eph. 4:12). The gift of the Spirit *is* the gift of community. True Christian spirituality, therefore, is spirituality that is born in the church, is nourished and grows in the church, and exists for the sake of the church's ministry to the world.

Some Christians (as well as non-Christians) are suspicious of the "institutional" church or the church as an "organization." They find its worship and preaching a boring and irrelevant routine without passion or commitment, its teaching the half-hearted communication of Christian truth by half-converted leaders, its fellowship one of "merely nominal" Christians whose lives have not been touched by the renewing power of the Holy Spirit. They often believe that the only way to find and nurture genuine spirituality is to form a small group of truly Spirit-seeking and Spirit-filled Christians like themselves outside or perhaps within the larger church—separated in one way or another from "those other" Christians who are not real Christians at all.

We must take very seriously this criticism of the church. Later we will give a whole chapter to the "problem" of the church. But those who reject the larger church and seek the presence of the Spirit by withdrawing from it into small groups of "real" Christians cut themselves off from the very Spirit they seek. This becomes clear when we look at two things the New Testament tells us about the inseparable connection between the Holy Spirit and the church.

First, according to the New Testament, the "fellowship of the Holy Spirit" is a fellowship of people who are different from each other, not one of congenial people whose religious experience, interests, and goals are exactly the same. In the early church it was a community of Jews and Gentiles, slave and free, male and female—people who were united in Jesus Christ by the Spirit of Christ despite all the religious, social, and political differences that in the surrounding world separated them from each other and made them hostile to each other. And so it is in our time too. The Holy Spirit does not bless but overcomes the animosities and exclusiveness that divide people into "insiders like us" and "outsiders like them." How can Christians expect to experience the reconciling and uniting power of this Spirit in their own lives if they are unwilling and unable to live in community even with fellow Christians who are different from them (not to mention other people)? How can they expect others to be impressed with their witness to the reconciling and uniting power of the Spirit if they themselves only echo the "us-them" mentality that divides the world into hostile groups? More specifically, how can Christians hope to receive the Spirit's gift of love (by definition, the mutual love of people who are different from each other) if they cannot or will not even love fellow Christians who are different from themselves? How can they expect others to believe what they say about the Spirit's gift of love if they are unwilling and unable to demonstrate it in their own community? How can they receive the Spirit's gift of new truth if they are unwilling and unable to learn even from fellow Christians in the church whose Christian experience, faith, and life are expressed in ways different from their own? How can they expect others to be open to learn new truth that comes from God if they themselves are unwilling and unable to learn it in their own community? To withdraw from the larger church into the company of a few "real" Christians just like us is to *refuse* the true spirituality that comes from God's Holy Spirit. It is to flee from the very gifts of the Spirit we seek for ourselves and to belie the very promise of the renewing power of the Spirit we proclaim to the world. When we confess our faith with the Apostles' Creed, "I believe in the Holy Spirit" and "the Holy Catholic Church" go together.

Second, among the gifts of the Spirit mentioned in the New Testament are whole lists of gifts promised specifically to the "organized church."[4] Paul identifies as gifts of the Spirit functions such as preaching, teaching, leadership (administration!), pastoral guidance and ministry, and prophecy (probably the gift of some to bring the Word of God to bear on contemporary social and political situations).[5] We may think here also of rituals of the church such as baptism (which in Acts is always connected with the Spirit's gift of faith and new life) and the Lord's Supper (which nourishes and strengthens the faith and life of the church). The preaching and teaching of the church may indeed often seem uninspired and unconvincing, even false. Its sacraments may indeed often seem "empty rituals." The work of its professional leaders and incessant committee meetings may indeed often seem more a matter of maintaining an all-too-worldly organization than of nurturing a fellowship of the Holy Spirit. It may indeed sometimes seem so concerned about doing "good works" in the world that it neglects the spiritual needs of its own members. But according to the New Testament, the presence and power of the Holy Spirit are promised and experienced precisely in the church's Sunday-by-Sunday preaching and teaching of the Word of God, its not-too-exciting everyday life, and its ministry to the world outside its own membership. Of course, the Holy Spirit can work when, where, and how the Spirit pleases, even apart from the church. But when spiritually hungry Christians reject the life and work of the organized church and encourage other spiritually hungry people to do so, when they withdraw from the church themselves and invite others to do so in order to tend to their own spiritual development apart from the church—then they deprive themselves and other people of the very renewing power and gift of the Spirit they yearn for.

Like the other gifts of the Spirit, the gift of community is one we cannot give ourselves. But what we have just seen about the nature of the new community that is the gift of the Spirit indicates some things we can do to open ourselves to receive this gift we cannot give ourselves:

1. If we really want the true community that is the gift of the Holy Spirit, we will listen very carefully to fellow Christians and others who criticize the church as it is. In fact, just because we yearn for the true fellowship of the Spirit, we will ourselves be the church's most severe critics. But we will criticize it as its "loyal opposition" who seek to correct and build up rather than to reject and tear down. We will criticize it as insiders who love the church rather than as outsiders who leave it altogether or form within it little groups of "true Christians" who have the same spiritual experience (or the same "politically correct" liberal convictions or "theologically correct" conservative convictions) in opposition to "those others" whom we suspect may not be real Christians at all.

2. If we really want the true community that is the gift of the Holy Spirit, we will criticize our own as well as other Christians' or "the church's" understanding of Christian faith and life. We will ask ourselves whether the spiritual gifts we want or think we have already received contribute to the "common good" of the whole Christian community and contribute to the mutual love, encouragement, comfort, and help of all its members—or whether they only satisfy our own personal needs and those of others like us.

3. If we really want the true community that is the gift of the Spirit, we will seek the gifts of the Spirit for the sake of the church's ministry in and for the world, not just for the sake of the warm fellowship Christians enjoy with each other.

4. If we really want the true community that is the gift of the Spirit, we will always be ready to recognize and receive the new life and new truth of the Spirit that is offered in the ordinary "routine" preaching, teaching, worship, and life of the church as well as in the experience of extraordinary manifestations of the Spirit in our private worship or in

the company of a few like-minded Christians who gather for prayer and praise. Instead of setting the public, institutional life of the church as an organization in opposition to our private or small-group exercises in spiritual development, we will let each of these mutually inform and correct the other.

5. If we really want the true community that is the gift of the Spirit, we will remember that there are "varieties of gifts" of the Spirit (1 Cor. 12:4), "gifts that differ according to the grace given to us" (Rom. 12:6). Christian unity does not mean Christian uniformity. Different Christians have different gifts. No one has all the gifts. The Christian community needs this variety and diversity to be a whole community. We will prove our desire for such a community when we gladly welcome other Christians whose gifts are different from our own; when we are grateful for other Christians who contribute experiences, insights, and abilities to the church we ourselves cannot offer it; when we rejoice in the opportunity to learn what genuine Christian love means in the company of other Christians who are different from us.

The gift of a new life of love, the gift of new truth, the gift of a new community different from other communities—these are inseparable gifts of the Holy Spirit and marks of true Christian spirituality. We cannot give them to ourselves. But if we earnestly desire them and do what we can to open ourselves to receive them, then we may pray an ancient prayer of the church, confident that it will be answered in surprising ways in our own lives, in the church, and in the world around us: "Come, Holy Spirit."

FOR FURTHER REFLECTION AND STUDY

1. Do you agree that the Holy Spirit is also at work in the world outside the church, among and in people who are not Christians? Could the Holy Spirit be at work in a shopping mall? In a session of the United States Congress? At a baseball game? How could we tell whether or not the Spirit is at work in such unexpected places?
2. Why is it important to insist that the Holy Spirit is the Spirit of Christ?
3. Read Paul's discussion of the gifts of the Holy Spirit in 1 Corinthians 12—14. What gifts are mentioned? Why are they given? Do they conflict with each other? Do all Christians receive the same

gifts? What is the greatest gift? What does Paul think of "speaking in tongues"?

4. In light of the biblical understanding of the meaning of the word *spiritual,* what would be a spiritual relationship between a husband and wife? Between friends? Between an employer and his or her employees?
5. What does it mean to be "born again"? How can we recognize a born-again Christian when we see one?
6. If faith, hope, and love are gifts we can receive only from the Holy Spirit and are not gifts we can achieve for ourselves, should we blame or condemn people who do not have these gifts?
7. How can we be faithful to the Christian convictions we already hold and yet let ourselves be corrected by the Holy Spirit?
8. Could the Holy Spirit lead us to "new truth" that is not specifically given us in the Bible? Could the Spirit lead us to think and act differently from the way Christians who respect the authority of scripture have traditionally thought we should think and live?

16

Are You a Christian?

The Doctrine of Justification

Are you a Christian? How would you answer someone who asked you point-blank? Many of us would suspect that it is a trick question meant to trap us. Any answer we give involves us in embarrassing self-contradictions.

Suppose I answer, "Yes, I belong to the church." Then your questioner is likely to ask whether belonging to the church and being a Christian are the same thing. Because there are so many denominations, with so many versions of Christianity, how do you know yours is the really Christian one? Why is there so much un-Christian pettiness and feuding in the church? Why does the church so often simply echo the class and race prejudices of its environment and spend all its time keeping the organization going instead of serving the world? Church membership is no guarantee that I take seriously either Christian faith or Christian life.

Suppose I answer, "Yes, I am a Christian. I believe in Jesus Christ as my personal Lord and Savior." Then my questioner can begin asking uncomfortable questions about my life. If you believe in Christ, then why are you so impatient with your children? Why do you talk about other people behind their backs? Do you pay your employees a fair wage? What are you doing to obey Jesus' command to minister to the poor, oppressed, and imprisoned? It does not take long to expose the contradiction between my professed faith and my life. But if I begin to argue that it is not what I *do* but what I *believe* that makes me a Christian, I open myself to the charge of being a fake and a hypocrite.

Suppose, then, I am more cautious and answer, "Well, I try to be a Christian." That invites my questioner to take another tack. How hard do you try? The temptation is to begin adding up the score: I go to church, read the Bible, pray, try to be kind to other people, and so on. But the total score will not stand close examination. Is it enough? Why do you do all that? Is it really out of love for God and other people, or is it at least partially out of a desire to earn the approval of God and the admiration of others? So long as I allow the conversation to turn around my achievements in living the Christian life, it will always be doubtful both to myself and to others whether I am even trying very hard to be a Christian, much less how well I have succeeded.

But on the other hand, if I try to turn the conversation from myself and the authenticity of my Christian faith and life to talk about God and what God has done and is doing in my life and the world around me, I seem to be avoiding the original question about whether *I* am a Christian.

What does it mean to be a Christian? How are Christian faith and Christian life related? What is the connection between what God gives us and does for us, and what God requires us to do? In other words, how do we receive and make our own the Holy Spirit's gifts of faith and new life described in the last chapter? These are the questions we will deal with in this and the following chapter. The church has answered them with the doctrines of justification and sanctification, and these are the doctrines that will guide our discussion. Study them not only to learn in general what a Christian is, but to discover how you would answer the question "Are *you* a Christian?"

THE PROBLEM OF JUSTIFICATION

Everyone who knows anything at all about Protestant beliefs knows that the doctrine of justification by God's grace through faith was what got the Reformation started. Luther was a man tormented by doubts about how he stood with God. He knew that God was a righteous God who would not let sin go unpunished, and he was terrified that he was not good enough to escape God's wrathful judgment. "How can I find a gracious God?" was the question that plagued his life. He became a monk and gave himself full time to the attempt to earn God's acceptance by an extraordinary religious life. But the harder he tried, the more he realized that he would never be good enough to merit salvation, and the more anxious, despairing, and guilt-ridden he became. Finally, he stumbled across the Good News of the New Testament that we do not have to save ourselves by "being good" to satisfy God's righteous demands. What we cannot do for ourselves, God has done for us in Christ. We are "justified"—made right with God—not by our own efforts to climb up to God but by God's free grace in coming to us. Just when we give up the futile attempt to merit God's love, acknowledge that we are and always will be unworthy in ourselves, and trust God's goodness instead of our own—just then we will discover that salvation is not a prize to be won by our good works, but a gift to be accepted by faith.

Most Protestants (and many modern Roman Catholics) agree in theory that Luther was right. But the words "justification by faith" no longer evoke in us the same overwhelming joy and sense of glorious freedom they gave Luther and the first Protestants. Why? Probably one reason is that it is hard for us to see that we are in the same desperate predicament that Luther was in when he "discovered" this doctrine. Quite apart from whether we ought to or not, how many of us take God and God's righteousness so seriously that we live in daily terror that we might be eternally damned? Who of us could say that every day, all day, our life is soured by the fear that God does not love us. Who of us ever thought seriously of giving up everything in order to escape the wrath of God and earn salvation by striving to live a perfect life? If we are to grasp something of the joy and freedom of justification, we must first translate the desperate situation to which it speaks into more contemporary terms. When we have done that, we will then speak of what the doctrine itself can mean to us modern people.

Most of us do not try to justify ourselves as young Luther did. But we have other ways of doing the same thing—with the same result.

Many of us Americans try to justify ourselves not so much by good works as by just plain work. Hard work and success make us feel that we are "worth" something and can win for ourselves the approval and admiration of other people. So we work harder and harder and longer and longer, feeling guilty whenever we stop to rest or play. But the very work that was supposed to give our lives meaning becomes a cruel slave driver that turns them into a treadmill. Our work was supposed to give us self-respect, but we are constantly threatened by the fear that we have not performed well enough or climbed high enough. And we are constantly tormented by the dread of failure, loss of work, or retirement. The work that was supposed to have made us responsible people takes so much time and energy that we neglect our families and friends. It was supposed to win the approval of others but instead turns them into rivals and opponents to be defeated and dominated. The very work that we thought would justify our existence to ourselves and other people becomes self-destructive and alienates us from them.

If we can believe television, many American men and women try to justify themselves by working constantly and frantically to stay young and physically attractive. How can we accept ourselves or expect to be loved otherwise? Every new wrinkle, every additional pound, every gray hair is a source of anxious concern. If we are constantly preoccupied with ourselves and our lovableness, how can we love anyone else or give ourselves to be loved? We offer not ourselves but youth and beauty to be loved. We are so concerned about ourselves that we are not free to love other people. The very quest that was supposed to make a loving relationship or a marriage work destroys it.

Some of us try to justify ourselves by being critical of other people, thinking that if we can make them look little, we will look big. But the need to run down others is itself a sign of our own insecurity and of our desperate need to be able to accept ourselves and to be accepted by them. The more we try to build ourselves up by tearing other people down, the more insecure, unlovable, and lonely we become. We are trapped and condemned by the very means by which we thought to save ourselves.

Others of us, on the other hand, try to justify ourselves by being critical of *ourselves*, thinking that the more humbly self-accusing and self-rejecting we are, the more admirable we will be. But the need to run down myself is not a sign of genuine humility; it is a sign of arrogant pride: I'm more humble than everyone—and therefore better than everyone. Such self-depreciation sometimes seems to lead to self-sacrifice and "selfless" service of others, but in fact it is only self-serving and a means of manipulating others. The very means by which we try to justify ourselves condemns us to a lonely, guilty life of self-centeredness.

Still others of us try to justify ourselves by trying to be good—not so much, like Luther, to win God's approval as to convince ourselves of our own worth and to win the love of other people. If I cannot justify myself by being rich or powerful or intellectual or attractive, perhaps I can do it by achieving moral superiority. Even if I cannot be anything else, I can be good! Or can I? The quest for self-justifying virtue is also self-defeating. It leads to constant, anxious circling round and round ourselves. Have I forgotten something? Have I done enough? Am I really good? Even when the quest does get beyond self-criticism, it never really reaches others. I only use other people as objects on whom to practice my goodness. I am not really interested in them, but only in the warm glow their thankfulness and indebtedness give me. How can I expect them really to love and respect me, when they sense that I am only using them to build up my own ego and satisfy my own needs? The very quest that should justify me in fact damns me. The very means by which I thought to buy the love of other people alienates me from them.

Depending on what is important to us and what is possible for us, all of us spend our lives trying to justify ourselves in one way or another. But whatever the means, the result is always the same. We are either too proud or too despairing of our own worth. Our lives are driven, anxious, guilty. No matter how hard we try, we cannot save ourselves or buy the respect, love, and acceptance of others. Those who look to themselves and try to measure and guarantee their worth by their own achievements destroy themselves, alienate themselves from others—and miss the one way in which their existence can be justified: God's grace.

That means that the predicament of us modern people, though it is expressed in a different way, is exactly the same as the predicament of Luther! Perhaps the New Testament truth he stumbled upon is after all more relevant than we thought. Maybe it is not just an appropriate theme for Reformation Sunday once a year, but a truth that could make a difference every day of our lives.

JUSTIFICATION BY GRACE

You cannot justify yourself. That was our first point. The doctrine of justification is a call first of all to give up. Surrender. Stop trying to be something you are not. Put aside all the ways by which you so desperately and futilely try to convince God, yourself, and other people that you are deserving of admiration, love, and respect. It won't work. You can't bring it off—not even by the negative way of trying to prove that you are deserving of admiration, love, and respect because you are so humble and selfless, or because you so earnestly beat your breast and confess that you are a no-good sinner. You cannot justify yourself. Only God can make things right within you and in your personal relationships.

But we will never understand the first point until we understand a second one: You *can* give up all your attempts to justify yourself, because you do not *need* to give yourself to the anxious, frantic, self-defeating task of justifying yourself. Only God *can*, but God *does* justify us. Now we will try to understand what this means in our relation to God. Later we will see how we also become right with ourselves and with other people as we become right with God.

The meaning of justification is really very simple. It seems complicated to us only because it sounds too good to be true. Justification by grace, as a "gift" (Rom. 3:24), means quite simply: You do not have to try to buy God's love and acceptance, because you are *already* loved and accepted by God—without any qualification or prerequisites.[1] God does not say, "I will love you *if* you are good, *if* you prove yourself worthy, *if* you do so and so, *if* you first love me." God does not even say, "I will love you *if* you first have faith in me or *if* you first humiliate yourself and grovel on the ground before me." God says simply, "I love you just as you are—*you,* not your righteousness, your humility, your faith, or your accomplishments of one kind or another."

That does not mean that God's love is blind. God sees us as we really are. Justification is a big "nevertheless." God says to us: "You may fool other people, but you cannot fool me. I see behind all the masks and defenses and pretensions by which you try to convince yourself and other people that you are somebody and not nobody. I see *you*—even more clearly than you see yourself when no one else is around and you admit to yourself who the real you is behind the front you usually hide behind. Nevertheless I love and accept you, *despite* your open and secret sins, *despite* your unworthiness and unlovableness, *despite* what you do to other people and yourself by your inability and unwillingness to love and let them love you."

Justification means that despite the fact that things are not right in our inner lives and our personal relationships, God forgives and accepts us. Therefore, there is no need for our compulsive, anxious, defensive attempts to make things right ourselves or to give up in despair because we cannot do so.

How do we know this is true? Because "while we were still weak, at the right time Christ died for the ungodly. . . . [W]hile we still were sinners Christ died for us" (Rom. 5:6–8). God is not for those who first do what they can to help themselves, but for those who cannot help themselves. God is not for those who first believe in God, but for those who have lived without and against God. God is not for the righteous, but for the unrighteous—including those who are unrighteous just because they think they are righteous, or because of their self-righteous confession that they are unrighteous! Christ means that God's love is not a reward for what we have done or confess that we have not done, but a *gift* given absolutely freely, with no strings attached.

And the result? We are justified—in Christ. That means that things are "made right" between us and God—not because we love God, but because in Christ God loves us. Our existence is "justified" not insofar as we make ourselves worthy of being loved, but simply because in loving us God gives us a worth we do not have in ourselves. It is not what we do for God but what God has done for us, not what we *give* but what we *receive* that makes us "somebody" and not "nobody."

THE JUSTICE OF JUSTIFICATION

We can better understand the meaning of justification by grace if we look at what it means in the light of a problem traditionally considered in connection with this doctrine. The problem arises from the fact that its terminology is borrowed from a law court. God is a righteous, or just, Judge. We are accused and convicted of unrighteousness. Justification means that the Judge declares us to be just, or righteous, in the eyes of the law. We who are guilty are forgiven and set free. This analogy raises obvious difficulties. If God is a just Judge, how can God forgive or declare righteous those who are in fact guilty? If God accepts us as righteous and treats us "as if" we were what we are not, does God not wink at sin and pretend that a lie is the truth? Traditionally, the answer has been that when God judges us, God looks at Christ's righteousness and accepts us for Christ's sake, on the basis of *his* merit. But the problem still remains. Can righteousness be transferred? Are we not still guilty? Even if God lets us get by, are we not still trapped in our sin?

The problem is unsolvable so long as we take the legal imagery literally and think of justification in exclusively moral or ethical terms. What the legal imagery intends to say is not that God pretends we are not guilty and falsely declares us to be morally perfect and thus deserving of salvation. Justification has to do not so much with morality as with our personal relationships. It says that in Christ God has acted to make right not just the wrong things we have *done* but the wrong persons we *are*. It deals not just with our sin and guilt but with the cause of sin and guilt within us. It means that in Christ God was and is at work not just to enable us to escape the price we ought to pay for our sins, but to heal the twisted relationships that lie at the bottom of all our particular sins. It is not a matter of God's pretending that we are something we really are not, but God's freeing us to become something we are not.

Perhaps we can best understand this by an analogy. Think of a problem child in school. He is noisy, uncooperative, insolent with his teachers, a troublemaker and bully among his fellow pupils. What should be done with such a child? "Justice" might demand that he be punished. But punishment does not solve his problem; it only makes him more hostile even if it squelches him.

Or think of the child who is a problem because she withdraws into herself. She does poor work because she is paralyzed by the fear of her own inadequacy, and she is rejected by her fellow pupils because in her withdrawal she seems "stuck-up." It might seem proper to warn her that if she does not work harder and listen to the teacher, she will fail; that if she does not make an effort to get along better with other people, she will never have any friends. But threats and pep talks only make her feel more insecure and afraid, so that she withdraws and fails all the more.

Any good psychologist knows that what both children need is first of all to be loved. If the troublemaker learns that he is accepted for himself, he no longer has to draw attention to himself by rebellion against authority and order. If the withdrawn girl learns that someone cares about her, she is freed from the insecure self-depreciation that defeats and isolates her from other people. Neither punishment nor threats can change either child or solve his or her problem. But love can.

Justification is something like that. It says God loves you. God accepts you. God forgives you—without demanding that you be punished, without demanding that you torment and punish yourself, without demanding that you do anything to make up for what you have done or not done. Is that just? In a sense, no. No judge in any court could treat guilty people that way. If the just requirements of the law are not met, the guilty party must pay up and suffer the consequences in one way or another. But on the other hand, the good news of justification does not simply leave us where we are, overlooking all the ways we put ourselves in the wrong with God and our fellow human beings. It means that the relationship between ourselves and God is changed. God restores fellowship where for one reason or another we have rejected or destroyed fellowship. And that new relationship with God inevitably *changes* us.

There are many ways to express how the good news of God's love *for* us results in a real change *in* us. First John 4:18 says it this way: "Perfect love casts out fear." When we learn that God loves us just as we are, then we are freed from the fear that expresses itself in hostile or defensive attempts to buy off or manipulate God and other people in order to build up ourselves. We are freed from the fear that expresses itself in despairing, self-hating attempts to escape God and other people by running and hiding from them to nurse our insecurity in self-centered isolation. Seemingly just punishment, threats, and demands only increase fear and lead to increased alienation and separation. But seemingly unjust love does away with fear and leads to reconciliation with God, our fellow human beings, and ourselves.

The love, forgiveness, and acceptance of God in Christ, in other words, make possible within us precisely what God's righteousness and justice demand of us—that we love God with our whole beings and our neighbor as ourselves. Justification is God's way of giving what God demands. It is not God's denial of the truth and pretending that everything is in order in our lives. It is God's way of beginning to *create* order just because God knows very well how hopelessly "fouled-up" we are.

JUSTIFICATION BY GRACE THROUGH FAITH

Suppose we begin to understand what justification by grace means. The question still remains, "How can we have this assurance of God's love that frees us *from* ourselves and *for* God, other people, and true self-fulfillment?" The church answers this question by speaking of justification through *faith.*

We have deliberately waited until the end of our discussion of justification to speak of faith because we wanted to avoid a common misunderstanding. It is often said that instead of the idea that our good works make us acceptable to God, Protestantism teaches that all we have to do is have faith in order to win God's approval and acceptance. This is a serious distortion, because it only substitutes another requirement that we must fulfill in order to earn salvation. In the last analysis it makes us just as insecure as does justification by other means. Instead of anxiously examining my life to discover whether it is good enough, now I must anxiously examine my faith to see whether it is sure and strong enough to earn God's love. Justification by faith in this sense is only another means of self-justification and self-salvation.

According to scripture (and true Protestantism), neither our good works *nor* our faith justifies us. God alone does it by God's free grace in Christ. It is not confidence in the goodness of our life *or* in the strength of our faith, but confidence in God that gives us the assurance that we are right with God. Robert McAfee Brown puts it this way: "The gospel does not say, 'Trust God and he will love you,' the gospel says, 'God already loves you, so trust him.' Faith is not a 'work' that saves us; it is our acknowledgment that we are saved."[2]

This does not mean that faith is unimportant. Although it is not the cause of God's loving us, it is the indispensable means by which we accept and live from God's love. Faith does not make us right with God, but no one is made right with God without faith.

Another analogy from human relationships can help clarify the part faith plays in justification. If a man's wife does not already love him, his faith in her cannot force her to love him, no matter how complete it is. But on the other hand, no matter how much she loves him, he can neither receive nor return her love if he does not have faith in her. If he constantly doubts whether she is really faithful to him, or if he constantly questions whether he is good enough for her, the marriage will be hopelessly spoiled by his suspicion of her or anxiety about his lovableness. The marriage can be a happy one only when he believes that her declarations and demonstrations of love are genuine.

So it is with us and God. Our faith does not force or enable God to love us, but it is our way of acknowledging, receiving, enjoying—and returning—the love that God had for us long before we ever thought of loving God. We are not made right with God *by* our faith, but we are made right with God *through* our faith. Our faith does not change God from being against us into being for us, but it does change us from being closed to being open to receive the love God has always had for us.

What is this faith we have been talking about? In order to answer this question, we have only to underline what we have already said not only in the present discussion of justification but also throughout this book. Very simply, faith is trust. It is not intellectual acceptance of biblical or theological doctrines, not even the doctrines of Christ or justification. It is confidence in God. Faith is not believing in the Bible; it is not, in Calvin's words, "assent to the gospel history" (*Institutes* 3.2.1). It is not believing in a book, but believing in the God we come to know in the book. Christian faith is not confidence in faith that saves ("saving faith") but confidence in the *God* who saves. The faith we have been talking about, in other words, is a kind of personal relationship—a total commitment of ourselves to the living God whose trustworthiness has been proved by God's powerful and loving action for us in the life, death, and resurrection of Christ. Calvin puts it this way: Faith is "a firm and certain knowledge of God's benevolence toward us, founded upon the truth of the freely given promise in Christ, both revealed to our minds and sealed upon our hearts through the Holy Spirit" (*Institutes* 3.2.7).

How can we have such faith? How can we be so sure of God's love that we are freed from the unnecessary, self-defeating attempt to justify ourselves? How can we trust God so completely that we do not have to trust our own goodness or faith? Here we run again into the problem we wrestled with in the previous chapter. Faith, trust, or assurance in God is a *gift*. We can no more simply decide to trust God than we can by sheer willpower decide to trust another human being. The faith that trusts in the love of God is itself the work of God's love, "revealed to our minds and sealed upon our hearts through the Holy Spirit."

Yet the fact that we cannot give ourselves faith does not mean that we must say fatalistically that everyone either has or does not have it, that God either does or does not give it, and that there is nothing we can do about it. As we said in the last chapter about all the gifts of the Spirit, there are some things we can do to put ourselves in situations in which the gift of faith is promised and received. In the present context, we mention three specific things we can do. Especially the last two raise questions that lead us to the two following chapters.

1. If we want a faith that trusts in the love of God that frees us from the necessity of trying to justify and save ourselves, we can admit honestly that none of us has such faith, at least not always. Even those who do not have intellectual doubts about the truth of biblical and Christian doctrines do not have so much confidence in God's love that they are free from the fearful or proud compulsion to build themselves up in one way or another before God and other people, and in their own self-estimation. None of us has faith in the sense of the relaxed, anxiety-free trust Jesus speaks of in Matt. 6:25–33. If we want real faith, therefore, we must paradoxically admit that we do not have it, and pray every new day that we may receive it. "I believe. Help my unbelief."

2. Faith (trust in God's love) becomes possible when we put ourselves in a situation in which we can hear about and experience God's love over and over again. Such a situation is first of all the church, the community of God's people.

Just as a child, spouse, or friend needs to hear over and over again that he or she is loved, so we Christians need to hear over and over again the unbelievably good news that God loves, forgives, and accepts us despite everything we have been and done—or not been and done. Trust in God becomes possible as we hear constantly anew how trustworthy God is. That happens in the church as it tells itself over and over again, Sunday after Sunday, the story of God's steadfast love for a sinful world and sinful human beings (each one of us included).

But hearing is not enough. A child could not trust a parent, a spouse his or her partner, or a friend his or her companion if there were not visible demonstrations that the other's love is genuine. It is not enough simply to hear the words that God loves us; we need to experience God's love. Again, it is above all in the church that this happens. It happens when people are baptized or remember their own baptism as they watch another being baptized—when they see a visible demonstration of the assurance that God knows each one of us by name and has "adopted" us to be God's dearly beloved children. It happens when it is not the good and worthy but precisely the needy, guilty sinners who are invited to the Lord's Table to receive nourishment for the new life they cannot give themselves. It also happens when we experience God's forgiveness, acceptance, and love as we experience the forgiveness, acceptance, and love of other people in the life of the Christian community. The church is by definition the community of those who live by God's forgiveness for guilty people, God's acceptance of those who in themselves are unacceptable, God's love for those who know they cannot earn the right to be loved. It is the place where people can risk putting aside all their defenses and masks, knowing that they will be accepted just as they are, with all their faults, whatever they have done, however unacceptable they are by the moral and social standards of the world. How can those who know themselves to be forgiven sinners not forgive other sinners?

We cannot give ourselves the gift of faith that is trust in God's love for us just as we are. But we can put ourselves in the situation—in the church—where we can hear about and experience God's faith-creating love. To say this, of course, raises the disturbing question whether the church (even when the gospel is "truly preached" and the sacraments "rightly administered") really is a community where God's and Christians' love and acceptance "happen" as we have claimed. We run again into the "problem" of the church that we will have to deal with later. But whatever has to be said in criticism of the church as it is, it still is the body of Christ, the fellowship of the Holy Spirit. God promises to make God's justifying grace real and effective in this all-too-human community of sinners who need it just as much as anyone else—perhaps more than anyone else! We can recognize, experience, and trust God's love everywhere when we first find it here.

3. What can we do to put ourselves in the situation where faith becomes possible? We can admit that we do not have it, but need ever afresh to receive it. We can participate in the community of faith. Finally, we can risk beginning to do what faith requires. Faith in God is

only possible when we live by faith. How will we ever learn that God is trustworthy until we give up trusting in ourselves? How can we trust God if we do not willingly and thankfully obey God? How can we believe that we unworthy, undeserving people are forgiven, loved, and accepted until we begin to forgive, love, and accept other unworthy, undeserving people? How can we believe that we are made free for a right relationship with God, other people, and ourselves until we risk giving up our self-destructive, self-destroying attempts to ignore or use God and other people to serve ourselves, and learn that we find ourselves by losing ourselves in serving them? Faith comes with obedience. Without obedience, there can be no faith. Or to put it in the classical language of the doctrine of justification, we are not made right with God *by* good works, but we are not made right with him *without* good works.

Dietrich Bonhoeffer beautifully describes the connection between faith and obedience in an imaginary conversation of a man with his pastor:

> "I have lost the faith I once had." "You must listen to the Word as it is spoken to you in the sermon." "I do; but I cannot get anything out of it; it just falls on deaf ears as far as I am concerned." "The trouble is, you don't really want to listen." "On the contrary, I do." And here they generally break off, because the pastor is at a loss what to say next. . . . The pastor feels himself confronted with the ultimate riddle of predestination. God grants faith to some and withholds it from others. So the pastor throws up the sponge and leaves the poor man to his fate. And yet this ought to be the turning-point of the interview. . . . The pastor should give up arguing with him, and stop taking his difficulties seriously. That will really be in the man's own interest, for he is only trying to hide himself behind them. It is now time to take the bull by the horns and say: "Only those who obey believe. . . . You are disobedient; you are trying to keep some part of your life under your own control. That is what is preventing you from listening to Christ and believing in his grace. You cannot hear Christ because you are wilfully disobedient. Somewhere in your heart you are refusing to listen to his call. Your difficulty is your sins. . . . Tear yourself away from all other attachments and follow him."[3]

"No one should be surprised at the difficulty of faith," Bonhoeffer writes, "if there is some part of his life where he is consciously resisting or disobeying the commandment of Jesus—some sinful passion, some animosity, some selfish hope."

> If so, you must not be surprised that you have not received the Holy Spirit, that prayer is difficult, or that your request for faith remains unanswered. Go rather and be reconciled with your brother, renounce the sin which holds you fast—and then you will recover your faith! If you dismiss the

> word of God's command, you will not receive his word of grace. How can you hope to enter into communion with him when at some point in your life you are running away from him? The man who disobeys cannot believe, for only he who obeys can believe.[4]

We have come to the point where the doctrine of justification leads to the doctrine of sanctification, the subject of our next chapter. We must begin there where we leave off now, with the connection between Christian faith and Christian life. Now it is important to see this much of the connection: If we want to receive the gift of the assurance of God's love, forgiveness, and acceptance that frees us in turn to accept God, other people, and ourselves, we must be willing to enter into the life of faith, do what faith requires.

By way of conclusion, let us go back to the question with which we began this chapter: Are you a Christian? According to the doctrine of justification, Christians are people who know that they are guilty of offending God and of hurting other people and themselves by their attempts to justify themselves. They are people who believe that nevertheless, despite everything, they are forgiven, loved, and accepted by God's grace in Jesus Christ. And as they experience freedom from the anxious or proud need to justify themselves, they also experience a new freedom for God and other people, and a new freedom to accept and be themselves. On the basis of what you have learned in this chapter, how would you begin to answer the question "Are *you* a Christian?"

POSTSCRIPT: JUSTIFICATION AND SOCIAL JUSTICE

In this chapter we have tried to interpret for our time the classical Reformation doctrine of justification. As we have seen, it has its roots in Luther's having a tormented conscience because of his inability to fulfill the demands of a righteous God, his desperate quest for a gracious God, and his discovery in Paul's letter to the Romans the good news that in Christ God loves, forgives, accepts, and promises to save guilty sinners. Ever since Luther, the church has understood the doctrine of justification to deal with God's justifying grace as it bears on the relationship between individuals and God, and consequently on their self-understanding and personal relationship with other people.

Although not rejecting this interpretation, contemporary biblical and theological scholars have criticized it for being too individualistic and self-centered.[5] They have emphasized the fact that in scripture the justifying grace of God makes things right not only in the lives of individuals but also in human society. It has to do not only with the reconciliation and salvation of individual persons but also with the reconciliation and salvation of *groups* of people and thus with social justice. This wider understanding is supported by Romans itself, where Paul's primary concern is not with the salvation of isolated individuals but with the salvation of the world as Jews and Gentiles are reconciled to God and each other (Romans 9—11).

One way to think of justification in such a way that it includes both its individual and social implications is to define it this way: *Justification means that God helps those who cannot help themselves and gives rights to those who have no rights.*

On the one hand, justification does mean good news for each one of us sinful human beings. We are trapped and helpless in our sinfulness. We can never do enough to escape the judgment of God that we deserve, and we can never earn the right to claim God's love and help. The good news of Jesus Christ is that God has come to the aid of us poor sinners who cannot help ourselves to give us "free of charge" the right to count on God's love for us.

But throughout scripture God's justifying grace also means that God helps and gives rights to people who are (1) poor, helpless, and without rights because they are ignored and excluded by the rich and powerful; (2) victims of unjust social systems; (3) denied the opportunity to care for their own and their family's health and welfare; (4) deprived of the "civil rights" and freedom others enjoy. Moreover, as God's justifying grace gives poor sinners oppressed by their own sinfulness all the "rights and privileges" of belonging to God's beloved people without having to do anything to deserve God's acceptance and help, so it also gives those who are politically poor and oppressed all the "rights and privileges" that belong to all human beings in a just and humane society without their having to prove themselves "worthy" of them.

We do not have to decide between justification that makes things right between individuals and God, and justification that makes things right in human society. Both are biblical. But the test of whether we really believe and live by the good news that God helps those who cannot help themselves and gives rights to those who have no rights is whether we reflect this good news also in the social-political sphere. If we do not see its implications there, then we have good reason to ask whether we really believe and live by it in the religious sphere either.

FOR FURTHER REFLECTION AND STUDY

1. Read Paul's doctrine of justification in Rom. 3:21–26. Compare his statement with Jesus' parable in Luke 18:10–14. Does Jesus' story help you to understand what Paul was talking about?
2. At the beginning of this chapter we spoke of various ways in which some people try to justify themselves. Do you recognize yourself in any of these examples? In what other ways do we try to justify ourselves before God, other people, and ourselves?
3. Is self-depreciation more Christian than self-exaltation?
4. Why is it impossible to earn the love of God? Why is it impossible to earn the love of other people?
5. Why do some Christians believe an overemphasis on justification by grace is dangerous? Do you agree?
6. How would you answer the objection that it is impossible for a God who is a just and righteous Judge to forgive, accept, and love sinful people?
7. Do you agree that it is wrong to speak of "saving faith"? Defend your answer.
8. If God loves us anyway, why does it matter whether we love God in return?
9. What is faith?
10. Do you agree that the main way we experience God's love, forgiveness, and acceptance is through other people? In what other ways could we experience them in our daily lives?
11. Compare Bonhoeffer's description of the relation between faith and obedience with what Paul says about it in Rom. 6:1–23. Do they say the same thing?
12. What is the relation between justification and social justice?

17

Are You a Christian?

The Doctrine of Sanctification

Albert Camus, a remarkably sensitive agnostic who fought courageously with the French Underground during World War II, was once asked to speak to a group of Christians. Taking them to task for their compromising silence or safely ambiguous theological jargon while millions of Jews were slaughtered, he spoke some words relevant to all Christians in all times:

> What the world expects of Christians is that Christians should speak out, loud and clear, and that they should voice their condemnation in such a way that never a doubt, never the slightest doubt, could rise in the heart of the simplest man. That they should get away from abstraction and confront the blood-stained face history has taken on today. The grouping we need is a grouping of men resolved to speak out clearly and to pay up personally. . . . Perhaps we cannot prevent this world from being a world in which children are tortured. But we can reduce the number of tortured children. And if you don't help us, who else in the world can help us do this? . . .
>
> It may be, I am well aware, that Christianity will answer negatively. Oh, not by your mouths, I am convinced. But it may be, and this is even more probable, that Christianity will insist on maintaining a compromise or else on giving its condemnations the obscure form of the encyclical. Possibly it will insist on losing once and for all the virtue of revolt and indignation that belonged to it long ago. In that case Christians will live and Christianity will die. In that case the others will in fact pay for the sacrifice. In any case such a future is not within my province to decide, despite all the hope and anguish it awakens in me. I can speak only of what I know. And what I know—which sometimes creates a deep longing in me—is that if Christians made up their mind to it, millions of voices—

> millions, I say—throughout the world would be added to the appeal of a handful of isolated individuals who, without any sort of affiliation, today intercede almost everywhere and ceaselessly for children and for men.[1]

What this unbeliever wants to hear is that Christians take seriously their own doctrine of sanctification.

Let us put it another way. In order to answer the question "Are you a Christian?" we spoke in the last chapter of the doctrine of justification, which describes how a people become Christian. Giving up all attempts at self-justification they come to trust in God's forgiving acceptance of them despite the fact that they are not good and deserving in themselves.

Yet that is only a part of the answer. If I am asked whether I am a Christian, it is not enough for me to answer, "Yes, I am a sinner who believes that nevertheless I am accepted, loved, and forgiven by God through Jesus Christ." Christians are not just people who passively trust God to accept them as they are, solve their problems, meet their personal and family needs, comfort, and save them. They are people who respond to God's love, forgiveness, and acceptance with thankful obedience in every area of their lives. To be a Christian is not only to believe and receive but to live and serve as a Christian. In other words, we cannot answer outsiders' criticisms of Christians and the church, or answer the question whether we ourselves are Christians, until we move from the doctrine of justification to talk about the doctrine of sanctification.

Justification tells us how a person becomes a Christian. Sanctification tells us how a person grows in the Christian life.

Justification tells us about God's gracious action toward us. Sanctification tells us about our response with obedient action toward God.

Justification tells us that God is *for* us, forgiving and saving us from sin. Sanctification tells us that by the Holy Spirit the same God works *in* us, helping us to leave our sin behind and begin a new and radically different kind of life.

In justification the covenant-making God makes a promise: "I will be your God." In sanctification, the same God also gives an inescapable command: "You shall be my people."

Justification tells us that Christ is our Savior who died for us. Sanctification tells us that the same Christ is our Lord who commands us to live for him.

Justification tells us that God adopts us to be God's children. Sanctification tells us that God expects and helps us to *live* as God's children—and therefore as brothers and sisters of one another.

Justification tells us that we are made free *from* the self-justification that breaks relationship with God and our fellow human beings, and therefore ruins our own lives. Sanctification tells us what it means to live as free people—free *for* God, *for* others, and therefore free *for* our own true self-fulfillment.

Justification and sanctification are related as gift and task, creed and deed, theology and ethics, faith and life, passively receiving and actively giving in return. No one is a Christian until he or she is both justified *and* sanctified.

That is what we have to try to understand in this chapter. It is all the more important that we learn what sanctification means because we live in a time in which outsiders are highly critical of the church, not so much because its faith is out of date as because it does not practice the faith it confesses. And it is all the more important because so many of us insiders like to hear about God's love and forgiveness but are angered by or simply cannot imagine the kind of costly Christianity Camus yearned to see.

We will think first about the relation between justification and sanctification as we have defined them. Then we will think in more detail about what sanctification as such means.

CHRISTIAN FAITH AND CHRISTIAN ACTION

The Reformed confessions deal with the problem of the relation between justification and sanctification in terms of the relation between faith and good works, or faith and the fruits of faith. We mean the same thing when we speak of Christian faith and Christian action. The point we have to make in several different ways is the point the Reformers made: Justification-faith and sanctification-action must be distinguished from each other, but they can never be separated. They are two different aspects of the one gracious work of the same God.

There can be no Christian faith without Christian action. It is easy enough for all of us to agree in theory with this general statement. We know that faith without works is dead (James 2:14–26). But in practice, we mainline Protestants have so strongly emphasized salvation by grace alone that we are often suspicious of any talk about good works. Some versions of Christian orthodoxy have so exclusively emphasized right Christian belief and pure doctrine that they simply ignore the Christian life; all that matters is to believe the right things. Some forms of pietistic Christianity have been so exclusively concerned with the salvation of souls that in practice if not in theory they have acted as if all that matters is leading people to make a confession of faith and join the church. Once they are saved, they can be forgotten. Their growth in the Christian life can be ignored, while we go out to win more converts.

This split between Christian faith and Christian life, justification and sanctification, lies behind many of the arguments in the church today.

There is an ongoing debate in the church whether evangelism should emphasize Christ as the Savior who saves us from our sins *or* Christ as the Lord who calls us to serve him in every sphere of everyday life. Is the mission of the church to save souls *or* to engage in Christian social action that tries to bring the good news of God's love and justice to bear on life in the world?

Many people really cannot understand why preachers do not "stick to the Bible" and talk about "spiritual things" rather than "meddling" by talking concretely about what it means to live as a Christian in face of the sexual, racial, social, and political crises of our time.

The result of thinking that we can be saved or justified without obediently living as those who have been forgiven and saved is what Bonhoeffer calls "cheap grace."[2] Cheap grace is grace without obedience. It means that we are not freed from our sins, but that we can settle down comfortably with them, assured that God will forgive, whatever we do—so long as we believe in the doctrine of justification. It says that because grace alone does everything, everything in our lives can remain as it was before. It reasons that because we depend on God's grace and not our works for salvation anyway, we can model our lives on the world's standards. It means that the Christian life is reduced to middle-class respectability that makes no costly demands and is safe and painless. "The upshot of it all is that my only duty as a Christian is to leave the world for an hour or so on a Sunday morning and go to church to be assured that my sins are forgiven."[3]

The Christian answer to this split between justification and sanctification and the cheap grace that follows from it is that there is no such thing as Christian faith without Christian action. To be justified or saved is to commit our whole lives to the God who justifies and saves us.

To know God is to know the God who not only graciously forgives, accepts, and loves us as we are but has a claim on our lives. How is this relation between God's grace and God's command expressed in Deut. 6:20–25? In Ex. 20:1–18?

To be elected or chosen by God is not to be given special privilege as God's elite or only to be guaranteed salvation when we die. It is to be chosen in order to serve God here and now. How is this said in Eph. 1:4 and Col. 1:21–22?

We cannot know Christ as Savior *for* us without acknowledging him also as Lord *over* us. To have faith in him means inevitably also to follow him. How is this said in Matt. 7:21?

To receive the Holy Spirit is not just to get an emotional charge or to experience God's nearness and love. It is to be renewed *to go to work,* living a different kind of life. How is this life described in Gal. 5:22–25?

To belong to the church is not just to belong to a community of believers who come together only to "get something out of" a church service, to be "fed" and "blessed." It is to belong to a community of people who come together to be renewed so that they can go back into the world to serve God as they serve their fellow human beings. How does 1 Peter 2:9 say this?

Just when we take the Bible seriously, we discover that it hardly ever speaks of faith without corresponding obedience, of theology without corresponding ethics. What relation between justification and sanctification is implied, for instance, in the great christological passage, Phil. 2:1–13?

> Can we believe that we are justified without doing good works? That is impossible. For to believe in Jesus Christ is to receive him as he is given to us. He promises not only to deliver us from death and to restore us to favor with his Father, through the merit of his innocence, but also to regenerate us by his Spirit, that we may be enabled to live in holiness. (Calvin's Geneva Catechism, Q. 126)

That is the first thing we have to emphasize. There is no such thing as Christian faith without Christian life. Christian faith does not free us *from* but *for* Christian action. God does not forgive, accept, and love us *on condition that* we become righteous, but God does forgive, accept, and love us *in order that* we may become righteous.

God's action makes possible our action. When we considered justification, we said that by ourselves we cannot achieve a right relationship with God and other people, or a meaningful life for ourselves. We are totally dependent upon God's forgiveness, acceptance, and love. Do we not contradict ourselves now when we being to talk about Christian action and quote Camus' call for Christians to get to work to make the world a better place to live in? Does not the doctrine of sanctification shift the emphasis from trusting in God's grace to trusting in our good works?

This would be a legitimate objection if a popular view were correct in saying that justification means that God does God's part to forgive and help us, and sanctification means that we take it up from there, working on our own to do our part. But this is not the Christian view. Sanctification is just as much the work of God's grace as justification. Effective Christian action in our individual relationships and in the life of the world is possible not because we are optimistic about "human potential" in general or even what Christians can accomplish but because we are optimistic about the renewing power of God in our lives. We can confidently give ourselves to obedient Christian action, and we can hope for progress in our own lives and in the world not because we have faith in ourselves and our own goodness but because we have faith that God does not stop with forgiving our sins, loving, and accepting us. God promises also to be at work in us, accompanying us every step of the way, enabling us to do what we could never do alone, helping us to achieve results we could never hope for if we were left to ourselves. How does Paul emphasize this in Phil. 2:13?

It is not individual and social Christian action but the apparently pious pessimism that refuses to engage in Christian action that is faithless. Christian faith in God's grace alone is not an excuse for us to do nothing, hopelessly sitting around waiting for God to do something. It is the courage to risk challenging all the difficulties, dangers, and obstacles of our own and the world's sinfulness just because we believe in a God who is with us not only at the beginning but throughout our Christian lives. Sanctification, in other words, means that an emphasis on human action does not exclude faith in God's action. On the contrary, it is faith in God's action that gives us the ability, courage, and hope to act. *We* cannot make the world a better place to live in, but *God* can—working in and through us.

This means, by the way, that obedient Christian life is not a terrible burden and necessity we unfortunately have to accept if we are really Christians. For Christians, God's law is not the threat that we had better obey or else suffer the consequences. Sanctification means that God promises to give us the ability to do what God commands us to do. God says to us not only "You *must* do what I command" but "By my grace you *can* do whatever is necessary to obey my command." The Christian life is not easy. It is difficult and costly. But it is not a life of grim, teeth-gritting determination. Christians can take on the serious responsibilities of the

Christian life with a kind of light-hearted, cheerful confidence precisely because they know that God gives what God demands. How is this attitude toward Christian obedience to the requirements of God expressed in Matt. 11:28–30 and 2 Cor. 4:7–12?

In summary: Sanctification means (1) that faith in God's action does not exclude but includes Christian action in the world, and (2) that the Christian life is not only a great task but a great privilege. How are both these points underlined in John 14:12–24?

Being a Christian is growing up. Justification has to do with becoming a Christian, sanctification with living out the Christian life. In justification we receive God's grace by faith. In sanctification by God's grace we become active servants of God and neighbor.

Does this mean that when we are sanctified, we leave justification behind us, switching from one kind of grace to another? There is a kind of Christian perfectionism that interprets the relation between justification and sanctification in this way: Once we are converted and receive the Holy Spirit, we no longer have to live from God's forgiveness. We can live from our own righteousness (which of course is acknowledged to be God-given). We no longer have seriously to confess our sin and ask for forgiveness. This way of relating justification and sanctification in a temporal sequence (first one, then the other) is unbiblical. "If we say that we have no sin, we deceive ourselves, and the truth is not in us" (1 John 1:8). Jesus taught us to pray over and over again, "Forgive us our debts." We *never* leave behind us our need to receive God's forgiveness for what we do to God, other people, and ourselves by our lack of love and refusal to let ourselves be loved. Sanctification—the Christian life, Christian action—does not mean that we who once were sinners can now congratulate ourselves and thank God that we are no longer sinners. Such a "sanctified" life would be the very essence of sinfulness!

How then can we understand the Christian life? We have said on the one hand that we cannot remain passive, helpless babies in the Christian faith. New birth to Christian faith in God's grace leads to strong, confident, responsible Christian action by God's grace. But now we seem to say that we never get past the beginning of the Christian life. No matter how long we live, every day we have to confess all over again what we confessed the very first day we knew what it is all about: "God be merciful to me, a sinner."

There is a biblical image that helps us clarify this seemingly complicated situation. It summarizes not only everything we have been trying to say about the relation between justification and sanctification but also everything we have tried to say about what it means to be a Christian.

The image is that of the growth of a child (Eph. 4:13–16). To be a Christian is to be "growing up." It means to be moving toward "maturity"—the complete or whole humanity that is the "full stature of Christ." Seen from this point of view, the question we have to ask ourselves (and be willing for people like Camus to ask us!) is not: "How close to perfect are you? What degree of righteousness have you achieved?" The question is: "Are you *growing*? Have you settled down comfortably with the growth you have behind you, or are you willing to keep up the painful, constant struggle to keep on growing? Is your Christian life an attempt simply to hold on to what you think you have already achieved in your relation to God and other people? Or are you willing to risk what you have already learned and accomplished to explore new and more complete ways of loving God and other people? Do you spend your life defending and protecting yourself as you are, or are you willing to subject yourself to the dangers of admitting that you are still immature in your beliefs and way of life and need to plow into new ways of thinking and living?"

To be a Christian is not to have arrived at some state or condition of Christian existence. It is to be constantly having growing pains. It is not to *be* something but to be *becoming* something. It is not to have arrived but to be constantly on the way (Phil. 3:12–16).

Thus, we never leave our need for the justifying grace of God. Even when we do keep growing, we never reach the point at which we no longer need God's forgiveness, love, and acceptance of us despite our "immaturity." In fact, the more progress we make toward the whole or complete humanity of Christ (sanctification), the more sensitive we become to our own inhumanity and need for forgiveness and renewal (justification). A Christian is one who every day, all through his or her life, lives both from God's sanctifying *and* justifying grace.

What is this "maturity," this "full stature of Christ" or complete and whole humanity Christians are moving toward? What does genuinely Christian life and Christian action look like? That is what we have to consider next.

IN BUT NOT OF THE WORLD

There are many ways we might try to describe the Christian life. In the context of the doctrine of sanctification, the obvious way is to describe it as a *holy* life. The verb "to sanctify" means "to make holy." Growth in sanctification is growth in holiness. Christians are by definition holy people. That means that they are "saints," for that is the translation of the New Testament word for "holy ones."

Most of us probably react negatively at first when we hear that Christians are supposed to be saints who lead holy lives. Our minds jump from "saint" to "superhuman," from "holy" to "holier-than-thou," from "sanctified" to "sanctimonious." We think of very pious people who live by a long list of thou-shalt-nots and are rewarded for their sacrifice of a normal life in the world by the assurance that they are superior to everyone else.

If we are to understand the true meaning of holiness, we have to get rid of this negative, self-righteous, world-denying view. But at the same time we must not fall into the opposite view that the Christian life means only a kind of mild moral respectability that fits comfortably into the world and its standards. We can avoid both extremes if we remember what holiness means in the Bible.

The root meaning of the word *holy* is "separate" or "different." The Old Testament people of God are called a holy people and the New Testament church is called a communion of "saints" because they are set apart from other people by virtue of their belonging to God. God's people are not "conformed" to the world but are "transformed" by the renewal of their minds in order to serve God by living in a way quite different from the way every "normal" person lives (Rom. 12:1–21). Jesus said, "My kingdom is not from this world" (John 18:36). Christians have their "citizenship" not on earth but in heaven (Phil. 3:20). We could cite many other passages that make it clear that Christians are not of this world. They are *holy* people, people whose lives are different from the lives of other people. They are "resident aliens" in the world.[4]

However, a Christian life is not one that flees the problems and responsibilities of life in the world. Christians are not different or separate in that they retire from the world into a spiritual realm of tranquil isolation and safety. The communion of the saints is not a purely religious community divorced from and uninterested in secular affairs. "I am not asking you to take them out of the world," Jesus prayed. "As you have sent me into the world, so I have sent them into the world" (John 17:15, 18). If Christians are resident *aliens,* they are also *resident* aliens! To be holy, in other words, means to live *in* the world but not *of* the world.

We can see why this is so and what it means by discussing first of all the holiness of God and then Christian holiness that reflects it.[5]

The Holiness of God

In the Old Testament the God of Israel is "different" from all the other gods in that this God is completely free of any dependence on the world and the claims of people in it, a "most high" God of absolute power, majesty, and righteousness who does not owe anyone anything and cannot be bribed. Yet this absolute superiority to all other gods and absolute freedom from human manipulation does not mean that Israel's God is too proud or too good to have anything to do with lowly, sinful human beings. The Holy One of Israel is a God who enters into covenant with an insignificant, all-too-human and all-too-sinful people, remains faithful to them, and promises to work through them for the good of the whole world. Yahweh is holy not *despite* but *because of* Yahweh's just and compassionate involvement in the very worldly history of a very worldly people.

In the New Testament, Jesus is called the "Holy One of God" (Mark 1:24; John 6:69). Throughout his life he demonstrated as no one before or since him the perfect holiness demanded by a holy God. But it was just in fulfillment of this holiness that Jesus accomplished his work not only in the synagogue and his private devotional life but in his encounters with people in the marketplace, on public roads, in a courtroom, and at the place where garbage and criminals were disposed of. He was holy not *despite* but *because of* the fact that he entered into the world, lived a fully human life in it, and was the friend of very unholy people.

We learn from the holiness of God and Jesus that holiness does not mean being unrelated to the world but being related to it in a particular way—specifically, to be both against it and for it at the same time.

Holiness That Is against the World

The kingdom of the holy God is not only different from the kingdoms of this world; it *invades, confronts, opposes,* and *contradicts* them. Christians are different in that they refuse to conform to the world; their loyalty to God takes precedence over all other loyalties. Holiness means a protest against the ways and claims of the world. In the words of Camus, whom we quoted at the beginning of this chapter, to be a Christian in such a world as ours means inevitably "condemnation," "revolt," "indignation."

Yet how can an effective holy protest *against* the world be made except *in* the world? A Christianity that refuses to have anything to do with political and economic questions, or does nothing to question the generally accepted way of life around it, can make no holy protest. By its inactivity and silence it gives an unholy *consent* to the worldly status quo. Its very otherworldliness lends support to the sinful world by letting it go unchallenged. A holy protest can be made only by those who "loud and clear," in word and action, call into question the ideals, institutions, and way of life that have unquestioned validity for other people.

We can make the same point in another way. The New Testament makes it unmistakably clear that a holy life in following the Holy One involves self-denial, cross bearing, and sacrifice (Mark 8:34–36; Rom. 12:1). Jesus often warned that those who followed him would be so at odds with the world that they would be hated and persecuted (John 15:18–21; Mark 13:9–13).

This kind of costly holiness is only possible when Christians are different from the world *in* the world—when they openly do what others do not do, and do not do what others do; when they publicly refuse to conform automatically to the political systems and ideologies, business practices, and even the standards of family responsibility and moral integrity others around them take for granted. A Christianity that withdraws into a purely religious church or restricts itself to purely private spirituality will obviously stir up no trouble and therefore demand no cross bearing, cost no sacrifices. The world may shrug off such a harmless, inoffensive Christianity. It may laugh at its pious pretentiousness. But the world will not be threatened enough by such an otherworldly Christianity even to take it seriously, much less to hate or persecute Christians.

This is not to say that Christians are to go out looking for trouble, seeking to be martyrs. It is to say that as with Christ, *the* Holy One, so also with his followers—to be holy means to risk being different *within* the structures of the world and to be prepared to "pay up personally" when that holy protest has painful repercussions. What is the alternative to such holy worldliness? Camus put it bluntly: "Christians will live and Christianity will die."

Holiness That Is for the World

The holiness of God, of Christ, and therefore of Christians means protest against the sinful world. But they are *against* the world only in order to be *for* it. When the Holy God of Israel judges the sinful people, it is to help, reconcile, and restore them to their true calling as the people of God. Jesus stirred up so much trouble in the world of his time that they killed him; but he did it not "to condemn the world, but in order that the world might be saved through him" (John 3:17). The agnostic Camus's purpose, when he asked Christians to voice their condemnation, indignation, and revolt against the "blood-stained" world we live in, was to plead with Christians to join those who "intercede almost everywhere and ceaselessly for children and for men."

Other gods and other people may seek their own honor, glory, purity, and superiority above everything else. They may condemn or use people to defend and advance their own spiritual or material interests. But the holy God and God's people are "different." They are holy just because they are willing to risk their own honor, power, and self-interest for the sake of other people. To be holy means to be not only for oneself but for others. It means to look not only to our own interest but to the interests of others (Phil. 2:4). It means not to serve oneself, but to serve God and to serve other people. This is how Christians are different, separate, not of the world.

That means, once again, that the truly holy life can only be lived *in* the world. How can we possibly be genuinely and effectively with and for other people if we withdraw into a self-serving church or a self-serving, private religion? How can we possibly be holy as God is holy so long as we think that to be holy means to be a spiritual elite who preserve their holiness by refusing to have anything to do with people, institutions, and places that are not holy? To be holy in the biblical sense is to abandon a self-protecting, world-denying concern for our own safety and purity—even for our own salvation (Mark 8:35)! It is to risk denying and sacrificing ourselves to "intercede for children and for men" wherever and however they are hurt or destroyed in the world.

THE HOLINESS JESUS COMMANDS

So far we have spoken of the holy life in but not of the world in a very general way. Now we will become embarrassingly and controversially concrete. We will look at some examples of the kind of life Jesus required of those who would follow him. The sayings we will look at are radical and difficult to interpret. Here are some guidelines to help you: (1) Remember that Jesus spoke always to particular people in particular situations. It would be wrong automatically to conclude that everyone, always, is required to do exactly the same thing he required of them, in exactly the same way. (2) On the other hand, it would also be wrong to spiritualize all the hard sayings of Jesus. We cannot escape the holy life he demanded by saying that he did not mean it literally, that we have only to take his commandments in a "spiritual" sense. Jesus spoke specifically and concretely about how his disciples should live in the world. Although we cannot make a legalistic set of general rules out of his commands, we must try to learn what it means faithfully and obediently to echo his attitude toward these worldly realities in our everyday lives. (3) Because he spoke as the "Holy One," we may expect Jesus to criticize the attitudes and practices the world takes for granted. He demands a costly nonconformity. On the other hand, because he spoke as the Holy One who gave himself for the world, we may expect that his hard commandments will also bring freedom—freedom *from* enslaving loyalties to the world, freedom *for* God and *our* fellow human beings.

Holiness and Money

Read Matt. 5:40–42; 6:24–33; Mark 10:17–22. Jesus said again and again that those who would follow him must give up their attachment to material possessions. The lives of other people (and of some churches?) may be determined exclusively by what is good business, by practical financial considerations, by sound fiscal policies, and by what will pay off with a good financial return. But the followers of Jesus are to be holy—different from other people in the world. They have to be willing to give up what belongs to them. Why? Not because wealth is bad and poverty is good, but because individuals (and churches!) cannot place their faith and hope in God and in financial security at the same time; because trust in God frees people from the anxious, self-seeking, self-destructive trust in possessions. Surely it is no accident that Jesus mentioned poor people as the beneficiaries of such a loose attitude toward money. To be holy means to risk one's own material comfort and security for their sakes.[6]

Impractical? Meddling in nonreligious business affairs and economic problems? Of course! Jesus was talking about what it means to be holy *in* the world.

Holiness and the Use of Force

Read Matt. 5:38–39, 43–48; 10:28; 26:47–54; Luke 9:51–56. Some people may believe that self-defense is automatically the right response when they are attacked or taken advantage of. They may assume that violence is self-evidently justified and even mandated against enemies who threaten their own or their people's self-interest and way of life. But not the followers of Jesus. They do not live by the standards and "self-evident" assumptions of the world. They are neither to fear force when it is used against them, nor exercise it against others, nor even passively allow someone else to do the dirty work for them. They are to be like the Holy One who did not defend himself or attack even when he could have had twelve legions of angels to fight for him and his cause.

Why this "pacifism" of Jesus and his followers? Its purpose is not the preservation of their own moral purity and superiority. They are pacifists because they do not hate, maim, and slaughter but *love* their enemies; because the kingdom of God's justice and compassion comes not through violence but through self-giving sacrificial love.

Unrealistic? Dangerous? Subversive? Of course! We are talking about *holiness*—not conforming to the generally accepted ways of the world but being transformed. We are talking about being in but not of the world.

The point is not to argue for pacifism in principle or to say that there are no conditions under which the use of force may be legitimate and necessary—to defend the victims of injustice or for the sake of order, justice, and peace in society, for instance. But it is to ask seriously whether at the very least Christians should not give sympathetic support to those who follow quite literally the commands of Jesus himself, and whether, even if they cannot be pacifists themselves, nonviolence (including nonviolent resistance) ought not seem the normal rather than the exceptional way of handling personal and social conflict.

Holiness and Family Responsibilities

Read Matt. 10:34–39; Luke 9:57–62; 14:25–26. For some people nothing may be more important than husband or wife, children or parents, brother or sister. Other people may believe everything else should be sacrificed for the good of their own family. Me and my family, my family and me—nothing can take precedence over our happiness, comfort, security, and responsibility to and for one another.

However, the disciples of Jesus are called to be holy. They do not live by the standards of the world—not even by its highest standards. They are commanded to renounce any absolute attachment to family. They may have to break with family, sacrifice the best interests of family, disturb peace and harmony within the family. They may actually be called to hate not father and mother, spouse and children as such, but the idolatrous worship of family and the enslaving hold family members can have on one another.

Why this family-threatening holiness of Jesus and his followers? It is not because the Christian faith is against sex, marriage, and family life as such, but because God and God's kingdom call into question all other attachments and loyalties. Holiness is a protest made for the sake of right worldly relationships. An exclusive, self-centered withdrawal into a clannish concern only for me and mine means that the needs and rights of other people (whom God loves as much as God loves us) are ignored and trampled. When family is made absolute, the warmth of family attachments becomes smothering; the closeness of family relationships a prison! Children are so tied to parents that they are prevented from growing up into mature, independent human beings. Husbands and wives lose their identity and become simply the echo or tool of the other. The lives of parents become empty and meaningless when the children are gone.

The family-threatening holiness Jesus demands does not destroy the family; it cuts the apron strings and breaks the tyranny that family members exercise over one another when the family is the be-all and end-all.

In any case, the holiness Jesus commands with his harsh sayings about the family is far more than that of religious activities. It has to do with such things as sex, the family budget, the letting-be and letting-go of family members, and proper care for the aged. It is holiness *in* the world.

Holiness and Piety

Read Matt. 5:21–48; 6:1–16; Mark 2:15–3:6. Some people may think they are good when they obey the law (not killing, committing adultery, stealing, swearing, and so on); when they pray, go to church, and give a little money to help others; and when they preserve their own moral and religious integrity by avoiding the company of those whose morality, patriotism, and religious sincerity are questionable. But Jesus and his followers are different. They are not merely moral, religious, and pure; they are holy.

On the one hand, their righteousness is more than that of others. Strict legal faithfulness to one's spouse does not make one an "innocent party" in the marriage and the marriage itself a sound one. Inner fidelity is what really matters; one can be legally innocent and yet just as guilty of adultery as someone who sleeps around. Not killing is not enough;

hating another person is just as bad. Loving only those who are like oneself in tastes, way of life, political and theological views, and race is not enough; holy people love their enemies.

On the other hand, the nonconforming holiness of Jesus and his followers can break moral and religious conventions that seem absolute to others. Those who follow Jesus may seem irreligious because they refuse to advertise their piety. They do their praying in private rather than at football games. They do their giving in secret rather than publicizing their tithing. They risk seeming immoral and politically subversive because they have the wrong friends and do not let their friendship with undeserving sinners be stopped by the warning that "birds of a feather flock together."

Why Jesus' harsh criticism of law-abiding, God-fearing people? Why this suspicious nonconformity to the moral and religious conventions of the "best" people? It is not because Jesus and his followers are against morality and religion as such (Matt. 5:17). Rather, not being of the world, they are more concerned about the verdict of God who sees into the heart than about the approval or condemnation of other people. Christian holiness is *against* the world only in order to be *for* it. Christians criticize and refuse to conform to conventional morality and religion for the sake of true morality and religion. They are holy—different—just because they have learned from Jesus that the needs of human beings take precedence over conventional moral and religious rules. People are more important to Jesus and his followers than legal purity and reputation. People do not live for the sake of laws; laws are there to be obeyed—and sometimes broken!—for the sake of people (Mark 2:27).

Such holiness is dangerous and costly, of course. One can get a bad reputation with it. One may be rejected by some solid citizens and by some pious church members. One may even get into trouble with the law (like Jesus and Paul). But that is just what it means to be holy—to run the risk of being in the world without being of the world, to be transformed instead of conformed to the world.

A serious investigation of the radical requirements Jesus made of those who follow him results in a sequence of thoughts that lead us to look first backward, then forward, in the course of our study.

The first result is painful self-examination. "If *that* is what it means to be a Christian, do I really want to be one? Am I willing to pay the cost of discipleship? Do I really want to be holy, if holiness means not just a little moral respectability, a little religious piety, a little orthodox theology, but such a dangerously different, nonconforming life? Many people who were with Jesus at first turned away when they heard him spell out what was involved in following him. Could it be that the same thing would happen today if we took seriously the call of Christian discipleship to 'speak out clearly and pay up personally'? Not everyone wants to be a Christian. Perhaps not even everyone whose name is on the church roll. Do I?"

The second result of listening to Jesus' description of the life his followers must live is thankful remembrance that sanctification never leaves justification behind. Even when we seriously want to, who of us ever obeys the radical call of Jesus so completely that we do not have to pray at the end of every day, "Forgive us our debts"? What good news to know that we do not *have* to depend on our own holiness, but that at the end of every day we can remember again that God forgives, accepts, and loves us despite our failures! That does not excuse us from the life of discipleship. It does give us the courage and confidence to keep starting out all over again every new day—to keep growing.

Third, the requirements of Jesus remind us that holiness is a gift. Who of us ever has the wisdom to make faithful yet responsible decisions on the Christian use of money? In knowing what to say and do about the use of force? In being a good husband or wife, parent or child? In knowing when to obey and when to disregard the usual rules or moral and religious behavior? Even when we do know what we should do, who of us has the courage and ability to do it? The good news of Christ is that we are not left to ourselves to make decisions and act alone. We have the promise of the guidance and help of God's Spirit to help us when we cannot help ourselves.

Yet to speak of the gift of holiness only raises again the same problem we have wrestled with in talking about other gifts of the Holy Spirit: How can we have this gift? In the present context one particular answer stands out. It is significant that in the New Testament no individual person—except Jesus himself—is ever called holy or a holy one (saint). Paul, for instance, addresses his letters to the "saints" in this or that Christian community, but he never calls any one of them (or himself!) a saint. Holy people or saints are found only in the plural, as a part of a community of people who are called and held together by the only Holy One. In other words, no one can be holy by himself or herself. The Spirit's gift of holiness is given and received in the body of Christ, the church.

What that means and whether we can believe it (does your church look like a communion of saints?) is what we have to consider in the next chapter.

FOR FURTHER REFLECTION AND STUDY

1. What is the relation between God's action and the Christian's action in Phil. 2:1–13?
2. Should evangelism emphasize Christ as Savior or Christ as Lord?
3. Some Christians argue that Christians should have nothing to do with organizations such as the Peace Corps or the United Nations, because our hope is in salvation through Christ, not in human efforts toward world improvement. What do you think?
4. Why do you think the Heidelberg Catechism places the title "Thankfulness" over its exposition of the Ten Commandments?
5. Is it correct to think of sanctification in terms of growing toward maturity? Would an outsider like Camus be satisfied with such thinking?
6. Describe in your own words what it means to be in but not of the world. How are Christians both *against* and *for* the world at the same time?
7. Do you think that we ought to take Jesus' commandments in the Sermon on the Mount literally?
8. On holiness and money:
   a. Defend or criticize the old saying that money is the root of all evil.
   b. Evaluate this bumper sticker from a Christian point of view: "I fight poverty—I work."
   c. Should Christians support tax increases that do not directly benefit them and their families? What about tax increases that would lower their own standard of living?
9. On holiness and the use of force:
   a. Evaluate this controversial statement from the Confession of 1967 (9.45): The search for cooperation and peace "requires that nations pursue fresh and responsible relations across every line of conflict, even at risk to national security, to reduce areas of strife and to broaden international understanding. . . . [T]he church which identifies the sovereignty of any one nation or any one way of life with the cause of God denies the Lordship of Christ and betrays its calling."
   b. Under what circumstances, if any, should Christians and the

church support violent revolution as a means of overcoming political injustice and oppression?

c. When we think of violence, we usually think of overt physical violence. In what other ways can people exercise violence against others? In what other ways can a society do violence to some of its members?

10. On holiness and family responsibilities:
    a. What factors should be considered in the decision to keep an aged parent in one's own home or to place him or her in an institutional "home" for the elderly?
    b. What should Christians think of such expressions of family love as the following: "She worships the ground he walks on." "He adores her." "They live only for their children."
11. On holiness and piety:
    a. In light of Matthew 6:5ff., what do you think of prayers over the loudspeaker before a football game? What about a prayer of invocation or thanks before a public gathering in our "pluralistic" society?
    b. Should the church receive into its fellowship alcoholics and drug addicts? Men and women known to be sexually promiscuous? Homosexuals? People with questionable occupations?
    c. Is civil disobedience ever allowed or required of people who take the Christian faith seriously?

18

Living or Dead?

The Doctrine of the Church

The following are common complaints about the church in our time. Check those that express your opinion.

It's too worldly. It silently accepts or openly supports (even in the lives of clergy) the steady erosion of biblical standards or personal responsibility and moral integrity, especially in the area of sexual and family relationships.

It's too worldly. It only echoes the same sexual, racial, and class discrimination that is destroying society outside the church.

The preacher's sermons proclaim vague, unrealistic generalities that give me no help in making concrete ethical decisions in my everyday personal, business, and social life.

Preachers meddle too much in practical questions that are none of their business. They ought to stick to talking about religious values and the salvation of souls.

All the church does is serve itself. All it cares about is its own power and influence in society and the satisfaction of the needs of its own members. It ignores the terrible suffering and social problems in the world around it and spends all its time bickering about such trivial issues as what color to paint the sanctuary or whether to get new choir robes.

The church is getting to be too much of a social welfare organization. It has forgotten that its true task is to preach the gospel and evangelize the unchurched; it spends all its time talking about "social justice" and supporting the latest liberal programs for improving the world.

It's so eager to be "inclusive" that it compromises the theological and ethical integrity of the Christian faith. As long as you make a pledge of financial support, it doesn't matter what you believe or how you live.

It's too exclusive and intolerant. You are not welcome if you are not the right color, don't wear the right clothes, don't have the right sexual orientation, don't support the right political ideology, don't accept without question "what our church has always taught and believed."

The church is too liberal or too conservative, too chummy or too cold, too intellectual or too superficial. Its worship is too traditional or too Hollywoodish. There is too much or too little hellfire-and-damnation preaching, too much or too little concern about our pluralistic society.

We could extend the list indefinitely. The point is that everyone is unhappy about the church for one reason or another. Some of the gripes are petty. Some of them simply reflect the general confusion and unrest in our rapidly changing world. Some of them are serious calls for a new reformation of the church according to the Word of God. But they all confirm the fact that the church is in bad trouble today. (It does not help much to point out that it has *always* been in bad trouble for one reason or another!) Evidence of the current troubles of the church has been collected in many books and articles analyzing from a sociological, psychological, or theological point of view what is wrong with the church and why the mainline churches are losing thousands of members every year.

Survey after survey shows that although religion is still popular in our country, the Christian church and its message do not significantly influence the lives of church members. Their attitudes about sex, marriage, and divorce; their ideas about race, poverty, war, and other social issues; their attitudes about work and money; their dread of old age, attitude toward death, and the way they conduct their funerals—in all areas of life church members are generally indistinguishable from other people. They consider religion to be a good thing only so long as it gives them personal comfort, meets their felt needs, and confirms what they already think about themselves, other people, and the world around them.

Thousands of "baby boomers" born since World War II and their children are simply not interested in the church anymore—not even interested enough to attack it and debate its beliefs. They simply ignore it as harmless and irrelevant, and live their lives as if it did not exist. Some people are leaving churches they consider too liberal to join more conservative "evangelical" churches, but most of those who leave are simply dropping out altogether.

The church *is* in trouble. On the inside it is torn by confusion and strife, or endured with a listless going through the motions of business as usual. On the outside it is increasingly ignored or laughed at for its irrelevant piety.

This is the situation in which we have to talk about what it means to say, "I believe in the Holy Spirit, the holy catholic church, the communion of saints." We cannot let the present situation determine what we believe about the church. We have to learn that from the biblical source of our faith. But neither can we ignore the present situation and act as if all we have to do is hold firmly to past ways of thinking and doing things. To be a Reformed Christian is by definition to be constantly reforming in obedience to the living God in every new time and situation.

In this chapter, then, we will look at the classical Protestant doctrine of the church and ask what it could mean for a renewal of the church in our time. We will not solve all the problems and answer all the questions we have raised. No one knows exactly how the church should go about fulfilling its task in our time. But perhaps we can at least identify the real problems and legitimate criticisms. Perhaps we can discover which possibilities are closed and which are open for further exploration if we are to learn what it means to be a faithful and relevant church in an increasingly pluralistic age.

This will be our procedure: First we will try to understand what it means to say that the church is the people of God and the body of Christ. Then we will discuss the nature and task of the church in terms of the classical description of it in the Nicene Creed as the one holy catholic and apostolic church. In following this procedure, we will not try to summarize everything that could be said about the doctrine of the church. We will concentrate on those points at which there seems to be widespread misunderstanding and confusion today.

THE PEOPLE OF GOD

The Greek word used in the New Testament for church means "called out." The church is a community of people who (along with the community of Israel!) are called out of the world to be God's people. The purpose of their coming together is twofold. First, it is to receive God's judging, forgiving, renewing grace. Second, it is to be sent out again to be agents of God's judgment, forgiveness, reconciliation, and renewal in the world. We will speak later of the gift and task involved in church membership. Now we are concerned only to say what it means that the church is a community of people called together by God.

You are the church. The church is not a board or agency with "headquarters" in this or that American city (not to mention Geneva or Rome). It is not just the ordained preachers and leaders of the church. When we talk about the church, we are not talking about "them" but about "us." *We* are the church. Whenever a group of Christians are gathered in the name of Christ, there the church is. In the New Testament it is first of all and primarily a local congregation—the church in Jerusalem or Antioch or Rome. It is not limited to individual local congregations, of course. Paul could also speak of the church in a wide geographical area. Nor do the individual congregations exist independently and self-sufficiently. They exist in mutual cooperation and support, united as members of the one body of the one Lord. Nevertheless, the church always exists concretely whenever a group of Christians are together. Thus, when we say "Why doesn't the church do so and so?" or "The trouble with the church is," we are asking why *we* don't do so and so and are complaining about *our own* faults.

The church is a community of people, not a building. It is hard for us to grasp this, because we are so used to thinking of the church as centered in a building that stands in the neighborhood where its members live (or perhaps across town in another neighborhood where we can come together with our own kind of people.). But is has not always been so. For the first three centuries the church had no buildings. Christians met together in homes (1 Cor. 16:19; Col. 4:15) or in places where their secular occupations brought them together (Phil. 4:22, "the emperor's household"). Later, when buildings were built they were not built in local neighborhoods but at the crossroads of life—in market towns or places of central government. It was not until the Middle Ages that the kind of parish church we know came into being.

It is important in our time to understand that the church does not depend on a church building. This raises some serious questions about our present church structures and suggests some interesting possibilities for the future. Have we given so much time, money, and effort to erecting, furnishing, and maintaining buildings that we have lost sight of the real nature and purpose of the church—not to serve ourselves but to serve God and our fellow human beings in the world? In removing churches from homes and from centers of business and government where secular life brings Christians of all races and classes together, have we come to think that Christian faith and life have to do only with what goes on in an isolated building once or twice a week when people of the same sociological groups come together?

As our society changes, our lives are less and less centered in the neighborhood where we live. Many people find their friends, do their business, take their leisure—spend most of their lives—outside the neighborhood where their homes are. Can we continue to think of the church primarily as a neighborhood institution? If the church is wherever and whenever Christians come together for worship, study, and service in the name of Christ, do they not just as surely "go to church" when they meet downtown during their lunch hour, when they join together in service projects away from the church building, when they meet for prayer and study in someone's house?

The point is not to deny that the local church building is still important. It is to say that as our society changes and the neighborhood becomes less and less important in many people's lives, the church does not have to be less and less important. We can be open to experiment with new and (to us) strange forms of the church, because the church is not a building. It is God's people, whenever, wherever, however they come together.

God creates and governs the church. A final implication of the fact that the church is a people called out and called together by God is that, for churches in the Presbyterian-Reformed tradition (in distinction from churches in some other traditions), the church is not a "voluntary association of believers" who get together and decide to form a church. It is *God* who creates the church and calls people into it. The church, therefore, is not like a club or group of like-minded people who enjoy each other's company, form an organization for their mutual benefit and enjoyment, and set up a constitution, rules of membership, and policies and goals to suit themselves. It is not "our" church but *God's* church.

This understanding of the church is dramatically emphasized by the practice of infant baptism.[1] It makes clear that before we loved and chose God, God loved and chose us. Before we decided to become members of God's family, God "adopted" us to belong to it. God wants us to respond to our "election" or "adoption" with thankful obedience and freely chosen participation in the life and work of the church. But it is *God* who initiates, governs, and maintains this community. It is *God's* will its members are to express in their life together, not the (liberal *or* conservative) will of the church's leaders or the (conservative *or* liberal) popular will of the church's membership. The church belongs to God, not the clergy *or* the laity, the local congregation *or* official church assemblies *or* various boards and agencies. Of course, it is not always easy to know what God is calling the church to say and do, but it makes all the difference when we remember who it is to whom we belong and whose will it is we are called to serve. Then clergy and lay people, parish ministers and church bureaucrats, and Christians who are different from each other in race, sex, class, and theological and political convictions will seek common ground for Christian faith and life in the will and work of God instead of fighting to see whose point of view and agenda are going to win and whose are going to lose.

THE BODY OF CHRIST

One of the main images used in the New Testament to talk about the church is that of the "body of Christ." Christians are related to each other as parts of the human body, and they are related to Christ as the body is related to the head. This image will guide us throughout the rest of our thinking about what the church is.

The first thing implied by it is that it is just as impossible for anyone to be a Christian by himself or herself as it is for an arm or a leg to live and function apart from the body and the head. To be Christian is by definition to belong to the church. There is no such thing as a purely individualistic relationship to Christ. "There is no private Christianity, for to be in Christ is to be in the church and to be in the church is to be in Christ, and any attempt to separate relation to Christ in faith from membership in the church is a perversion of the New Testament understanding."[2]

Notice that we have not said that in order to be good or moral one must belong to the church. The old claim that "you can be just as good without going to church" is certainly true. We only have to look around us to see that many people who never darken the door of the church are not only morally beyond reproach but fine, sensitive, upstanding people. Remember the unbelieving Camus we spoke of in the last chapter! Many non-Christians put some Christians to shame by their personal integrity, their warm and loving family life, and their willingness to "speak out and pay up" in behalf of those whom society in general ignores or rejects. Why should we not be happy and grateful—and repentant—when we meet such people?

However, to be a Christian means inevitably to belong to the church. To believe in and follow Christ is to join the community of followers he draws around himself. To be reconciled to God in Christ is to be reconciled also with other people; it is to be led out of a sinful attempt to live in self-sufficient, autonomous isolation above, apart from, or against others, and to be drawn into the community where all barriers that separate people from each other are broken down. To be open to receive the Holy Spirit and the Spirit's gifts of faith, hope, and love is to be a part of the community to whom the life-renewing power of the Spirit is promised. To be saved is not just to be assured that I will go to heaven when I die; it is to enter into a new relationship with God and fellow human beings in the community of God's people here and now.

How can I know that the forgiveness, love, and help of God in Christ are real if I do not experience them through the community of people who are God's people? How can I be a Christian if I do not participate in the life and work of the community gathered and empowered by God's Spirit to share with others the forgiveness, love, and help they themselves have received? Whoever tries to do without the church tries to do without Christ. Whoever is too good or too "spiritual" for the church (with all its weaknesses and faults) is too good or too spiritual for Christ himself, the God who sent him, and the Holy Spirit who continues his work.

This inseparable connection between being a Christian and belonging to the church has led some theologians to say that there is no salvation outside the church. Both Luther and Calvin took this position (see Calvin's *Institutes* 4.1.4 and Questions 104 and 105 of his Geneva Catechism). It is also expressed in chapter 16 of the Scots Confession and chapter 17 of the Second Helvetic Confession. The Westminster Confession (15.2) says more carefully that outside the church "there is no *ordinary* possibility of salvation."

Is the church that essential? We must be very careful here. It is not the church but the God whom we come to know in Christ who saves. Although it is true that the church is bound to Christ, it is not true that Christ is trapped in the church. He came to express God's love not just for Christians and the church but for all people, for the whole world. He is the risen Lord who is at work not only in the church but everywhere, even among people who do not recognize or acknowledge his liberating, reconciling, healing work. He himself said, "I have other sheep that do not belong to this fold" (John 10:16). God may provide some other way for those who are never reached by the church. Even Calvin said that "God's power is not bound to outward means" (*Institutes* 4.1.4). We cannot say, then, that there is no salvation outside the church.

What we can say is that although God is not bound to the church, we Christians are bound to it. That is where the Christ who is at work in loving and liberating power everywhere is specifically known, thankfully trusted, and voluntarily served. If that is so, then we are bound to the church ourselves, and we are bound to invite others into it so that they too may accept and live by the forgiveness, love, help, and command of the God who cared for them and was at work for their good even before they knew it.

A HOLY PEOPLE

"The *holy* catholic church, the communion of saints (holy ones)." What do we mean when we confess that the church is holy? From what we learned in the last chapter, it must mean that the church is set apart, or different, from other organizations. How is the church different?

Let us immediately clear away a misunderstanding church members all too often have about themselves, much to the world's amusement or disgust. The people of God are not holy in that they are morally superior to other people. Every sin that can be found outside the church can also be found in it, both in the lives of individual Christians (clergy as well as laity) and in whole denominations (Protestant as well as Catholic). Inside as well as outside the church there is prejudice and intolerance; personal immorality on the one hand and legalistic self-righteousness on the other; cut-throat competition; misrepresentation or misuse of the truth for personal or collective gain; lust for money, prestige, power, and success at all costs; pious rationalization for social injustice, nationalistic arrogance, bloody wars, and economic exploitation.

There is no point in denying or trying to explain this away. It is perfectly obvious to the rest of the world even if it is not to us Christians. Nor do we need to deny or try to hide it. The Bible is quite open about the sinfulness of God's people. Think of the prophet's preaching against the individual and social sinfulness that Israel tried to conceal with pious words and religious ceremonies (Isa. 1:1–17; Jer. 6:13; 7:1–26; Amos 5:21–27). Think of the sins to be found among the "saints" to whom Paul addressed his letters (1 Cor. 1:10–13; 5:1; 5:9–13; 11:20–22; Gal. 2:11–14;

Phil. 1:15–17). Whatever the holiness of the church may mean, it does not mean that unlike other organizations it is not sinful. We will never understand the holiness of the church until we get rid of the idea that it is a community of the pure who know better and live better than everyone else.

That leads us to three ways in which we can say that the church is holy or different:

First, the church is distinguished from other societies precisely in that it is a community of people who *know* they are sinners, freely admit that they are not good or superior, and *take responsibility* for their sinfulness without blaming someone else for it. Charles C. Morrison puts it this way:

> The church is not a society of good people; it is a society of sinners. It is the only organization in human society that takes sinners into its membership just because they are sinners. It is the only organization that keeps on saying week after week, year after year, age after age: "We have left undone those things which we ought to have done, and we have done those things which we ought not to have done."[3]

The church is the only "club" in the world that accepts as members only those who are not qualified to belong to it!

Second, the church is holy in that it is a community of *dissatisfied* sinners.[4] They are not satisfied with themselves or with the way things are in the world around them. They are gathered together not to justify their present way of life or to advertise their piety but to admit publicly that they need to be forgiven for what they are, want to change, and need help. The people of God, in other words, are holy not because of what they *have* or what they *are* but because of what they are seeking to *receive* and *become.*

Finally, the church is different from all other societies in that it is gathered in the name of Jesus Christ. Here we run again into the image of the body and the head. The body is holy because the Head is *the* Holy One. Holiness is not found in the church and its members as such but in him from whom they seek forgiveness, change, help, and new direction. When asked about the holiness of the church, Christians cannot proudly or defensively begin arguing about the church's (their own!) goodness, strength, purity, and wisdom. They can only point to *his* goodness, strength, purity, and wisdom.

On the other hand, it also follows from the fact that the church lives from the holiness of its Head that it cannot be only a passively receiving people. The Head directs and activates the body. The church freely admits its sinfulness; but if it is a community of dissatisfied sinners, it cannot settle down comfortably with its confession of sin. If it is serious about wanting to change and be helped to change, it can only be willing to be led by its Head. How can it claim to be the holy community gathered in the name of Christ if instead of reflecting his work of reconciliation it goes on reflecting the same social and personal hostilities as worldly people? How can its members live from him if, instead of reflecting his self-giving love for guilty and suffering people everywhere, they go on reflecting a worldly concern only for their own present and future happiness, peace of mind, comfort, and security? How can they say they believe in the truth he brings if in practice they think and live just like everyone else in the world around them?

Dependence of the body on the Head means the confession that the people of God are sinful and that he only is holy. But it also means the demand that they at least get up and start moving, set out on the way that leaves their sinfulness behind and moves toward his holiness.

That is what we learn and experience at the Lord's Supper.[5] On the one hand it is a way of reminding us that we do not live from our own strength. We have to be fed, nourished, given new life over and over again. On the other hand, the Lord's Supper means that we *are* fed, nourished, and given new life. We share in it not just so that we may flex our spiritual muscles for everyone to admire, but so that we may be empowered to be a community of people who are agents of the risen and coming Christ. This Christ is at work in the world to feed, nourish, and bring new life to people who are desperately hungry—hungry for bread to fill empty bellies, hungry for forgiveness and acceptance, hungry for new beginnings and fresh starts, hungry for justice, hungry for a God who cares.

A UNITED, CATHOLIC PEOPLE[6]

It follows from the fact that there is one Savior and Lord of the church that the community of people who are the body of Christ are united in faith, hope, love, worship, and service (Rom. 12:4–6; 1 Cor. 1:16–17; 12:4–27; Eph. 2:11–22; 4:1–16). Closely related to the idea of the church's unity is that of its catholicity. "Catholic" means universal. The church is catholic in that it unites in faith and life Christians in all times and places; of all races, classes, languages, cultures, nationalities; in all kinds of political, economic, and social situations. There is one Lord, one Spirit, one God, one baptism, one shared bread and cup—and therefore one body, the "one holy catholic church."

That is what Christians confess. But it is not what either non-Christians or Christians themselves actually see. What everyone sees is not *the* church but *many* churches: Eastern Orthodox, Roman Catholic, Lutheran, Presbyterian-Reformed, Methodist, Baptist, Pentecostal, and hundreds of others. Even churches that follow one or another of the great classical theological traditions are split into different churches, each of which claims that its interpretation of the tradition is the most authentic and faithful one. Moreover, there are separate denominations or congregations within denominations for ethnic majorities and for ethnic minorities who "would not feel at home" in each other's church, for "upper" and for "lower" classes, for those who do and for those who do not accept homosexual persons—and on and on.

Behind some of these divisions lie genuinely important differences of theological interpretation—differences, for instance, concerning predestination, the authority of scripture, baptism and the Lord's Supper, the gifts of the Spirit, holiness, and Christian hope for the future. However, sometimes doctrinal differences are only the excuse to split the church along the same racial, cultural, and class lines that separate secular society into groups that are openly hostile or simply indifferent toward each other. In either case, the splintering of the church into many churches screams that the church is *not* one, *not* catholic (and therefore not holy either). And that implies that in fact we do not have one but many lords, are led not by one but by many spirits.

What can we say about the scandalous contradiction between the church Christians confess and the many churches they actually see and live in? We will first discuss two nice-sounding but unsatisfactory ways of arguing that the divisions among and within the churches do not in fact destroy the church's unity and catholicity.

The first argument is that the true church is invisible. There is an invisible "spiritual" unity and catholicity that remain in spite of external divisions. The different denominations or factions within them may not talk together, worship together, sit at the Lord's Table together, or work together. They may be suspicious and afraid of each other, question the authenticity of the other's faith, work in competition with each other. Yet they are "spiritually" one!

There is a sense in which the true nature of the church is indeed invisible. There is no external proof that God is uniquely present and at work in this very ordinary group of people—just as there is no proof that God was uniquely present and at work in a Jew named Jesus. As with Jesus, so it is with the church; we cannot *see* but only *believe* that it is so. Yet as in Jesus, so in his body, the church, God works in a very this-worldly, *visible* way. It simply will not do for us to try to explain away the embarrassing facts by piously talking of a disembodied "real" church somewhere above or apart from the concrete church organizations we see around us. The world may not be able to see *why* it is so, but it ought to be able to see *that* in and among all the churches gathered in the name of Jesus there are present the fruits of his Spirit that are mentioned in Gal. 5:22–25, Eph. 4:30–32, and Phil. 2:1–3.

When you look at your own local congregation, your denomination, and the relation between denominations in your country, what do you see? Love, joy, peace, patience, kindness, generosity, faithfulness, gentleness, one mind? Or bitterness, anger, wrangling, slander, conceit, competition, envy, selfish ambition? Be careful how you answer. It would be faithless and ungrateful if we falsely claimed too little in order to avoid falsely claiming too much for the church(es). Through the centuries and in our time, too, God has been faithful to God's promise to be present in the church with sustaining and transforming grace. But it is true that all talk about the church's "invisible" unity and catholicity is only pious nonsense unless there are very visible signs of that grace at least here and there, now and then, once in a while.

A second way of arguing that our divisions do not contradict our unity and catholicity is the "branch theory." The various denominations and groups within them are like different branches of the same tree. It is just natural for rich and poor, educated and uneducated, various ethnic groups, liberals and conservatives to come together with their own kind and seek a version of Christianity that appeals to them and meets their particular needs. (There are theologians who argue that if we want "effective" evangelism that produces "successful church growth," we must establish "homogeneous" churches in which various kinds of people can feel comfortable as they come together with others like themselves.) But of course all these divisions are still bound together by their common faith in Christ!

There is something right about this argument, too. According to the New Testament, the unity of the body of Christ is not a rigid uniformity. There are legitimate differences among the various members of the body (1 Cor. 12:14–31; Rom. 12:4–8). But in the first place, the differences mentioned in the New Testament are not sociological or even theological differences but differences of gift and task. Second, nowhere does the New Testament suggest that the different members of the body can live in self-sufficient isolation or in downright opposition to each other. On the contrary, Paul's point is that they all need each other and must live together in mutual cooperation if the whole body is to be healthy and function properly. "To each is given the manifestation of the Spirit for the *common* good" (1 Cor. 12:7, emphasis added).

The branch theory that separates Christians according to natural or sociological differences is a plain contradiction of the reconciling work of Christ, who breaks down and overcomes the natural barriers between people of the world. Donald Miller puts it this way:

> There is diversity within a large family—different aptitudes, different tastes, different personal characteristics. It would be a strange family, nonetheless, which would set up separate living arrangements to satisfy the particular peculiarities of each member. In a real family, the diversity is held within the unity of the family. The family lives in the same house, eats together, carries forward its group activities as a unity. In this way, the diversity enriches the whole family life, and each benefits from the other.[7]

Insofar as the branch theory attempts to justify denominational and factional separation, therefore, it is no more acceptable than the invisible church theory. In fact, it is helpful only insofar as it works in the opposite direction.

What then can we do about the glaring contradiction between the unity and catholicity of the church we say we believe in and its brokenness in practice? Acknowledging once again that like all the gifts of the Spirit the gift of unity and wholeness is one we cannot give ourselves, what can we do to open ourselves to receive it?

1. If we want the community-creating work of the Spirit within and among the churches, we can give up all attempts to justify, excuse, or explain away the scandal of the church's disunity and brokenness that contradicts everything we say about one Lord, one Spirit, one faith, one baptism, one God of us all. We can acknowledge the sinfulness of the wrangling within and the divisions between churches and denominations that call themselves the body of Christ.

2. If we want the Spirit's gift of community, we can examine ourselves before we criticize the faith and life of other denominations and groups within our own denomination. Is it really our steadfast holding to biblical truth that separates us from others—or perhaps only the desire to insist on the superiority of our limited and self-serving

interpretation of it? If the church is split into warring churches and factions with churches, is it because of "their" or *our own* unwillingness to be instructed and corrected by the gospel? When we reject and refuse to have anything to do with people and groups of people who understand Christian faith and life differently from us, is it really because we seek the integrity of the church—or perhaps because what we really want is for people like us to have controlling power (us males or females, heterosexuals or homosexuals, rich or poor people, political and theological liberals or conservatives)? Is the disunity and brokenness of the church due to someone else's or our own sinfulness?

3. If we want the Spirit's community-building power among us, we will be open to talk and listen to other denominations and groups within our denomination. What if the Spirit of God is also at work among them? If we are too afraid or too suspicious to have anything to do with them, might we not deprive ourselves of something very important the Spirit is saying to us and doing for us through them? Unless we let them speak for themselves, how can we know whether their version of Christian faith and life is as foolish or corrupt as we think? Have we rejected fellowship with them on the basis of what they really believe and how they really live, or only on the basis of the prejudiced caricatures we have made of them? Do we listen to everything they have to say, or do we hear only what we "knew" beforehand they would say? How can we be open to the reformation of the church if we are not open to listen to, learn from, and let ourselves be corrected by other Christians and churches who read the same Bible in their efforts to be guided by and follow the same Lord we want to follow? "Dialogue" is not a magic solution to the problem of the church's lack of unity and catholicity, but the problem can never be solved without dialogue.

4. If we want the Spirit's gift of community, we will recognize that unity does not mean uniformity. Within Christian community there are "varieties of gifts, but the same Spirit; and there are varieties of services, but the same Lord; and there are varieties of activities, but it is the same God who activates all of them in everyone" (1 Cor. 12:4–6). All Christians do not have to think or live exactly alike. Are we sure that the different interpretations of Christian truth and practice among other denominations and parties are of community-splitting significance? Even if others seem to be one-sided in one direction or another, might we not need fellowship with them to correct one-sidedness on our part? True unity does not mean a boring and sterile sameness; it is a unity in which there is exciting and mutually enriching diversity. Of course, Christian diver-

sity does not mean a wide-open "pluralism" in which "anything goes." It is not the same thing as relativism. There are limits to what Christians can believe and do if it is the one Lord, one Spirit, one God of scripture they confess and serve. It may indeed sometimes be necessary to decide that some do not really belong in the church—not because we have excluded them but because they have excluded themselves. If it is the Spirit's unity-in-diversity we seek, we will be very careful not to draw these boundaries too rigidly or narrowly, and will always be open to learn that the God of Jesus Christ is more "inclusive" than we might have expected (as the early church had to learn in its dealings with uncircumcised Gentiles).

Of course, all this is easier said than done. But how can we refuse to take the risks and run the dangers of such attitudes and actions if we really want the one holy catholic church we confess?

AN APOSTOLIC PEOPLE

"The one holy catholic and *apostolic* church." "Apostolic" means "in line with the apostles." Some churches have interpreted this to mean that the bishops of the church are connected by historical succession with the original apostles and therefore speak and act with the same authority. The Presbyterian-Reformed tradition (with some other Protestant traditions) interprets apostolic to mean that the church must let itself be constantly judged and corrected by the original apostles. "Apostolic," in other words, is synonymous with "biblical"—one holy catholic church that is governed by *biblical* authority.

Even if we consider ourselves correct in this interpretation, we must confess that just at this point we run into a very serious weakness not only in the classical confessions of the Reformed churches but in Calvin himself. According to them, the "marks" of a true apostolic or biblical church are the "pure preaching of the Word of God and the right administration of the sacraments according to the institution of Christ," with proper administration of church discipline sometimes added (Scots Confession, 18; Second Helvetic Confession, 17; Calvin, *Institutes* 4.1). What is wrong with this orthodox doctrine of the church is not what it does say but two things it does *not* say.

The Mission of the Church in the World

The classical definition of the church says nothing about the church's having a *task* to fulfill. Preaching, sacraments, and internal discipline are indispensable, but they are all ways in which the people of God are *ministered to.* A too exclusive emphasis on them has resulted in the idea that the main function of the church is to care for itself and tend to the spiritual needs of its own members. But that is only half of it. The New Testament Greek work for apostle means "one who is *sent out.*" According to the New Testament, Christians enter into the company of God's people by baptism, hear the Word of God preached, receive new life and strength as they break bread together, and discipline themselves in order to be sent back into the world as servants or "ambassadors" of Christ (2 Cor. 5:20). After all, the Christ who is proclaimed in word and sacrament was the original "apostle"—one sent by God into the world not to be served but to serve and give his life for many (Mark 10:45). His followers heard him say not only "Come unto me" but "Go!" "As the Father has sent me, so I send you" (John 20:21). If we listen to what our Reformed forebears themselves taught us about the authority of scripture, therefore, we have to go beyond them at this point to say that an apostolic people of God not only listen to sermons and receive the sacraments when they come together among themselves; they are a people who are *called* out in order to be *sent* out, *loved* and *saved* by God in order to *serve* God—and therefore also the world God loves and wills to save. In short, an apostolic church is by definition a church commissioned with a mission to fulfill in and for the world.

We can be grateful that the Confession of 1967 (9.31) has recovered this biblical understanding (though in gender-specific language we would no longer use) of the apostolic nature of the church that has been so sadly neglected in the church's confessions and theology of the past:

> To be reconciled to God is to be sent into the world as his reconciling community. This community, the church universal, is entrusted with God's message of reconciliation and shares his labor of healing the enmities which separate men from God and from each other. Christ has called the church to this mission and given it the gift of the Holy Spirit. The church maintains continuity with the apostles and with Israel by faithful obedience to his call.

The Mission of All Christians

Before we talk about how the church fulfills its mission, we must correct another serious failure of the classical Reformed definition of the church. Who does the work of the church? As long as we stick to the old definition, the only answer is that it is the church's "professional" ordained ministers. It is they who do the preaching, baptize, and preside over the distribution of the bread and wine. All that lay people have to do is listen to what preachers say and receive from them the sacraments. Active clergy and passive laity—that is the consequence of the orthodox doctrine of the church we have learned. Already disastrous in the inner life of the church, it becomes even more disastrous when we think of the apostolic mission of the church. Who is called out and sent out to be agents of the liberating and reconciling work of God in the world? Ministers and other professional Christians! It is their job, and the task of the laity is only to pay them to do it.

That is not what the Bible says. According to Ex. 19:6, all God's people were called to be "priests" (mediators who bring God to people and people to God). According to the New Testament, certain functions such as preaching, teaching, and church leadership are given to only a few, but nowhere does the New Testament suggest that only a few are called to be priests or servants of God to minister to other people. As in the Old Testament, all God's people are called to this task (1 Peter 2:9).

Luther saw this and emphasized it with his doctrine of the "priesthood of all believers." He did not mean by this simply that every person is his or her own priest with his or her private access to God. He meant that every Christian is called to be a priest to every other person. However, the doctrine of the priesthood of all believers was soon lost in Protestantism, partly as a result of defining the church only in terms of word and sacrament. The consequence was the split lasting right down to our time between the clergy, who are "full-time" active representatives of Christ in the world, and those "second-class" Christians, the laity, whose only task is to receive passively the benefits of the church or at best to be part-time helpers of the clergy.

As Reformed churches (along with others, including the Roman Catholic)[8] have rediscovered the biblical idea that "apostolic" means sent with a task or mission to fulfill, they are also rediscovering the biblical and Reformation understanding that the apostolic task is given not just to a few people with a special calling but to the whole Christian community and every one of its members. Only a few may be called to stand behind a pulpit or baptismal font or communion table. But the task and privilege of the ministry of reconciliation is given to all, clergy and laity alike. To believe in an "apostolic" church is to believe that every Christian is called and sent out to be a minister, missionary, and servant of God—not just part-time but full-time, whatever his or her occupation. That means *you!*

THE TASK OF THE ONE HOLY CATHOLIC AND APOSTOLIC CHURCH

How then does the one holy catholic church go about its apostolic work? Following are some suggestions meant to apply both to the church as a whole and to every individual Christian. They draw together and summarize some themes that have often been emphasized throughout this book.

The Servant Church

The purpose of the church and its members, like that of Jesus himself, is to serve God and fellow human beings. The goal of the church in its preaching, teaching, and missionary and evangelistic work is not to build itself up so that it can become as big and powerful as possible in order to compete successfully with other churches and control and dominate society around it. And the goal of Christians is not just to find meaning for their own lives, to be assured that God is with and for them now and for all eternity, and to enjoy warm fellowship in the company of other Christians. Whether clergy or laity, no matter how involved we are in church activities and how committed to the work of the church, we are only using God and the church to serve ourselves when we are motivated by such concerns—and other people will very quickly recognize our self-serving religiosity. As the one who was *the* Servant of God gave himself (and at the same time found himself) in love for God and others without asking what he personally would get out of it, so will his body and its members give (and find) themselves—even if the result is failure and not success, weakness and not power, a cross and not a crown. How does Jesus say this in Matt. 20:25–28 and Mark 8:34–35?

The Church for the World

As Christ gave himself for a sinful humanity in a sinful world because he loved them, so the church and individual Christians are *for* the world into which they are sent. We cannot look at people outside the church with suspicion, belligerence, or contempt as enemies to be conquered, forced to surrender, and placed under the control of the church and its beliefs. Sometimes the church has given itself to evangelism and missions in order to defeat "godless secularism" or some other ideology. Sometimes Christian individuals approach the unchurched as potential "customers" to be "sold" or as opponents to be out-argued or frightened by threats into giving up and joining up. As if victory for "our side" were our main concern! That cannot be the way of a church and its members who follow their Head. We go into the world not as conquerors but as agents of reconciliation, not with hostility for sinful non-Christians, but with the compassion with which Jesus looked on those who were trapped in the inhumanity of their alienation from God, other people, and themselves. Without participating in their personal or social sinfulness, without in any way condoning it, not hesitating to speak against it, Jesus was their friend and gave his life for just such people. That must be our model also. However great their unbelief, however shocking their immorality or equally sinful self-righteous morality, however wrongheaded their political and social ideologies, we will be interested in them as human beings whom God loves, not only as potential converts to our way. We will listen as well as talk to them—and be open to hear something worth listening to. We will not only expect them to come to us, but we will be willing to go to them wherever they live and work and play, even if it means going into dangerous inner cities or sinful suburbs, union halls or executive suites, cheap taverns or posh country clubs, jails or the P.T.A.

The Church with the World

We must be careful when we say that like Christ himself the church and individual Christians have a servant's task to fulfill for the sake of the sinful world. We are not Christ (not even "little Christs," as Luther said), and we cannot do what he does. We Christians are in no position to judge sinners; we ourselves are sinners who *are* judged. We cannot forgive the sins of others; we need forgiveness for our own sins. We are not the saviors of the world or even soul-savers of a few individuals; we are just as dependent on God for salvation as anyone else. We cannot reconcile people to God and each other; we ourselves are disobedient, unloving people who constantly need to *be* reconciled. We cannot solve the problem of injustice and all the suffering it causes in the world; we are part of the problem ourselves. Sometimes the church and individual Christians have thought they could approach unbelieving or other-believing people in a sinful world as the wise to the foolish, the strong to the weak, the righteous to the unrighteous, the superior to the inferior. In a condescending, patronizing, or pitying way we have spoken and acted as if we Christians are called to help or force others to think and live as we do. No wonder people outside the church have been angry—or only laughed—at such arrogance!

We will properly fulfill our servant task in and for the world only when we never forget that we are *not* Christ (not even little Christs) and cannot do what he does. We are only his body and its members, and we are just as dependent on his compassion, forgiveness, and liberating power as anyone else. We never stand *above* the guilty, needy world. We can only stand *with* it, knowing that we share its sin, guilt, and need for forgiveness and renewed humanity. We are not sent into the world to point to ourselves, our spiritual or moral achievements, our superior social and political programs. We are sent to point to him and the new humanity he brings.

Body and Soul

There is an old argument about whether the church should be more concerned about the souls and the spiritual needs of people or about their bodies and physical needs. The biblical answer is that we should be concerned about neither bodies nor souls but about *human beings—people.* There are no such things as bodiless souls or soulless bodies. What kind of ambassadors for Christ would we be if we said in effect, "God loves you—but of course God only cares about saving your soul. God is not interested in whether you are hungry, poor, sick, homeless, overworked, and underpaid. All that is unimportant." On the other hand, what kind of ambassadors would we be if we said in effect, "God loves you, wants you to have everything you need to lead a safe, healthy productive life in a free and just society. But God is not interested in the fears, hostilities, prejudices, and idolatrous worship of false gods that enslave you, ruin your life, and sour your relationship with God and other people. That's your problem to work out as best you can." In both cases, the response would quite correctly be, "The church and its God may be interested in my soul or in my body, but they are not interested in *me.*" Like Christ himself, who healed bodies *and* broken relationships with God and other people, the church and individual Christians are sent to minister to human beings who are body and soul in their inseparable interconnection.

Individuals and Society

Another big debate concerning the mission of the church is about whether we are sent as representatives of Christ only to individuals or to the society in which they live. Is social action a part of the church's task or only the evangelization and nurture of individuals? As we have already learned, this is another false alternative.

If people cannot work to support themselves and their families because they do not have the skills to work in a computerized economic system; if they are exploited and discriminated against because of their race or sex; if they are so poor that they have no home at all or have to live in a rat-infested inner-city neighborhood—how can we expect them to believe us when we proclaim the good news that Christ loved and died for them and is now risen Lord over the whole world for their good too? How can we refuse as servants of this Lord to do what we can to make the justice, love, and freedom of his kingdom visible in the economic, social, and political spheres that shape the lives of individuals? If we do not take our own gospel about the lordship of the risen Christ seriously, how can we expect anyone else to take it seriously?

On the other hand, how can we expect people to believe the promises and accept the requirements of the gospel we proclaim if we are in fact more interested in this or that social or political cause than in their personal hurts, problems, and needs? Victims of injustice and poverty, for instance, resent Christian social proclamations and service projects when they suspect that we are only using them to practice our Christianity in order to salve our guilty consciences or to show what fine Christians we are. Middle-class and affluent people resent and reject a proclamation of the gospel that suggests Sunday after Sunday that God is for justice and peace in the world but is not interested in what is going on in *their* lives; or that God loves the poor and oppressed but not despicable people like them. Rich, poor, or middle-class, male or female, how can people hear and receive the good news of Jesus Christ if they are not personally included, or if what they hear is only a gospel indistinguishable from the platform of this or that political party or advocacy group?

The Christ who sends us into the world as his ambassadors knows and cares for every single individual (without any ideological strings attached). At the same time, he proclaims and brings not just personal salvation but a kingdom of justice, compassion, freedom, and peace that is for all people everywhere (not just for any one group). Our assignment is not to make one or the other but both facts known by what we say and do.

Everything we have said about our being sent into the world means that as a church and as individual Christians we have been given a very difficult task to perform. It would be an impossibly difficult one if our mission were to "take" Christ to the world or "win the world" for Christ or "bring in" the kingdom of Christ—as if we were his sponsors, defenders, and protectors.

Our understanding of the task changes completely when we are modest enough to acknowledge that we Christians and our church are neither required nor allowed to think that we have to be the saviors and lords of the world; when we recognize that it is the crucified, risen, and coming Christ who is and will be the world's Savior and Lord. Then our task becomes an unbelievably confident, even carefree, enterprise.

There is no place we can go where Christ is not already at work before us—no nation, no home, no place of work or entertainment, no hospital, no place where the homeless, unemployed, and untended sick huddle together. We do not have to go into the hostile or callously indifferent world anxiously, defensively, or belligerently. We can go thankfully, confidently, and joyfully, because we go not to *take* but to *meet* him. Long before we ever thought of going into the world, he entered into it and identified himself with it. Long before we became concerned about people suffering from their own and others' inhumanity, he cared for them and suffered with and for them. Long before we ever dreamed of going to do battle with the forces of darkness, evil, and death in the world, he triumphed over them. Long before it ever occurred to us to go as ministers of reconciliation to live among and minister to unbelievers and outsiders near at hand or far way, he was living among them, ministering to them. Wherever we look, wherever we go, he is already there—he to whom a torn and broken world already belongs and will belong. That is the comfort and certainty, joy and freedom, of our apostolic mission. We do not have to shoulder the impossibly heavy burden of doing his work for him. We are simply invited to participate with him in the work he has done, is doing, and will do.

We can summarize everything we have been trying to say about the task of the one holy catholic and apostolic church by quoting Matthew's version of Jesus' last word to his disciples. He left us a command: "Go therefore and make disciples of all nations." But *before* he gave us this task, he said, "All authority in heaven and on earth has been given to me." And *after* he gave it, he promised, "I am with you always, to the end of the age" (Matt. 28:18–20).

We began this chapter talking about what is wrong with the church today and the big trouble it is in. Then we discussed what the church is and is called to do according to the Bible and Christian tradition. All the way along we have tried to be both realistic and honest about what the church as we know it is really like, and to be faithful to what scripture and tradition teach us to believe about it. Have we succeeded? (Think of your local congregation, your denomination, the church in general.) The following suggestions for further reflection and study are intended to help you answer this question.

FOR FURTHER REFLECTION AND STUDY

On "The People of God"

1. When you hear the word *church,* what comes first to your mind?
2. What does your local church do other than what takes place within the church building?
3. What percentage of your local church's budget is spent on maintaining the building and activities that take place in it?
4. How does Presbyterian-Reformed church government differ from that of a congregationalist church? How does it differ from the form of government of the United States?

On "The Body of Christ"

1. Can a person be just as good without belonging to the church?
2. Can one be a Christian without belonging to the church?
3. Is everyone who does not belong to a Christian church going to hell? Is it true that there is no salvation outside the church?

On "A Holy People"

1. Evaluate this observation from a late medieval manuscript: "The church is something like Noah's ark. If it weren't for the storm outside, you couldn't stand the stink inside."
2. Is it true that church members are just as sinful as other people?
3. Do you think we were realistic and honest when we said that the church is a community of dissatisfied sinners who want to change? Is it true of you? Does this affect your social and political views? Your theological views?

On "A United, Catholic People"

1. Do you agree that denominational divisions are a sinful denial of the unity and catholicity of the church?
2. Do you agree that in practice the disunity of the church in our country is caused more by sociological and ideological than by theological differences?
3. What could the denominations do, without losing their integrity, toward making the unity we have in Christ visible?

On "An Apostolic People"

1. To what extent would it be accurate to say that your church is an apostolic church? In what ways do its members go beyond a purely passive relationship with the church to live as people sent out with a ministry of reconciliation?
2. "The world does not exist for the sake of the church, but the church for the sake of the world." Do you agree?
3. Discuss the following statements in the light of Matt. 28:18–20:
   a. It is wrong to speak of the "soul-saving" work of the church.
   b. It is wrong to speak of "taking" Christ to the world, "winning the world" for Christ, or "bringing in" the kingdom.
4. How would you define the church's task of missions and evangelism?
5. How could Christ be at work among people who never heard of him or having heard of him do not accept him as Savior and Lord?

19

What's Going to Happen to Us?

The Doctrine of the Christian Hope for the Future

You are going to die. So is everyone you love—your husband or wife, your children, your parents, your friends. It may happen tomorrow or the day after tomorrow or not for several years. It may come quickly and easily or slowly and painfully. But we are all going to die. One day we will be cremated or put in a hole in the ground and covered up with dirt. Or like millions of other people in our time, we may be blown into irretrievable bits and never buried at all. But in one way or another, sooner or later, we are all going to die—you, I, every one of us.

We may try to fool ourselves and other people. We may do everything we can to look young. We may count calories and exercise faithfully. We may prolong life with medical techniques undreamed of a generation ago. We may try to live as if there were no tomorrow. But finally it won't work. Every day we are one day nearer to death, the end.

Is there any more hope for the world in general than for us individuals? Early in the twentieth century we fought the war that was supposed once and for all to "make the world safe for democracy." Is the world better off now than it was then? Is there any less hatred, greed, brutality, or equally cruel indifference among human beings now than there was a thousand years ago? Is it realistic to hope that even in the next thousand years we will reach the point at which there will be no more wars or rumors of wars, injustice, poverty, crime, oppression of minorities, the physical and psychological crippling of children as the result of the inhumanity of their elders? The forms of our inhumanity change, of course. We have nuclear weapons instead of bows and arrows; economic exploitation instead of slave trade and colonialism. But can we really expect that human beings themselves will change, even if the United States could have its way all over the world? Even if Christians and their church could control everything?

It is considered bad taste in our time to talk about dying. Death has replaced sex as the subject too obscene for polite conversation. (Now we say "passed on" instead of "died," and "memorial park" instead of "graveyard.") And it is downright un-American to suggest that we cannot eventually solve all our own and the world's problems if we work at it long and hard enough, if we only can convince or enable the rest of the world to follow the American way of life. But that is the way it is: We are all going to die. The suspicion will not go away that the American Dream for ourselves and the rest of the world is *only* a dream.

In this last chapter we are going to consider what Christians have to say about these brutal facts of life and death. It is the good news of hope for the future even when personal experience and world history seem to say there is no hope. Christian hope for *individuals* is hope in the God who raised Jesus from the dead; it is therefore hope for our own resurrection—hope for "the resurrection of the body" and "the life everlasting" (Apostles' Creed). Christian hope for the *world* is hope that through the risen Christ the God who created the heaven and the earth at the beginning will create a *new* heaven and earth at the end; it is the hope that Christ "will come again in glory to judge the living and the dead, and his kingdom will have no end" (Nicene Creed).

It will help us to understand and claim the true meaning of this great Christian hope if we first eliminate some tempting alternatives to it (some of them clearly unchristian, some less clearly so and often mistaken for the Christian position). Then we will suggest some guidelines for asking the right questions about what Christians can hope for. With this preparation behind us, we will finally discuss the meaning of the creedal affirmations we have quoted.

CHRISTIAN HOPE, HOPELESSNESS, AND FALSE HOPES

Whether obviously or less obviously unchristian, all alternatives to Christian hope for the future have in common the fact that from the Christian point of view they are either too optimistic about human power over sin and death or too pessimistic about the power of God over them. Or to put it another way, they are based either on a false hope in human potential or on hopelessness about God's potential. We will discuss the Christian response to four such alternatives, the first two having to do with the future of the world and the last two with the future of human individuals. We can summarize quickly what needs to be said in the first two points because we have already emphasized it repeatedly in past discussions (see especially our discussion of the kingdom of God in chapter 14). The last two points will take a little more time.

Christian Hope Versus Historical Optimism

Against all optimism about human potential in history, Christian hope for the world is hope that God will overcome inhuman and unjust social, political, and economic structures. The justice, freedom, and peace of the kingdom of God will not come *within* history as the result of human efforts; it will come at the *end* of history as the result of what only God can and will do. For Christians that means the end of all idealistic or utopian confidence in any political or social ideology. They know that the world cannot and will not be saved by a socialistic *or* by a capitalistic economic system, by a democratic *or* by any other form of government, by nonviolent pacifism *or* by "realistic" use of violence to achieve good ends, by revolution that hopes to correct everything that is wrong in human society overnight *or* by reform movements that hope for gradual change, by secular humanistic *or* by specifically Christian programs and crusades to combat personal immorality and/or social evil. Christian hope in the God who will come to straighten things out at the conclusion of history means the end of all optimism about what either non-Christians *or* Christians can accomplish with their liberal or conservative strategies to improve the world.

Christian Hope Versus Historical Pessimism

Christians are just as critical of hopeless pessimism as of overconfident optimism about the possibilities of human life in the world. The God in whom we hope is a God who not only *will be* but *is* the powerful and compassionate Creator and Ruler of the world. The crucified and risen Christ who *will* come to overthrow all the powers of darkness and evil that spoil God's good creation and human life in it has *already* triumphed over them and *even now* is at work to complete the work he has begun. The reconciling and liberating Spirit whom God will pour out on "all flesh" (Joel 2:28) is *already* "blowing where it will," also outside the little circle of Christians in the world. Therefore an openly unbelieving or apparently pious hopelessness about what can be accomplished in the world is just as impossible for Christians as secular or religious utopianism. We may understand and sympathize with others who fall into despairing resignation, weariness, inertia, and melancholy because they are overwhelmed by the massive suffering and injustice they experience in their own lives and in the world around them. But, to put it bluntly, for Christians to fall into such hopelessness is sin, lack of faith and hope in the triune God they confess.[1]

Christians do not believe in the perfectibility of humankind; but if we really believe in the sovereign power and love of a God who is the world's Creator and Ruler, we can and must do what we can to achieve at least a little more justice and humanity in a world that not only will be but is *God's* world. We cannot have faith and hope in either secular or Christian programs and organizations that seek to solve all the world's problems, but if we believe in a living Lord and a life-renewing Spirit who are present and at work in the world here and now (even where they are not recognized and acknowledged), we can and we must join forces with all people of good will, Christian or not, who seek to alleviate human suffering and restrain the destructive power of hatred, greed, and oppression. Hope in the triune God means that we will expect and work for preliminary signs of the new humanity and new world that we know are surely coming.

If Christians who hope in God always seem too pessimistic to optimists, they will also seem too optimistic to pessimists.

Hope in the Power of God over the Power of Death

For the fate of humans and the fate of animals is the same; as one dies, so dies the other. They all have the same breath, and humans have no advantage over the animals. . . . All go to one place; all are from the dust, and all turn to dust again.

As they came from their mother's womb, so they shall go again, naked as they came; they shall take nothing for their toil, which they may carry away with their hands. . . . [J]ust as they came, so shall they go; and what gain do they have from toiling for the wind?

Everything that confronts them is vanity, since the same fate comes to all, to the righteous and the wicked, to the good and the evil, to the clean and the unclean.

Enjoy life with the wife whom you love, all the days of your vain life that are given you under the sun, because that is your portion in life and in

> your toil at which you toil under the sun. Whatever your hand finds to do, do with your might; for there is no work or thought or knowledge or wisdom in Sheol [the realm of the dead], to which you are going.

These words were not written by an atheist. They were written by a "teacher" who could also say, "Fear God, and keep his commandments; for that is the whole duty of everyone." They are included in the book Christians believe to be the word of God. Stop now and read through the whole book of Ecclesiastes (we have quoted Eccl. 3:19–20; 5:15–16; 9:1–2, 9–10; 12:13).

What can we make of such strangely pessimistic words coming from the Bible itself? Here are some conclusions we may draw from Ecclesiastes. Some of them are debatable, so you had better examine them carefully.

First, if death has the last word and there is no hope for a future beyond death, then my life here and now will be meaningless. All I can do is live like "the teacher," swinging back and forth between a weary, depressed cynicism and a frantic, joyless attempt to wring what little pleasure I can from this fleeting life. An empty future means an empty present.

Second, it is not true (as some Christians have argued) that only the promise of heaven and the threat of hell can prevent lawless, godless living. Who can fail to admire "the teacher" and others like him who are honorable, morally responsible, courageous, even deeply religious people even though they have no hope for a final reward or fear of final punishment for themselves, and no hope for a final balancing of the books when the wicked of the world who have been successful and the innocent who have suffered unjustly will finally get what they deserve?

Third, compassion and not condemnation is called for when we meet people like "the teacher." How can we fail to sympathize with people who, having no future, can only swing back and forth between paralyzing despair and the desperate attempt to escape the emptiness of life in simple earthly pleasures and hard work? People who are trapped in meaningless lives need to be loved, not damned. They are already tragically damned.

Finally, no one can talk convincingly about life after death who does not face as honestly as "the teacher" the stark reality of death and the cloud it casts over all of life. No cheap talk about a final happy ending will do. If we are honest with ourselves, who of us does not sometimes suspect that what he tells us is the truth about our own lives and the lives of everyone else?

However, Christians who believe what they have heard about the resurrection of Christ and therefore the resurrection of all the dead know that although death is real and certain, it does not have the last word. For us there can be no ultimate pessimism about the future—and therefore no cynicism about the value of life in the present (the value of other people's lives as well as of our own). We know that we move not only toward the *end* of life but toward its *fulfillment*—toward the genuinely full human life that God willed for all human beings from the beginning, which God is at work here and now to restore and renew, and which God will finally give to everyone. There may be some question about how seriously we Christians take our own gospel. (Do Christians in fact find more joy and meaning in life because of their hope for the future?) But the gospel itself declares that all gloomy philosophies of life like that of "the teacher" in Ecclesiastes have been superseded by the promise of another "teacher" in 1 Corinthians 15:54–57: "Death has been swallowed up in victory. . . . [T]hanks be to God, who gives us the victory through our Lord Jesus Christ."

Hope in God's Power over Death, Not Our Own Power

We have been talking about a point of view that from the perspective of Christian faith is falsely pessimistic because it takes death too seriously: it has no hope for the future because it either does not know about or does not believe in a God who is stronger than death. Now we have to talk about a point of view that from the perspective of Christian faith is falsely optimistic because it does not take death seriously enough. Its hope for the future is based on confidence in a capacity we have within ourselves to survive death rather than on confidence in God's power over it. Because the position we are about to criticize and reject is just what many believe is the very foundation of Christian hope for the future, we emphasize from the very beginning that we criticize and reject it not to destroy hope for eternal life but to defend an authentically biblical-Christian hope for it that is far better and far more trustworthy.

We refer to belief in the immortality of the soul. This doctrine was not taught by the biblical writers themselves, but it was common in the Greek and oriental religions of the ancient world in which the Christian church was born. Some of the earliest Christian theologians were influenced by it, read the Bible in light of it, and introduced it into the thinking of the church. It has been with us ever since. Calvin accepted it

(*Institutes* 1.15.2, 6), and so did the classical confession of the Reformed churches (Scots Confession, 17; Westminster Confession, 34).

According to this doctrine, my body will die but I myself will not really die. My body is only the shell around my true self. It is not *me*. It is only the earthly-physical house in which I live temporarily, or the earthly-physical prison in which I am trapped for a while. My true self is my soul, the spiritual part of me that is like God and therefore shares God's immortality (inability to die). What happens at death, then, is that my immortal soul escapes from my mortal body. My body dies, but I myself live on and return to the spiritual realm from which I came and to which I really belong.

If we follow the Protestant Reformation in seeking to ground our faith on "scripture alone," we must reject this traditional hope for the future based on belief in the immortality of the soul (even if the Reformers did not follow their own advice at this point).[2] There are several reasons why it is unacceptable from a biblical point of view.

1. Bible-believing Christians must reject the doctrine of the soul's immortality because it is based on an unbiblical understanding of what the soul is. According to scripture, the soul is not the inward divine (and therefore immortal) part of us that comes from God and returns to God; it is simply the God-given "breath of life" that makes us living creatures (see our discussion of body and soul in chapter 10). It is true, then, that when we die the soul "departs" and is "gone." But that does not mean that the immortal divine part of us has departed to live on somewhere else. It means that *life* has left us, that our lives have come to an end, that we are "dead and gone." According to scripture, in other words, my soul is just as human, creaturely, finite—and mortal—as my body; it is simply the life of my body. This does not mean that there is no hope for "life after death," but it does mean that we have no hope at all if our hope is in our own built-in immortality.

2. We say the same thing in another way when we say that biblically based Christian faith rejects hope in the immortality of the soul because that doctrine denies the terrible reality of death. The Bible does not pretend that death is not so bad after all because we do not actually die at all but only "pass on" to a new form of existence when our souls escape our bodies. According to scripture, death is real, total, and dreadful. Jesus himself did not face death with the calmness of one only "passing over to the other side." He faced it with "loud cries and tears" (Heb. 5:7) and blood-sweating anguish (Luke 22:44). And there is no suggestion in

the New Testament that when Jesus died, his soul returned to God leaving only his body in the tomb; it says that he was completely cut off from God, really *dead.* Nor did Paul think of death as a "friend" to be welcomed because it meant only "entering into a wider room" or "sailing beyond the horizon"; for him it was an enemy, the "last enemy" that will finally be utterly destroyed (1 Cor. 15:26). In contrast to the doctrine of the immortality of the soul, there is no pious denial of the horror of death in biblical teaching. Christians face the reality of death with unflinching honesty: it is hideous because so far as we are concerned it means the end of *us,* not just the death of our bodies.

It is true that a life may be so wracked with pain, tormented by inner anguish, limited by physical or mental disability, or debilitated by the aging process that death seems preferable to life. But even when it comes as a "blessing," it is a sad one because it means a life that once was but no longer is. Whether it comes as release from intolerable suffering, or as sudden tragedy, or simply as the end of a long and fruitful life, death comes as the destroyer of life that cuts off all hope for future healing and growth, all hope for further accomplishment, all possibility of continued relationship with loved ones. It means the "dead end."

That is only the first and not the last word Christians have to say about death, of course. But it is the first word without which any other word (especially about the immortality of the soul) will sound like whistling in the dark, false comfort, and cheap piety.

3. We begin to see the Christian alternative to hope in the immortality of the soul when we mention a third reason that it is unacceptable from a biblical point of view. According to scripture, our hope is not in the indestructibility of human beings but in the creative power of God, who can call life into being out of nothing and make the dead live again. The New Testament is clear about this. God alone "has" immortality (1 Tim. 6:16). Our hope for life beyond death does not lie in a capacity we have within ourselves to live forever but in God's promise to *give* us eternal life, or immortality (Rom. 2:7). Biblical hope is not in our own ability to overcome the power of death but in the power of the God who raised Jesus from the dead. It is hope in the risen Christ, who triumphed over death for us so that we too might have eternal life. Is not hope based on what God in Christ can do, has done, and promises to do a far greater, far more certain hope than hope based on wishful thinking about the immortality of our souls? This brings us to a fourth point.

4. Biblically informed Christians reject the doctrine of the immortality of the soul because of the unbiblical split it makes between body and

soul, physical-earthly and spiritual-heavenly life. If the concept of the soul's innate "divine" immortality is unbiblically optimistic about the future that lies ahead of us, its contempt for the body is unbiblically pessimistic. The Bible does not teach that the body is an inferior, worthless shell or prison in which we are trapped and from which we long to escape. It teaches that we were created and *are* body (male or female body!) as well as soul, and that bodily as well as spiritual life is willed and blessed by God. It also teaches that our hope for the future is not for the soul's escape from bodily-physical life into some higher and better spiritual realm but for renewal of our *total* human existence as *embodied* souls and besouled *bodies*. So it was with Jesus: The New Testament does not tell us that his soul left his body and "went home" to be with God; it tells us that God raised him *bodily* from the dead and that the same earthly Jesus his disciples had known before (to be sure with a transformed "new" body) returned to the God from whom he had come. So it will be with us: We do not look forward to a finally bleak future in which our "naked" souls live on forever; we look forward to a future in which we, the bodily-creaturely persons we are now, will live (to be sure in a new way) in communion with God and other people. Whether we think about life in this world or in the world to come, contempt for our own (or any other person's) bodily life is unbiblical and unchristian. Biblical-Christian hope for the future is hope for human beings who are body and soul in their inseparable unity.

Here we have run into the very heart of the Christian hope for the future. We will ask presently what it means more specifically. The point now is that for the sake of a genuinely biblical-Christian hope for the future we must reject hope in the immortality of the soul. On the one hand, Christians are far more honest than that about the total threat and reality of death. On the other hand, Christian hope is far greater than that. Our hope is not in our own deathless spirituality but in the God who creates and re-creates whole human beings. When Christians confess their hope for the future, they say that they believe in "the resurrection of the *body*."

SOME GUIDELINES FOR ASKING THE RIGHT QUESTIONS

In discussing some false hopes or lack of hope for the future Christians cannot accept, we have already begun to see the outlines of the Christian alternative to them. Before we focus on the specific content of this

Christian alternative, however, we will first try to set some limits to the questions we may legitimately ask and answers we may expect to find if we want to understand it. This can save us from all the wild speculations and fantasies that are a danger especially at this point in Christian theology.

We must not want to know too much. "It is unwise for Christians to claim any knowledge of either the furniture of heaven or the temperature of hell; or to be too certain about any details of the kingdom of God in which history is consummated."[3] Why? First, because no one knows the answers to many of the questions, our curiosity leads us to ask about the future. The biblical writers do not and cannot tell us everything we would like to know: "What we will be has not yet been revealed" (1 John 3:2). Even Jesus himself did not know all the answers (Mark 13:32). So "it is foolish and rash to inquire concerning unknown matters more deeply than God wants us to know" (Calvin, *Institutes* 3.25.6). Moreover, as a rule the biblical writers were not even interested in the details of "what it will be like." They did not worry about the future because they understood their own and the world's future to be in the hands of the God who in Jesus Christ has triumphed and will triumph over all the powers of suffering, sin, injustice, and death. They had no time to sit around speculating and arguing about when, where, and how new life in the kingdom of God would come; they were too busy living here and now in joyful and confident anticipation of it.

We would do well to follow the example of the writers of the New Testament. Where the Bible is silent, we ought not ask too many questions or claim that we have too many answers. Our best response to questions in this area is often "I don't know and we don't need to know." Where scripture places its emphasis is where we ought to place ours too—on living in the present in light of our future hope, knowing that what is going to happen to us, our loved ones, and the world will be better than the very best we can imagine in our wildest dreams.

Biblical language about the future is metaphorical or symbolic. When Jesus or the biblical writers talk about the end of the world and what happens after death, they use images based on everyday human experience to talk about something that is beyond all human experience. They use categories of space and time to express truth that is beyond all spatial and temporal categories. Not only that, they do this in terms of human experiences and understanding of space and time that belong to an ancient culture quite different from ours. Therefore, we cannot take the images and pictures they use literally; we must try to understand the truth they want to convey with those images and pictures. Some examples follow.

When Jesus said to the thief on the cross. "Today you will be with me in *Paradise*" (Luke 23:43), he used a word that was originally a Persian word for a nobleman's park or garden, the most beautiful place anyone in the ancient world could imagine. If we want to understand what heaven is like, we will not investigate what a rich man's property in the ancient Near East was like; we will try to imagine what it might mean to be *with Jesus.*

When Jesus spoke about his coming again, he said he will be "coming on the clouds of heaven" (Matt. 26:64). We have only to ask the question that naturally follows to see how absurd it would be to take such a statement literally: *Where* will he appear riding on the clouds? Palestine? New York? Alabama? South Africa? The point obviously is not *how* and *where* he will come but that God in Christ will be the Judge and Savior of the whole world at the end of history.

Paul pictures Christ coming "with the sound of God's trumpet" (1 Thess. 4:16). Paul's point is surely not that God will blow a big God-sized horn but that a great victory is coming.

In the New Testament, hell is sometimes described in terms of "fire" (Matt. 18:8–9; 25:41), but sometimes as "darkness" (Matt. 8:12; 22:13; 25:30). How can it be both fire and darkness at the same time? The problem is solved as soon as we stop thinking of these as literal descriptions of hell and consider them as images that say the same thing in different ways. For the people of Jesus' time, "fire" was a symbol of the destruction of everything displeasing to the holy God. "Darkness" was the opposite of the light, which was a symbol for salvation. The images were not intended to describe the physical characteristics of hell but what it means to be cut off from God.

On the other hand, although we must recognize that the Bible speaks of what lies beyond human experience in symbols and metaphors drawn from human experience, we must also remember that they do stand for something significant and real. Symbols by definition symbolize something. Metaphors tell us what something or someone "is."

As with the particular images we have used as examples, so in general we may apply two rules for the proper interpretation of all biblical language describing the future: (1) It is not to be taken as a literal description of *how* things will be but as a symbolic description of the fact *that* at the end of our individual lives and at the end of history God will be there as Judge and Savior. (2) The Bible uses earthly human categories of time and space not to describe literally *where* we will be and *how* we will exist "after time" but to describe *who* we will be. It is not primarily interested in "the furniture of heaven" or the "temperature of hell" but in *people* and what it will mean for them to be together with or separated from God.

Scripture offers us not one but several hopes for the future. In the writings of the Old Testament for the most part there is no hope at all for life beyond life in this world. Individuals may hope that God will bless the righteous and punish the unrighteous in this life, but after this life there is no heaven and no hell, nor any real life at all. Everyone who dies goes to the same place, Sheol, "the land of gloom and deep darkness" (Job 10:21), a region where all the dead have a kind of shadowy existence completely cut off from God and forgotten by God (Ps. 88:4–6, 10–12; 115:17). Israel's hope for the world is not hope for a new heaven and earth that will come at the *end* of world history but hope for the coming of a new king like David (a "Son of David") who will bring a political kingdom of prosperity, justice, peace, and true religion for all people *within* history.

Toward the end of the Old Testament period, Israel's hope for the future changed when the people were carried off into exile. It became clear that in this life it is not the godly who prosper and the ungodly who suffer but just the opposite. There was no longer any realistic hope for a Davidic kingdom before which the nations of the earth would bow. There arose an "apocalyptic" hope for a great cosmic battle between God and all the demonic forces of evil at the end of history, at the end of which God will be victorious. At that time all the dead will be raised to "everlasting life" or to "shame and everlasting contempt" (Dan. 12:2) to receive the reward or punishment they did not receive in this life, and God (not this or that political leader) will establish an eternal kingdom of righteousness *beyond* history.

In the New Testament, the book of Revelation develops this apocalyptic hope for the future in greatest detail, but it is also the framework for Jesus' own proclamation of the coming of the kingdom of God and for the theology of the New Testament writers. As a result of Jesus' preaching and especially his death and resurrection hope for a final world judgment, the resurrection of the dead and the coming of "a kingdom not of this world" became the foundation of Christian faith. It is important to note, however, that there is no agreement in the New Testament about just when and how all this will happen. Jesus himself seems to have thought that the end of the world and the resurrection of the dead would come very soon (Mark 13:30). In his earlier writings, Paul still expects the end to come very soon (1 Thess. 4:13–18), but in his later writings (e.g., Romans) he seems to postpone the end to an indefinite future.

We are not concerned here to trace the details of this development[4] but only to make this one point: We cannot expect to find one neat biblical timetable for the future. Nor can we expect to combine all the relevant texts into one neat scheme describing the way everything will happen. The details of the biblical hope change from time to time and from situation to situation. What we do learn (from the New Testament at least) is that however conflicting and difficult to harmonize are the pictures we are given in different writings, at different points in the development of biblical thinking, they all agree on two basic points: (1) God in Christ stands at the end of history in general; and (2) God in Christ stands at the end of the life of every individual person. In the last analysis that is all we know and all we need to know.

The best insight we have into what God will do is found by looking at what God has done. What may we expect to happen at the end of our individual lives and at the end of the world? We may expect the confirmation and victory of what God intended from the very beginning in creating the world. We may expect the confirmation and victory of what God was at work to accomplish in Christ two thousand years ago. The most certain clue to what will happen to us in the *future* is what God has been doing with and for us all along in the *past*. As someone has said, Christians *remember* the future. We may draw two conclusions, one negative and one positive, from this past-oriented Christian hope for the future.

The negative conclusion is this: The clearest biblical sources for helping us to understand Christian hope for the future are not Daniel and Revelation, which speak most exclusively and explicitly about the future. We do not say that they are not true or that nothing is to be learned from them. We say only that they are not the clearest sources for understanding the future Christians look forward to. They are highly symbolical, filled with all kinds of weird beasts, angels, demons, visions, mystical numbers, and cosmic conflicts that are utterly strange to us. Some people spend years making charts, timetables, and diagrams trying to figure out what all this means. Churches have been split and new churches formed because of different interpretations of this one part of scripture. We will do well to follow the example of Calvin and the Reformed confessions in not getting bogged down in these apocalyptic books.[5] Christians ought not place their hope in all kinds of fantastic predictions and speculations about a future they cannot really know anything about. They place their hope in the God they know, the God whose plans and promises are made known to us in the whole story of Israel and in the life, death, and resurrection of Jesus Christ. This means that when we think about the future, we cannot forget about all the rest of the Bible and read it only in terms of Daniel and Revelation. On the contrary, we must read these difficult books in light of what we already know from the rest of the Bible.

The positive conclusion to be drawn from the relation we have suggested between past and future is this: What we look forward to is not the destruction but the renewal of the life of our created world and our creaturely lives in it. To look forward to a final judgment of the world is not to look forward to the annihilation of the world and a purely spiritual, otherworldly kingdom of God, but to look forward to a "new heaven and a new earth"—the completion and perfection of *this* world, which in itself always has been and always will be God's good creation. To look forward to "life after death" is not to look forward to becoming disembodied heavenly spirits but to becoming a "new *creation*" (2 Cor. 5:17), part of a "new *humanity*" (Eph. 2:15). It is to expect, not escape from, but the completion and perfection of our humanity—the human existence God willed for us from the very beginning and was at work to restore to us and in us through Jesus Christ.

That means that everything we say about the future of the world or about our future as individuals must take the form of good news we can thankfully and gladly hear. For the future hope of Christians is not a world-denying hope disinterested in or contemptuous of a genuinely human, earthly life. The "end" we Christians look forward to is not only the conclusion (*finis*) but the fulfilled goal and purpose (*telos*) of our earthly, worldly, human life here and now. To say what this good news means in more detail is our task in the rest of this chapter.

CHRISTIAN HOPE FOR THE WORLD

Will it always be this way—a world in which the little drama Gen. 3:1–4:16 tells us took place at the beginning of human history is repeated over and over again, in constantly new variations, with ever more disastrous consequences, as long as human history continues? Will history always be the story of human beings' rebellion against God and enmity toward one another—until we finally destroy the whole human race and take our planet with us? No! "He is coming to judge the quick and the dead" and to create "a new heaven and a new earth." That is the promise we have to try to understand in this section.

The Last Judgment

When we hear this phrase, even those of us who have not seen Michelangelo's picture of it in the Sistine Chapel or other medieval pictures of the "last day" probably think of a stern sword-wielding Christ separating those on the right who are floating upward into rosy clouds from those on the left who are being dragged down by hideous demons into all kinds of horrible torture. (Why is it that those at the bottom of such paintings are so much more interesting than those at the top? Is it because the "blessed" are so sweetly and boringly passive, whereas something is at least going on among the "damned"?) If we are to think biblically about the future of the world, we have to get rid of such half-pagan mythology and think in a quite different way about what is going to happen on "judgment day."

"In the Biblical world of thought the judge is not primarily the one who rewards some and punishes the others; he is the man who creates order and restores what has been destroyed."[6] The first thought that comes to Christians when they think about the end of history ought not be anxious or vindictive speculation about who will be "in" and go "up," and who will be "out" and go "down." It ought to be the thankful and joyful thought that we may confidently look forward to the time when the will of the world's Creator, Reconciler, Savior, and Renewer will prevail once and for all—when justice will triumph over injustice, love over hatred and greed, peace over hostility, humanity over inhumanity, the kingdom of God over the powers of darkness. The last judgment will come not against but for the good of the world. It means that "evil will be condemned and rooted out of God's good creation" (Declaration of Faith, 10.2). That is good news not just for Christians but for everyone!

Hope for the restoration and renewal of all creation does of course involve a final day of judgment. In the ominous words of the Westminster Confession (consistent with the warning of Paul in Rom. 2:6–7), all must "appear before the tribunal of Christ to give an account of their thoughts, words and deeds; and to receive according to what they have done in the body, whether good or evil" (33.1). If that were the whole story, the medieval pictures of the last judgment would be justified. In fact, they would be too optimistic, for no one will survive if salvation depends on the absolute purity and obedience demanded by God. All of us would have to look forward to the end with stark terror. Who of us, no matter how moral or religious, will not be counted among the wicked for our failure to love God with our whole being and our neighbor as ourselves?

The whole picture changes as soon as we remember who the Judge will be. Not a vengeful or even an unbiased "blind" judge, but Christ himself! The one who will judge sinners is the very one who loved and gave his life for them. The triumphant Judge who stands at the end is none other than the dying Jesus on a cross, who has already taken the judgment of God on himself for the sake of the whole world. We think again of two confessional statements we have quoted before: "We should not then fear the last judgment and have a horror of it?" Calvin asks in his Geneva Catechism. "No, since, we are not to come before any other Judge than he who is our Advocate and who has taken our cause in hand to defend us" (Q. 87). "What *comfort* does the return of Christ to judge the quick and the dead give you?" asks the Heidelberg Catechism. "That in all affliction and persecution I may await with head held high the very Judge from heaven who has already submitted himself to the judgment of God for me and has removed all curse from me" (Q. 52). Because the judge will be *this* judge, we can look forward to the final judgment not with terror but "with head held high."

What about those who have not confessed this judge to be their Lord and Savior either because they have never heard of him or because they prefer to stand on the record of their moral and religious innocence in thought, word, and deed? We have already dealt with this question in our discussion of other doctrines, and we will return to it soon. At this point, however, we make the following observation: If we listen to the gospel our Reformation forebears taught us to trust above all else, we cannot follow them in the almost sadistic pleasure with which they seem to look forward to the time when God "will cast all his enemies and mine into everlasting condemnation" (continuation of the statement from the Heidelberg Catechism we have just quoted), or when we will "see the terrible vengeance which God shall execute on the wicked" (Belgic Confession, Art. 37). The good news of Jesus Christ is that God does not hate and will the destruction of sinful people who are God's enemies; God loves them and wills their reconciliation and salvation. God also commands *us* to love them, not gleefully look forward to the time when we can enjoy seeing them "get what they have coming to them" and say "I told you so." Moreover, if we know that while we ourselves were "helpless," "ungodly" sinners and enemies of God, Christ died for us (Rom. 5:6–11), how can we not do what we can by our attitudes, words, and actions to let those other sinners and enemies know that the same good news is for them too? If we do not believe it for them, how can we believe it for ourselves? If we know that the hope any of us has is that all of us will one day stand before the Judge who is the "friend of sinners" (Luke 7:34), must we not hope *for* rather than *against* the wicked who are "his enemies and mine"?

The New World

We have said that we must not speculate about what the future will be like in detail. So if we come now to talk about the "new heaven and new earth" the last judgment will bring, we must be careful not to begin thinking about streets of gold, fluffy clouds, white robes, halos, harps, and the like. Nevertheless, without giving us any literal descriptions, scripture does tell us something of what the coming kingdom of God will be like (and therefore also something about the meaning of our lives here and now).

1. *No more church!* "I saw no temple in the city, for its temple is the Lord God the Almighty and the Lamb" (Rev. 21:22). What a relief to know that it will not be like being in church all the time! What could be more boring than to spend eternity sitting around singing hymns, listening to sermons, praying, and listening to prayers (some of which already seem to last forever)! When the kingdom of God comes in its fullness, God will be loved, praised, and served without ceasing, but there will be no more church. Why? Because there will be no more need for it. At the end of history there will no longer be only a limited number of people who know about the rule of God and the new humanity brought by Christ. *Everyone* will know. There will no longer be only a relatively small community of people in the world who acknowledge the liberating lordship of Christ. *Every* knee in heaven and on earth will bow before him and *every* tongue confess him (Phil. 2:10–11). There will be no more need for missions and evangelism to invite hostile, alienated people to find their own true selves as they are reconciled to God and their fellow human beings in Christ. "All things, whether on earth or in heaven" will be reconciled and united in him (Col. 1:20; Eph. 1:10). The church's task will have been accomplished. We may eagerly and joyfully

look forward to the day when the church will be out of business once and for all.

This good news about the future demise of the church underlines something we have already learned about the nature and task of the church "between the times." The world does not exist for the sake of the church but the church for the sake of the world. Its task is to announce that God is for the world, not just for Christians and their church. It is more interested in the liberating and reconciling work of God in the world than in its own power and influence. For when its proclaimed kingdom of God comes in power and glory, it is not the world but the church that will disappear.

2. *We will all live in the city!*[7] We continue the same line of thought when we say that the New Testament uses political (not churchly) language to talk about the new world to come. The new earth and new heaven we hope for will be like a city, a "New Jerusalem" (Rev. 21:1–27), and we will be its "citizens" (Phil. 3:20). This urban image is not the only one the New Testament uses to talk about the coming kingdom of God, but it is one that is especially suggestive in our time.

We do not have to look forward to an eternal life of isolated loneliness (as pictured in the typical cartoon of someone sitting all alone on a little private cloud in a vast empty sky). Nor do we have to think of a lazy pastoral scene in which there is nothing to do but sit around for eternity in bored idleness. The Bible chooses rather the picture of city life to talk about what eternal life will be like. A city is a place where there is work to be done, where there is excitement and action, where new building and new ways of doing things are always in progress. It is a complex, cosmopolitan place where all kinds of people, of different races, classes, nationalities, and religions have to learn to live together, work together, depend on each other, cooperate with each other, be responsible to and for each other if they are to survive. On the other hand, a city is a place where there is room for real individuality, freedom from the smothering conformity and rigid conventions often imposed on people who live in small towns.

That is what the City of God will be like. It will not be a place of "retirement" in which there is nothing more to think, do, or achieve. Rather, it will be a place in which there will always be new things to learn, new things to do, new tasks to perform in service of the living God who not only once was but always will be a living, creative God who does "new things." In the "New Jerusalem" there will be community without uniformity, individuality without irresponsibility. The problem of individual rights versus community welfare will be solved in such a way that community serves individual freedom and free individuals serve the common good. Does not this city image draw together everything we are told that God willed from the very beginning in creating human beings to find self-fulfillment as they live in community with God and other people? Does it not helpfully summarize the new humanity promised us in Christ—the true humanity that frees us to be ourselves as we are reconciled to God and to other people who used to be strangers and enemies?

If we are right in this train of thought, then new light is thrown on the ever-growing urbanization of society in our time and the church's task in face of it. Middle- and upper-class Protestants in the United States tend to be suspicious of this development. They are threatened by the way it breaks down old patterns of life and threatens to destroy traditional moral values. They are frightened by the difficult social, economic, political, racial, and religious problems that arise when all kinds of people are forced to live together in a complex system of interdependence and cooperation. They long for the good old days when everything was simpler, clearer, and easier. When they can, they move their families—and their churches—as far away from inner cities as they can.

This reaction is certainly understandable. The City of God is hardly reflected in the smog-polluted, traffic-congested, crime-ridden, heartless cities people live in now. Modern cities only magnify and multiply the brutal competitiveness, alienation, loneliness, and indifference to the needs and suffering of others that were there in the good old days too but were easier to ignore and hide. Nevertheless, if we Christians look forward to life in a new heaven and a new earth that will be like life in a city, how can we fail to welcome the challenge and opportunities of urbanization? Urban life has been hallowed by the word of God; it says that is what the kingdom of God will be like—the kingdom that keeps breaking into the world here and now.

Of course, the risen Christ is at work making all things new in rural, small town, and suburban areas too. But to the extent that the church flees the city, does it not also flee the new world that is on the way? Does it not flee the God of justice and compassion who in the risen Christ may be especially at work in our crumbling, self-destructing inner cities? If we are not willing to recognize the presence of God and the promise of the New Jerusalem there, will we be able to recognize it anywhere else?

CHRISTIAN HOPE FOR INDIVIDUALS

Having discussed the Christian hope for the world, we turn to discuss the hope of Christians for individual persons. What is going to happen to *me* and those whom I love? Christians answer: "I believe in the resurrection of the body and the life everlasting."

The Resurrection of the Body

We have said that hope for the resurrection of the body is the Christian alternative to hope for the immortality of the soul. If we are to make this Christian alternative our own, we must answer three questions: Why do we confess it? What does it mean? When does it happen?

1. *Why hope for bodily resurrection?* The idea of the resurrection of the dead did not originate with Jesus or the early church. It originated in the apocalyptic eschatology of late Judaism. Jesus' ministry took place in the midst of a hot debate already going on between the Pharisees who affirmed it and the Sadducees who rejected it. But the first Christians did not hope for resurrection of the dead because Jesus and they agreed with the arguments of the Pharisees. Nor did they hope for it because they preferred it to speculations and theories about the immortality of the soul. They hoped for it because they believed that it had *happened:* a dead man actually lived again! Not just *a* man (so that the event could be considered a freak exception to the rule that dead people stay dead), but one in whom they believed God's plan for the future of all human beings was revealed. Because God raised Jesus from the dead, we may be sure that God will do the same for everyone. How is this connection between what happened to Jesus and what will happen to all of us made in 1 Cor. 15:12–22 and Rom. 8:11? Once again we see that Christian hope for the future is based on what has already happened in the past.

2. *What does it mean?* We began to answer this question in our discussion of the resurrection of Jesus. We take up here where we left off there. The key to understanding hope for bodily resurrection lies in the fact that for the biblical writers "body," or "flesh," is a synonym for "human being." Resurrection of the body means resurrection of a *person.* To hope for it is to hope that my human self, the person that "I" am, will live again. I will not be someone or something different from who and what I am now. I will be *myself.* The same holds true, of course, for other people.

Now for the biblical writers (as for realistic modern people), it is impossible to think of a human being without a body. How can anyone be a distinct, recognizable individual person without a body? Without ears, eyes, mouths, hands, feet, and the male or female identity that make us the men or women we are, how could we love, praise, serve, and live in communion with God? How could we recognize, communicate with, and relate personally to other people? Resurrection of *persons* means necessarily resurrection of their *bodies*.

This does not mean hope for the revivification or resuscitation of our present physical bodies. The writers of the New Testament knew as well as we do that these bodies may be deformed or disabled, and that in any case after death they decompose and "return to dust." Straining to express the inexpressible, Paul said that we will have perfect "spiritual bodies" (1 Cor. 15:42–44). We cannot and need not try to conceive exactly what that might mean. But if we follow the rule that our best clue to what is going to happen to us is what happened to Jesus, we may say that our resurrected "spiritual" bodies will be something like his resurrected body. First John 3:2 says that we do not know what we will be, but we do know that we will be "like him."

According to the Gospel stories of Jesus' postresurrection appearances (Matt. 28:9–10; Luke 24:13–50; John 20:11–29; 21:1–13), the disciples recognized the risen Jesus as the same earthly Jesus they had known before. He was no disembodied ghost. He walked and talked, ate and drank, and could be touched. He had a *body*. But it was a mysteriously *different* body. It was so transformed that even those who knew him best did not always recognize him. He could suddenly vanish from sight or appear in a room with locked doors. Whatever we make of the details of these strange stories, they tell us that there was both continuity and discontinuity between the physical-earthly and the spiritual-resurrected Jesus. He was the same person in a different way.

Something like that is what we may hope for as we look forward to life in the "spiritual bodies" Paul tells us about. We will not (as some versions of the doctrine of the immortality of the soul teach) lose our personal identity and be dissolved into some kind of universal spirit or realm of spirituality like a drop of water returning to the ocean. In an unimaginably different and better way we will still be the individual human beings we are now, with the ability to have a genuinely personal relationship with God and other people (including those who have gone before us and those who will come after us) in the eternal "communion of the saints."

3. *When will our resurrection happen?* The New Testament gives us two different answers to this question. On the one hand we are told that

immediately at death we may expect to be with Christ. In Luke 23:42 Jesus says to the dying thief, "Today you will be with me in Paradise." In Philippians 1:23 Paul expresses his longing to "depart and be with Christ." On the other hand, Paul tells us that there is something like a waiting sleep of all the dead until they are all raised at the same time in what was later called a "general resurrection" at the end of history (1 Cor. 15:51–52; 1 Thess. 4:13–18).

Classical Protestant tradition neatly solved this problem by combining the doctrines of the immortality of the soul and the resurrection of the body. When we die, God assigns each of us our eternal destiny. Our souls go immediately to heaven or hell, whereas our bodies remain in the grave. On the last day our bodies are raised and reunited with our souls for a final judgment and assignment to heaven or hell (see chap. 34 of the Westminster Confession). This explanation can be criticized for several reasons: (1) Its separation of body and soul, even temporarily, is unbiblical. (2) The final judgment seems superfluous if the souls of the righteous and the wicked have already been assigned their permanent places immediately after their death. Why do it all over again? (3) The traditional explanation confuses the categories of time and eternity. After death a person is beyond our creaturely categories of space and time. Our distinctions between present and future and the time between them (as well as our categories of up and down) are no longer applicable. The Bible recognizes this when it says that "with the Lord one day is like a thousand years" (2 Peter 3:8). Events that from our point of view are widely separated in time may happen simultaneously from the standpoint of "God's eternal Now," which includes past, present, and future all at once. (4) Although the traditional explanation does combine two expressions of the New Testament hope for the future, the New Testament itself does not seek to reconcile or combine them but is content to let them stand in their seeming contradiction and leaves unanswered our questions about exactly when and how it will all happen. Should we not do the same?

Without trying in an unbiblical way to know or say too much about what is called the "intermediate state" of the dead between the time of their death and the final judgment, perhaps we can nevertheless say one thing about it based on what we do know about the coming of the rule of God who raises the dead and will make all things new. We may believe that Jesus' promise to the thief on the cross applies to each one of us: *This day,* at the very moment of death, we will be raised to be with Christ. For us, all the heartache, pain, suffering, and injustice that are part of human life in this world will be over once and for all. But they will not be over for those who still live and will yet live in such a world. If God is a God who loves and suffers with and for a suffering world, then that is also true of those who live in communion with God. As God will never rest until God's plan to create a whole new heaven and earth is fulfilled, so the dead who are with God will not find perfect rest until then. Until that time comes, those who have died and share God's eternal life still live in their own way as we do "between the time." For them too the kingdom of God has already come in all its fullness, but they too still wait for the time when there will be no more mourning or crying or pain or death anymore, for anyone, anywhere (Rev. 21:4). They do not wait to get their bodies back so that their own personal eternal happiness may be complete; they wait for the restoration of all creation, for their own joy in living with God will not be complete until it is shared by everyone.

This "already–not yet" character of the life of those who are already with the Lord may be bad news for those who want total, instant gratification for themselves in the next life as in this one. But it is good news for Christians. For one thing, it means that we can be comforted by the knowledge that not only God but also the whole heavenly company (including our own loved ones who have gone before us) know and care about us and our problems, suffering, and needs. It also means that after we die, as in this life, we will be given the privilege of sharing in God's own compassion for suffering people in a suffering world until that great day when there is a fulfilled new humanity for *all* people in a brand new world that once and for all will be God's good creation.

The Life Everlasting

The New Testament teaches that there are two kinds of future life: life in heaven and life in hell. If we are to think correctly about this great either-or, we must follow the rules we have learned for all Christian thinking about the future: (1) We must not take literally but seek the meaning of the symbolic language of Jesus and the writers of the New Testament. (2) We must remember that the clearest clue to what is going to happen in the *future* is what God has been doing in the *past.*

What then is *heaven?* Not a place located somewhere in outer space where we will escape from our humanity to become angels or disembodied spirits. Heaven is an eternal life of genuine, completely free realization of our humanity in a new heaven and a new earth. It is the life originally willed for us by God the Creator of heaven and earth, lived for us by Jesus Christ (true God *and* true human being), and promised and worked in us by God's life-renewing Holy Spirit. It is the eternal life of the self-fulfillment that comes in loving, praising, and serving God, and in living in peace with fellow human beings. Life in heaven can be described as entering into "rest" (Heb. 4:1), but that does not mean lying down and doing nothing forever. It means rest from all the frustration, conflict, and self-contradiction that result from our self-destructive attempts to live without or against God and other people. It means coming to rest or peace with our true selves as we live in free and open community with them.

And what is *hell?* Not a fiery or dark place of eternal torment located somewhere underground between the United States and China. It is living apart from or in hostility toward God and other people, and therefore denying one's own true humanity—forever. It is living forever in loneliness that results from the inability or unwillingness to love and be loved. It is *never* coming to rest but living *forever* in the frantic, self-destroying attempt to be what one is not and never can be. Hell, in other words, is not a kind of eternal life at all; it is a kind of eternal *death.*

Who is going where? We will not repeat here what we have already said about salvation and damnation in general (see chapter 7 on predestination). In the present context we will only try to correct a common misunderstanding of the meaning of heaven and hell.

The misunderstanding is that heaven is the reward for being good and hell the punishment for being bad—like an eternal lollipop or eternal spanking promised good or bad children. According to Jesus and the writers of the New Testament, the truth is just the opposite: *Heaven is for sinners and hell is for "good" people.* To whom did Jesus address gracious words of invitation and promise? To people who were obviously guilty sinners—dishonest tax collectors, prostitutes, political and social outcasts rejected by respectable people, and religious heretics condemned by orthodox believers. And to whom did Jesus address his sternest warnings and threats of hellfire and eternal misery? He almost never mentioned hell except when he spoke to the scribes and Pharisees—the moral, religious, church-going people of his day who wanted above all else to preserve the "moral values" and "religious traditions" that "once made our country great." In Matt. 21:31 he says it with shocking bluntness: "Truly I tell you, the tax collectors and the prostitutes are going into the kingdom of God ahead of you." Again and again Jesus predicted that when the kingdom comes there will be a surprising reversal of the situation of "insiders" and "outsiders," the "first" and the "last" (Matt. 19:30; 20:1–16; 25:31–46; Luke 13:29–30).

Why is there this complete contradiction of our popular understanding of the way God ought to dispense rewards and punishments? The point, of course, is not that God approves of godlessness and immorality, and condemns religious piety and morality. The point is that only people who are unworthy sinners and know it can be aware of their need for the acceptance, forgiveness, love, and help of God and their fellow human beings. Only they can love the God who loves *sinners*. Only they are moved to care for other undeserving sinners. Only those who know that they do not *have* the true humanity that comes from living in a fellowship of mutual love with God and other people can *seek* and *find* it.

On the other hand, there are those who are convinced that they are morally and spiritually in good shape and can take care of themselves. They do not know a God who cares for us as good earthly mothers and fathers care for their children even when they do not deserve it or ask for it. Such people know only a great heavenly Paymaster who pays off for services rendered or demands retribution for debts not paid. Therefore they do not know the true God at all. And they do not know other people as brothers and sisters whose forgiveness, love, and help they need; they know them only as rivals or inferiors to be ignored, rejected, or used to practice their superior virtue and wisdom on. They cut themselves off from their true humanity as they cut themselves off from their fellow human beings. As long as they persist in their proud inhumanity without God and neighbor, they can never enter the kingdom of God, nor will they even want to on the terms on which it is offered.

So heaven is for sinners and hell is for "good" people. To say this is to take seriously the consequences of Protestant insistence that salvation comes by God's freely given grace alone and not by our good works (not even by our faith considered as a good work). When we understand this, then talk about heaven and hell is no longer a pagan matter of adding up the score to decide who will be in and who will be out with God. It becomes the essence of the good news of Jesus Christ. This good news does have two sides, warning and promise. But it is warning to "good" people and promise to sinners.

This is the warning: Do you (with others like you) want to be autonomous, self-sufficient people who need neither God nor other people for anything except perhaps to recognize and reward your superior moral insight and integrity, your correct liberal or conservative political position, your true religion? Do you want to be able to judge, accept, or reject other people (and perhaps even God and the Word of God) according to whether they agree with your views of correct sexual, familial, and social behavior and relationships; and according to your understanding of what people must believe, say, and do if they want to be "saved"? Do you want to live as if everyone who thinks and lives differently from you (maybe including God) needs to be forgiven, instructed, and corrected by you, whereas you have no need to be forgiven, instructed, and corrected by them? Do you want, in other words, to live as if God and other people may need your love and help but you do not need theirs? Very well, you may *have* what you want. You (with others like you) may live in the godless and inhuman loneliness of your moral superiority and religious self-sufficiency now and forever. You will go to hell (already live in hell) not because God "sent" you there but because you have chosen to live there. (But you need to know that even if you "make your bed in hell" God will still be there—the God who is for and not against you. You will never be able to escape the relentless love of God in Jesus Christ that is for hell-bent people just like you. This relentless love longs for you to find your own true humanity in community with the God and fellow human beings you were willing to go to hell to get away from.)

And this is the promise: Are you willing to admit that no matter how moral and religious you are, you are just as prone as the most immoral and irreligious to get lost in life, lose sight of who you are, become confused about how you (and other people) ought to live? Are you willing to admit that it is your fault—that you keep losing your own identity because in one way or another (in your immorality and lack of religious faith or precisely in your too confident morality and piety) you have cut yourself off from God and the fellow human beings who alone can enable you to find yourself? Are you willing to risk the pain of giving up your proud or anxious self-sufficiency to be reconciled with God and other people (*all* of them)? Do you want to be born again to be a truly free, truly human man or woman—free to be yourself as you are free for the disturbing, demanding love of God and other human beings? Then you may enter the kingdom of God, no matter how sinful you may have been in your religious piety or lack of it, your immorality or morality. You may have eternal life not only in the future but already now. All you have to do is choose the God who in Jesus Christ has chosen just such lost sinners as you. That is, all you have to do is find yourself in surrender to the Christ who was totally with and for God, totally with and for other people, and therefore totally human.

That is the Good News addressed both to sinful outsiders and to sinful insiders. For God so loved the world—the *sinful* world—that God came in Jesus Christ to bring eternal life to those who believe in him. He came not to *condemn* the world but that the world—the whole world!—might be *saved* through him (John 3:16–17).

FOR FURTHER REFLECTION AND STUDY

On "Christian Hope, Hopelessness, and False Hopes"

1. Read the book of Ecclesiastes now if you have not already read it. Should this book be in the Bible? What can Christians learn from it?
2. Is it true that if there is no hope for the future, the present will be meaningless?
3. Some Christians have argued that we ought not be overly concerned about all the suffering and death caused by social injustices and war, for this life is not really all that important anyway. Do you agree?
4. Summarize the reasons for arguing that the doctrine of the immortality of the soul is less than Christian? Do you think they are valid?

On "Guidelines for Asking the Right Questions"

1. Does talk about the symbolic character of the New Testament's language about the future undermine the authority of scripture? What about the assertion that there is a development and inconsistency in biblical hope for the future?
2. Why is the past the clearest indication of what the future will be like?
3. Do you agree that it is better not to try to give a detailed description of the end of the world based on Daniel and Revelation?

On "Christian Hope for the World"

1. Why is it important to emphasize that *Christ* will be the judge of the world?
2. Do you agree that it is wrong for Christians to look forward to the time when God "will cast all his and our enemies into everlasting condemnation"?
3. Were you glad or sorry to read that in the life to come we will not be idle but will have work to do?
4. What do you think of the argument that life in God's new creation will be city life?

On "Christian Hope for Individuals"

1. Read 1 Cor. 15:35–50. What does Paul think our resurrected bodies will be like? Does 1 John 3:2 help with this question?
2. Does our discussion of the resurrection of the body help answer the familiar question whether we will recognize our loved ones in heaven?
3. Do you think we were right in our criticism of (and alternative to) the classical Christian understanding of what happens between the death of an individual and the final judgment of the world?
4. Jean-Paul Sartre wrote a play about hell called *No Exit*. He has one of the characters say: "There's no need for red-hot pokers. Hell is—other people!"[8] What do you think he meant? Does his interpretation of what hell is like agree with the interpretation given in this book?
5. Would it be more biblical and Christian to think about eternal life in heaven as an angelic or divine life rather than as a fulfilled *human* life?
6. How would you try to comfort someone who is dying? Someone who has recently lost a loved one?

Notes

PART 1
THE METHOD AND TASK OF THEOLOGY

1. This question is the first question of several Christian catechisms.

CHAPTER 1
WHO IS A THEOLOGIAN?

1. Rules of interpretation are discussed in the Scots Confession, chap. 18; the Second Helvetic Confession, chap. 1; the Westminster Confession, chap. 1; The Confession of 1967, I.C.2; A Declaration of Faith, 6.3. The most often cited confessions in this book are found in the *Book of Confessions* of the Presbyterian Church (U.S.A.), published by the Office of the General Assembly, 100 Witherspoon St., Louisville, KY 40202–1396. For A Declaration of Faith, see *The Proposed Book of Confessions* (Atlanta: Presbyterian Church in the United States, 1976). For other collections and discussions of the creeds and confessions of both Reformed churches and other churches, see John H. Leith, *Creeds of the Churches* (New York: Doubleday & Co., 1963); and the three-volume work of Philip Schaff, *Creeds of Christendom* (Grand Rapids: Baker Book House, 1966). Lukas Vischer has collected twentieth-century confessions and statements of faith of Reformed churches around the world in *Reformed Witness Today,* published by the *Evangelische Arbeitsstelle Oekumene Schweiz,* Sulgenauweg 26, Bern, Switzerland.

2. Quoted by Karl Barth, *Church Dogmatics* I/2 (Edinburgh: T. & T. Clark, 1956), 607.

CHAPTER 2
WHO SAYS SO?

1. For a more complete discussion of creeds and confessions, see "The Confessional Nature of the Church," a study paper commended to the church

for study by the 198th General Assembly (1986) of the Presbyterian Church (U.S.A.).

2. From Franklin H. Littell, *The German Phoenix* (New York: Doubleday & Co., 1960), 180ff.

3. John H. Leith, *Creeds of the Churches* (New York: Doubleday & Co., 1963), 5.

4. Quoted by Karl Barth, *Church Dogmatics* I/2 (Edinburgh: T. & T. Clark, 1956), 658.

PART 2
GOD AND HUMAN BEINGS

1. I am indebted in this section to Paul Tillich's definition of faith as "ultimate concern" and to his understanding of any person's god as that about which he or she is ultimately concerned. See his *Dynamics of Faith* (New York: Harper & Row, 1957).

2. John Calvin, *Institutes of the Christian Religion*, ed. John T. McNeill, trans. Ford L. Battles (Philadelphia: Westminster Press, 1968), 1.1.1. Subsequent references to this work will be identified in parentheses in the text; for example, (*Institutes* 1.1.1).

CHAPTER 3
HOW CAN WE FIND GOD?

1. Karl Barth, *Theological Existence Today* (London: Hodder & Stoughton, 1933), 52.

2. George S. Hendry, *The Westminster Confession for Today* (Richmond: John Knox Press, 1960), 23.

3. Quoted in J. Dillenberger and Claude Welch, *Protestant Christianity Interpreted Through Its Development* (New York: Charles Scribner's Sons, 1954), 216.

4. Quoted in Charles C. West, *Outside the Camp* (New York: Doubleday & Co., 1959), 56.

CHAPTER 4
HOW DOES GOD FIND US?

1. Luther speaks specifically of the way in which scripture "holds" Christ: "Here you will find the swaddling clothes and the manger in which Christ lies. Simple and little are the swaddling clothes but dear is the treasure, Christ, that lies in them" (quoted by B. A. Gerrish, "Biblical Authority and the Continental Reformation," *Scottish Journal of Theology* [December 1957]: 343).

2. The classical confessions of the sixteenth and seventeenth centuries emphasize scripture as the word of God. But the Westminster Confession (1.1; emphasis added here and in the following) knows the distinction between scripture and God's original revelation in Israel's history and in Christ: "It pleased the Lord, at sundry times, and in diverse manners, to reveal himself and

to declare his will unto his church; and *afterwards* for the better preserving and propagating of the truth . . . to commit the same wholly unto writing." And the Second Helvetic Confession (chap. 1) strongly emphasizes *preaching* as the word of God: "Wherefore when this Word of God is now preached in the church by preachers lawfully called, we believe that the very Word of God is proclaimed and received by the faithful."

But it is especially contemporary confessions that emphasize the unity and distinction between the three forms of the word of God. The Confession of 1967 (I.C.2) says: "The one sufficient revelation of God is Jesus Christ, *the Word of God incarnate,* to whom the Holy Spirit bears unique and authoritative witness through the Holy Scriptures, which are received and obeyed as *the word of God written.*" The Declaration of Faith (6.1) says that "we confidently listen for his Word in Jesus Christ, in holy Scripture, in preaching and the sacraments." The chapter then follows this outline: Jesus Christ is the *living* Word of God, the Bible is the *written* Word of God, preaching *communicates* the Word of God, the sacraments *confirm* the Word of God.

3. See the statement on the relation between Christians and Jews, the church and Israel, in the Declaration of Faith (7.3). It concludes: "We are bound together with them in the single story of those chosen to serve and proclaim the living God."

4. Declaration of Faith (1.5): "God is at work beyond our story. We know that God is not confined to the story we can tell. The story itself tells us God works his sovereign will among all peoples of the earth. We believe God works beyond our imagining throughout the universe."

CHAPTER 5
WHO IS GOD?

1. Sallie McFague, in her *Models of God: Theology for an Ecological, Nuclear Age* (Philadelphia: Fortress Press, 1987), develops a doctrine of the Trinity as Mother, Lover, and Friend.

2. This is the suggestion of Leonardo Boff, *Trinity and Society* (Maryknoll, N.Y.: Orbis Books, 1988), 121, 170ff.

3. On the "Wisdom" of God, see Rosemary Ruether, *Sexism and God-Talk: Toward a Feminist Theology* (Boston: Beacon Press, 1983), 57ff; and Boff, *Trinity and Society,* 41.

4. Jürgen Moltmann, *The Way of Jesus Christ* (San Francisco: HarperCollins, 1990), 83. On the feminine Holy Spirit, see also Boff, *Trinity and Society,* 196ff.

5. Perhaps the best discussion of the development of the doctrine of the Trinity in the ancient church is J.N.D. Kelly, *Early Christian Doctrines* (London: A. & C. Black, 1972). Excellent but less technical discussions are found in George S. Hendry, *The Westminster Confession for Today* (Richmond: John Knox Press, 1960), chap. 2; and in William C. Placher, *A History of Christian Theology* (Philadelphia: Westminster Press, 1983), chap. 6.

6. For feminist criticisms of a monarchical understanding of God and a search for an alternative, see the works of Sallie McFague and Rosemary

Ruether mentioned above, and Anna Case-Winters, *God's Power: Traditional Understandings and Contemporary Challenges* (Louisville, Ky.: Westminster/John Knox Press, 1990). For a new statement of Trinitarian theology in conversation with Eastern Orthodoxy, see the excellent work of Boff, *Trinity and Society,* and Jürgen Moltmann, *The Trinity and the Kingdom of God* (San Francisco: Harper & Row, 1981).

CHAPTER 6
WHAT IS GOD LIKE?

1. See George S. Hendry, *The Westminster Confession for Today* (Richmond: John Knox Press, 1960), 46–48.

2. Karl Barth, *Church Dogmatics* II/1 (Edinburgh: T. & T. Clark, 1956), 386.

CHAPTER 7
WHAT DOES GOD WANT WITH US?

1. C. P. Snow, *The Light and the Dark* (New York: Charles Scribner's Sons, 1947), 77, 238.

2. The Synod of Dort was convened in Dordrecht in the Netherlands in 1618. Reformed theologians from all over the continent came together there to debate the doctrine of predestination. They decided in favor of Calvin's doctrine of double predestination and rejected all alternatives to it. For a discussion of this debate, see "Dort, Synod of," in *Encyclopedia of the Reformed Faith,* ed. Donald K. McKim (Louisville, Ky.: Westminster/John Knox Press, 1992). See also the related article on "Arminianism."

3. For a similar discussion of Pelagianism, especially as it is related to evangelism, see Shirley C. Guthrie, "A Reformed Theology of Evangelism," in *Evangelism in the Reformed Tradition,* ed. Arnold B. Lovell (Decatur, Ga.: CTS Press, 1990), 75ff.

4. Karl Barth is the first Reformed theologian to have interpreted predestination exclusively "in Christ." We are indebted to him for many of the insights in this chapter. See *Church Dogmatics* II/2 (Edinburgh: T. & T. Clark, 1956), 3–509, for Barth's discussion.

5. Dietrich Bonhoeffer, *The Cost of Discipleship* (New York: Macmillan Co., 1963), 99.

PART 3
GOD THE CREATOR AND CREATION

CHAPTER 8
WHAT ARE WE DOING HERE?

1. In this discussion of the relation between the Christian doctrine of creation and modern science, I am especially indebted to Langdon Gilkey, *Maker*

of Heaven and Earth: The Christian Doctrine of Creation in the Light of Modern Knowledge (Lanham, Md.: University Press of America, 1985). In general, this fine book remains a very helpful discussion of the doctrine of creation.

2. Most recent discussions of the doctrine of creation understand it in light of the ecological crisis of our time. See Jürgen Moltmann, *God in Creation* (San Francisco: Harper & Row, 1985), 20ff.; Daniel L. Migliore, *Faith Seeking Understanding* (Grand Rapids: Wm. B. Eerdmans, 1991), 80ff.; Sallie McFague, *Models of God: Theology for an Ecological, Nuclear Age* (Philadelphia: Fortress Press, 1987), pt. 1.

3. Strictly speaking, the church's doctrine of creation "out of nothing" is not a biblical doctrine. Borrowing from ancient Babylonian myths, the earliest accounts of creation in the Old Testament describe creation as the victory of God over a primal chaos, sometimes symbolized by a sea dragon. See, for instance, Job 26:12; Psalms 74:13–14 and 89:10; Isaiah 51:9. On the other hand, the doctrine of creation out of nothing finds some support in such New Testament texts as John 1:3; 1 Corinthians 8:6; and Colossians 1:16, which say that *all* things were created by God through Jesus Christ.

4. For a criticism of traditional theism and a discussion of the world as God's body, see McFague, *Models of God,* 59ff.

5. Moltmann's defense of Christian panentheism is found in his *The Trinity and the Kingdom of God* (San Francisco: Harper & Row, 1981), 108–11, and in his *God in Creation,* 13–19.

6. John Calvin, *Institutes of the Christian Religion,* ed. John T. McNeill, trans. Ford L. Battles (Philadelphia: Westminster Press, 1968), 3.10.1. Both chap. 10, "How We Must Use the Present Life and Its Helps," and chap. 19, "Christian Freedom," remain good discussions of Christian life in God's good creation.

CHAPTER 9
WHY DOESN'T GOD DO SOMETHING ABOUT IT?

1. Harold B. Kushner's widely read *When Bad Things Happen to Good People* (New York: Shocken Books, 1981) is an attempt to deal with this classical philosophical-theological statement of the problem of evil.

2. See Langdon Gilkey's *Maker of Heaven and Earth* (Lanham, Md.: University Press of America, 1985).

3. See Calvin's discussion of the doctrine of providence in his *Institutes of the Christian Religion,* ed. John T. McNeill, trans. Ford L. Battles (Philadelphia: Westminster Press, 1968), 1.16–18.

4. See Reinhold Niebuhr's discussion of this explanation in *The Nature and Destiny of Man,* vol. 1 (New York: Charles Scribner's Sons, 1949).

5. A number of recent thinkers have tried to understand the meaning of human suffering in light of God's own suffering. See Jürgen Moltmann, *The Crucified God* (New York: Harper & Row, 1974); Terence E. Fretheim, *The Suffering of God: An Old Testament Perspective* (Philadelphia: Fortress Press, 1984); Douglas John Hall, *God and Human Suffering: An Exercise in the Theology of the Cross* (Minneapolis: Augsburg Publishing House, 1986).

CHAPTER 10
WHO ARE WE?

1. With this expression and in the following discussion I follow Karl Barth's discussion of "The Basic Form of Humanity" in *Church Dogmatics* III/2 (Edinburgh: T. & T. Clark, 1956), 222ff. Our whole discussion of humanity in the image of God is influenced by Barth's interpretation of it in the volume just mentioned and in his discussion of "Man and Woman" in III/4, 116ff. I hope, however, that I have made clear my disagreement with Barth's tendency to maintain a traditional hierarchical view of the relation between men and women.

2. Letty M. Russell's works are especially helpful in enabling us to understand "partnership" as a key to the meaning of creation in the image of God. See her *The Future of Partnership* (Philadelphia: Westminster Press, 1979) and *Growth in Partnership* (Philadelphia: Westminster Press, 1981).

CHAPTER 11
WHY DON'T YOU JUST BE YOURSELF?

1. See Calvin's *Institutes* 2.1.11 for a discussion of this paradox. When the New Testament speaks of "natural man" as sinful or when the Reformed confessions speak of human beings as being sinners "by nature," they are referring to people who are helplessly trapped in their denial of their truly natural selves.

2. For a good discussion of sin in this form, see Daniel L. Migliore, *Faith Seeking Understanding* (Grand Rapids: Wm. B. Eerdmans, 1991), 130ff.

3. William Faulkner, *Requiem for a Nun* (Bungay, Suffolk, Eng.: Penguin Books, 1953), 233.

4. Franklin H. Littell, *From State Church to Pluralism* (New York: Doubleday & Co., 1962), 134.

5. George Bernard Shaw, *Man and Superman* (Baltimore: Penguin Books, 1952), 130.

PART 4
GOD IN CHRIST AND RECONCILIATION

CHAPTER 12
WHERE IS GOD?

1. In the following discussion I have been helped by Karl Barth's discussion of "The Miracle of Christmas," *Church Dogmatics* I/2 (Edinburgh: T. & T. Clark, 1956), 172ff.

2. Ibid., 192–96.

3. Good discussions of the story of Jesus are found in Hans Küng, *On Being a Christian* (Garden City, N.Y.: Doubleday & Co., 1976), 177ff.; and in Jürgen Moltmann, *The Way of Jesus Christ* (San Francisco: HarperCollins, 1990), 73ff.

4. Karl Barth was one of the first to understand the humiliation and

exaltation of Jesus in this way. See his *The Humanity of God* (Richmond: John Knox Press, 1960), 37ff. For a more systematic treatment, see his *Church Dogmatics* IV/1 (Edinburgh: T. & T. Clark, 1956), 132–35.

CHAPTER 13
IS GOD AGAINST US?

1. See George S. Hendry, *The Westminster Confession for Today* (Richmond: John Knox Press, 1960), 110ff.

2. See Jürgen Moltmann's development of a "trinitarian theology of the cross" in *The Crucified God* (New York: Harper & Row, 1974), especially chap. 6, "The 'Crucified God.' "

3. For the development of this analogy I am indebted to Donald Baillie, *God Was in Christ* (New York: Charles Scribner's Sons, 1948), 171ff.

4. In his book *God of the Oppressed* (San Francisco: Harper & Row, 1975), 226ff., James Cone argues persuasively that there can be no true reconciliation between oppressed people and their oppressors without liberation of the oppressed. All talk about reconciliation without liberation only blesses injustice. But it is also true that there is no true liberation without reconciliation. True liberation means liberation also from the hostility and alienation that destroy the humanity of both oppressed people and their oppressors.

CHAPTER 14
WHO'S IN CHARGE HERE?

1. See Jürgen Moltmann, *The Crucified God* (New York: Harper & Row, 1974), esp. chap. 6, "The 'Crucified God.' "

2. Roman Catholic theologian Hans Küng gives a good exposition of this interpretation in his *On Being a Christian* (Garden City, N.Y.: Doubleday & Co., 1974), 214–26.

3. Following the apostle Paul and many theologians in the history of the church, we have not made a distinction in this chapter between the meaning of Jesus' resurrection and the meaning of his ascension. We have assumed that "he ascended into heaven" does not add anything theologically new to "he rose again." In support of this assumption it can be pointed out that whereas all four of the Gospels tell the story of the resurrection, none of them tells the story of the ascension. But Acts 1:6–11 does tell this story, and if we can get beyond our tendency to read it as a "mythological" story of a first-century space trip, we can see that it tells us some important things that enrich our understanding of the significance of the resurrection:

1. The story of the ascension tells us that the earthly history of Jesus has come to an end and that after this he will be present with his followers in a new way with the coming of his Spirit and the witness of the Christian community (Acts 1:8). The ascension sets the stage for the continuation of the story of God's work in Jesus with the story of Pentecost and the birth of the church.

2. The story of the ascension underlines what the resurrection tells us about the extent and purpose of Jesus' lordship. Jesus' ascension to "be seated at

the right hand of God" does not indicate the geographical location of the ascended Christ; it is imagery from the ancient world that recognized the authority of one who sits at the right hand of a ruler to speak and act in the ruler's behalf. So if Jesus now sits at the right hand of "God, the Father almighty, creator of heaven and earth," he is Lord not just in the hearts of individual Christians or in the church but over the whole world. His work is not just to save believers but to create a whole new heaven and earth for all people.

3. The ascension tells us something about ourselves and how we stand with God. The risen Jesus who ascended into heaven to sit at the right hand of God is the one who was the friend and not the enemy of sinful people, who defended the cause of all who are helpless, poor, and oppressed. That means, to use the traditional language of the church, that all such people (every one of us in one way or another) have in the risen and ascended Jesus an "Advocate," one who is on our side, in the presence of God. More than that, it means that the Jesus who shared our humanity has taken it with him into the very "inner circle" of the communion of God the Father, Son, and Holy Spirit. If *Jesus* lives in the very heart of God, then we do too, for he was one of us. If he made the cause of humankind his own cause, then we may be sure that it is God's cause too.

A good discussion of the meaning of the ascension may be found in Jan M. Lochman's fine exposition of the Apostles' Creed in *The Faith We Confess* (Philadelphia: Fortress Press, 1984), 163–70.

PART 5
GOD THE HOLY SPIRIT AND NEW LIFE

CHAPTER 15
WHAT'S NEW?

1. Daniel L. Migliore, *Faith Seeking Understanding* (Grand Rapids: Wm. B. Eerdmans Publishing Co., 1991), 174.

2. On the Holy Spirit in creation and in the history of Israel, see Hendrikus Berkhof, *The Doctrine of the Holy Spirit* (Richmond: John Knox Press, 1967), 94ff. See also Jürgen Moltmann, *The Spirit of Life* (Minneapolis: Fortress Press, 1992), 39ff.

3. See 1 Corinthians 12:8–10; 12:28; 14:6; Romans 12:6–8; Ephesians 4:11.

4. On the institutional aspect of the church, see Berkhof, *The Doctrine of the Holy Spirit*, 51ff.

5. See the lists of gifts of the Spirit in note 3 above.

CHAPTER 16
ARE YOU A CHRISTIAN? JUSTIFICATION

1. No one has said this more movingly than Paul Tillich in his great sermon "You Are Accepted," in *The Shaking of the Foundations* (New York: Charles Scribner's Sons, 1948), 153ff.

2. Robert McAfee Brown, *The Spirit of Protestantism* (New York: Oxford University Press, 1961), 63.

3. Dietrich Bonhoeffer, *The Cost of Discipleship* (New York: Macmillan Co., 1963), 75–76.

4. Ibid., 72–73.

5. See, for instance, Krister Stendahl, *Paul among Jews and Gentiles* (Philadelphia: Fortress Press, 1976); Jürgen Moltmann, *The Spirit of Life* (Minneapolis: Fortress Press, 1992), 123ff.

CHAPTER 17
ARE YOU A CHRISTIAN? SANCTIFICATION

1. Albert Camus, *Resistance, Rebellion and Death* (New York: Alfred A. Knopf, 1961), 71–74.

2. Dietrich Bonhoeffer, *The Cost of Discipleship* (New York: Macmillan Co., 1963), chap. 1.

3. Ibid., 34.

4. Stanley Hauerwas and William H. Willimon, *Resident Aliens* (Nashville: Abingdon Press, 1989).

5. The rest of this chapter roughly follows Karl Barth, *Church Dogmatics* IV/2 (Edinburgh: T. & T. Clark, 1956), 543–53.

6. An excellent study of the relationship between Christian discipleship and possessions in Luke and Acts is found in Luke T. Johnson's *Sharing Possessions* (Philadelphia: Fortress Press, 1973). Johnson cites the story of Jesus' friendship with the rich man Zacchaeus (Luke 19:1–10) as evidence that Jesus was not against money and possessions as such. He also points out texts indicating that Jesus and the early church did not believe that to be a Christian is necessarily to give away everything one has. Luke 8:3 speaks of some women disciples who supported Jesus "out of their resources." Acts 10:2 speaks approvingly of Cornelius, a devout man who "gave alms generously to the people." Acts 9:36 mentions Tabitha, who was "devoted to good works and acts of charity."

"Sharing possessions" as well as giving everything away can be forms of authentic Christian discipleship. For Christians, the fundamental issue is not how much one has but how possessions are acquired, how highly they are valued, and how generously they are shared.

CHAPTER 18
LIVING OR DEAD?

1. On baptism in general and the issue of infant baptism in particular, see Daniel L. Migliore, *Faith Seeking Understanding* (Grand Rapids: Wm. B. Eerdmans, 1991), 211ff.

2. Claude Welch, *The Reality of the Church* (New York: Charles Scribner's Sons, 1958), 165.

3. Quoted in Robert McAfee Brown, *The Spirit of Protestantism* (New York: Oxford University Press, 1961), 99.

4. Karl Barth calls them "disturbed" sinners: *Church Dogmatics* IV/2 (Edinburgh: T. & T. Clark, 1956), 524.

5. On the traditional doctrine of the Lord's Supper and new developments in it, see Migliore, *Faith Seeking Understanding,* 220ff.

6. In the following discussion, I have been helped especially by Donald G. Miller, *The Nature and Mission of the Church* (Richmond: John Knox Press, 1957), 119ff.

7. Ibid., 126.

8. See "Decree of the Apostolate of the Laity," in *The Documents of Vatican II,* ed. Walter M. Abbott, S.J. (New York: America Press, 1966), 489ff.

CHAPTER 19
WHAT'S GOING TO HAPPEN TO US?

1. Jürgen Moltmann makes this point very clearly in his *Theology of Hope* (New York: Harper & Row, 1965), 22ff.

2. On the teaching of the New Testament on this question, see Oscar Cullmann, *Immortality of the Soul or Resurrection of the Body* (New York: Macmillan Co., 1958).

3. Reinhold Niebuhr, *The Nature and Destiny of Man,* vol. 2 (New York: Charles Scribner's Sons, 1949), 294.

4. A fine, easily understood summary of the development of eschatological hope in the Old and New Testaments is found in John Macquarrie, *Christian Hope* (New York: Seabury Press, 1978).

5. In agreement with the position taken by the Reformed tradition in general, the Westminster Confession ends with these words: "As Christ would have us to be certainly persuaded that there shall be a day of judgment, both to deter all men from sin, and for the greater consolation of the godly in their adversity: so will he have that day unknown to men, that they may shake off all carnal security, and be always watchful, because they know not at what hour the Lord will come; and may ever be prepared to say, Come, Lord Jesus, come quickly. Amen."

6. Karl Barth, *Dogmatics in Outline* (New York: Philosophical Library, 1949), 135.

7. See Harvey Cox, *The Secular City* (New York: Macmillan Co., 1965). This book, widely and enthusiastically read when it was written, sounds unrealistically optimistic about the future of cities when we see what they have become since the 1960s. It is nevertheless still a helpful book in its vision of what the City of God will be like.

8. Jean-Paul Sartre, *No Exit* (New York: Vintage Books, 1958), 47.

Index of Scripture

Genesis

1 147
1:1 150
1:2 85, 293
1:26 150
1:27 74, 159, 194, 195, 198, 202, 210
1:28 148, 150, 164, 196
1:30 195
1:31 64, 158
2:7 195, 293
2:16–17 219
2:17 196, 226
2:18 197, 198, 207
3 158, 181
3:1–4:16 386
3:1–13 218
3:16 196, 197
3:4–5 219
3:5 196
3:6 218
9:6 213
18:22–33 115
22:15–18 139
50:20 188

Exodus

13:21–22 122
19:6 365
20:1–17 215, 227, 347
20:1–18 333
20:2 57
20:2–3 77
20:3 30
20:4 74, 100, 239
20:12 30
31:1–6 293
33:7–23 101
33:11 101
33:20 101
35:31 293

Leviticus

17:11 259
19:17–18 14

Deuteronomy

4:32–40 55
6:4 77
6:4–5 14
6:20–25 333

1 Samuel

2:12 55

1 Kings

8:27 111

Job

10:21 384
23:3 39
26:12 405 n.3
32:8 293
38—41 190

Psalms

19 46
19:1 48
22:1 184, 185, 187
23:4 187
24:1 149
31:15 114
34 184
36:5–8 108
51:5 222, 223
72 184
72:1–4 108
72:12–14 108
74:13–14 405 n.3

Psalms (cont.)
77:5 184
77:11 184
88:4–6 384
88:10–12 384
89:10 405 n.3
98:7–9 108
103:6 108, 293
103:15 169
103:17 114
104:15 160
104:30 293
115:17 384
139 113
139:8 398
139:13 15
146 293
146:7–9 108

Proverbs
3:12 110

Ecclesiastes
3:19–20 377
5:15–16 377
9:1–2 377
9:9–10 377
12:13 377

Song of Solomon
1—8 160, 165

Isaiah
1:1–17 356
1:3 55
1:10–31 255
1:17 255
3:13–15 108
11:1–2 294
11:1–5 108, 294
40:6–7 169
42:1 294
42:1–4 139–40, 294
42:8 77
42:9 115
42:14 75, 99
45:8 108
49:6 140
49:15 75
51:9 405 n.3
55:6–9 102
55:8 6, 48
55:8–9 56, 74
57:15 102
61:1 294
61:1–2 108
61:1–4 294
66:13 75, 99, 292

Jeremiah
2:8 55
6:13 356
7:1–26 356
16:21 55
31:3 105

Ezekiel
25:14 55

Daniel
1:17 293
12:2 384

Hosea
3:1 105
6:6 255
11:1–3 99
11:9 102

Joel
2:28 376

Amos
3:2 110
5:21–27 356
5:22–24 255

Micah
6:6–8 255

Malachi
3:6 114

Matthew
1:18–2:23 248
1:20 294
1:21 243
1:23 79, 231, 243
2:3–5 235
2:16 235
3:16 294
4:1–11 245
5:1–7:27 347
5:17 345
5:21–22 215, 245
5:21–48 344
5:27–28 215
5:38–39 342
5:40–42 342
5:43–48 342
6:1–16 344
6:5 348
6:9 102, 111
6:10 288
6:11 159
6:12 264, 336, 346
6:13 288
6:16 263
6:24–33 342
6:25–33 324
7:21 334
8:12 383
9:12–13 241
10:28 342
10:34–39 343
11:19 160
11:27 48
11:28 364
11:28–30 336
12:28 180, 280, 294
13:10–17 281
15:13–14 242
16:13–20 246
16:23 246
16:25 140–41, 215

17:20 301
18:8–9 383
18:20 50
18:23–35 269
19:30 397
20:1–16 397
20:25–28 366
21:21 301
21:31 396
21:31–32 216
22:13 383
22:14 121
22:34–40 14
22:37–39 210
24:3–14 168
24:3–35 279
25:30 383
25:31–46 125, 263, 397
25:41 180, 383
26:47–54 342
26:53 343
26:64 383
27:46 57, 97, 240
28:1–20 272, 287
28:9–10 393
28:13 273
28:17 273
28:18 280, 282
28:18–20 370, 372
28:19 80, 95, 364

Mark

1:1 243
1:24 339
2:5–7 245
2:15–3:6 344
2:15–27 198
2:27 345
3:22 180
8:18 281
8:33 180
8:34–35 366
8:34–36 340
8:35 341
8:35–38 243
9:1 288
9:24 324
10:17–22 342
10:45 252, 364
11:23 301
12:28–34 14
12:29–30 77
13:1–37 279
13:9–13 340
13:30 288, 385
13:32 239, 382
14:22–24 255
15:34 57, 97, 185, 187
15:39 246
16:1–19 272, 287
16:8 273
16:11 273
16:13 273

Luke

1:5 235
1:26–56 248
1:32–33 245
1:38 236, 237
1:46–55 249
1:51–53 165, 235
1:52–53 108
1:53 235
2:1–20 248
2:2 235
2:52 239
4:18 108, 294
4:18–19 242
6:20–24 242
6:20–25 165
6:20–26 235
7:34 108, 389
8:1–3 165, 242
8:3 409 n.6
9:24 267
9:35 140
9:51–56 342
9:57–62 343
10:17 280
10:18 180
10:25–28 14
10:29–37 216
10:38–41 242
11:2 102, 111
11:3 159
11:12 288
13:29–30 397
14:25–26 343
15:2 241
15:8–10 99
15:11–32 75, 126
18:10–14 216, 329
18:13 336
18:18–25 165
18:25 242
19:1–10 165, 409 n.6
19:10 105
21:5–36 279
22:44 379
23:21 242
23:42 394
23:43 383
24:11 273
24:13–16 275
24:13–50 393
24:1–51 272, 287
24:30–31 275
24:36–39 273

John

1 79
1:1 57, 79, 150
1:1–3 96, 165
1:1–14 62, 234, 238
1:3 85, 405 n.3
1:5 167, 190, 235
1:14 235
1:18 58
1:29 123, 255
2:1 160
3:1–21 313
3:4–6 292
3:8 67, 294, 301, 376
3:16 106
3:16–17 105, 399

John (cont.)
3:17 123, 341
3:19 227
4:7–26 242
4:18 321
4:34 79
5:19 79
6:42 244
6:69 339
7:53–8:11 105, 241
8:31 133
8:36 133
8:44 180
10:16 356
10:30 79
10:38 92
12:12–24 336
12:31 175, 180
14—15 295
14:6 48, 54, 69
14:9 58, 79, 102
14:15–18 80
14:16 80, 295
14:26 295, 305
14:30 175
15:18–21 340
16:11 175
16:12 295
16:13 305
17:9 121
17:15 338
17:18 338
18:36 338, 384
19:6 242
20:1–21 272, 287
20:11–29 393
20:14–17 275
20:21 364
20:24–28 273
20:25–27 272, 287
21:1–13 393

Acts
1:6–11 407 n.3
1:8 407 n.3
2:1 295, 308
2:4 96
2:21 128
2:22–36 234
2:36 231, 276, 280
2:44–45 165
5:29 163
7:48 112–13
8:9–11 245
9:31 292
9:36 165, 409 n.6
10:2 165, 409 n.6
10:38 294
10:42 259
13:44 62
14:16–18 46
17:22–31 46, 49
17:23 51
17:28 157

Romans
1:16–32 51
1:18 260
1:18–23 46
1:21–25 49
2:6–7 387
2:7 380
2:12–16 46
3:10–11 221
3:21–26 108, 329
3:24 252, 319
3:25 255, 259
4:17 151
5:6–8 105, 319
5:6–10 108
5:6–11 256, 389
5:8 258
5:9 260
5:12–21 221, 227
5:15–21 197
5:18 123
6:1–14 265
6:1–23 329
6:23 110, 226
7:14–25 174
8:3 217
8:3–4 241
8:9 80
8:11 274, 392
8:12 217
8:18 302
8:28–30 119
8:28–37 141
8:28–39 138
8:35 137
8:37–39 180
8:38 162, 302
8:38–39 186
8:39 137, 157
9—11 65, 121, 132, 138, 141, 328
9:13 121
9:18 121
10:2–4 196
10:3 219
10:9 22, 31, 287
11:13–24 141
11:30–36 141
11:32 123, 132, 134
11:32–36 123
12:1 340
12:1–21 338
12:4–6 358
12:4–8 360
12:6 312
12:6–8 408 n.3
14:1–23 227

1 Corinthians
1:10–13 356
1:16–17 358
1:20–25 48
1:23 234
1:23 56
2:2 214
2:9 56
2:9–13 74
2:9–16 48
2:11 80
5:1 356
5:7 255
5:9–13 356
5:18–19 96
6:11 80
6:20 252, 258

7:23 252, 258
7:40 80
8:1–13 227
8:4 77
8:5 37
8:5–6 37, 38
8:6 405 n.3
11:20–22 356
12—14 303, 312
12:3 287
12:4 80, 312
12:4–5 95
12:4–6 362
12:4–27 358
12:7 309, 361
12:8–10 408 n.3
12:14–31 360
12:28 408 n.3
13 303
13:9 308
13:12 308
14:4 309
14:6 408 n.3
15:3 214
15:3–4 234
15:3–8 31, 272, 287
15:12–22 392
15:17–19 271
15:21–22 221
15:22 123
15:24–28 180, 253
15:25 279
15:26 380
15:35–50 400
15:42–44 393
15:45–49 197
15:51–52 394
15:54–57 378
16:19 352

2 Corinthians

1:19 132
3:17 80
4:4 175, 197
4:7–12 336
5:10 107, 259
5:14–15 265
5:16–21 256
5:17 151, 386
5:18 259
5:19 85, 106, 231, 268
5:20 364
5:21 241
11:14–15 180
12:7–10 115
13:13 70, 80
13:14 95

Galatians

2:11–14 356
2:19–20 266
2:20 265
3:13 252–53
3:28 203
4:4 238
5:19–21 217, 304
5:22–23 303
5:22–25 334, 360

Ephesians

1:3–10 123
1:3–11 119, 121
1:3–14 141
1:4 122, 334
1:10 132, 134, 389
1:15–23 138
1:16–23 69
1:19–23 180
1:21 78, 162, 282
1:23 156
2:1 226
2:11–22 358
2:14 106, 267
2:15 386
2:18 85
3:14–19 55
4:1–16 358
4:4–6 31, 80, 95, 358–59, 361
4:6 77
4:11 408 n.3
4:12 309
4:13 31, 106
4:13–16 337
4:30–32 360
4:31–32 303
5:6 260
5:25–26 96
5:26 86

Philippians

1:15–17 357
1:23 394
2:1–3 360
2:1–13 334, 347
2:3–8 267
2:4 341
2:5–11 31
2:6 197
2:9 274
2:9–11 280
2:10–11 389
2:11 22, 287
2:13 335
3:6 196
3:8–11 55
3:12–16 337
3:13 264
3:20 338, 390
4:8–9 293
4:15 352
4:22 352

Colossians

1:13 180, 186, 253
1:15 197
1:15–16 165
1:15–20 69
1:16 96, 157, 162, 405 n.3
1:19–20 123, 256
1:20 389
1:21–22 334
2:9 79
2:15 186, 253
3:5–6 260
3:10 214
3:11 156
4:15 352

1 Thessalonians
4:13–18 385, 394
4:16 383
5:23 86, 96

1 Timothy
2:3–4 105, 259
2:4 123, 133, 134
6:10 165
6:16 102, 380

2 Timothy
3:16 62

Titus
2:14 253
3:4 96

Hebrews
1:1 14
1:1–2 165
1:2 96
4:1 396
4:15 240
5:7 379
8—10 255
9:9 259
9:14 259
10:10 96, 259
10:13 279
10:14 259
12:6–7 110
13:8 116
13:12 259

James
1:17 114
2:14–26 332
3:9 213

1 Peter
1:18 253
2:9 334, 365
3:13–16 287

2 Peter
1:19–21 62
2:4 179
3:8 394
3:9 123
3:13 386, 387

1 John
1:8 336
2:4 55
3:2 382, 393, 400
3:14 226
3:14–18 227
4:1 297
4:8 104, 116
4:11 267
4:12 60
4:14 105
4:16 116
4:19 258

Jude
6 179

Revelation
3:19 110
3:20 128
5:6 254
5:12 254
17:14 180, 280, 282
20:10 180
21:1 151, 386, 387
21:1–27 390
21:4 395
21:22 389

Index of Subjects

Abbott, S. J., Walter M., 410 n.8
abortion, xii, 127
accidents, 172
acid rain, 148
adultery, 215, 225, 227, 344
aging, 160, 168–69, 173, 380. *See also* evil
AIDS, xii, 166, 270
alcohol, 162, 163, 217, 227
alcoholism, 177, 348
American culture, 4, 263, 316, 317, 374
Anselm, 19, 257–58, 259
antisemitism, 11, 238–39
Apollinarianism, 236
Apostles' Creed, 32; deficiency, 230–31
Arminianism, 404 n.2
astrology, 163
atheism, 51, 53, 97, 153; atheist Christians, 78
atonement, doctrine of, 250–69; and ancient religion, 256–57; and relationships, 267–68, 269; biblical images, 251–62; blood theology, 255; costly love, 260; death of sinners, 265–66; financial image, 252–53, 258; forgiveness, 263–65; God's initiative, 257–59, 262; legal image, 255–56, 259, 264; military image, 253–54; sacrifice, 259, 268; sacrificial image, 254–55, 258–59; satisfaction theory, 258, 259; substitutionary, 230, 250. *See also* reconciliation
attributes of God, doctrine of the, 97–117; changeable, 115; consistency, 122; eternity as presence, 113; goodness, 112; gracious, 121; immutability for all, 114–15; interpersonal, 125; justice, 106–11, 121, 134, 250; love, 104–6, 121, 134, 257–59; loving and sovereign, 101–4; omniabsence, 184; omnipotence in weakness, 111–12, 117, 124, 247–48, 302; omnipresence for all, 112–13, 157; omniscience as friend, 113, 122–23; righteousness (*see* justice); wrath of love, 109–10, 125, 131, 250, 254, 259, 260–62, 268, 315
Augustine, 19, 126, 222, 258

authority, the problem of, 20–35, 313

Baillie, Donald, 407 n.3
baptism. *See* church
Barmen Declaration, 34
Barth, Karl, x, xii, 17, 34, 44, 107, 138, 168, 236, 387, 401 n.2, 402 nn.4,1; 404 nn.2,4; 406 nn.1–2; 406–7 n.4, 409 nn.5,4; 410 n.6
Battles, Ford L., 402 n.2, 405 nn.6,3
Berkhof, Hendrikus, x, 408 nn.2,4
bias, xii, 8, 10, 11, 15, 26, 49, 133, 174, 215, 273, 308
Bible. *See* scripture
birth defects, 168. *See also* evil, natural evil
blood of Jesus. *See* atonement, doctrine of
Boesak, Allan, xii
Boff, Leonardo, xii, 403 nn.2–4; 403–4 n.6
Bonhoeffer, Dietrich, 141, 326–27, 329, 333, 404 n.5, 409 nn.3–4,1;
Book of Common Prayer, 51
Book of Confessions, 32, 401 n.1
Brief Statement of Faith, 34
Brown, Robert McAfee, 322, 408 n.2, 409 n.3
Brueggemann, Walter, xiii
Buddhism, 270
Bullinger, Heinrich, 32

Caesar, 22
Calvin, John, x, 16, 18, 30, 32, 33, 38, 44, 58, 67, 102, 103–4, 109, 111, 120, 127, 129, 132, 135, 160, 171, 258, 259, 270, 271, 299, 308, 323, 324, 334, 355, 356, 363, 378, 382, 386, 388, 402 n.2, 404 n.2, 405 n.6, 405 n.3, 406 n.1
Calvinism, 103, 137, 175, 225
Camus, Albert, 330–31, 332, 334, 337, 339, 340, 341, 347, 354, 409 n.1
cancer, 166, 168, 170, 190, 270. *See also* evil, natural evil
Canons of the Synod of Dort, 33
capital punishment, 110, 127, 269
capitalism, 77, 127, 177, 375
Case-Winters, Anna, 403–4 n.6
Catechism of Geneva, 32
catechisms, 24
charismatic movment, 291
Christ. *See* Jesus Christ
Christian arrogance, 66
Christian hope for the future, doctrine of, 373–400; and non-Christians, 388–89; and scriptural language, 382–84; City of God, 390–91, 400, 410 n.7; communion with God, 381; community without uniformity, 390–91; completion of our humanity, 386, 389, 394, 400; confirmation of the past, 385; creation reconciled, 389–90; death, the end of us, 380; false hopes, 374–81; God at the end, 385; God's power over death, 376–81; God's promise, 380; heaven (*see* heaven); hell (*see* hell); historical optimism, 375; historical pessimism, 375–76; hope for the world, 386–91; human potential, 375; humanity of soul and body, 379; immortality of the soul, 378–81, 392, 399, 410 n.2; individual hope, 392–99; individuality without irresponsibility, 391; kingdom beyond history, 384; kingdom of God, 374, 375, 387; kingdom within history, 384; last judgment, 387–89, 394, 400; life with Jesus, 383–84; new heaven and earth, 374, 384, 386, 389–91, 407–8 n.3;

New Jerusalem, 390–91; reality of death, 379; renewal of human existence, 381; resurrection not resuscitation, 393; resurrection of the body, 374, 392–95, 400; resurrection of the person, 392–93; several future hopes, 384; sin of hopelessness, 376; ultimate fulfillment, 386. *See also* resurrection, doctrine of

Christian life: and the Apostles' Creed, 230–31; communion of the saints, 338, 347; cost of discipleship, 345; difficulty of faith, 326; faith as gift, 324; faith as obedience, 326; faith as trust, 323; faith as ultimate concern, 402 n.1; holiness of, 338; hypocrisy of, 314–15, 330–31; in but not of the world, 337–41; resident aliens, 338. *See also* sanctification, doctrine of

Christmas. *See* incarnation, doctrine of

Christology: as interpretation of history, 230. *See* God in Christ and Reconciliation, 229–88

church, doctrine of, 349–72; a fellowship of the Holy Spirit, 295, 308–12, 325; agents of reconciliation, 367, 370; always following Christ, 370; and predestination, 137–41, 359; and the kingdom of God, 64, 185, 190, 278 (*see also* kingdom of God); apostolic authority, 363; apostolic people, 363–65, 371; becoming holy, 357; Body of Christ, 59, 325, 354–56, 368, 371; branch theory, 360; called and sent with Israel, 351, 364, 403 n.3; Christians bound, God unbound, 356; definition of, 325; diversity in gift and task, 360–61; equal dependents, 367, 368; essentially corporate, 354; following a non-ideological Christ, 369–70; for the world, 366–67; God creates and rules, 353–54; Holy People, 356–58, 371; homogeneity, 360; invisibility versus visibility, 359–60; Jesus Christ is Head, 357–58, 367; listening community, 367; mission for the world, 363–64; mission of all Christians, 364–65; no monopoly on goodness, 354–55, 371; not morally superior, 356; people needing nourishment, 358; people not a building, 352–53, 371; People of God, 351–54, 371; priesthood of all believers, 365; reformed and always being reformed (*see ecclesia reformata...*); servant church, 366, 367–68; sinfulness of, 59, 360–62, 371 (*see also* sin, doctrine of); society of dissatisfied sinners, 357, 371; task of, 366–71; united and catholic, 358–63, 371; united in diversity, 358–63; we are the church, 352; wholistic ministry, 368–69; with the world, 367–68. *See also* church

church, 15; administration, 310; and compromise, 190; and faith development, 324–25; and non-Christians, 105, 136; and pluralism, 351, 362–63; and Pollyanna sentimentality, 167; and racism, 21, 45, 77–78, 96, 277, 359; and the Trinity, 81; Baby Boomers, 350; baptism, 45, 59, 310, 325, 353, 359, 364, 409 n.1; birth of, 271, 407 n.3; Christ's present rule, 282; decline, 350; discipline, 363, 364; diversity of, 309, 312,

church (cont.)
354; evangelism, 356, 368–70, 372; idolatry of, 68; indistinct from nonmembers, 350; institutional, 309, 310–11; kingdom of Christians, 278; Lord's Supper, 59, 310, 325, 358, 359, 364, 410 n.5; mission, 310, 334, 364, 372; necessity of dialogue, 362; pastoral care, 310; polity, 371; preaching, 59, 309, 310, 311, 364, 402–3 n.2; prophecy, 310; Reformation Sunday, 318; special revelation, 59; teaching, 309, 310, 311; triumphalism, 254; unity not uniformity, 312, 360, 362; word and sacraments, 325, 363, 365, 402–3 n.2; worship, 309, 311. *See also* church, doctrine of
Church Reformed and Always Being Reformed. *See ecclesia reformata semper reformandum*
civil disobedience, 163, 348
civil rights, 209, 211; movement, xi
class and classism, 4, 8, 111, 161, 163–64, 186, 359, 362
clear-cutting, 148
cold war, xi, 270
Coleman, Will, xiii
communism, 53, 77. *See also* political ideology
Cone, James, xii, 407 n.4
Confession of 1967, 34
confessional documents, the Reformed family, x, 2, 12, 15, 386
conservatism. *See* political ideology
Council of Constantinople (381), 32
Council of Nicaea (325), 32
Cousar, Charles B., xiii
Cox, Harvey, 410 n.7
creation, doctrine of, 145–65; and ancient myth, 146; and body-soul split, 152, 195, 210, 216, 380–81, 394; and evil, 152–53, 158 (*see also* kingdom of God); and human dignity, 151; and idolatry, 163–64; and Satan, 280, 281, 288; and the Holy Spirit, 305, 408 n.2; anthropocentrism, 147–49; as protest against dualism, 152–53; as witness, 146; asceticism, 159–60, 176; beginning of creation, 150–52; biblical and scientific understandings, 145, 165, 404–5 n.1; chaos, 181, 405 n.3; confidence in God, 161; continuous creation, 151; Creator in three tenses, 151; demonic powers, 162–63, 179–82; ecological crisis, 148–50, 155, 161, 277, 286, 405 n.2; fearless living, 162; geocentrism, 148–49; God's image as task, 150; God's transcendence and immanence, 153–58; good but corruptible, 162; goodness of creation, 158–61; goodness of temporal life, 160–61; human creation, 147–48, 150; human freedom, 164; materialistic faith, 159, 210; mutual interdependence, 150; mystery, 158; myth of progress, 161, 165, 225; new creation, 159; out of nothing (*ex nihilo*), 152, 236, 405 n.3; Owner and Landlord, 149–50; panentheism, 156–58, 165, 405 n.5; pantheism, 154–56, 165; stewardship, 150, 164, 196–97, 201; subleasers of God's world, 150; theism, 153–54, 165, 405 n.4; theocentrism, 149–50; through Christ, 405 n.3; victory over tyranny, 162–63; world-affirming faith, 159

Creed of Chalcedon, 32
creeds and confessions: and bias, 26; and culture, 24; and education, 23–24; and heresy, 23, 31; and history, 22, 31; and justification and sanctification, 332; and preaching, 23; and scripture, 23, 26, 30; and the church, 23; and the Holy Spirit, 26, 29; and witness, 23, 24; and worship, 22; authority of, 20, 25, 29; communal, 23; earliest, 31, 271, 287; examples, 32–35; limitations of, 24, 25, 29; nature and purpose of, 22–24; prevalence of legal imagery in, 256; Reformed tradition and, 25; signposts, 31; subordinate standard, 26; threefold word of God in, 62, 402–3 n.2
crime, 177, 223, 270, 373, 391
criminal justice, 116, 225, 269
Crow, Jim, 22
Cullmann, Oscar, 410 n.2
culture: impact on theology and ethics, 24
cursing, 215

Damascus, John of, 91, 248
David, 234, 384; and Jonathan, 202
de Bres, Guido, 33
death, 168–69, 171, 190, 226–27, 270–71, 374, 379. *See also* evil, natural evil
death of God. *See* God, death of
Declaration of Faith (1977), 34
Declaration of Faith for the Church in South Africa, 35
Declaration of Independence, 51, 200
Deism, 43, 114, 151
democracy, 225. *See* political ideology
denominationalism, 16, 227, 359, 371
Dillenberger, J., 402 n.3
disabilities, 163, 168–69, 204, 380; blind, deaf, mute, but human, 204
divorce, 202
docetism, 237
domestic violence, 166, 177, 270, 373
doubt, 5–6
drugs, 163, 348
dualism. *See* creation, doctrine of; *see also* evil
Dutch Reformed Church, 35

earth, xii; exploitation of, 148–49; God's body, 155–56, 405 n.4; mother of us all, 149
Easter, 186, 252, 253, 270–71, 273, 274, 275–87. *See also* resurrection, doctrine of
Eastern Orthodoxy, x, 76, 81, 83, 84, 88, 91, 253, 359, 403–4 n.6
ecclesia reformata semper reformandum, ix, 17–18, 19, 27, 31, 351; creeds and confessions, 25
ecology. *See* creation, doctrine of
ecumenicity, 16
election, 66, 203, 334, 353; of Israel and the church, 65–66, 138, 351, 364, 403 n.3; sign of, 138. *See also* predestination
environmental movement, 148–49
eschatology. *See* kingdom of God; Christian hope
eternal punishment, 125, 131, 254, 316, 396, 399
ethnocentrism, 163–64
evil, 166–91; and education, 176, 210; and God's presence, 170–71; and God's will, 170–71; and human sensuality, 176; and Satan, 175, 176, 179–82, 196, 198, 220, 246, 253, 271, 279, 288 (*see also* Tempter); and social influences, 177; and the kingdom of God, 284–87; and the people of God's

evil (cont.)
presence, 188; and the witness of science, 170–71; and the witness of scripture, 170–71; chaos, 181; cross, 168, 186; definition of, 176; demonic powers, 179–82 (*see also* creation, doctrine of); enslaving power, 174; existence of its own, 174; fallen angels, 179; free will, 178; human finitude, 168–69; human responsibility, 171–72; idolatry of life, 168–69; ignoring it, 167; inhumanity, 181; moral evil, 167, 173–75; mystery of, 173; natural evil, 166–67, 168–73, 270–71; natural law, 169–71; neutrality of Mother Nature, 170; omelet theory, 167; origin of, 175–79, 190; parasitical power, 182; realism, 167; relative dualism, 175; serving God's love, 188–89; slaves of sin, 178, 226, 253 (*see also* sin, doctrine of); solution in memory and hope, 191, 302; the Big Lie, 182; universal and endless, 177. *See also* creation, doctrine of
evolution, 151

failure, 171
faith. *See* Christian life
Faulkner, William, 221, 227, 406 n.3
feminist theology, xii, xiii, 73, 76, 89, 155, 218, 403 n.6
food, 162
foreigners, 211
Forsyth, P. T., 6
freedom: and the Holy Spirit, 29; individual, 27 (*see also* predestination); of God (*see* God, freedom of); of the Holy Spirit, 304–5; relative, 29
Fretheim, Terence, 405 n.5
Freud, Sigmund, 9

Gandhi, 225
gender, 8, 73–76, 202–4. *See also* Jesus Christ, gender of; Trinity, and gender
general revelation, 39–52; and evangelism and mission, 45, 46; and evil, 53, 191; and God's transcendence, 48, 49; and human sinfulness, 47 (*see also* sin, doctrine of); and idolatry, 48, 49; and John Calvin, 44; and Karl Barth, 44; and Roman Catholicism, 44; and scripture, 46; and the doctrine of creation, 143; and world religions, 50; arguments against, 47; arguments for, 45; art, 50; conscience, 42, 47; five senses, 45; natural sciences, 50, 146; natural tragedy, 47, 168, 270–71 (*see also* evil, natural evil); nature of God, 47; origin of world, 41; personal experience and, 41–42; philosophy, 50; psychology, 50; purpose of universe, 41; rational world, 42, 43; spiritual awareness, 42; world history and, 41
German Evangelical Church, 45
Gerrish, B.A., 402 n.1
ghosts, 163
Gilkey, Langdon, 403–4 n.1, 405 n.2
Gloria Patri, 70
God: absence of (*see* God, hiddenness of); and evangelism and mission, 87, 244, 249; and human beings, 37–142 (*see also* human beings, doctrine of); and natural tragedy, 47, 270–71 (*see also* resurrection, doctrine of); and sanctification (*see* sanctification, doctrine of); attributes (*see* attributes of

God, doctrine of); Creator and creation, 10, 64, 66, 82, 85, 86, 143–228, 146, 147–58, 161, 162, 175, 200–201, 294, 375–76, 387; crucified, 271, 407 nn.2,1; death of, 53, 97, 116; evidence for (*see* general revelation); Father, 74, 104, 111, 155; Father, Son, and Holy Spirit, 80 (*see also* Trinity, doctrine of); freedom of, 65, 120, 304–5, 339; Friend and Companion, 83, 101, 108, 154, 187, 199, 403 n.1; Giver of new life, 83, 214; great big Male up in the sky, 74, 116; great heavenly Granddaddy, 98, 101, 102, 116, 125; great heavenly Idea, 98, 116; great heavenly Male, 75; great heavenly Paymaster, 397; great heavenly Tyrant, 98, 101, 102, 116, 125; heavenly Bookkeeper, 56; heavenly Parent, 130–31; Helper, 82, 86, 199; hiddenness of, 48, 57, 97–99, 116, 183–85, 186; Highest Being, 100; holiness of, 339; Holy One of Israel, 102, 339, 341; immanence, 101–4, 153–58; impartial, 107; Judge, 55, 86, 109, 125, 134, 255–56, 261, 320, 329, 341; Liberator, 64; living, xi, xiii, 3, 11, 12, 18, 22, 26, 55, 63, 65, 71, 99, 114, 115, 122, 171 (*see also* Holy Spirit, doctrine of); Lover, 403 n.1; maternal Father, 75; Mind, 42; Moral Power, 42; Mother, 75, 99, 102, 104, 111, 155, 157, 292, 403 n.1; mystery of, 6, 61; oneness, 77, 152, 175; Owner and Landlord, 149–50; paternal Mother, 75; personal but not human, 99–100; preferential option for the poor, xii, 107–9, 116, 187–88, 238, 293–94, 328; Presence, 82; Preserver, 85, 147, 149, 161, 294; Protector, 85; Provider, 166; Reconciler, 10, 64, 143, 214, 387; Redeemer, 82; Renewer, 10, 143, 147, 149, 161, 387; Ruler, 82, 85, 86, 111, 147, 149, 152, 154, 161, 162, 175, 375–76, 387; Savior, 86, 123, 147, 149, 234, 387; self-communication of (*see* special revelation); self-humiliation of, 247–48; silence of (*see* hiddenness of); Stranger in our midst, 61; Superior Power, 201; Sustainer, 82; the Holy Spirit, 80, 289–400; the Son (*see* Jesus Christ); the supreme Male, 90; transcendence of, 6, 48, 49, 56, 74, 101–4, 153–54; Ultimate Reality, 41; unconditional acceptance by, 319, 408 n.1. *See also* Trinity, doctrine of

Good Friday, 186, 252, 253, 259, 262, 265, 266, 273, 287

gossip, 314

gourmet food, 217

Grant, Jacquelyn, xii

greenhouse effect, 148

Guthrie, Shirley, 404 n.3

Gutiérrez, Gustavo, xii

Hall, Douglas John, 405 n.5

Handel's *Messiah*, 270, 271

Hauerwas, Stanley, 409 n.4

heaven, 111, 135, 377, 382, 383–84, 394, 395–99; definition of, 395–96

Heidelberg Catechism, 33

hell, 113, 126, 141, 227, 371, 377, 382, 383–84, 394, 395–99, 400; definition of, 396

Hendry, George S., 402 n.2, 403 n.5, 404 n.1, 407 n.1

heresy, 6, 23, 31, 86–88, 124, 236, 237; and orthodoxy, 6

Hinduism, xi
Hitler, Adolf, 21, 22, 47, 225
Hodge, Charles, 17
Holocaust, 11, 47, 97, 185, 190, 238, 330
Holy Spirit, doctrine of, x, 289–313; Advocate, 295; always working, 301–2; and conception of Jesus, 236; and creeds and confessions, 26; and culture, 293; and individuals, 28, 29, 61–62, 296 (*see also* spirituality); and Jesus, 239; and justice, 87, 96; and money, 87, 299; and nature, 296; and non-Christians, 96, 297, 308, 372; and other spirits, 296–98; and scripture, 13, 14, 61, 62, 298, 300, 307–8, 402–3 n.2; and sex, 87, 96, 299; and spirituality (*see* spirituality); and the church, 30, 45, 61, 186, 296, 308–12, 325; and the life of love, 303–4, 313; and the New Testament, 294–95, 297, 302, 309–12; and the Old Testament, 293–94, 297; and the Reformation, 296; and worship, 304, 309; femininity of, 292–93, 403 nn.1,4; freedom of, 304–5; gift of new community, 308–12, 361–62; gift of new life, 303–5; gift of new truth, 305–8; gifts of, 302–12, 355, 359, 408 n.5; giver of faith, 323–24; Giver of life, 291, 293, 296, 303–5; identity of, 292–98; justification (*see* justification, doctrine of); maternity of, 292–93; of heart and mind, 305–8; of Jesus Christ, 294–95, 297, 312; of Jesus of Nazareth, 61; of the Creator, 305; of the Father and the Son, 80; of the God of Israel, 293–94, 296, 297, 299, 408 n.2; personality of, 292–93; preferential option for the poor, 293–94; promised to the church, 295, 299, 308; Reconciler, 186, 296, 387; renewal, 302–12; Renewer, 85, 291, 302–12; sanctification, 85, 346 (*see also* sanctification, doctrine of); source of all truth, 307–8; special revelation, 64–65; Spirit of truth, 295, 305–8; teacher, 295, 296, 305–8; Transformer, 85, 186; unique work of, 296
homelessness, xi, 140, 166, 207, 211, 277, 370. *See also* evil
homosexuality, xii, 127, 202, 268, 348, 359, 362
hope. *See* Christian hope; kingdom of God, doctrine of
horoscope, 163
human beings, doctrine of, 192–211; Adam and Eve as negation, 197, 241; all handicapped, 204; and God, 37; balancing individuality and community, 209–10; besouled bodies, 195, 381; co-humanity, 202; created for fellowship, 199; created for fidelity, 202; embodied souls, 195, 381; exaltation of, 247; eye-to-eye, 204–5; fellowship with God, 199–201; finitude, 49, 67, 168–69; free will (*see* predestination); human life in community, 202–4; human sciences, 193; idolatry, 37, 48, 49, 50, 77, 155–56, 215; image of God, 74, 100, 150, 159, 193, 194–204, 406 n.1; image of God in relatedness, 198, 241–42, 406 n.2; individuality, 207–10, 211; Jesus Christ, true human being, 197–98; knowledge of self and God, 38,

54; listening to speak, 205–6; male and female for community, 202; masking ourselves, 205; moral capacity, 195–96, 210; mutually dependent, 206–7, 210; partners in stewardship, 201; partnership of equals, 203, 406 n.2; partnership of unequals, 199, 200; purpose, 40; rationality, 194–95; self-image, 192–93; sexuality, 159, 199, 202, 217, 240, 344, 381; sinfulness, 133, 262–63 (*see also* evil, moral evil; sin, doctrine of); soul, 195; thankful dependence, 200, 210; togetherness in difference, 203–4; will-to-power, 196–97
hunger, 166, 167, 172. (*see also* evil)
hymns: A Mighty Fortress, 163, 253; Holy, Holy, Holy, 70; Jesus Loves Me, 96; Silent Night, 233

Immaculate Conception, 222, 241
Immanuel, 58, 59, 60, 63, 79, 103, 110, 154, 168, 175, 231, 234, 238, 239, 240, 243–48, 253, 258, 259, 294
incarnation, doctrine of, 233–49; Christmas, 233, 235–36, 242, 243–48, 249, 406 nn.1–2; mystery, 237, 248; particularity of, 234; reversal, 246–47
inclusive language, xiii, 73–76, 275–76, 364
income tax, 191
individual rights, 208–9, 211
individualism, 28, 77, 164, 207–8, 211, 283
Institutes of the Christian Religion: **1.1.1** 38, 402 n.2; **1.5.9** 104; **1.15.2,6** 379; **1.16–18** 405 n.3; **2.1.11** 406; **2.2.15** 67, 308; **2.2.16** 67; **2.16.4** 258; **3.2.1** 323; **3.2.7** 323, 324; **3.7.1–5** 299; **3.10.1** 160, 405 n.6; **3.10,19** 405 n.6; **3.21–24** 120; **3.25.6** 382; **4.1** 363; **4.1.4** 355, 356
intellectualism, 164
Irenaeus, 19
Islam, xi, 69, 72, 270
Israel, 15, 40, 45, 55, 58, 62, 63, 65, 77, 101, 102, 107, 112, 114, 122, 138, 154, 183–85, 188, 203, 255, 257, 339, 341, 351, 356, 364, 403 n.3, 408 n.2; memory and hope, 183–85, 191, 386; messianic hope, 294; songs of, 183–85, 208. *See also* Jews

Jeremiah, 208
Jesus Christ: action of, 78, 241–42; actions, 230; Advocate, 109, 388, 407–8 n.3; and economics, 22; and family, 22, 343; and force, 342–43; and his disciples, 202, 243, 262; and human experience, 239–40; and money, 342; and nation, 22; and Satan, 198, 245–46, 253; and the Gospels, 239, 281, 294, 393, 407 n.3; and the Holy Spirit, 239; and the kingdom of God, 57, 78, 87, 185, 242, 262, 275–87, 294 (*see also* kingdom of God); and women, 13, 236, 242; ascension of, 271, 407 n.3; authority of, 22, 44, 78, 407–8 n.3; baptism of, 294; Chosen One of God, 140; cross, 261, 262–68, 271; crucified Messiah, 186, 231, 242, 271; death of, 110, 257, 259, 269, 274, 379–80 (*see also* atonement, doctrine of); deity of, 78, 102, 237; fatherless, 236; Friend of friendless, 102,

Jesus Christ (cont.)
105, 198, 241, 248, 249, 263, 266, 295, 339, 367, 389, 407–8 n.3; gender of, 239; God-with-us (*see* Immanuel); Holy One, 342; hope of the world, 279; humanity, definition of, 10, 239, 247; humanity of, 10, 198–99, 237–43; Jewish preacher, 58; Jewishness of, 238; Judge, 78, 102, 259, 261, 263, 383–84, 388, 389, 399; King, 102, 275–87; lamb, 254; Liberator, 78, 85, 285; limited, 239, 245–47, 249; Lord, 78, 102, 186, 231, 234, 238, 272, 275–87, 288, 333, 334, 347; lordship of, 22, 186, 275–87, 407–8 n.3; moral hero, 243; mystery of, 10; peasant baby, 58; perfect relatedness, 241–42, 249, 339; preferential option for the poor, 198, 238, 293–94; Priest, 254, 255, 263; radical subversive, 242, 249; real God (*see* incarnation, doctrine of); real human being (*see* incarnation, doctrine of); Reconciler, 78, 85; Redeemer, 78, 252–53; renewer of humanity, 266, 275, 285; representative, 254, 265; resurrection of, 393–94 (*see also* resurrection, doctrine of); risen presence, 244, 252, 272, 273, 370; Savior, 78, 85, 102, 238, 333, 334, 347, 383–84; second coming of, 279–81; Second Adam, 197; self-giving, 276; sexuality of, 249; sinlessness of, 222, 240–42; Son, 74, 78; Son of David, 384; Son of God, 234, 243, 244, 245–47; special revelation, 58; Spirit-filled, 294–95; Suffering Servant, 102, 140, 272, 275, 366; the true human being, 197–98; totally dead, 274; two natures (*see* incarnation, doctrine of); unity and distinction within God, 79; unity of person and work, 230; warrior and Victor, 253–54, 279; Wisdom, 75, 403 n.3; Word of God, 18, 57, 62, 74, 79, 234, 402–3 n.2
Jews, 11, 65, 69, 72, 81, 183–85, 186, 190, 203, 211, 265, 328, 330, 403 n.3; chosen people, 65, 121, 141, 203; monotheism, 77. *See also* Israel
Job, 39, 208
John, 18
Johnson, Luke T., 409 n.6
Joseph, 234
Judaism, xi, 270, 276, 392
judgment day. *See* Christian hope
Jüngel, Eberhard, x
justification, doctrine of, 314–29; and Catholicism, 316; and God's preferential option for the poor, 328; and sanctification, 251, 331–32; and scripture, 322; and social justice, 327–28, 329; and the Reformation, 315, 327; by grace, 318–20, 329, 397; certainty of, 318; cheap grace, 333; effects change, 321–22; faith as trust, 323, 329; forgiveness not punishment, 320–21; free gift for faith, 316, 319–20; gift of faith, 324; God's nevertheless, 319; God's unconditional acceptance, 319–20; individualistic, 327–28; instillation of worth, 320; justice of, 320–22; legal terminology, 320; meaning of, 319–20; problem of, 315–18; relationships not morality, 320, 329; self-justification, 316–18, 329; through not by faith, 315, 322–27

Kazantzakis, Nikos, 249
Kelly, J.N.D., 403 n.5
King Jr., Martin Luther, 188, 225
kingdom of God, 275–87; and sexist language, 275–76; and the New Testament, 278; apocalyptic, 279, 384; battle against evil, 285–86; between the times, 283–87, 289, 302; dawn not dusk, 284; dialectical lordship, 284, 288; future reality, 279–81; God bigger than, 285; here and now, 281–83; ideal, 277–79; non-dependent upon Christians, 278; realized eschatology, 281; seriousness of evil, 284–86; undemocratic, 276; versus a kingdom of Christians, 278. *See also* Christian hope; church, doctrine of
Kline, C. Benton, xiii
Knox, John, 33
Koheleth, 376–78
Küng, Hans, 406 n.3, 407 n.2
Kushner, Harold B., 405 n.1

Larger Catechism, 34
Last Temptation of Christ, The, 249
Lawrence, Bishop, of Massachusetts, 51–52
laws of nature. *See* natural law
Leith, John H., 22, 401 n.1, 402 n.3
liberalism. *See* political ideology
liberation theology, x, xii, xiii, 76, 89, 218, 253, 407 n.4
Littell, Franklin H., 21, 402 n.2, 406 n.3
Lochman, Jan M., 407–8 n.3
Lombard, Peter, 222
Lord's Prayer, 102, 111, 159, 288
Lord's Supper. *See* church
Lovell, Arnold B., 404 n.3
Luther, Martin, 19, 59, 127, 129, 151, 159, 162–63, 253, 315, 316, 317, 318, 327, 355, 365, 367, 402 n.1

Macquarrie, John, 410 n.4
marriage, 202, 208, 215, 227, 301, 323, 344, 346
Marx, Karl, 9, 53, 280, 288
Marxism, 21
McFague, Sallie, xii, 403 n.1, 403–4 n.6, 405 nn.2,4
McKim, Donald K., 404 n.2
McNeill, John T., 402 n.2, 405 nn.6,3
Menken, 19
mental health, 163, 166, 225, 409 n.4
Michelangelo, 387
Migliore, Daniel L., 405 n.2, 406 n.2, 408 n.1, 409 n.1, 410 n.5
militarism, 77
Miller, Donald, 361, 410 nn.6–7
Moltmann, Jürgen, x, 17, 156, 403 n.4, 403–4 n.6, 405 nn.2,5,5; 407 nn.2,1; 408 n.2, 409 n.5, 410 n.1
money, 162, 164, 165, 288, 299, 342
Morrison, Charles C., 357
Moses, 18, 101
murder, 215, 225, 344

Naomi and Ruth, 202
nationalism, 34, 48, 163, 227, 344
natural knowledge. *See* general revelation
natural revelation. *See* general revelation
nature, natural environment, xii. *See* creation, doctrine of
nature versus nurture, 165
Nazi regime, 21–22, 47, 141, 284
new age movement, 291
New Testament, 11, 13, 15, 22, 102, 109, 179, 197, 230, 238, 241, 244, 255, 256, 258, 259, 266, 271, 272, 274, 275, 278, 281, 287–88, 292, 302, 309–12, 315, 338, 339, 340, 346, 352, 354, 360–61, 364, 365, 380, 381, 382, 383, 384, 385, 390, 393–94, 395, 396, 399, 405 n.3, 406 n.1, 410 n.4
Nicene Creed, 32

Niebuhr, Reinhold, 405 n.4, 410 n.3
Nietzsche, Friedrich, 97
Noah's Ark, 371
nonviolence, 77, 163, 343, 375
nuclear war, xi, 176, 285, 373

Old Testament, 10, 13, 15, 100, 102, 107–8, 109, 138, 154, 179, 183, 188, 198, 238, 259, 292, 293–94, 339, 365, 384, 405 n.3, 410 n.4
Olevianus, Casper, 33
overpopulation, 148

pacifism. *See* nonviolence
pain, 168–69, 171, 380. *See also* evil, natural evil
panentheism. *See* creation, doctrine of
pantheism. *See* creation, doctrine of
parasychology, 163
patriarchy, 177
Peace Corps, 347
Pelagianism. *See* predestination
Pelagius, 126
Pentecost, 295, 407 n.3
physical laws. *See* science, natural
Placher, William C., 403 n.5
pluralism, xii
political correctness, xi, 164, 208, 311
political ideology, 4, 77, 129, 164, 165, 211, 277, 297–98, 307, 340, 362, 375
political oppression, 163
political science, 10
pollution, 148, 391
Pope, 22
positive thinking, 167
preaching. *See* church, preaching
predestination, doctrine of, 34, 66, 118–41, 326; and evangelism and mission, 135, 136, 139–41, 404 n.3; and external condition, 136–37; and infant baptism, 353, 409 n.1; and John Calvin, 120, 127, 129, 132, 135, 404 n.2, 405 n.3; and non-Christians, 132, 134–36; and self-examination, 137; and the church, 137–41; and the sacraments, 139; as adoption, 353–54; conditional love, 130–31; cost of discipleship, 140–41; double predestination, 120–24, 126, 134, 141, 404 n.2; for service, 139–41, 334, 364; free will, 124, 128–29, 132–33, 141; gift and task, 139–41; God's grace in Christ, 136, 404 n.4; good news, 123, 125, 131; good works, 126–27; human initiative, 129–30; justice without love, 120–24, 125; laws and commandments, 126–27, 134, 215; love without justice, 124–26; mystery of, 131; Pelagianism, 126–31, 141, 404 n.3; Pelagianism, pure, 126–27; Pelagianism, semi, 127–31, 178; security of salvation, 130; self-salvation, 129–30; sign of, 138; source of freedom, 133; total biblical witness, 131; universalism, 124–26, 134, 141
prejudice. *See* bias
Presbyterian Church (U.S.A.), 32, 33, 34, 401 n.1
Presbyterian Church in Taiwan, 35
Presbyterian Church in the Republic of Korea, 35
Presbyterian Church in the United States, 401 n.1
Presbyterian Church of Southern Africa, 35
Presbyterian-Reformed Church in Cuba, 35
promiscuity, 202
property, 162, 163, 164, 165
Proposed Book of Confessions, The, 401 n.1
prostitutes, 180, 198, 396

Protestant Orthodoxy, 33, 34
Protestant Scholasticism, 33
providence, doctrine of, 166–91; and idolatry, 48; biblical witness, 183–86; church's memory and hope, 185–87, 191, 302, 386; confession, not proof, 183; cross as God's power, 186; evil serving God's love, 188–89; foretasting the future, 186; God's proleptic triumph, 189; hope, 189–90; Israel and Jesus Christ, 183–86, 188; Israel's memory and hope, 183–85, 191, 386; kingdom of God, 185, 190, 272, 275–87 (*see also* kingdom of God); lordship of Jesus, 186; motive for ministry, 187–88; perseverence, 189–90; resurrection of Jesus, 185–86, 188 (*see also* resurrection, doctrine of); Spirit of Jesus, 186; suffering as sign of God's presence, 188, 405 n.5; witness of the poor, 187
psalmist. *See* Israel
psychology, 9, 10, 19, 50, 297, 308

race, 4, 8
racism, 21, 34, 45, 96, 111, 161, 163–64, 177, 207, 223, 270, 277, 373
reconciliation, 34, 186, 229–88, 254, 267–68; center of Christian faith, 229; mystery of, 229. *See also* atonement, doctrine of
Reformed Church of America, 33
Reformed family, 15–18; ecumenical, 25. *See also* confessional documents, the Reformed family
religious background, 5, 8
resurrection, doctrine of, 270–88; and bias, 273; and the kingdom of God, 275–87 (*see also* kingdom of God); ascension, 271, 407 n.3; center of history, 272; faith without proof, 272–74; historicity of, 287; nature of, 274–75; political imagery of, 276; resurrection of the person, 392–93. *See also* Jesus Christ, Lord; Christian hope for the future
revealed knowledge. *See* special revelation
Roman Catholicism, 28, 81, 88, 126–27, 222, 283, 298, 316, 356, 359, 365
Ruether, Rosemary, xii, 403 n.3, 403–4 n.6
Russell, Letty M., xii, 406 n.2

sanctification, doctrine of, 330–48; against the world, 339–40, 347; and evangelism, 333, 347; and family, 343–44, 346, 347; and force, 342–43, 346, 347–48; and justification, 251, 331–32; and money, 342, 346, 347, 409 n.6; and piety, 344–45, 347; as action, 332–37; as corporate phenomenon, 346; as deed, 332; as ethics, 332, 334; as gift, 346; as giving, 332; as good works, 332; as growth, 336–37; as obedience, 331, 334; as privilege, 336; as service, 334, 336, 364; as task, 332; as the fruit of faith, 332; for the world, 340–41, 347; God's gracious work, 334–36; holiness Jesus desires, 341–47; holy worldliness, 340; not condition, but purpose, 334; Savior or Lord? 333; versus Christian perfectionism, 336. *See also* Christian life
Sartre, Jean-Paul, 400, 410 n.8
Satan, 124, 168, 175, 176, 179–82, 196, 198, 220, 245–46, 253, 271, 281, 288. *See also* Tempter

Schaff, Philip, 401 n.1
Schleiermacher, Friedrich, 210–11
sciences, natural, 10, 19, 24, 43, 50, 146, 169–71
scripture: and bias, 13, 49; and creeds and confessions, 20, 23, 26, 30; and diverse interpretive community, 13; and God's will, 12; and personal experience, 11, 298; and relative dualism, 175; and science, 68, 145–47, 164; and slavery, 12; and the doctrine of creation, 147–52; and the Holy Spirit, 13, 14, 26, 62, 307–8, 402–3 n.2; and the problem of evil, 171; and women, 12, 13; anthropomorphic, 99–101; as witness, 12, 146; authority of, xii, 11, 12, 23, 64, 76, 313, 359, 363, 364, 399; christological principle, 13; continuity of, 238; human words, 59; idolatry of, 63, 68; interpretation of, 11; literary and historical context, 14; metaphorical language, 382–84; patriarchal, 99; political ideology, 307; purpose of, 12; rule of faith, 13; rule of love, 13; rules for interpreting scripture, 12–14; self-interpreting, 12; special revelation, 58–59; totality of, 12–13; trust in God not scripture, 323; word of God, 62, 402–3 n.2; worldview, 12, 145–47; spectacles, 67
second coming, 230. *See also* Christian hope
Second Helvetic Confession, 32
secularism, 77, 97, 366, 375
Segundo, Juan Luis, xii
seven deadly sins, 159
sex ethics, 227
sexism, 163–64, 207
sexual promiscuity, 348
sexuality, 3, 159, 162, 163, 198, 202, 217, 240, 344, 374
Shaw, George Bernard, 227, 406 n.5
Sheol, 384
Shorter Catechism, 34
sickness, 168–69, 171, 172. *See also* evil
sin, doctrine of, 212–27; Adam and Eve, 218, 221–22, 223–24, 241; and death, 226–27; as disobedience, 214–15; as distrust, 219; as predicament, 224; as pride, 218; as self-contradiction, 212–13; as self-sufficiency, 218; as sensuality, 216–18; as the desire to be good, 218–20; broken relationships, 220–21, 223; consequences, 224–27; desire to know like God, 219; enmity against one another, 220; fall upward, 219; inevitable, 212–13, 221, 253, 406 n.1; inherited sin, 222, 227, 240; natural man, 406 n.1; of the heart, 217; of the person, 217; original sin, 221–24; passive self-denial, 218; rebellion, 219–20; root and essence of, 219; self-destructive, 220; sex as the origin, 222; social influence, 223; total depravity, 224, 227; universal, 221, 406 n.1; unnatural, 213–14, 227
Sistine Chapel, 387
slavery, 11, 225
Snow, C. P., 118, 119, 122, 124, 126, 131, 141, 404 n.1
Sobrino, Jon, xii
socialism, 77, 127, 177, 375. *See also* political ideology
Son. *See* Jesus Christ
Sound of Music, 167
special revelation, 39–40, 53–69; a human limitation, 67; and God's hiddenness, 57–58, 183–85, 187; and God's

transcendence, 56, 58, 61; and Karl Barth, 44–45; and non-Christians, 67, 372; and the church, 59; God's condescendion, 58; God's self-communication, 54; good news, 56; indirect, 57–58, 60; Israel, 58, 402 n.2; Jesus Christ, 58, 402 n.2; living God, 55, 63; newness of, 56; of a Person, 54; ongoing, 63; particularity of, 65, 67; personal, 55; scripture, 58–59; word and action, 56; word and sacrament, 59; world religions, 68
species extinction, 148
spiritualism, 77
spirituality, 298–302; and experience, 298–99, 303–4, 305–7; and ordinary life, 300–301; and relationships, 313; Catholic tradition, 298; Christ-centered, 299; gifts of the Spirit, 302–12, 355, 408 n.5 (*see also* Holy Spirit, doctrine of); importance of scripture, 298–99, 307; this-worldly, 299–300; within and for the church, 308–12
stealing, 215–16, 344
Stendahl, Krister, 409 n.5
Stoicism, 160
Stroup, George, xiii
suffering. *See* evil
summer homes, 172
superstitions, 163
Supreme Court, 107

technology, 162, 169–70, 286
Tempter, 167, 179–82, 218–19, 245–46. *See also* Satan
Ten Commandments, 215–16, 227
terrorism, 111
theism. *See* creation, doctrine of
theological correctness, 311
Theological Declaration, 35
theology, method and task, 1–35; analogical and metaphorical, 74; and Bible study, 11; and confessing faith (*see* confessional documents; creeds and confessions); and personal background, 3; anthropomorphic, 100; bias, 8–9 (*see also* bias); task defined, 9–15; language, 7–8; rules for interpreting scripture, 12–14; Who is a theologian? 3–19
Tillich, Paul, 402 n.1, 408 n.1
tithing, 215
Trinity, doctrine of, x, 70–96; and gender, 73–76, 403 nn.1,4; and God's attributes, 73; and heresy, 86–88; and interreligious dialogue, 72; and monotheism, 72, 77, 89; and nonbelievers, 86; biblical roots, 76; church's doctrine, 81; community of persons, 92; covenant-making, 93, 331, 339; Creator, Savior, and Life-renewer, 84; critique of Western monotheism, 90–91; Father, Son, and Holy Spirit, 80; free society of equals, 94; heavenly board of directors, 81; implications of social Trinity for human community, 93–94; language of, 73–76; Mother, Lover, and Friend, 403 n.1; mystery, 71, 84, 95; necessity of, 71; one big boss and two subordinates, 82; one essence (substance), three persons (*hypostases*), 83; one social person, 92; *perichoresis*, 91–95; persons as simultaneous self-expressions, 84; relational integrity, 74, 76; social Trinity, 88, 199; three indivisible works, 85, 95, 257, 407–8 n.3;

Trinity (cont)
three players on a football team, 82; woman who wears three hats, 82
truth, 9

United Church of Christ in Japan, 35
United Nations, 347
United States Congress, 312
universalism. *See* predestination
Ursin, 19
Ursinus, Zacharia, 33

Vietnam, xi
virgin birth, 230, 233–34, 236, 240, 243–44, 294; and Jesus' humanity, 237
Virgin Mary, 222, 233–34, 241, 243, 249
Vischer, Lukas, 401 n.1
Voltaire, 106

war, 166, 167, 190, 373, 399
Warfield, Benjamin, 17
weather, 168, 170, 172. *See also* evil
Welch, Claude, 354, 402 n.3, 409 n.2
welfare system, 117, 127, 207
Wesley, John, 306
West, Charles C., 402 n.4
Westminster Assembly, 34
Westminster Standards, 34
Wilberforce, William, 51
Willimon, William H., 409 n.4
womanist theology, xii
women: status, xii, 127, 186, 225, 236
word of God, 62–65; as Jesus Christ (*see* Jesus Christ); as proclamation (*see* church, preaching; creeds and confessions, threefold word); as scripture (*see* scripture); distinctions in form and priority, 62
world religions, 10, 18, 19, 45, 50, 72; interreligious dialogue, 209, 211
World Alliance of Reformed Churches, 17
World War II, 284, 330, 350

Index of Reformed Confessions

Apostles' Creed ix, 16, 20, 22, *31*, 32, 70, 77, 85, 143, 147, *153*, 164, 179, 214, 229, 230–31, 233, 236, 238, 244, 248, 287, 289, *310*, 351, 356, 374, 381, 387, 392, 407–8 n.3
Barmen Declaration (Germany, 1934) 22, 34; **1–3** 21, 52; **6** 23
Belgic Confession (Netherlands, 1561) 29, 33, *43*; **Art.2** 39; **Art.14** 224, 225; **Art.15** 222; **Art.37** 388
Brief Statement of Faith (United States, 1991) x, 34, *75*, 76
Catechism of Geneva (1541) 32, 120; **Q.73** 270; **Q.87** 109, 259, 388; **Q.104** 355; **Q.105** 355; **Q.126** 334
Child's Catechism 239
Confession of 1967 (United States) 34; **preface** 27; **I.C.2** 13, 14, 401 n.1, 403 n.2; **9.31** 364; **9.45** 347
Confession of Faith (Japan, 1954) 35
Confession of Faith (Cuba, 1979) 35
Confession of Faith (Taiwan, 1979) 35
Confession of the Synod of Berne (1532) 26
Council of Toledo (675) 75
Creed of Chalcedon (451) 32
Declaration of Faith (United States, 1977) x, 34, *401*; **1.5** 403 n.4; **2.1** 147; **6.1** 403 n.2; **6.3** 13, 14, 401 n.1; **7.3** 403 n.3; **10.2** 387; **10.5** 135, 190, 286
Declaration of Faith for the Church in South Africa 35
Heidelberg Catechism (1563) 33, 120; **Q.1** 1; **Q.5** 213, 216, 227; **Q.6** 196; **Q.7** 224; **Q.26** 170; *Q. 28 171*; **Q.52** 388; **Part III** 347
Nicene Creed (325) 20, 32, 293, 351, 363, 374
Our Confession of Faith (Korea, 1954) 35
Scots Confession (1560) 33, 77, 120; **preface** 26; **9** 255; **16** 355; **17** 379; **18** 13, 363, 401 n.1
Second Helvetic Confession (1566) 32, 120; **1** 401 n.1, 403 n.2; **2** 13–14; **8** 196; **9** 225; **10** 135; **17** 355, 363
Small Catechism (Luther) *151*, 159
The Canons of the Synod of Dort (1619) 33, 120, 404 n.2; **Art.15** 120
The Gallican (or French) Confession (1559) 33

The Larger Catechism (1646) 34; **Q.1** 1; **Q.9** 89; **Q.109** 100
The Shorter Catechism (1646) 34; **Q.1** 1
Theological Declaration (Dutch Reformed Church, 1979) 35
Westminster Confession (1646) 24, 34, *43*, 120, 271; 1 401 n.1; **1.1** 39, 45, 402–3 n.2; **1.2** 12; **1.9** 12; **1.10** 27; **2.1** 100, 103, 114; **2.2** 103; **2.3** 83; **3.1** 122; **3.3** 120; **3.7** 120; **3.8** 123; **4.2** 196; **6** 225; **6.3** 223; **8.5** 257; **8.8** 253; **11** 225; **15.2** 355; **33.1** 387–88; **33.3** 26; **34** 379, 394; **35.3** 410 n.5

CPSIA information can be obtained at www.ICGtesting.com
Printed in the USA
LVOW12s0345190814

399747LV00002B/135/P